WE'RE STILL HERE

WE'RE STILL HERE

The Rise, Fall, and Resurrection
of the South Bronx

by JILL JONNES

The Atlantic Monthly Press

BOSTON / NEW YORK

FIRST EDITION

Photograph credits: pages 16–17, Courtesy of The New-York Historical Society; 21
top, U.S. History, Local History & Genealogy Division, The New York Public
Library, Astor, Lenox and Tilden Foundations (Gift of Randall Comfort); 21 bottom,
Museum of the City of New York; 30–31, U.S. History, Local History & Genealogy
Division, The New York Public Library, Astor, Lenox and Tilden Foundations; 38,
Museum of the City of New York; 52, Collection of Vincent Ciulla Designs Inc.;
54–55, Alliance for Progress; 68, AP / Wide World Photos; 76, Farmers Security
Administration, Courtesy of the Library of Congress; 92, Copyright of the Bronx
County Historical Society Collection; 101, Al Fenn, Life Magazine; 129, UPI / Bett-
mann Archive; 157, N.Y. Daily News Photo; 172, Neal Boenzi / The New York
Times; 195, Don Hogan Charles / The New York Times; 207, Courtesy of The New-
York Historical Society; 238–239, Michael Abramson / Gamma-Liaison; 254, Mu-
seum of the City of New York; 255, Harry T. Johnson; 262, Harvey Eisner; 263,
Harvey Eisner; 314 top, UPI / Bettmann Archive; 314 bottom, Jerome Liebling;
315, Tyrone Dukes / The New York Times; 334, AP / Wide World Photos; 335, AP /
Wide World Photos; 343 top, Lisa Limer; 343 bottom, Sepp Seitz, Woodfin Camp
& Associates; 373, N.Y. Daily News Photo; 380, Joan Baren; 381 top, Jon Love;
381 bottom, Joan Baren; 386, UPI / Bettmann Archive

LIBRARY OF CONGRESS CATALOGING-IN-PUBLICATION DATA
Jonnes, Jill, 1952–
  We're still here.

  Bibliography: p.
  Includes index.
    1. Bronx (New York, N.Y.)—History. 2. Bronx
(New York, N.Y.)—Social conditions. 3. New York (N.Y.)
—History. 4. New York (N.Y.)—Social conditions.
I. Title.
F128.68.B8J65 1986   974.7'275   85-47632
ISBN 0-87113-020-3

MV

Published simultaneously in Canada

PRINTED IN THE UNITED STATES OF AMERICA

For my parents

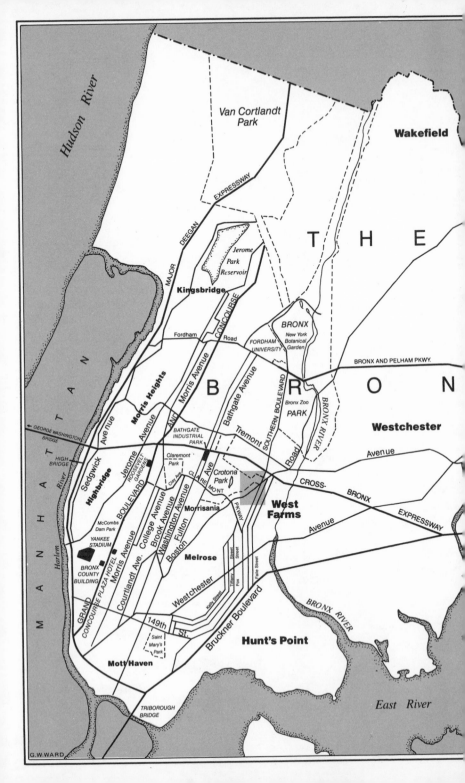

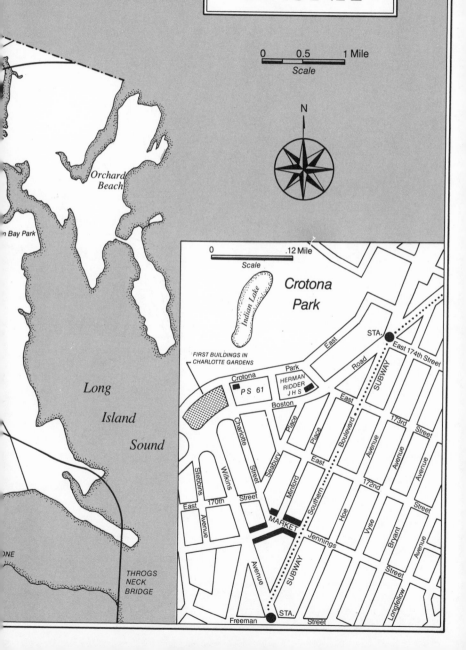

THE BRONX

0   0.5   1 Mile
Scale

N

Orchard Beach

n Bay Park

Long

Island

Sound

THROGS NECK BRIDGE

ONE

0   .12 Mile
Scale

Crotona Park

Indian Lake

FIRST BUILDINGS IN CHARLOTTE GARDENS

Crotona

PS 61

HERMAN RIDDER JHS

East

Park

Road

STA.

East 174th Street

SUBWAY

Boston

East

173rd

Street

Charlotte

Place

Street

Seabury

East

Place

Boulevard

Avenue

172nd

Street

Avenue

Stebbins

Wilkins

Street

Street

Mintord

Southern

Hoe

Vyse

Bryant

Avenue

Longfellow

East

170th

Avenue

MARKET

Jennings

Street

Street

Avenue

Avenue

SUBWAY

Freeman   Street

STA.

Acknowledgments

I AM very grateful to numerous people for their support and encouragement. Professor Penn Kimball of the Columbia Journalism School introduced me to the Bronx in 1977 and later reviewed the manuscript. Paul Brodeur's work in the *New Yorker* set a high standard for me, as did his journalism-school writing class. Alan Oser and Dee Wedemeyer of the *New York Times* encouraged me to write about housing in New York City, an interest that led me to the Bronx in 1981. There Detectives Bruce Rivera and Richard Hake of the Forty-fourth Police Precinct gave me the tour that sparked this book. From the time that I first contemplated writing a history of the South Bronx, my literary agent, Harriet Wasserman, has been a staunch and loyal enthusiast.

In the early stages of research and reporting, Victor Marrero gave hours and hours of his time to discuss the Bronx of the Model Cities era and then provided entrée to other Bronxites important to the story. At this same time, Seymour Durst made extended loans of several histories of the borough that were otherwise unobtainable. *Daily News* librarian Merrill Sherr generously opened the paper's morgue, enabling me to read expeditiously reams of Bronx and New York City stories. Mike and Alice of the *New York Post*'s Reader Service went out of their way to provide requested articles.

Others who opened their files, providing invaluable documents or articles, were the Reverend Neil A. Connolly, Ed McCarthy, Genevieve Brooks, John Pratt, Ralph Alvarado, William Prott, Janet Murphy, Veralyn Hamilton, Jim Gelbman, the Ben Gilhooleys, Richard Flynn, the Northwest Bronx Community and Clergy Coalition, Alan V. Davies, Leo Levy, Michael Hoyt, and Togetherness Housing.

From the start, the Kingsbridge Historical Society applauded my interest and urged me on. Dozens and dozens of

Bronxites shared their recollections and opinions. To all of them, especially those featured as Voices, I am grateful. Special thanks to Jim Buckley, whose declaration, "We're still here," provided a title.

A small stipend from Professor Emita Hill of Lehman College and her Bronx Community History Project supported the very early stages of writing. Professor Davis Ross of that same institution kindly shared his Bronx census data. The Ford Foundation provided much-appreciated funding for the completion of the book.

The late Harry T. Johnson was a good companion and guide to the Bronx who did many favors, including taking photos and reviewing the manuscript. Others who generously supported my endeavors in a variety of ways were my parents, Lloyd and Marilyn Jonnes, Donald J. Reis, Bob and Peggy Sarlin, Susan Farkis, Amy Dunkin, Gioia Diliberto, Mary Mealey, David Ruggiero, Clare Romano, John Ross, Grace Glueck, and Mitchell Sviridoff. Jan Goldin, who did much of the word processing, was always cheerful about deciphering revised manuscripts and about our marathon sessions. Both Joanmarie Kalter and Bronx historian John McNamara read the manuscript.

Above all, deepest thanks to Peter Davison, my editor at the Atlantic Monthly Press, who made numerous important suggestions and was unfailingly enthusiastic. He was a pleasure to work with, as was his assistant, Sarah McFall. Natalie Greenberg, then of the Atlantic Monthly Press, was a kindly and knowledgeable guide through the thickets of pre-publication.

And finally, thanks to my husband, Christopher, who always believed in this book.

Contents

Foreword by Daniel Patrick Moynihan   xv

Introduction: Do Not Give Way to Evil   3

1. "It Is a Veritable Paradise"   1639–1900   11
2. The First Boom   1900–1922   27
3. Boss Flynn   1922   41
4. "The Bronx Is a Great City"   1923–1929   51
5. "Hard Hit by the Depression"   1929–1932   65
6. The New Deal Years   1933–1939   78
7. War Fever   1939–1945   85
8. The Diaspora after the War   1946–1953   91
9. "There Was No Standing Still"   1952–1953   105
10. "Moses Thinks He's God"   1954–1959   117
11. The New Boss   1959–1963   127
12. "Horse Was the New Thing"   1960   137
13. The New "Other Half"   1962–1966   144
14. The Pondiac's Last Hurrah   1961–1967   153
15. The Puerto Rican and the Priest   1962–1967   164
16. Mau-mauing the City   1967   175
17. Who Will Be Caudillo?   1968–1969   182
18. "The Whole Place Was Caving In"   1969–1970   199
19. Interlude: Sweet Days on Charlotte Street 1925–1951   205

20. Charlotte Street: It Was Not a "Good" Neighborhood 1951–1961   219

21. Charlotte Street: "What a Madhouse It Was" 1961–1968   225

22. Charlotte Street: The Fires 1969–1973   231

23. Charlotte Street: The Gangs 1970–1975   236

24. Charlotte Street: The Collapse 1973–1975   249

25. The Grand Concourse 1965–1969   268

26. The Hotel and the Concourse 1969–1976   281

27. Roosevelt Gardens 1974–1975   288

28. The Grass Roots 1974–1977   300

29. The President's Magic Visit 1977–1978   311

30. Disenchantment 1979–1980   324

31. Charlotte Street and National Politics 1980   333

32. "The Next Part of the South Bronx" 1972–1978   345

33. "We're Still Here" 1978–1982   363

34. White Picket Fences 1984   376

Notes   389

Bibliography   399

Index   409

Illustrations

The Bronx from 179th Street and Bryant Avenue,
  circa 1904   16–17
Charlotte Street at Boston Road in 1906   21
Doc Fisher's Saloon, circa 1885   21
The Grand Concourse in 1924   30–31
Southern Boulevard at 163rd Street, 1913   38
A postcard of Yankee Stadium, 1923   52
The Concourse Plaza Hotel and 161st Street, 1926 54–55
Franklin D. Roosevelt, Fiorello LaGuardia, Eleanor
  Roosevelt, and Edward J. Flynn, 1939   68
Bathgate Avenue near 172nd Street, 1934   76
James Lyons and Harry Truman, 1948   92
Puerto Rican families arrive in New Jersey, 1947   101
Cross-Bronx Expressway under construction in 1962 124
Charles A. Buckley and John F. Kennedy, 1962   129
Herman Badillo campaigning in 1973   157
Ramon Velez leaving the polls, 1974   172
Father Louis Gigante in Hunt's Point   195
Skaters in Crotona Park, circa 1910   207
Youth gang, 1970s   238–239
Faile Street at 165th Street, circa 1925   254
Faile Street at 165th Street, 1984   255
Firemen train their hose on an old wooden house, 1972 262
Burning building at 174th Street and Southern Boulevard 263
Jimmy Carter on Charlotte Street in 1977   314

Burned-out buildings on Charlotte Street, 1977   314

Herman Ridder Junior High School and Charlotte Street   315

Ronald Reagan on Charlotte Street in 1980   334

Parade of Hiroshima survivors on Charlotte Street, 1978   335

Street scene in Hunt's Point, 1982   343

Children playing on Faile Street, 1978   343

Anne Devenney and the Northwest Bronx Community and
   Clergy Coalition   373

Houses built on Tiffany Street in the early 1980s   380

Ed Logue on Charlotte Street, 1984   381

A woman keeps an eye on her block, 1984   381

Herbs being grown on Bathgate Avenue in 1983   386

Foreword

by DANIEL PATRICK MOYNIHAN

NEW YORK is the richest city in the world; the richest city in the history of the world. It is also a city in which more than a third of the children now live below an official poverty line, and in which it is forecast that half the children now being born will be on welfare before reaching age eighteen.

Of the ten poorest congressional districts in the nation, four are to be found in New York City. One of these directly adjoins the richest congressional district in the nation, the "silk stocking" Fifteenth District of Manhattan's East Side. Directly to the north is the Eighteenth District of the South Bronx — in the words of the *Almanac of American Politics*, "the nation's most famous slum."

'Twas not ever thus. Oh, no. In the Great Depression of the 1930s, the Bronx was called "the city without a slum." It had the lowest unemployment rate of any of the five boroughs of New York, and, as reported by Lloyd Ultan, was during this period one of the few areas of the country that experienced privately financed residential construction.

The first European settler was a Swedish sea captain, Jonas Bronck, who was serving the Dutch, and in 1639 got the polyglot tradition of the borough going nicely by starting up a farm worked by Dutch, Danish, and German servants. A rural county was formed. Lewis Morris, one of the four signers of the Declaration of Independence from New York, tried to persuade Congress to set up the nation's capital there (in the area we now call Morrisania) but Thomas Jefferson prevailed and we went off to a swamp on the banks of the Potomac. After that not much happened until the subways —"Els," actually — arrived in the first decade of the present century.

It was a time of enormous urban energy; very different from the entropy we so frequently encounter today. The builders were there waiting for the subways, and most of the high-rise apartments of the South Bronx were built between 1906 and 1917.

It was a time also of great political energy. New York City and State were the centers of much of the political innovation of the first three decades of the century, creating the principal forms of contemporary state and city government. To the bafflement of reformers, then as now, the indispensable elements in this transformation were the extraordinarily powerful and *stable* urban Democratic party organizations of the period. "Machine" was a pejorative term of the press, along with "Bosses." To the men and women involved in that most honorable of callings in a republic, the corresponding terms were Organization and Leaders. (The former, by common usage, pronounced "Ahrganization" with a slight brogue.)

In Manhattan, Charles Francis Murphy, for twenty-two years head of Tammany Hall, nurtured the career of Alfred Emanuel Smith, first in the State Assembly, then as New York county sheriff, then as governor. The New Deal that Franklin D. Roosevelt brought to Washington was in considerable measure fashioned in Smith's Albany. At about this time, Murphy gave his blessing to a young Bronx lawyer, Edward J. Flynn, who followed Smith's pattern as an assemblyman and county sheriff, but then followed Murphy's, becoming the democratic leader of Bronx County. Roosevelt, who had succeeded Smith as governor, appointed Flynn his secretary of state, the chief political office in state government. Flynn became a political mentor of sorts to the president-to-be. In 1940, as chairman of the Democratic National Committee, he managed the third-term election, and so through many adventures.

The Bronx County Democratic organization, essentially an alliance of Irish Catholics and Eastern European Jews, enjoyed enormous influence and stability. The influence extended to the greatest affairs of the American state: who would be president, who would succeed him should he die in office.

At the local level, James Lyons, an affable and deceptively simple Irishman, served as borough president of the Bronx for thirty years.

What the Bronx political organization never enjoyed was a reputation for good government. This puzzled me as a young man. As a youth I rarely ventured there from Manhattan's West Side; I went twice in the late 1930s to Yankee Stadium to see Lou Gehrig. The Bronx was a *place*. Not everybody belonged there, nor felt free to sojourn. Anyway, you remembered your visits. In the late 1950s Nathan Glazer and I were writing *Beyond the Melting Pot,* a study of the ethnic groups of New York City, and nothing daunted, I made my way uptown to visit the Fordham University campus, where, *mirabile dictu,* the student newspaper had printed some irreverent notices and cartoons concerning the *Tablet,* the then majestically autocratic newspaper of the Catholic Diocese of Brooklyn. I got mildly lost, asked directions of a policeman, who courteously pointed me on my way, and then in a stage whisper asked, "Why are all the Protestants heading for Fordham today?" (So much for the influence of the brothers at Holy Name on West Ninety-seventh Street!) But I am getting lost again: I mean only to suggest a place that lived somewhat by itself and by its own rules, and not badly. I suppose it seemed improbable that it could have been no more than it appeared to be. Flynn's career was ruined when a county maintenance crew fixed up his courtyard with "Belgian" paving blocks. There seems little doubt Flynn did not know of this, and there is no conceivable reason he would have wanted it done, but a furor arose, not least in Washington, where his association with Roosevelt made him a valuable target. The president had chosen him to be ambassador to wartime Australia, a not unimportant position. The nomination was dropped. Flynn began to withdraw from politics and died in Dublin, young at age sixty-one, and I suspect bitter.

This is as good a point as any to begin the saga of the South Bronx: in Dublin, whose medieval coat of arms bears the inscription "Obediantia Civium Urbis Felicitas" (By the Obedience of the People Is the Happiness of the City Ensured).

It is not a thought that promptly commends itself to modern sensibilities; but then it is not a thought at all: it is a fact. Obedience to law, and by extension a sense of obligation to others, is the foundation of any civil order of free men and women. It is surely the pride and ought on occasion to be the boast of those who govern themselves. We fought a revolution, after all, to win the right to enact our own laws; presumedly in order to abide by them.

The first fact, then, is that this ceased to be the condition of society in the South Bronx. Not to start here is to get nowhere. Law and order collapsed in this part of the City. It happened quietly at first. Appearances were kept up, or for that matter didn't much change. The Bronx Democratic organization, now headed by Flynn's chosen successor, Congressman Charles A. Buckley, seemed as solid as ever. (And Buckley was to have a considerable influence in the nomination and election of John F. Kennedy in 1960.) But *crime* was beginning to be a problem; not crime so much as delinquency. In the mid-1950s I spent four years in Albany on the staff of Governor Averell Harriman. I became a close friend of Mark McCloskey, whom Harriman had appointed head of the State Youth Division. McCloskey was a rare sort of the kind New York used to produce. A product of Hell's Kitchen on Manhattan's West Side, he went off to World War I and then to Princeton, where he became an accomplished Latinist, and thence back to the West Side, where he spent his life as a social worker until Harriman summoned him to Albany. McCloskey's Hell's Kitchen had more than its share of self-destructive young males. But they lived in a setting of institutions that were stronger than they and always in the end prevailed over them. Prohibition had been a close-run thing, but even then there were controls.

By the mid-1950s something new was stirring. A new kind of delinquent was coming onto the state net. The new delinquency was different, and it disturbed McCloskey. He couldn't find the controls.

He was right. As Jill Jonnes recounts in her absorbing narrative, at about this time drug use was becoming epidemic among the newly arrived Puerto Rican settlers in the South Bronx. The wide use of heroin (developed, incidentally, by the Bayer pharmaceutical company in Germany at the turn of the century) among lower-class youth brought social devastation to the neighborhoods where it took hold. It may be argued that the appearance of large quantities of distilled alcohol two centuries earlier had a similar impact on cities, and history may settle the question. For the moment it is enough that drugs suddenly assaulted the tenement communities of Manhattan and the Bronx and the authorities were thoroughly unprepared, even unaware. But most important, within the community itself there were simply no institutions strong enough to insist that drug use was lawbreaking and would be punished and stopped. (And to demand this not least of the City police and the federal government. It is the responsibility of the federal government to prevent drug smuggling.)

Of the institutions that had kept order in McCloskey's Hell's Kitchen, none was so important as the family, reinforced by a stern Jansenist church that made few allowances for human failings, and none whatever for social tolerance. Later generations would not understand, but the people involved understood: there was no choice. This was equally clear to the Yiddish-speaking inhabitants of Charlotte Street in the Bronx in its early days. Ms. Jonnes writes:

> no matter how bitterly the couples might quarrel, or however leaden the silences between them, they persevered in their marriages. There was no possibility of separation, much less divorce. It was not socially acceptable. Think of the children, think of the shame.
>
> It was not economically possible, either. Tellingly, the one divorced mother in the neighborhood had been married to a man who became wealthy and could easily support separate domiciles, but no other man in the neighborhood could possibly underwrite two households. A man who left his family did so knowing they would end up as wards of charity. There was no welfare or relief

system for them to fall back on, and they would suffer a most shameful fate.

What social psychologists would come to call delayed gratification was a way of life and children were its focus.

In the Jewish culture the family was too cherished to be easily cast aside.

Ultimately, everything was for the children. These immigrant-parents had no illusions that their own lives would ever transcend the unremitting struggle to provide. Very few had even a high school education, much less complete command of that mysterious language, English. Yiddish was the mother tongue of Charlotte Street. Some women attended special evening classes to learn English, but it was hard to wrestle with such strange words after an exhausting day of children, making meals, and cleaning the house.

The powerful energy and will of these Jewish immigrants, especially the mothers, was channeled into the next generation. The women hoarded their nickels and dimes and opened secret savings accounts to pay for special lessons or anything else that would enrich their children's lives.

One of the baffling questions of our age is how these elemental truths got lost as society became more generous. It is not a question to be settled here, but the facts need to be recorded. New York in the 1950s began to develop a welfare *population*. That is to say, social settings, neighborhoods, in which it was as normal for a family to be "on" welfare as not to be.

Early on, Glazer spotted this among the new Puerto Rican community. He did not claim to understand it; but simply recorded that these were not a people prone to dependency when they arrived here. By the mid-1960s, now in Washington, I had assembled a set of statistics and correlations that argued that a welfare explosion was about to take place, and it did. Jonnes records: "By 1970, of 3,181 families living in the Charlotte Street neighborhood, 1,467 families, or almost half, were on welfare." As with the epidemic drug use, those responsible in City government (or state, or national government) could not for the longest while recognize that something *different* was abroad, that a profoundly destabilizing condition was developing.

The urban riots of the late 1960s of necessity focused government attention, and within the limits of its understanding, government did respond.

But the crisis of the South Bronx sort of crept up on everyone, not least the people who lived there. There were no explosions. The kids started to behave badly, but not all that badly at first. The men started drifting away, but again, not all at once. There were fires. Well, where weren't there fires in a big city? Why all those fire escapes the City Council had decreed three generations earlier; why all those fire alarms and fire trucks? Then one day the situation became irreversible. To my limited knowledge, the most graphic of early accounts of the trouble appeared in July 1979 in an article by Adele Chatfield-Taylor in the *Livable City,* a publication of the Municipal Arts Society. Focusing on Charlotte Street, that soon to be Avenue of the Presidents, the report found that

> by 1968, the place was beyond description. Wild dogs roamed the streets, tearing in and out of buildings and through the trash that covered the sidewalks and the streets. Persons scarcely recognizable as human were prey and predator to one another. Fires burned everywhere — in cans on the corners, in empty lots, in all kinds of buildings. Over the months, buildings could be seen to catch the disease and die. What is truly miraculous is that all of the South Bronx has not ended up like Charlotte Street. . . .

Soon, of course, president and would-be presidents were arriving for the photo opportunity and the ritual reference to Berlin after World War II. (Actually, the South Bronx in the 1970s did come to resemble Berlin in the late 1940s, part cleared rubble, part buildings half collapsed, and another part simply burned-out buildings, and everywhere a certain life in the ruins.)

Which brings us to the failure of government. To be sure, citizens failed: broke laws, broke rules. It *is* a rule, is it not, that a man provides for his children and looks to their future? It was a rule in Puerto Rico. Why not in the South Bronx? Part of the answer has to be that the welfare administrators in New York City, as Armageddonic night began to fall on the South Bronx, never made this clear to the newcomers. This was mindless indulgence of educated, perhaps overeducated, sensibilities by assorted elites, much as drug use was not taken seriously, and the associated crime wave dismissed as exaggerated.

These propositions might be about any number of cities in the United States in the 1950s and '60s. New York is singular in one respect, which is the government's involvement with housing, and it is well to keep in mind that the crisis of the South Bronx is elementally a crisis brought on by the destruction of rental housing. *Rental* housing. That is the clue. Something like 85 percent of New Yorkers rent homes, typically apartments in four- or five-story buildings (made possible by the genius of the City's water engineers at the turn of the century, who devised a means to lift water four to five stories without any expenditure of energy). "Slum clearance" was an early enthusiasm of reform elements in city politics, and public housing became a standard feature of the City's political agenda, regardless of party or faction. After World War II rent control or stabilization was added to the list. Such were politics in a liberal city in which tenants greatly outnumbered landlords. (Tenants, incidentally, on Park Avenue as well as Charlotte Street, to the far greater advantage of the former.)

Students of the subject differ, but there is strong evidence that housing is a dependent variable in social development. When jobs are available and families stable and crime is controlled — housing gets created. Surely it is not the other way around. In any event, one certain fact is that when rental housing becomes unprofitable it begins to disappear. Daniel Rose, at once a careful student and accomplished practitioner in this field, has put the matter plainly enough: "Our state and city political leaders must recognize that capital *flows* to where it is rewarded." That this still had to be stated in 1983 suggests the extent to which government had become the problem. The City of New York allowed housing to disappear everywhere, and in the case of the South Bronx you could even say the place disappeared.

Another enthusiasm of government at this time was the creation of neighborhood organizations to deal with various social and economic matters. The beginnings of the development, curiously, can be traced to a juvenile delinquency program begun under the Kennedy administration on the Lower East Side of Manhattan. It became widespread as the Community Action component of the "war on poverty" and carried over into the Model Cities program of the Johnson administration. Much of Ms. Jonnes's narrative concerns such programs in the South Bronx. The great question about these programs — and it brings roaring disagreement even now — is whether they actually *retard* the development of political institutions and influence in the neighborhoods where they are established. It is fairly clear the Bronx Democratic organization could not or would not find a place for the newly arrived Puerto Ricans in the borough. Had the organization been less under attack on principle — machines were bad, bosses were bad — it might have had greater resources and greater confidence. We will not know. We only know that the power of the indigenous political organization declined. First Washington, then City Hall — City Hall far away downtown — set about creating new organizations to do what the old ones had done. As with housing, isn't this getting directions wrong? Politically viable organizations reflect a politically viable populace; they do not create one. Charles V. Hamilton of Columbia University has shown a disturbing coincidence between increased federal funding for poverty programs in certain New York City neighborhoods and decreased voter registration and voting. His theoretical explanation is simple enough: the successful entrepreneurs in the new system were those who could get grants from above, as against turning out voters from below. In any event, the *Almanac of American Politics* records that "the 18th district has the lowest voter turnout in the United States — even though the turnout of Puerto Ricans in Puerto Rico is higher than the turnout in any American state."

Joseph P. Fitzpatrick, S.J., of Fordham University has devoted a lifetime to the study of the Puerto Rican community of New York, and has no peer in the quality of his work. He has recently calculated from the 1980 census that 50.3 percent of all Hispanics in the New York Archdiocese are under seventeen years of age and, further, that Puerto Ricans are the poorest segment of the New York City population. In combination this gives us the stark proposition: "It is the Puerto Rican children who constitute the majority of the poor" of the City. In the end, he writes, renewal will come from "the calling up again of the strengths and vigor of the deep roots of Puerto Rican culture. The family is the fundamental basis for identity and community strength. Absence of a father and dependence of the family on welfare leave the family incapable of fulfilling both these functions." There are things government cannot do, and probably should not try. But, says Fitzpatrick, there are things it can and must do, and of these the first is to provide a standard of welfare benefits for dependent children that keeps them above poverty. It is not much, and it is *our* future we'll be paying for, or giving up on.

Ms. Jonnes writes of *The Rise, Fall, and Resurrection of the South Bronx*. I have touched on the rise, and lingered on the fall. I will leave to her the final and hopeful segment, asking only that I be allowed to note the essential event. After much travail, and much failure, and much avoidance of the obvious, the people of the South Bronx and the Catholic church got together and have set to work. And the Lord's work it is.

And more. It is news. *Good news.* Traveling in Asia recently, I picked up the *International Herald-Tribune* to learn: "Crotona Park Pool is Pride of the Bronx . . . In its first full summer of operation, more than 2,000 bathers a day find respite from the heat in the shimmering oasis that Robert

Moses, former New York City parks commissioner, built in
1936." Crotona: named by a City engineer for the Greek city
in southern Italy where Pythagoras was born. We are in Ms.
Jonnes's debt for her reminder that we used to have City
engineers who knew about such things. Allow an admirer to
note also that Crotona was scarcely the only park Robert
Moses built in the half century of extraordinary public service
that began in the administration of Al Smith — the Cross-
Bronx Expressway being an exception, but then we were
building such urban freeways all over America at the time.

It is not over. It is scarcely begun. Yet a people who endure
and an institution that endures are joined in a great effort to
deal with a problem that endures also. Is it not strange, in
passing, that with all that has changed, so little has changed
since that conversation between a young English nobleman
and a perfect stranger which Benjamin Disraeli recorded in
his novel *Sybil,* published across the sea some one hundred
forty years ago:

'It is a community of purpose that constitutes society,'
continued the younger stranger; 'without that, men may
be drawn into contiguity, but they still continue virtually
isolated.'

'And is that their condition in cities?'

'It is their condition everywhere; but in cities that condition is aggravated. A density of population implies a
severer struggle for existence, and a consequent repul-
sion of elements brought into too close contact. In great
cities men are brought together by the desire of gain.
They are not in a state of cooperation, but of isolation,
as to the making of fortunes; and for all the rest they
are careless of neighbours. Christianity teaches us to love
our neighbour as ourself; modern society acknowledges
no neighbour.'

'Well, we live in strange times,' said Egremont, struck
by the observation of his companion, and relieving a
perplexed spirit by an ordinary exclamation, which often

denotes that the mind is more stirred than it cares to acknowledge, or at the moment is able to express.

'When the infant begins to walk, it also thinks that it live in strange times,' said his companion.

'Your inference?' asked Egremont.

'That society, still in its infancy, is beginning to feel its way.'

'This is a new reign,' said Egremont, 'perhaps it is a new era.'

'I think so,' said the younger stranger.

'I hope so,' said the elder one.

'Well, society may be in its infancy,' said Egremont, slightly smiling; 'but, say what you like, our Queen reigns over the greatest nation that ever existed.'

'Which nation?' asked the younger stranger, 'for she reigns over two.'

The stranger paused; Egremont was silent, but looking inquiringly.

'Yes,' resumed the younger stranger after a moment's interval. 'Two nations; between whom there is no intercourse and no sympathy; who are as ignorant of each other's habits, thoughts, and feelings, as if they were dwellers in different zones, or inhabitants of different planets; who are formed by a different breeding, are fed by a different food, are ordered by different manners, and are not governed by the same laws.'

'You speak of —' said Egremont, hesitatingly.

'*The rich and the poor.*'

Daniel Patrick Moynihan

August 10, 1985

WE'RE STILL HERE

Do Not Give Way to Evil

"The building of cities is one of man's
greatest achievements. The form of his
city always has been and always will be
a pitiless indicator of the state of his
civilization."

Edmund Bacon
Design of Cities

THE South Bronx of New York City has become a national
symbol, a disaster area invoked as the epitome of urban
failure. This extraordinary, sprawling cityscape of twenty square
miles in the southwest portion of Bronx County today encom-
passes large stretches of eerie necropolis — charred ruins;
fields lumpy with detritus; disemboweled, abandoned buildings — brought to life here and there by thriving, busy shopping streets, factories, and small domains of well-tended homes,
apartment houses, and parks, each preserved, shored up, or
resurrected from the maelstrom that engulfed and destroyed
the South Bronx in the 1970s.

The story of the South Bronx is not just the story of one
unfortunate corner of New York City. The borough's history
parallels that of many old American cities and urban neighborhoods, though the particularities of its time and place made
for a more spectacular demise than many. Sierras of rubble
and ranks of vacant, shattered buildings became a place of
pilgrimage for anyone concerned about cities. The South Bronx
made a terrific stage for passing politicians, a Pope, radicals,
journalists, assorted do-gooders, and hustlers of every hue.

While the Bronx was burning they came, basking briefly in its lurid glow.

But long before the "South Bronx" got its name, there was just the Bronx, one of the five boroughs of New York City, a bucolic backwater. Then, in the first decade of this century, the Manhattan subway lines pushed north, setting off a frenzy of development. Brick walk-ups and sturdy elevator buildings came to line street after street, transforming the Bronx into a city in its own right. The more successful immigrants who crowded lower Manhattan sought a better life in the Bronx: the Irish settled in the neighborhoods of Mott Haven, Melrose, and Highbridge, the Italians in Morrisania and Belmont, and the Jews, by far the biggest contingent, in Hunt's Point, West Farms, East Tremont, and bordering the Grand Concourse, the wide boulevard sweeping up the length of the borough. Young families filled the new apartment houses and reveled in the tree-lined streets, verdant public parks, good schools, and shopping. "The neighborhood was a complete universe for the majority of its residents," remembers Donald Sullivan, a professor of urban planning who grew up in the Bronx. "Social life revolved around the stoops and courtyards of the apartment buildings. The fabric of community life was tight, ordered, and internal."

The Bronx of the 1920s, 1930s, and 1940s became a staging ground for the American Dream, the unremarkable home of 1.5 million first- and second-generation Americans. Fathers set off daily to toil in the small printing shops and garment factories of midtown Manhattan, or as blue-collar civil servants, unionized painters, or clerks. Parents encouraged their children and believed they would live a better life. And many Bronx offspring fulfilled that dream: Clifford Odets, Paddy Chayefsky, Lauren Bacall, Herman Wouk, Jules Feiffer, Anne Bancroft, Dr. Jonas Salk, Irving Howe, Armand Hammer, George Segal, J. P. Donleavy, Jake La Motta, Sal Mineo, George Meany, Stanley Kubrick, and Tony Curtis. Families worked hard and participated happily in local politics and neighborhood life.

These ordinary citizens provided the foundation of the powerful Bronx Democratic machine led by the urbane and inaccessible Boss Edward J. Flynn, master politician and close adviser and friend to Franklin Delano Roosevelt. Observing the travails of his working-class county during the Depression and its leftward tilt, Flynn steered the Democratic party toward liberalism on a national level. On the local level his clubhouses dispensed traditional favors and spearheaded tremendous voter turnout on election day.

The postwar world of the Bronx was roiled by relentless change and social and physical disruption. Huge immigrations of impoverished Puerto Ricans and blacks jammed Harlem and East Harlem and then overflowed into the oldest Bronx neighborhoods, creating new slums, while the white residents fled to the suburbs or areas farther north in the Bronx. Yet no one saw any warning in the neighborhoods' decline, for in the history of New York (and of every other American city) one class has moved, ceding its old dwellings to the less well-to-do. While expanding ghettoes sundered the social fabric of the lower Bronx, the Cross-Bronx Expressway plowed through the heart of the county, laying waste to one neighborhood after another and uprooting thousands of families. Elsewhere in the Bronx, enormous public housing projects, designed to alleviate New York's perennial housing crisis, wiped out established neighborhoods.

In Samuel Lubell's 1952 classic *The Future of American Politics,* he focused on the plebian working-class enclaves of the East Bronx as prototypical American city neighborhoods, as indeed they were. He observed how the neighborhoods were handling the influx of poor blacks and Puerto Ricans and found "an almost perfect example of the new zone of political insurgency developing in our cities," a testing ground for minorities coming up the ladder who had to coexist with whites and use the traditional political framework for their own ascent.

Not even Lubell, a prescient journalist who studied voting and census patterns to predict the emergence of special-interest politics, foresaw the disaster. Why should he have? The Bronx was still a solid, vital city, even at the time he came to record its troubled racial transition. Lubell understandably failed to appreciate such imponderables as the disruption caused by the massive public works, or the difficulty black and Puerto Rican newcomers would encounter in establishing an economic foothold. At one time lack of education and training would not have mattered, but unskilled jobs were disappearing in the postwar years as small businesses and whole industries closed or relocated. The well-worn path to the middle class was crumbling just as the new pilgrims were starting their own journeys. Without jobs, families foundered.

Unrelenting poverty in the new ghettoes fostered a culture of despair that fell back on welfare, drugs, and crime as survival techniques. "People began to fear for their property, for their families," remembers one Hispanic woman. "The young men and women who were the pride and hope of the community became preying lepers — no longer in control of their actions and driven by their insatiable urge to secure the most expensive drug on the black market — heroin." Residents were held up on the streets by desperate junkies. White flight accelerated, leaving behind a population that was overwhelmingly minority, poor and without hope. The city responded to this growing underclass by expanding welfare benefits. The old Bronx political machine, once so masterful at serving its constituents, had fossilized, but an undaunted, activist federal government launched the Great Society programs to bring hope to the slums. When the War on Poverty proved too threatening to City Hall and too raucous, it was supplanted by the Model Cities concept, with yet more programs to uplift those trapped in the terrible poverty of the inner cities. But in the Bronx, fierce local feuding largely dissipated the effects of these programs.

When Co-op City opened in 1968, it served as a cheap, safe escape hatch from the neighborhoods coming apart psychologically and physically. Located in the far northeastern corner of the borough, Co-op City offered fifteen thousand brand-new, subsidized apartments in massive towers. Recalls one young man, "I remember when my mother and I went to see our congressman. We wanted to talk to him about what was going on and see if we couldn't get the neighborhood working to fight this change, to stem the tide. He said, 'Move to Co-op City.' "

In the late sixties in the Bronx the rental apartment building (a form of housing invented in ancient Rome and reliably lucrative in every era thereafter) suffered a dramatic demise as an economic entity, becoming in short order a worthless investment. Costs had soared, rents remained controlled, while rent delinquency and vandalism were rampant. Some landlords just abandoned their buildings, others "milked" them — paying no taxes, providing no services, but collecting what rents they could. The most venal turned to arson to recoup their losses. Concurrently, "finishers" (whose vocation was invented in this time and place) and junkies mined the dying apartment houses for every item of worth. They set fires to force out tenants so that they might more easily extricate pipes and other valuables. Welfare tenants, desperate to escape buildings without heat or hot water and often under siege, torched their apartments in order to get priority on city housing lists.

Arson emerged as a sordid solution, a fact New York City stolidly denied for years. The borough's dense development, and its almost exclusively rental housing stock, rendered each apartment building vulnerable to the fate of its neighbors. One bad building in an otherwise decent block could poison life for everyone. In a frenzy of arson, greed, and destruction, many willingly reaped the gains — landlords, tenants, junkies, and finishers — while others pretended not to see. And so the tragedy unfolded, and — perhaps unique in the history of civilization — a citizenry annihilated its own city for profit.

In truth, it would be hard to exaggerate the dimensions of this unnatural disaster. An epidemic wave of arson broke in 1969, and for years the fire engines screamed endlessly through the lower borough, futilely extinguishing blaze after blaze. Engine Company Eighty-two was routinely answering forty calls in each twenty-four-hour tour. In the South Bronx, more than 12,000 fires blazed a year. The very air smelled seared. The fires accelerated the abandonment, destroying about 5,000 apartment buildings with 100,000 units of housing and guaranteeing that no one could return and rebuild without tremendous expense. Bronx politicians seemed either impotent, frustrated, or cynically indifferent to the ravaging of their county. A defeated officialdom conceded finally its bafflement about what to do.

At this chaotic time, the term "South Bronx" was attached to each new neighbohood stricken by the vicious cycle of poverty, drugs, crime, and then arson. Originally, the South Bronx had been a small, one-mile-square neighbood in the far southeast corner of Mott Haven. For unknown reasons, this old name was transformed into a traveling curse. As crime, abandonment, and arson engulfed each successive neighborhood in the lower, and then the middle, Bronx, each came to be stigmatized as the "South Bronx." Bronxites mourned, not just the destruction of these old neighborhoods, but the disappearance of their very names. Year by year as the arson epidemic raged, Melrose, Mott Haven, Hunt's Point, Morrisania, West Farms, Tremont, Concourse, Highbridge, and Morris Heights were overwhelmed, immobilized, destroyed, and subsumed by the "South Bronx." No one who observed this South Bronx cancer could believe the rapidity with which it struck. By 1980, the city of New York and the media had redefined the boundaries of the infamous South Bronx to include everything south of Fordham Road, or twenty square miles.

In 1977, President Carter made a surprise visit to Charlotte Street in the South Bronx, and his televised ruminations amidst the rubble riveted the attention of an appalled world. This old city neighborhood, once solidly lined with brick apartment buildings and stores, had been laid waste in peacetime as thoroughly as if it had been bombed in a savage war.

Overnight, Charlotte Street and the South Bronx became the new shame of the cities, national symbols of urban collapse. The *New York Times* declared editorially that seeing the South Bronx was "as crucial to the understanding of American urban life as a visit to Auschwitz is to understanding Nazism." This was not just another slum, but a city almost obliterated. The 1980 census showed the decimated Eighteenth Congressional District of the president's visit to be the poorest place in the nation.

By 1981, the fires had banked, and a tenuous peace had enveloped the remains. Those who had struggled and survived were shoring up their isles in the ruins, and the curious and caring who still continued to come around were astonished and inspired by the tenacity, pluck, and good humor of those who refused to run. These people — many are Catholic clergy — have emerged as the leaders of grass-roots groups, the scrappy organizations whose dogged persistence is testimony to the human will to prevail and even flourish. The South Bronx has bottomed out, and in these small realms the rebuilding is impressively underway.

Those who preached the creed, The Bronx Shall Rise Again, can point to the taming of the frenzy of arson, abandonment, and crime. The gangs are gone, and the younger generation of street kids have funneled their energy into inventing breakdancing, which in its way took the nation by storm. But above all, there is one constant in the long history of the county: location. The South Bronx sits right across the river from golden Manhattan and remains a prime piece of real estate for families and industry.

The story of the South Bronx has never been fully explored — perhaps because its disintegration occurred in such a swift fury of destruction. It is an intensely American tale, for all the destructive social changes that swept our cities swept the South Bronx. And no people better personify the American struggle to succeed and prevail than the men and women now rebuilding the South Bronx, whose perseverance has given new meaning to the official motto of Bronx County, *Ne Cede Malis:* Do Not Give Way to Evil.

1

"It Is a Veritable Paradise"
1639–1900

THE Bronx is the sole borough of New York City situated on the American mainland. Just south of Westchester County, the Bronx covers a large, splayed peninsula that is split neatly into two lobes by the Bronx River. The eastern-most lobe, marshy flatlands washed by the waters of the East River and Long Island Sound, seems a world apart from New York, a suburb of bay views and beaches. The Bronx west of the river, however, is the City, separated from upper Man-hattan only by the narrow, sinuous Harlem River. Even a century of intensive urban development has not obliterated the borough's distinctive geological features: three gnarled ridges, worn rocky backbones of the old Appalachian Moun-tains, running north to south. Left behind when the glaciers melted, the easternmost of these Fordham Gneiss ridges rises in the Wakefield section and slopes through Bronx Park and Crotona Park. The majestic central ridge crests under what is now the Grand Boulevard and Concourse. The high bluffs of the third ridge overlook the Hudson River and the Palisades of New Jersey and, farther south, the Harlem River and Man-hattan.

This once unspoiled rocky wilderness of forests, valleys, meadows, and streams was the realm of various Indian tribes — the Mohegans, Weckquaesgeeks, Siwanoy, Sint Sincs, Kitch-enwonks, Manhattan, Tankitekes, and Taekmucks. In 1639 the first white settlers arrived in the persons of Jonas Bronck and his wife, Antonia Slagboom. Bronck, a Scandinavian with the Dutch West India Company, bought a five-hundred acre tract (everything south of what is now 150th Street) from the

Mohegan sachems Ranachqua and Tackamuck for the price
of "two guns, two kettles, two coats, two adzes, two shirts,
one barrel of cider, and six bits of money."[1] Bronck built a
stone house with tile roof, a barn, barracks for his workers
and servants, and several tobacco houses. This settlement,
called Emmaus, was spread over a small hillock fronting on
the Harlem River. Its eastern border was defined by the Aquahung ("high bluff or bank") River, later to be known as the
Broncks' River, a name applied in time to the whole region.
A pleased Jonas Bronck wrote in a letter to Holland: "The
invisible hand of the Almighty Father surely guided me to
this beautiful country, a land covered with virgin forest and
unlimited opportunities. It is a veritable paradise and needs
but the industrious hand of man to make it the finest and most
beautiful region in all the world."[2]

Four years later Bronck died, and his estate passed through
various owners until 1670, when it was bought by the Morris
family, who added to it until their holdings covered 1,920
acres. In 1697 Colonel Lewis Morris, a good Quaker, got
himself proclaimed the first lord of the manor of Morrisania.
Several generations of Morrises lived in the Bronx, distinguishing themselves as scholars, judges, legislators, and pa-
triots. Lewis Morris, great-grandson of the first colonel, signed
the Declaration of Independence, even though one of his
brothers warned it was against their best interests. The im-
perious Morris cried, "Damn the consequences, give me the
pen!"[3] This same Morris subsequently lobbied to locate the
new nation's capitol on a portion of his property in Morrisania,
which he extolled as conveniently accessible by water, "perfectly secure from any dangers either from foreign invasion
or internal insurrection," and salubrious in climate, a spot
where invalids were "speedily reinforced in health and vigor."
Furthermore, it was defendable by "the hardy sons of New
England on the one side and the inhabitants of the populous
City of New York on the other."[4] His fervor persuaded no
one. In truth, the Bronx and its small settlements had been
ravaged by the Revolutionary War. Many Bronx farmers for-

sook their ruined acreage and moved on to more fertile farm-
land opening elsewhere in the young country.

Lewis's half brother, the Honorable Gouverneur Morris,
was a patriot and statesman of even greater renown. Gouverneur Morris joined General George Washington at Valley
Forge, where he helped reorganize the ragtag army. During
a sojourn in Philadelphia he established the decimal system
of American currency and invented the term "cent." In 1787
he attended the constitutional convention. Theodore Roosevelt, in his biography of Gouverneur, tells us "it was he
who finally drew up the document [the Constitution] and put
the finish to its style and arrangements, so that as it now
stands, it comes from his pen."[5] Subsequently Morris served
as the American minister to France during the Reign of Terror
and then as a U.S. senator from New York. He delivered the
eulogy at Washington's funeral. He was also an important
force behind the building of the Erie Canal.

For all Gouverneur's statesmanlike qualities, a later historian called him "conspicuous for his disregard of the opinions of the respectable portion of the community."[6] A great
wit and ladies' man, he did not marry until the age of fifty-
seven. He drove his phaeton like a hellion, smashing it up in
a terrible accident that cost him his left leg. John Jay heard
the rumors that he was eluding a wrathful husband and wrote
him, "I have learned that a certain married woman after much
use of your legs has occasioned your losing one."[7] Thereafter
Morris stumped around with a wooden leg (the floor of his
Morrisania mansion was pockmarked by it). He rebuked one
well-meaning sympathizer that he "had so handsomely argued
the advantage of being legless as to make me almost tempted
to part with my remaining limb."[8] In his later years, Gouverneur Morris grew disenchanted with American democracy
and complained of how the power of the old gentry was dim-
ming. The bodily remains of this illustrious family lie today
in a vault and small graveyard in Saint Ann's Church, a lovely
stone building erected on their property by Gouverneur's son
in memory of his mother. They are otherwise immortalized

in the Bronx by the many places named in their honor: Morris
Avenue, the neighborhood known as Morrisania, Morris High
School, Morris Heights, and the Gouverneur Morris housing
project.

The Bronx of the Morrises was still heavily forested, divided
into sizable estates interrupted here and there by small farms
and a few minuscule villages and townships along the New
York–Boston Post Road. The arrival in 1841 of industrialist
Jordan L. Mott heralded the introduction of the machine age
into the bucolic landscape. Mott bought from Gouverneur
Morris II a site bounded by Third Avenue, 134th Street, and
the Harlem River. After the sale he asked if he might name
his new settlement Mott Haven. "I don't care what he calls
it," said Morris. "While he is about it, he might as well change
the name of the Harlem [River] and call it the Jordan."[9] Mott
erected a sprawling Victorian factory, dominated by a tall
brick smokestack. This was the first major industry in the
Bronx — an iron foundry that produced sinks, ornamental
ironwork, and an iron cooking stove. Having settled near his
factory, Mott sought to persuade others to join him. In 1848,
a group of mechanics and laborers who wanted to escape the
tenements of Manhattan and build homes on their own land
asked Mott to act as their purchasing agent. He bought two
hundred acres from the Morris family for $37,622 in the vi-
cinity of what is now Washington Avenue and 160th Street,
which came to be known as Morrisania.

The same year that Jordan Mott erected his foundry, 1841,
the New York and Harlem Railroad crossed the Harlem River
and pushed through the wilds along Park Avenue. Wherever
stations were located, stores and houses soon followed. Further west, the Croton Aqueduct, bearing pure water to Manhattan's large reservoir, was also under construction. Thick
cast-iron water pipes ran south under University Avenue before emerging to cross the river under the twenty-five-foot-
wide walkway of the new City-built High Bridge, whose elegant hundred-foot-high granite arches vaulted across the
Harlem River, connecting the Bronx to Manhattan. The
promenade offered spectacular vistas up and down the river

and was a popular destination for strollers. (Edgar Allan Poe, who lived in a small country cottage in the north Bronx in the late 1840s, often walked down to the High Bridge.)

The aqueduct was to service the burgeoning port city of New York. On any day a visitor to the busy wharves of lower Manhattan could view hundreds of sailing vessels lining the piers. Longshoremen lumbered on and off the high-masted ships, unloading cargo and filling the holds with the myriad manufactured goods that had earned New York City the reputation of being the country's biggest, richest metropolis, "the greatest commercial emporium of North America." The completion of the Erie Canal in 1825, and then of the railroads, had dramatically increased New York's wealth, for it made the City the conduit not only for goods to and from Europe, but also for everything coming in and out of the Midwest. The City, its business and trade expanding exponentially, was itself growing at a prodigious rate. Wholesalers, auction houses, and warehouses overwhelmed once-residential streets near the harbor downtown, while new residential neighborhoods sprang up farther north. New York was a frenetic, driven city, dirty, crowded, cacophonous, and ripe with opportunity. In 1820 the population was 123,706; by 1860 it had reached 812,660.

Almost half of these New Yorkers were recent immigrants from Europe. The terrible potato famines in Ireland had driven the starving Irish to flee to America in the cargo holds of ships sailing for New York. The one million Irish who poured off the ships in the 1820s, 1830s, and 1840s were unschooled, and completely unfamiliar with and unequipped for urban life. Many moved on to other cities or to farms, but the worst jobs and rankest housing fell to the lot of the two hundred thousand who remained in New York. The men, with only their muscles and hands to offer, worked as longshoremen, day laborers, boatmen, chimney sweeps, bootblacks, and teamsters. The women toiled as laundresses, house servants, and waitresses.

The history *Manhattan Moves Uptown* describes a report by the *Courier and Enquirer* in 1853: "In one building, a twelve-by-twelve room housed five families, a total of twenty people. Two beds made up the entire furnishings; there were

Taken around 1904, this view of the Bronx from 179th Street and Bryant Avenue shows the suburban character of the borough. The completion of the West Farms elevated line—visible in the distance here—led to intensive development that filled these blocks with apartment houses.

no chairs, no tables, rugs, or partitions for privacy. The scenes in this building were so awful that the *Courier and Enquirer* thought that words did not adequately convey the 'gaunt and shivering forms and wild ghastly faces living in hideous squalor and the deadly effluvia, the dim undrained courts oozing with pollution, the dark narrow stairways decayed with age, reeking with filth and overrun with vermin, the rotted floors . . . and windows stuffed with rags.' "[10] Onetime backyards were built over with even taller tenements, obliterating what air and sunlight had filtered through to those miserable warrens. The first slums were the converted family homes, abandoned by the middle class and wealthy as they fled the immigrant hordes converging on and filling lower Manhattan. The houses were soon superseded by tenements newly built to hold as many families as possible, giving no consideration to light, ventilation, or such amenities as water or garbage removal.

The impoverished Irish inundated almshouses, courts, and jails. Although by the 1850s the Irish were one-third of the populace, they accounted for 55 percent of the arrests (about half for drunkenness) and two-thirds of the paupers. Police vans were dubbed "paddy wagons" after their most frequent occupants. Illegitimacy was commonplace. Native-born Americans reviled the Irish as lazy, filthy, drunken brawlers who bonded into young gangs and terrorized the streets. The Five Points section, an Irish slum of great notoriety, became one of *the* tourist sights for genteel visitors to New York. They shivered at the dirt and depravity and marveled at the vilest slum of all, a former Coulter's Brewery that was home to more than a thousand people.

Alhough their Roman Catholic religion only made the Irish further suspect, it was also their source of strength, and it gave them a powerful champion early on. When the public school system refused to share its money with Catholic schools, the church created a parallel system, catering largely to its Irish parishioners. The Irish also displayed a genius for politics, and by the mid-nineteenth century they had seized control of the Democratic party in New York City.

The Germans landed soon after the Irish, fleeing their own

smaller potato blight and then, after the 1848 revolution, political repression. While the Irish who stayed in New York were mostly peasants, the Germans who flocked there in the second half of the nineteenth century were often skilled artisans and industrial workers. Their superior earning power may explain their easier assimilation into the booming city. The Germans made up 10 percent of the populace and had a tenth of their people in the jails and poorhouses.

Very shortly both the Irish and the Germans found their way to the Bronx. The Irish first saw the Bronx when they were sent up in gangs of laborers, the brawn that constructed the New York and Harlem Railroad and the High Bridge. In 1847 they built the Hudson River Railroad in the northernmost Bronx. This was exhausting, dangerous work and led to the saying that American railroads had "an Irishman buried under every tie." Many of those Irish workmen, finding the Bronx a lovely and quiet change from frenetic Manhattan, stayed on and settled down with their families in Highbridge, near the aqueduct spanning the Hudson, and in Melrose, where the railroad entered the Bronx from Manhattan.

When the Germans moved to the Bronx, many turned to farming, but the more ambitious bought cheap land to open their own breweries (they disdained the weak American beer). These huge Victorian edifices were soon producing such famous Bronx brews as Haffen's, Ebling's, and Eichler's beer, which were aged in natural caves. Other Germans opened piano factories to supply music for the new continent. Newspapers with names like *Tagblatt* and *Volksfreund* catered to the new communities. Many of the Germans were Catholic, like the Irish, and in 1852 they built their first church in the lower Bronx, the Church of the Immaculate Conception, on 150th Street. In 1888 that wood church gave way to a magnificent red-brick structure with a towering steeple visible for miles.

The most enterprising of the Irish and the Germans opened businesses large and small in the Bronx, and, as they prospered, they bought fine pieces of rolling land and built spacious homes — turreted, gabled, bedecked with ornamentation and encircled by wide porches for the hot summer days and nights. Most of the newcomers were workers, however — participants in the fledgling industrial revolution. Having escaped the slums of lower Manhattan, they lived in the Bronx in neat wooden frame houses, with pigs, cows, and chickens in the side yards, and cultivated vegetable gardens in the rear. Many commuted to jobs in Manhattan, but others sought work in the factories opening in the Bronx.

The Bronx, so near to Manhattan, and newly discovered by the workers, was already prized by the rich as an ideal country retreat. One local historian made a record of the influx throughout the early 1800s of this new urban gentry and their fancy-label farm animals: "Wealthy men of New York, recognizing the beauties of the hilly, river and bay-girt region, sought rest from their labors by purchasing some of the worn-out farms, and erecting costly mansions, laying out well kept pasture lands, tasteful plantations, and sloping lawns. The town Clerk only enlarged the Poll list . . . with many names known in the mercantile, professional, journalistic and literary life of the great Metropolis."[11] And so the great estates were laid out alongside the small villages and early factories. Richard March Hoe, inventor and manufacturer of the fast rotary press for newspapers, built Brightside on Faile Street in Hunt's Point near his brother Peter's estate. Paul N. Spofford, a capitalist and director of banks and railroads, built Elmwood in Hunt's Point, not far from where the Simpson family summered in Ambleside and later Foxhurst. The Lorillards, with their large tobacco fortune, bought a vast estate with rolling meadows and virgin hemlock stands and built a splendid mansion. They also planted a famous rose garden whose best blossoms were used to scent the fragrant Lorillard snuff.

While the wealthy Manhattanites were raising trotting horses and prize cattle on their Bronx country places, the good citizens — second-generation Irish and Germans — of the small townships of Morrisania and West Farms were agitating for better services and, above all, paved streets to banish the annual mud plague. There was even talk of annexing the Bronx to the City of New York, but this aroused opposition

Charlotte Street at Boston Road in 1906

Doc Fisher's Saloon at Railroad Avenue and
Fifth Street in Morrisania, circa 1885

from some of the more extensive land proprietors, "who were opposed to all progress." By 1868 a commissioner had been appointed to map out streets throughout the Bronx. The resulting map supported the general belief that the district's future lay with the City, not with rural Westchester County, for the street map extended the Manhattan grid across the Harlem River, starting with the southernmost cross street in the Bronx, 132nd.

In the ensuing years the district's fate was "warmly agitated" in the legislature. Finally, in 1874, after a favorable referendum, the City of New York annexed the first lobe, all the territory east to the Bronx River, 12,317 acres with a population of thirty-three thousand. On New Year's Eve, 1873, "amid general handshakings and outside firing of many guns, the old town of Morrisania and the towns of West Farms and Kingsbridge expired, and the City of New York reigned supreme over the new territory above the Harlem River."[12]

In 1895 another 14,500 acres — the second lobe, the rest of the peninsula out to Long Island Sound — was annexed from Westchester County. This area of forty-two square miles was known variously as the North Side or the Annexed District. In 1898 New York City consolidated all its territories into the Greater City, and the Bronx became a separate borough.

From the start, leaders of the North Side complained that their district was seen as "a mere suburban locality, that was more to be tolerated than looked upon as a part of the city," and few of the hoped-for improvements in services and roads were made.[13] Mud still ruled supreme. The local property owners' association hounded the legislature for a North Side streets commissioner to oversee a complete topographical survey, street laying, sewer installation, and paving. When a group of state senators came in person to review the matter they "got a very practical introduction to the celebrated mud of the district by having their carriages break down and in having been compelled to wade ankle-deep in their shiny patent leathers to terra firma."[14] The senators were sufficiently impressed, and shortly thereafter, in 1890, the Bronx got its own street commissioner, Louis J. Heintz of the Parks Department.

With that accomplished, the borough's businessmen and leaders organized the Bronx Board of Trade and set out to lure more industry and citizens to their wide-open spaces. Progress and accomplishment — the twin gods — would be measured by the number of streets paved, bridges erected, stores opened, schools dedicated, factories established, and houses built. The Bronx was determined to share in the glorious future that New York City was building. Trumpeted the Board of Trade in a promotional book: "Within this magnificent territory upon which nature has bestowed her bounties with such liberality we may expect to see developed the residence quarter of the Metropolis, dotted with homes of the thrifty and industrious of moderate means as well as the palatial mansions of the wealthy."[15]

By 1897 the newly formed Bronx Board of Trade could boast of many factories from which issued "a great variety of commodities, such as iron work of every description, including stoves, ranges and furnaces, refrigerating and ice-making machinery, church organs, pianos, refrigerators, artistic bronze goods, electric supplies, surgical instruments, beaten gold, china and enameled ware, naphtha launches, railway lamps, paper boxes of every design both as to utility and beauty, window shades, toys, segars, brushes, carpets, dyeing and printing work, mineral waters, tape, soap, silks, shirts, drums, varnish and other products of necessity and practical usefulness."[16] The Janes and Kirtland Iron Works had had the great honor of making, section by section, the 8,909,200-pound dome of the Capitol building in Washington, D.C., and setting it in place with horses in 1863.

As New York City's economy boomed, its leading citizens wrestled with how to accommodate the seething masses of immigrants surging off the boats from Europe. There was no thought of restrictions, for each new wave provided the cheap and ready labor that was the basis of the City's growing manufacturing might. Reformers had been railing for decades against the putrid slums in which the immigrants lived. Civic-minded

New Yorkers had realized back in the 1840s that these pes-
tilential conditions and the unprecedented crowding were
breeding not only cholera and yellow fever epidemics, but
violent crime. Diarist and onetime mayor Philip Hone complained that "the city is infested by gangs of hardened wretches,
born in the haunts of infamy, brought up in taverns . . . who
patrol the streets making night hideous and insulting to all
who are not strong enough to defend themselves."[17] A young
Englishwoman, Isabella Lucy Bird, wrote that "existence of
a 'dangerous class' at New York is now no longer denied
. . . and that probably in no city in the civilized world is life
so fearfully insecure. . . . Terrible outrages and murderous
assaults are matters of such nightly occurrence as to be thought
hardly worth notice."[18]

By the late nineteenth century, the crowding in lower Manhattan had reached scandalous proportions. Thousands of immigrants flowed off Ellis Island weekly into the ghastly tenements already packed to the gills. Some slum neighborhoods
had 290,000 persons living in a mile-square area, crowding
far worse than that of the famously teeming and squalid cities
of India. A young journalist named Jacob Riis shocked and
galvanized the City in 1890 with his muckraker about New
York's slums, *How the Other Half Lives.* An angry indictment
of the tenement houses, it laid out in disconcerting detail the
terrible conditions and social consequences of Manhattan's
immigrant slums. Like many reformers of his day, Riis believed that poor housing was largely at the root of social disarray and misery. He wrote: "in the tenements all the influences make for evil; because they are the hot-beds of epidemics
that carry death to rich and poor alike; the nurseries of pau-
perism and crime that fill our jails and police courts; that throw
off scum of forty thousand human wrecks to the island asylums
and workhouses year by year; that turned out in the last eight
years a round half million beggars to prey upon our charities;
that maintain a standing army of ten thousand tramps with
all that implies; because, above all, they touch family life with
deadly moral contagion."[19]

Albert Davis, a Bronx architect who worried that such conditions might spread across the Harlem River, denounced the tenements of Manhattan, noting that "the extent to which the morality, integrity, and civic virtue of a city are dependent on the character of the home life of its citizens cannot be overestimated." He had nothing but contempt "for those property owners of the North Side whose greed of gain has caused them to attempt a repetition of this undesirable feature of lower New York."[20] All the good intentions in the world could not compete with the profitability of these tenements, however, and soon the Manhattan-style tenement made its appearance in the Bronx, replacing old family homes along the side streets of Mott Haven and Melrose. It took legislation in 1901 to ban forever the construction of the "old-law" tenements.

Horrified by the grisly living conditions of the new immigrants, and certain that City land prices would never get any cheaper, civic groups rallied for rapid acquisitions of parklands in all the boroughs. In 1895 the City condemned and acquired almost four thousand acres in the Bronx for parks and connecting parkways. In the South Bronx there were Saint Mary's Park (29 acres) and Crotona Park (142 acres). A bit farther north were Bronx Park (662 acres), which was close to being a wilderness, and Claremont Park (38 acres). In the far northern reaches of the borough sprawled the almost-wild Van Cortlandt Park (1,131 acres), and bigger yet, Pelham Bay Park (1,756 acres). The latter was more than twice the size of Manhattan's 840-acre Central Park. The Bronx parks were an immediate success, proving the great need for such rural respites from the hurly-burly of downtown. "Anyone who has visited Van Cortlandt Park on a clear, bright winter day and seen the thousands of happy skaters flitting hither and thither on Van Cortlandt Lake or who has wandered amid the shady dells of Bronx Park on a quiet Sunday afternoon and seen the troops of children, the young men and maidens, and even the old folks enjoying the fresh air and the beautiful scenery of that most beautiful of parks, has had an argument presented to him so convincing nothing further is needed," wrote one advocate in 1897. "On Saturday afternoons when the band plays in the parks the people congregate in large numbers and the scene is as animated and attractive as any furnished by Hyde Park or the Bois de Boulogne."[21]

Both the New York Zoological Society and Botanical Garden were given acreage within Bronx Park, encompassing the old Lorillard estate. The Bronx Zoo opened on November 8, 1899, and men and women in all their Victorian finery promenaded about gazing at the hundreds of strange and wondrous beasts. The zoo showed great foresight in acquiring the native American bison then being slaughtered by the millions out west. Years later, bison from the Bronx repopulated the decimated herds of the plains. The model for the old Buffalo nickel resided at the Bronx Zoo.

The Botanical Garden was patterned after Kew Gardens outside London. The first officers were Cornelius Vanderbilt II, Andrew Carnegie, and J. Pierpont Morgan. Without too much difficulty they raised $250,000 to erect a museum building and conservatory, and before long the garden was swarming with delighted visitors. One brief history tells that on sunny weekends hundreds of people arrived hourly. "Residents of Manhattan's crowded Lower East Side tenements spent Saturdays and Sundays at the Garden, passing the night in the cool hemlock forest. Long lines of newly washed clothes would sometimes be seen drying in the sun near the Bronx River."[22]

2

The First Boom
1900–1922

BY 1890 the bucolic Bronx had a population of one hundred thousand, a mere fraction of the 1.5 million residents who filled booming Manhattan, or of the 3.4 million citizens constituting the newly consolidated City of New York. The tremendous wealth and industrial and commercial activity centered in Manhattan should have made it plain to the world that the intense urban environment was bound to burst its island borders and overwhelm the annexed districts. Yet, as with most obvious eventualities, few realized how thoroughly the then-rural Bronx would be transformed into a city. In the borough's subsequent extraordinary development, the man who played a pivotal role was the one who foresaw this and acted on it. His name was J. Clarence Davies.

A dapper man who sported a goatee and a pince-nez, Davies first saw the Bronx in 1889. While convalescing from a broken ankle (suffered while rushing pell-mell to pay his insurance on time), he used to take long country drives with his cousin from their Manhattan abodes. The cousins "had seen the vacant fields, and felt the chugging force of the city downtown; some day it was bound to overflow into the Bronx," and they set up a real estate office.[1] The cousin was discouraged by the initially meager activity and went his own way, but Davies hung on in his Melrose office just across from a bottling works. Next door stood a blacksmith's shop; on the opposite corner a pharmacy; a block above, the general store. Thin, wiry, and determined, Davies trudged the dusty country roads, scribbling notes in a small book. While he sold a home or a lot here and there, he also secured commissions to sell the large summer places of the great families — the Morrises, the Lorillards, the Harpers, the Pells, the Ogdens — as they moved on to the fashionable resorts of Newport and Narragansett.

Davies's perseverance, preparation, and patience were rewarded munificently in 1904 when the Third Avenue elevated subway was completed up to the West Farms station. An extraordinary land boom exploded, and the Bronx was gripped with a frenzy of acquisition, sales, and unheard-of profits.

The *New Yorker* reported that "lots leaped from five hundred dollars to five thousand dollars literally overnight. Farms were dismembered; the Lydig Estate, at the West Farms terminus, was almost torn apart by the bidders. Streets sprang up, twisting like tendrils of some quick-growing plant. Boom traders cleaned up. Householders went mad, sold lots on one street and bought on the next: won, lost. Through it all, Davies kept his head, and his confidence. In two months, his commissions on sales totaled more than a quarter-million dollars; he spent most of it buying land for himself.

"No one, conditions being what they were, could have stopped the boom in 1904; Davies' accomplishment is that he kept it going through the years that followed. The blocks of land he dealt in were huge, and he was shrewd enough to adapt his methods to their size. He advertised on a large scale, taking full pages when others were content with an inch or two in a column. It is not easy for the average man, except in the excitement of the boom, to picture a community of houses where he sees only barren meadows; Davies helped imagination along by hiring workmen to lay down streets and mark off building sites, before the sales began . . . it was nothing to sell off a hundred acres in an hour, to turn over a profit of a hundred and fifty thousand dollars in an afternoon."[2]

The 1929 *New Yorker* story named Davies as the virtual inventor of the "modern land sale" and more important, the force behind the development of "that surprising, long-lying, intricately patterned borough, the Bronx. He is the man who took these towns when they were scattered crossroads communities, boomed them, developed them, and wove them finally so closely into the pattern of the city that now they remain only as names to identify the stations in the subway's course through that vast, sprawling borough, the Bronx."

The Bronx that J. Clarence Davies was selling was still largely a rustic backwater of old farms, modest frame houses, and quiet dirt roads that attracted ambitious immigrant families who wished to bring up their children away from the hustle and bustle of Manhattan. These were people who had gotten "jobs the day after they got off the boat, worked hard, reared families that were never hungry, [who] worshiped as they pleased, and earned their simple pleasures."[3] Yet all through the first decade of this century, the vibrant, sophisticated city of Manhattan was growing, spilling across the Harlem River, engulfing the old villages. Slowly but surely the old family houses came down to make way for that most urban of structures: the apartment house.

Louis A. Risse, a Frenchman and chief engineer in the Parks Department, was responsible for laying out roads in the young borough. The elite Rider and Driver Club of Manhattan asked that he widen Jerome Avenue in the West Bronx to create a racing speedway for the fast horses of New York City society. Risse had another, far more ambitious plan than simply enlarging Jerome Avenue. He envisioned "one, wide clean road from Washington Square, up a widened Fifth Avenue, clear up to Van Cortlandt Park," the Bronx portion of which would run along the elevated ridge of an old hunting path of his youth.[4] Risse took his new boss, Louis J. Heintz, out to the ridge. "As I unfolded my plan to the Commissioner," Risse wrote later, "explaining how the broad avenue I purposed building on the ridge would serve both as a speedway and a connecting link between the Park systems, and how I intended the traverse streets to pass under the Concourse, he stared at me as though he thought I ought to be removed at once to an institution for the feeble-minded."[5] As a progressive man of his time, however, Heintz quickly grasped the beauty of the plan and was won over before descending the ridge. Risse was soon lobbying for construction to begin, ar-

The Grand Concourse in 1924. By this time the inner lanes were no longer reserved for horses and bicyclists.

guing that "public opinion on the North Side is emphatically and enthusiastically unanimous upon the question of the Grand Boulevard and Concourse."[6] Risse plugged away, and work finally started in 1902. By 1909 the broad, curving avenue, said to emulate the Champs Élysées in Risse's native France, carried motorists on the outer of its ten lanes, while bicyclists, pedestrians, and horse carriages each had unpaved inside roadways, all separated by traffic islands planted with trees. The four-and-a-half mile Grand Concourse swept up from 161st Street all the way to Van Cortlandt Park at the Westchester line, past the double rows of shade trees and the handsome houses. Commissioner Heintz's successor declared simply, "When completed, it will be the most magnificent thoroughfare in the world."[7]

Each year the Bronx lost some of its rural and suburban character, and as it grew more cosmopolitan, pressure mounted for the borough to become a separate county, with greater autonomy. The Bronx County Bar Association began lobbying to this end in 1905, backed by the borough's first daily newspaper, the *North Side News*. The bill was reported out of committee but sat moribund until 1911. As clamor for county status grew, six hundred Bronx organizations banded together and sent 450 delegates to besiege Albany, wearing derbies, topcoats, handle-bar mustaches, and white silk badges emblazoned "Home Rule and Bronx County." In the course of the legislative struggle, state Senator Franklin Delano Roosevelt emerged as a supporter of countyhood. Years later he told how those opposing the measure, seeing that its backers were not present in large numbers, tried to force a vote on the issue. The supporters rushed to escape the chamber to forestall the vote, but the doors were locked and they were trapped. After further wrangling, the legislature decided to lay the question before the voters of the Bronx in a referendum, which passed in November 1912. A court fight over the constitutionality of the referendum ended happily for the Bronx on March 14, 1913, when the Court of Appeals upheld its legality. In 1914 the Bronx became a county in its own right.

By the time the Bronx stepped up to countyhood, the original Dutch settlers had long since been supplanted by the Irish and Germans, and, as Manhattan spilled over into the Bronx, the third wave of settlers came — the Italians and Jews, who had begun to inundate the Lower East Side at the turn of the century. The Italians, like the Irish, were primarily peasants. They were not fleeing famine, however, but lack of land and opportunity. Without any special aptitude or training for urban life of the booming industrial age, the Italians initially worked at the lowest, most difficult jobs. Education had counted for little in the farms of southern Italy, and the Italians of New York saw little point in schooling. Their almost-feudal heritage had not encouraged them to think in terms of upward mobility.

Above all, the Italian immigrants were fiercely clannish. All loyalties centered in the family. Women were sheltered, and unruly behavior brought shame. Many Italian men came on their own seeking only to earn enough to return to southern Italy and Sicily and buy land. Those who stayed in America relied on their families and relatives in time of need. If the problem was too great to be dealt with by the family, then they could turn to that peculiarly southern Italian institution, the Mafia.

The Jews, fleeing Poland and Russia in droves, saw America in a far more romantic and glorious light. Here they would be free of the restrictive laws and the pogroms that had bedeviled their lives in the old country. For them there was no going back. The German Jews, long established in New York, were horrified at the tens of thousands of Eastern European Jews swarming out of the steerage compartments of boats. These new Jews were almost destitute; favored medieval dark dress, shaggy beards, and forelocks; still practiced a very strict, Orthodox Judaism; and spoke Yiddish, a lowly folk dialect. Scornful as the German Jews were of this motley, penurious horde of coreligionists, they felt compelled by a strong charitable tradition to help out. Thus the Eastern Jews became the first mass migration to benefit from the strong philanthropic ways, however grudging, of earlier cohorts. One of the recent arrivals complained, after visiting a German Jewish charitable agency, that "every poor man is questioned like a criminal, is looked down upon; every unfortunate suffers self-degradation and shivers like a leaf, just as if he was standing before a Russian official."

The Eastern Jews came with qualities that significantly aided their adjustment in America. Prevented from owning land and farming or residing in many cities, they had been forced into entrepreneurial activities. They had often functioned as go-betweens for farmers and city merchants or worked as small businessmen, trading and peddling. Unleashed in the mercantile mecca of turn-of-the-century New York, the Jews flourished. They opened small shops, peddled from carts, and worked in the sweatshops of the garment industry and fur trades. Before long they came to dominate the latter and were highly active in real estate.

An important factor in their swift rise in the economic ranks of New York was a reverence for education. In the Jewish tradition, the rabbi-scholars were always the most respected and honored members of the community. And unique among the immigrants of this era, the Jewish intellectuals, teachers, and artists made the journey along with the masses, thus providing a rich, transplanted cultural life. The intellectuals, knowing there was no return, plunged into American life with gusto. Free to express themselves and organize as they had never done in Russia or Poland, they provided much of the ideology and talent for the first labor unions and the early socialist and anarchist movements. The Jews organized constantly — synagogues, unions, credit leagues, social clubs, fraternal societies, choral groups, theaters, newspapers, and debating societies.

Despite its modern-day reputation as a melting pot, New York has never been hospitable to newcomers. Each immigrant group had to wrest what it could from those already established. Earlier arrivals and natives scornfully dismissed each new wave of people. When the Irish came, they were excoriated as "Celtic scoundrels" and debauched drunkards;

the Italians were patronized as "mainly a vagabond but harmless class of organ-grinders, rag-pickers, bear-leaders, and the like,"[8] Another writer observed, "Our Italian fellow-citizens are contented with being allowed to stab each other when the fancy seizes them."[9] It was the Eastern Jews, their sheer numbers transforming the City, who evoked the most interest and disdain. Lamented one critic, "The Poles, Russians and lowest class of Germans come to us embued with Anarchistic notions — notions which are fed by the misery and disappointment of their life in this country where they had looked for affluence without work, and fostered by the freedom of speech which is permitted by laws which were framed to govern a people of entirely different character to those who have been pouring in upon us from the slums of Europe." The Jews were reviled as "the most helpless and inefficient immigrants that have ever entered this country."[10]

Yet another writer of that time, however, marveled in a *McClure's* magazine article at the determination and ambition of the Eastern Jew, his "constant industry, his remorseless pacemaking," and his success: "His economic improvement is paralleled by that of no other immigrating race." Moreover, he noted approvingly, they were most grateful to be here. "His enthusiasm for America knows no bounds. He eagerly looks forward to the time when he can be naturalized."[11]

As the Jews and Italians gained some measure of success, they too began to move into the Bronx, filling up the modern apartment houses and whole new neighborhoods arising on former farms and estates. New buildings went up steadily. Owners vied with one another to provide better amenities, such special touches as courtyards with statuary and fountains. Many proud landlords christened their property with names of family members and hired stonemasons to chisel them above the stone entryways. By 1900 the population had doubled to two hundred thousand. The basic form of development had been established — five- and six-story rental apartment buildings lining street after street, housing for the workers of Manhattan and their families. There was an ebullience to the Bronx of that era. It was a milieu to aspire to, and its varied population gloried in the opportunities and freedom the wide-open borough represented.

Their self-congratulation was not without cause. English novelist Arnold Bennett, who was fascinated by the life and conditions of average people, was much taken when he observed the fast-developing Bronx. In *Harper's Monthly* in 1912 he wrote: "I was led to a part of the Bronx (Westchester Avenue and Southern Boulevard) where five years previously there had been six families and where there are now over 2,000 families. This was newest New York.

"A stout lady, whose husband was either an artisan or a clerk, I forget which, inducted me into a flat of four rooms, of which the rent was $26 a month. She enjoyed the advantages of central heating, gas and electricity and among the landlord's fixtures were a refrigerator, a kitchen range, a bookcase and a sideboard. Such amenities for the people — for the *petit gens* — simple do not exist in Europe; they do not even exist for the wealthy in Europe. . . .

"Thence I visited the flat of a doctor, seven rooms for $45 a month. Now I began to be struck by the splendour and cleanliness of the halls, tesselated landings, and stairs out of Holland; the whole producing a gorgeous effect — to match the glory of the embroidered pillowcases in the bedrooms.

"The Bronx is different, the Bronx is beginning again, at a stage earlier than art, and beginning better. It is a place for those who have learned that physical righteousness has got to be the basis for all future progress." What amazed Bennett was that capitalists and landlords, not well-meaning philanthropists, had created this luxurious housing. He found it nothing less than a "wondrous sign of the essential vigor of American civilization" and a proof of great "public spirit."[12]

Leon Trotsky, who lived with his wife and boys at 1522 Vyse Avenue in the West Farms district in 1917 while awaiting the Russian revolution, wrote: "We rented an apartment in a workers district and furnished it on the installment plan. That apartment, at $18 a month, was equipped with all sorts of conveniences that we Europeans were quite unused to:

electric lights, gas cooking range, bath, telephone, automatic-service elevator, and even a chute for the garbage. These things completely won the boys over to New York."[13]

Playwright Clifford Odets, who grew up on Southern Boulevard off 167th Street in some of the original elevator buildings, remembered fondly the "delightful nights 'around the block.' The streets were crowded with boys and girls; women and men sat on the stèps, on boxes, and talked of wonderful things.

"On Southern Boulevard the big, red open air trolley cars moved. The conductor swung himself along the narrow landing board and pulled on a bell. In the car women and men without coats leaned back indolently after the long hot day. Some people got off at our corner and if it was someone's father he was greeted with a shout."[14]

The Bronx of that time was most desirable. In the first successful talkie, *The Jazz Singer,* Al Jolson, stalking stardom on the vaudeville circuit, promises: "Mama dahlin', if I'm a success in this show, we're going to move up to the Bronx. A lot of nice green grass up there and a whole lot of people you know. The Ginsbergs. The Guttenbergs. The Goldbergs. Oh, a whole lot of Bergs, I don't know 'em all." Jolson returns triumphantly to his family's cramped tenement on the Lower East Side and whoops, "Mama, I'm rich! We're moving to the Bronx!"

In the history of Bronx County and its transformation into a metropolis in its own right, the year 1922 brought three developments of great significance: groundbreaking for the Concourse Plaza, a luxury hotel right at the entrance to the Grand Concourse at 161st Street; Colonel Jacob Ruppert's decision to take his baseball team out of the Polo Grounds and build his own stadium a mere pop fly from the new hotel; and the election of the county's convivial young sheriff, Edward J. Flynn, as leader of the Bronx Democratic party.

From its conception, the hotel was a great cause within the borough's business circles, proof of the county's new maturity and stature. An entire blockfront, from 161st Street to 162nd,

Shoppers and mothers with babies bustle along Southern Boulevard at 163rd Street in this scene taken in 1913

was bought for $120,000 (within two years it would be worth $310,000) and $1 million raised. Despite the fervor of the crusading sponsors, there remained "many skeptics whose croakings had to be silenced."[15]

In March 1922 the construction of the hotel commenced. Designed by architect Paul Revere Henkel of Maynicke and Franke, the hotel rose swiftly, a bulky twelve-story red-brick building with two large wings, a limestone façade at street level, and a few Grecian urns gracing a flat roof topped with two tall flagpoles. Bas-relief wreaths provided simple decoration. Its "predominating feature," declared the Bronx Boosters, a group of businessmen, "is its sumptuous, spacious ballroom . . . a vast hall, seventy-five feet wide and one hundred feet deep. Marble trimming and wainscotting adds a touch of richness equal to that of any similar hall in the country. . . . Expense has not been spared."[16]

Just down the hill from the Concourse Plaza site, ground was just being broken for the $2.5 million Yankee Stadium, the largest of its day. For years, the Yankees had played across the river at the Polo Grounds in Manhattan, where the New York Giants reigned and spectators sat in a few free-standing bleachers. Giants manager John J. McGraw didn't particularly mind the Yankees playing there as long as they remained a second-string sort of team, operating in the shadow of his heroic boys. Then the Yankees were bought by new owners: Colonel Jacob Ruppert, scion to a brewery fortune and an "avid collector of jade, first editions, race horses, yachts and St. Bernard dogs," and his partner, the inimitably named Colonel Tillinghast l'Hommedieu Huston. Both dearly wanted a winning team. They lured Babe Ruth down from Boston, and he blossomed into a star hitter and all-around celebrity who captivated first New York and then the nation. In 1921 Ruth, a large fellow with spindly legs and wide moon face and pug nose, hit fifty-nine home runs. The third-place Yankees began outdrawing the second-place Giants. McGraw was not about to be upstaged on his own turf and soon issued an eviction edict. "The Yankees will have to build a park in

Queens or some other out-or-the-way place. Let them go away
and wither on the vine," he decreed.[17]

On February 5, 1921, Huston and Colonel Ruppert, eligible
bachelor and four-term congressman, bought ten acres in the
Bronx bounded by 157th and 161st streets, from River Avenue
to Doughty, from the estate of William Waldorf Astor. As
Joseph Durso recounts in his history *Yankee Stadium,* in April
1922 the colonel approached White Construction Company
and told them, "We must play ball there next spring. Are you
interested?" They were, and construction was begun in May.

3

Boss Flynn
1922

WHILE the real estate and business development of the Bronx was progressing in a most satisfying manner in the spring of 1922, the political situation was not. Ever since the Bronx's incorporation as a county eight years earlier, Bronx Democrats had been dominated by the Manhattan Democratic organization, Tammany Hall, as were the other three counties that made up New York City. "The immigrants, being human, wanted friends, jobs, the chance to become citizens. Tammany was smart enough to offer all three, in return for lifetime and often second-, third-, and fourth-generation fealty to the party. It was as simple and obvious as that."[1] One attempt by the Brooklyn Democrats to break free of Tammany's yoke had been effectively squashed. The Bronx county leader, Arthur Murphy, was once described as related to Charles F. Murphy, Tammany's leader, "only as the puppet is related to the puppeteer."[2] (Tammany Hall in turn was firmly in thrall to the Irish.)

The Bronx and its Democrats in 1922 were but a fiefdom of Tammany when Arthur Murphy died, leaving no clear successor. "There was a great deal of maneuvering by various candidates for the Leadership," wrote Edward J. Flynn years later. "At least three of the candidates were well out in front. Each of these sought repeatedly to obtain a majority of the Executive Committee, but none was strong enough for that. This situation continued for some time, and ultimately reached truly alarming proportions. The time seemed to have arrived when only intervention from outside might restore order in the Bronx. . . . Unquestionably it was up to Mr. Charles Murphy to bring order out of chaos in the Bronx."[3]

Seeing that there was no clear consensus, Charles Murphy of Tammany decided to appoint a triumvirate made up of two of the district leaders seeking the leadership and the newly elected county sheriff, Edward J. Flynn. "This was one of the greatest shocks I have ever received," wrote Flynn in his political autobiography, *You're the Boss*. Although he was most reluctant, professing himself a political neophyte, he accepted, and observed the arrangement, at least intially, with amusement. "Once a week we would hire a funeral hack and the three of us would proceed in state to Mr. Murphy's house on East Eighteenth Street. We would be ushered into his overly elegant parlor, where we would sit and wait. After an appropriate pause Mr. Murphy would enter and with great solemnity, say, 'How are you Steve? How are you Tom?' and then to me, 'How are you, young man?' Then he would seat himself with his usual dignity and ask, 'How are conditions in the Bronx?' Each of us in turn would reply, 'Excellent.' This would conclude the conference. We would rise, get our hats, climb into the funeral hack, and proceed solemnly back to the Bronx. This was the sum total of our contacts with the Leader of the party in the city."[4]

By Flynn's own account he got into politics in 1917 when Jim Brown, district leader for the Irish neighborhood of Mott Haven, asked him to run for state assembly. Flynn consulted with his brothers and they advised him to do it. Flynn's family was quite prominent in the lower Bronx and certainly did not fit the Irish immigrant sterotype of penniless peasants fleeing the potato famine. His father was a Trinity College man who had immigrated from Dublin and gotten a minor executive job with the New York Central. The elder Flynn's true vocation lay not in his work, however, but in scholarship and tutoring his five children. It fell to his wife, Sarah, to make the family prosper with her real estate investments in the booming Bronx.

When Jim Brown induced him to enter politics Flynn was not long out of Fordham Law School and in practice. A tall, good-looking young man who was regarded in his neighborhood as quite a wit and a charmer, Flynn was elected to the assembly despite a "none too energetic campaign" and acquitted himself adequately during his four one-year terms there. The Citizens' Union rated him "not particularly attentive or effective . . . absent on important roll calls . . . unsatisfactory record of votes."[5] When that same good government group sent him a questionnaire, he replied that he would be delighted to answer if they in turn could furnish the names of twenty of his constituents who were members. He heard no more from the Citizens' Union.

Once Flynn saw how outnumbered the Democrats were in the legislature, he concentrated on "social relaxation." His escapades with the nephew of Governor Alfred E. Smith caused some small commotion during the two-month legislative session in Albany, and he was summoned forthwith to Smith's executive office. "I went in fear and trembling," recalled Flynn. "When I finally entered the great room, Governor Smith, in his usual rasping voice, gave me as stiff a dressing down as I have ever gotten. It ended with the dire prophecy that no good would ever come, either to his nephew or myself. I determined then and there to surprise him."[6] That episode and a sense of boredom persuaded Flynn that he had had enough, and he declined to run again, deciding to devote himself to his lucrative law practice and real estate investments.

Yet his district leader, Jim Brown, clearly saw some potential in young Flynn, and ignoring Flynn's demur that politics was not for him, kept pushing him for various posts. Brown and Bronx leader Arthur Murphy finally persuaded Flynn to run for sheriff of Bronx County, a sinecure that possessed considerable political clout: it had 62 of the county's 165 patronage appointments available to good party men. In the Democratic primary Flynn had the then-rare experience of opposition, and very tough opposition at that: Patrick J. Kane, a powerful and popular district leader.

With the organization using its considerable influence, the charming, handsome Flynn won first the primary and then the general election. Kane, who had resorted to running on the Republican line, was demolished 92,755 to 50,816. Flynn became the youngest sheriff in the United States. For one so reluctant to pursue politics, he was enjoying a meteoric ascent.

It was not long after Sheriff Flynn took office that Bronx leader Arthur Murphy died and Flynn found himself part of a three-way leadership. At first, the easygoing Flynn found the whole setup amusing, but as the weeks and months went by, marked by the ritual pilgrimage down to Mr. Murphy's ornate parlor, he became more and more dissatisfied.

"Finally, one evening when Mr. Murphy had put this inevitable question, and O'Neil and Nugent had chorused their usual 'Excellent,' the Commissioner turned confidently to me. I fairly exploded the word 'Rotten.' Mr. Murphy showed some surprise. But he quickly pinned me down with a 'What do you mean?' I said that one man should accept sole responsibility, because under the existing system it was literally impossible to get decisions when urgent questions arose. Nugent might be playing golf, O'Neil might be at the races, and I myself very likely busy at something equally 'vital.' I pointed out that by the time we three could get together, the patronage in question would be absorbed by some other county, or the question of policy would no longer be important."[7] A sober Mr. Murphy then directed the three to return to the Bronx and select a leader. Although the young Flynn gathered a majority of votes, the rules prevented him from prevailing, and time and again the executive committee met and then dispersed with no result.

An outraged Flynn stormed down to confront an astonished and then bemused Charles Murphy, who soothed the young man and promised, "There will be a meeting of the committee tomorrow, and you will be elected chairman." The next night two hundred district leaders, captains, and their followers milled about in front of county headquarters, waiting for the outcome of the struggle. At half past ten in the evening of May 15, 1922, Flynn emerged victorious, the youngest leader of a major political organization in the country. The *Bronx Home News*, now the county's daily paper, reported on Flynn's coup, remarking that "his rise to political prominence has been amazingly swift."

The Bronx Democratic party in the early days was a classic big-city political machine, controlled by the Irish and modeled, some say, on the Catholic church, the most powerful and successful organization in their experience. Each election district and its captain was comparable to a parish and its priest. The district leaders, one for each assembly district (the Bronx then had eight), were the political bishops, while the county leader was the archbishop. The faithful were registered Democrats, ministered to by an army of ardent Democratic club members whose rewards were varied — for the few, jobs, appointments, and contracts; but for the many, nothing much more than the pleasure of feeling in the know, the excitement of political contests, and the camaraderie of the political clubhouses. Anyone could come to a club — and many did — seeking help with the landlord, a job, or a son in trouble. The quid pro quo for service was that the recipient would register as a Democrat and vote accordingly.

The clubhouses, one to each assembly district, were the foundation of the political machine. Thus, when Kane lost the election, young Flynn wasted no time obliterating his rival's last base, Kane's political club located in the old Third Assembly District in the southeast Bronx, a teeming neighborhood of walk-up tenements, small factories, and busy market streets.

The new Flynn club, organized by lawyer Albert Cohn (father of lawyer Roy Cohn) during the election race, was named the Pontiac Club after the American Indian chief of the Ottawa tribe. Whoever registered the club misspelled the name as Pondiac, and so it remained, to the confusion of outsiders. The Pondiac Club opened its clubhouse on the second floor of a handsome corner bank building at 809 Westchester Avenue. The club entrance was on the avenue, in the shadow of the elevated subway tracks. The floor of the spacious foyer was tiled in elaborate mosaic swirls, the wide stairs laid in heavy white marble, the solid wood banister cradled in brass fittings. At the top of the stairs a simple hand-lettered sign stated "Pondiac Democratic Club," with an arrow indicating a door down the hall. All the ceilings were pressed-tin designs. The club itself had a huge main hall with numerous offices and rooms off it.

On many a Monday and Thursday evening, the traditional club nights, long lines of neighborhood folk snaked along the hallway, down the stairs, and out onto the street, all waiting stolidly to see someone about a problem. From the time the club was set up in 1921 the surrounding neighborhood was home to the working class, mainly Jews, many of whom hovered just above poverty. "Everyone worked in factories," remembers Judge David Ross, who grew up nearby and was long active in the club. "The union was very, very significant to those people and very frequently made the difference to survival."[8] The club also played an active economic role. In this it followed the classic tradition of the Irish political machines from the time they were built up at the end of the nineteenth century — personal service and jobs in exchange for votes.

Before the poor Jews moved up to the Bronx from the Lower East Side, they had learned to expect such constituent service as the Pondiac offered. In *How We Lived*, Henry Schimmel described the Ahearns and their local club. "When the chief rabbi of New York died in 1902 and a mob of Irish factory workers began throwing bricks at the Jewish mourners, Mr. Ahearn instructed his men to move in and break their heads. When a peddler received a summons to pay a fine for violating a city ordinance, someone from the clubhouse went to the court to straighten things out. When a widow with orphans needed coal in the winter or ice in the summer, Ahearn's men were there before anyone else. . . . The Ahearns did a lot of good. John Ahearn was the first district leader in New York City to nominate an East Side Jew for municipal court judge. His son Eddie could be counted on to get Jimmy Walker to do one of us a favor. They did for Jews what no Jew could do — until we grew stronger and finally replaced them."[9]

The Pondiac Club had about two hundred dues-paying members, mostly men. On club nights several dozen, including the locally elected officials, would appear for duty. The young lawyers all offered their services gratis. They sat in cubicles rimming the walls of the large main room and conferred with constituents parceled out by interviewers at several desks. The whole place throbbed with chatter, drifting smoke, and the intermittent clatter of the El outside. File cards were kept for each voter, noting the requests for help and the action taken. If, for instance, a young mother, children in tow, came to complain of a lack of heat, the club would contact her landlord and "work it out." Others came in desperation because they had bills they could not pay or eviction notices. Then the club opened its coffers and paid. It was an investment in the voters, and no one expected or wanted repayment. Once, when a grateful constituent presented the leader with a box of cigars, it was returned huffily. The club expected votes, that was all. There were myriad reasons to come by the club for help: a businessman who hoped to get special parking in front of his store, a post office worker who wanted a promotion.

Anyone who came to the club not registered as a Democrat would be so registered shortly thereafter. At election time the precinct workers, equipped with the file cards detailing favors done, climbed the stairs of the walk-ups ringing bells, summoning voters, then crossing the rooftop to the next building and down the stairs, knocking on one door after another, flushing out the Democrats and dispatching them to the polls. And according to the votes produced in their district, the members of the Pondiac Club were rewarded when headquarters meted out jobs and contracts. The turnouts in the Third Assembly District were spectacular compared with our current standards of 50 to 60 percent. They often hit 90 percent, and in hard-fought races could rise to 94 percent, indicating that every living voter had been hauled willy-nilly to the polls. In 1923, 15,367 of 16,383 registered voters turned out, or 93.7 percent. In 1940, 34,946 of 38,920 registered voters went to the polls, for a 89.7 percent turnout. Getting the registered Democrats to the ballot box did not guarantee they'd vote the party line. Socialist candidates perennially garnered two and three times their registered party members, indicating that many radical thinkers belonged to the Democratic party for its excellent personal services but voted with the Socialists, or later the American Labor party, because they backed these parties' programs to redistribute income and establish social programs to help the common man.

Politics in the Bronx was serious business, and Flynn's ascension to leader in 1922 was of great moment to the 109,051 registered Democrats. They were in for some shocks as Flynn established himself, for over at county headquarters a small revolution was in progress. Dispensing with the traditional notion that a good leader had to be one of the boys, available to referee disputes, give opinions, massage egos, and mix socially with the rank and file, Sheriff Flynn, as he liked to be called, deliberately cultivated the opposite image. He set up a new county headquarters in a handsome office building of white stone on Courtlandt Avenue, just off the bustling shopping district surrounding 149th Street, known as the Hub.

Flynn, an educated, literate man who enjoyed good books and was acquiring a taste for fine art and travel, regarded the intellectual aspect of politics as the most compelling and the rest as mechanics. He wanted his political organization to run like a business, rather than as "a neighborly affair, with the Leader being called upon at all times, both at his home and at his office, by any Tom, Dick or Harry whose business may or may not have been important. There was too much talk, too much wasting of time, with too little accomplished. I wanted to streamline the organization. I intended to keep my personal life entirely separate from my political life. . . . The change was revolutionary at the time."[10]

Sheriff Flynn abolished the practice of seeing long lines of petitioners in person, and instructed the district leaders that all requests for patronage or favors must be funneled through them, to be presented when Flynn held court at county headquarters. He never visited the clubhouses except for such rare and major events as selecting a new district leader; he graced only the most important political dinners. "He would never think of attending a clambake or passing out Christmas baskets to poor though registered voters, and the party workers and voters on whom his power rests all know that he is one of the most difficult men in the city to find, let alone see."[11]

Those who managed to wangle an appointment with Sheriff Flynn found a tall, well-built, clean-shaven man, with heavy eyebrows, deep-set hazel eyes, and a broad forehead. His dark hair, combed straight back, was greying prematurely at the temples. He carried his 190 pounds well and was always impeccably tailored in the broad-shouldered suits of the day, a fresh boutonniere in the wide lapel, and a carefully folded handkerchief in the breast pocket. He also had a penchant for lurid Charvet ties. He was almost always perched on the edge of an immense wooden desk and smoking a cigarette. If the meeting dragged on and the visitor showed no inclination to leave, Flynn would rise up to his full six feet and start shaking his guest's hand, at the same time guiding him to the door. The young leader had little patience for political gossip or chicanery. The many gifts that followed his elevation to boss of the Bronx were all promptly returned. The word quickly went out that any jobholder who got in trouble was on his own. And any disloyalty to the organization meant instant firing and eternal excommunication. To Flynn, the basis of muscular, successful organization was loyalty, jobs, and patronage.

Flynn had seized power in a Bronx that could no longer be ignored. Its growth was nothing less than phenomenal, as its biggest booster, the Board of Trade, proclaimed again and again. In a promotional pamphlet issued in 1923, the Board dubbed the Bronx "The Nation's Sixth City," and still growing, already bigger than such major cities as Saint Louis, Boston, and Baltimore. The borough, which had had one hundred thousand people in 1890, was fast approaching a population of one million! The majority of the buildings were still one- and two-family houses, but apartment buildings were catching up quickly. In its survey, the Board of Trade tallied 13,177 freestanding houses, 4,782 "old-law" tenements, and 6,185 "modern" tenements, with 3,326 residential buildings under construction. The Bronx in 1923 already boasted of eighty public elementary schools with numerous annexes, thirty-three parochial schools, a continuation school, three public high schools, and two universities of national renown (Fordham and the uptown campus of New York University), two hundred places of worship, 4,172 acres of park (including the world-famous Bronx Zoo and New York Botanical Gardens), nine vaudeville or drama theaters, seventy motion picture houses, and twenty banks. More than twenty-five thousand workers were employed in 1,370 Bronx industries.

4

"The Bronx Is a Great City"
1923–1929

IN the annals of the Bronx, the year 1923 was certainly one of its most triumphant, bringing to fruition the big plans of the previous year. Down on River Avenue, Yankee Stadium was rising steadily, a behemoth among stadia, as the construction workers pushed mightily to get the great sports arena ready. The sheer magnitude and speed of the job were stupendous. An undulating stream of trucks and carts had to haul forty-five thousand cubic yards of dirt, twenty-two hundred tons of structural steel, twenty thousand cubic yards of concrete, and eight hundred tons of reinforcing steel. By April, eleven months after groundbreaking, the final lush green sod had been laid and home plate installed. The Yankees were ready to play ball.

Opening day was Wednesday, April 23. The glorious spring morning was just dawning when one Malcolm Drummond stationed himself at the stadium ticket window, the first Bronxite in line. By ten o'clock police had been dispatched from the nearby Highbridge precinct house to keep order as fans surged off the extra trains, trolleys, and buses scheduled for the grand occasion. The throng swelled larger and larger, until it became obvious that even this mammoth new stadium of sixty-five thousand seats couldn't possibly accommodate the army of baseball fans clogging the surrounding streets. At noon the stadium opened its gates, and the crowds burst in, swarming up the aisles into the tall, freshly painted bleachers. The Bronx Board of Trade sat in a reserved block of fifteen hundred seats between first base and home plate, while the Rotary Club, whose membership largely overlapped, sat in the next section.

A postcard of Yankee Stadium from 1923, the year it opened and the Yankees won the first of many championships

A thousand Bronx Elks turned out, and two hundred Kiwanis, a new group for the Bronx. Outside, twenty-five thousand disappointed fans were turned away from what would be the first of many sellouts.

When every seat and available foot of standing room was filled to bursting with exuberant fans, the Seventh Regiment Band marched smartly onto the field, led by composer John Philip Sousa, followed shortly thereafter by the Yankees, sporting their new blue-on-white pinstripe uniforms. Bringing up the rear were their arch-rivals, the Boston Red Sox, "a symphony of red: red sweaters, red-peaked caps and red-striped stockings." There was rousing applause as Governor and Mrs. Alfred E. Smith were spotted descending to their box. With that, Judge Kenesaw Mountain Landis, the first high commissioner of baseball, strode onto the field with the Sousa band leading the way. The two teams surrounded the center field flagpole. The crowd quieted and rose respectfully for "The Star-Spangled Banner" and the flag raising. "As the last note of the national anthem died away and the halyards were made fast, the big crowd let loose a roar that floated across the Harlem and beyond."[1]

At Governor Smith's bunting-bedecked box, the news photographers got their pictures, the Babe was presented a boxed gift that turned out to be a bat (a hint), and finally the governor rose, took the ceremonial ball, and tossed it onto the field. The crowd roared again and the game was on — and what a game! The score was 0–0 when the Bambino came to bat in the third inning with two men on base. He hit a flawless homer into the right-field stand. As Ruth circled the bases, "the biggest crowd in baseball history rose to its feet, and let loose the biggest shout in baseball history."[2] The game was in the bag after that, and the Yankees won, 4–1. It was a delirious day. The season was sensational, and that fall the Yankees ruled as the world champions of baseball. Yankee Stadium was christened the "House That Ruth Built."

Just two blocks up the hill from the stadium, as the Yankees celebrated a great inaugural year, the Concourse Plaza Hotel was preparing for its grand opening, a formal dinner to be

In this view looking east on 161st Street in 1926, the
Concourse Plaza Hotel looms large and majestic

given in the autumn by the wealthy and powerful Bronx Board of Trade. Manager George Everart, formerly of the Plaza Hotel in Manhattan and the Ritz in London and Paris, was overseeing all the last-minute details before the Bronx's first (and only) luxury hotel opened its doors. A French chef put his squadron of sous-chefs through their paces daily, turning out the elaborate dishes featured on the restaurant menu.

On Monday evening, October 22, 1923, a brisk fall night, "the greatest assemblage ever witnessed in Bronx County" streamed through the doors.[3] With a nod to the liveried door-man, the gentlemen in top hats and formal black tie strolled up the marble steps into the gleaming, wood-paneled lobby, lush with thick white pillars, suspended lanterns, marble floor, and potted palms. The new hotel, aglow with lights in the crisp fall darkness, was every bit as deluxe as the Waldorf-Astoria in downtown Manhattan. The debut of the Concourse Plaza marked — with sedate fanfare and high style — the coming of age of the bumpkin borough.

To underscore the importance of it all, the governor of the state of New York had come to pay tribute and give the main address. As Alfred E. Smith rose on the dais to speak, the elated businessmen also rose, launching into "The Sidewalks of New York," the governor's favorite song. When the final chorus subsided, Governor Smith lauded the Bronx as the "most striking example of urban development in the United States" and then delighted the assembled Bronxites with tales of his own youthful vacations spent on a Bronx farm and of his sister, who had lived on Southern Boulevard in West Farms. "One day while she was pushing a baby carriage a cow came along," he related, "and she ran away, leaving the carriage and baby where they stood." The Bronx, however, as the governor's presence made clear, was no longer just a suburb of cows and hicks, it was a growing city in its own right and the hotel was proof. "Today," concluded the governor, "the Bronx is a great city. I want to extend my congratulations to you men who brought this great Concourse Plaza to realiza-tion, and I stand by at all times ready and willing to help in any way I can. After seeing this new structure, I am convinced that anything will go in the Bronx." The whole ballroom rose with a roar.[4]

From the night of its glittering opening, the Concourse Plaza Hotel was established as the social, political, and sporting center of the Bronx. Just about anything important that happened in the Bronx took place there — in the lobby with its marble floor and potted palms, the chandeliered Grand Ballroom, the quiet elegance of the Wedgewood Room, Terrace Room, or Gold Room. After a game at Yankee Stadium, the teams and fans alike — a mass of wide-lapeled suit jackets, baggy pants, and brimmed caps — walked up the hill to the imposing hotel, the players to relax briefly in their rooms, the fans to crowd the restaurants and lobby, rehash the game, and wait for their favorite players. Little boys hung about the front doors in clusters, darting forth to get an autograph or just to gaze up in awe. Legend has it that the one three-bedroom suite in the hotel, located on the top floor of the northern wing, was enlarged specially for Babe Ruth. His first wife, Helen, lived there for a while when they separated in the mid-1920s.

All the big fraternal organizations met at the Concourse Plaza, and some — the Rotary, Lions, Medical Society, and Automobile Dealers — even made it their headquarters. If an event was to be truly classy, it had to be at the Concourse Plaza, whether wedding, bridge or tea party, club meeting, political dinner, communion breakfast, or the myriad gatherings that marked the Bronx social rituals of the time.

It instantly became the best address, a smart abode for those who found the bustle of the hotel and its extensive service congenial. In its first years, the hotel, which was principally an apartment hotel, sought out an exclusive, permanent clientele, while setting aside some rooms for such glamorous worthies as the Yankees, and all the visiting college teams coming up to play Fordham. The hotel went all out to be as luxurious as any first-class hotel. Each of its 160 suites had its own kitchen and included the services of a "chambermaid, bathroom maid, charwoman, houseman, porter, and bellboy." There was restaurant service for the apartments at all hours and a commissary in the hotel, as well as a hotel laundry, barber, valet, hairdresser, and newsstand. On the hotel roof was an "open-air playground with an attendant in whose care children may be left during short absences, as when the mother desires to make an afternoon call or attend the matinee." Closets were lined with "Kilmoth" cedar, "permitting storage of furs."[5] Rents ranged from $125 a month for a two-room suite to $250 for four rooms.

The hotel anticipated serving the crème de la crème. By subway train it was "less than 30 minutes to Wall Street." The Concourse tenant clearly would be one of the elect. "Through his window in a upper story, the Concourse Plaza tenant views the world's metropolis from an airy and peaceful height," trilled the hotel's advertisements. "Looking to the south, one has the illusion that the Concourse Plaza is on a plane with the Metropolitan Tower and Woolworth Building. To the west one sees the Palisades of the Hudson and to the east the waters of Long Island Sound. To the north stretches the beautiful green parkway of the Grand Concourse. At night the myriad lights of the city are a fascinating sight."[6]

One woman remembers living in the hotel when it first opened. Her parents had sold their large Victorian home in booming West Farms, where apartment houses were rapidly encroaching. "The hotel was *the* place they wanted to move to. My father was in the manufacturing business, in silk. There wasn't anything better than the Concourse Plaza." Along the whole sweep of Risse's Grand Boulevard and Concourse, only one edifice, the Theodore Roosevelt Apartment Hotel, could compare, but that was many blocks north. The new ten-story hotel dominated, a stately vision with its canopied front, uniformed doormen, and striped awnings shading every window.

The last Saturday before the general election of 1924, John W. Davis, Democratic candidate for president, came to the Concourse Plaza in the Bronx for the first of what was to become a ritual event among the Democratic candidates — the Ladies' Luncheon. In the Grand Ballroom, festooned with patriotic bunting and campaign posters, one thousand lady Democrats of the Bronx — dressed to the nines — cheered their party's slate, from president to senator to City judge. Women in gowns of black satin with large, black, ostrich-trimmed hats, beaded crepe de chine, and smart little chapeaux applauded lustily as Davis reassured them "a Democratic victory is before us, I for one, have no doubt." Another candidate told the ladies, "Washington needs a housecleaning and there is no one who can clean house as well as the women."[7] (Naturally, Sheriff Flynn presided over this gratifying display of his own growing influence. Registered Democrats in the booming borough had increased in two years by 25,000 to 134,695.)

Even though the national election was a rout for Davis, as Calvin Coolidge swept the nation, Governor Smith was easily reelected and immediately set out to settle some old political feuds by installing his own mayor in New York City. Flynn cemented their nascent political alliance by backing Smith's choice, James J. Walker, a charmer with a flair for politics. After his election in 1925, a grateful Walker appointed Sheriff Flynn city chamberlain, a position akin to treasurer that paid $12,000 and required only an occasional appearance at the office. Flynn was now a rich man, thanks in large part to his real estate investments.

Flynn had joined forces with Monroe Goldwater, an old friend and neighbor from the Bronx who was considered one of the most brilliant lawyers in Manhattan. In time, they became Goldwater and Flynn, and the two partners and staff practiced out of luxurious offices in the Lincoln Building at 60 West 42nd Street in Manhattan. Their firm was the preeminent political law firm in New York City, but they actually did law work, as Warren Moscow explained in his book *What Have You Done for Me Lately?*: "Political law firms were accustomed to accepting fees for allowing their names to appear on briefs while another firm did the work. The lawyer with an 'in' might get $10,000, those who did the work, $40,000. Flynn and Goldwater combined the operation, insisting on using their skill as well as their 'in' to collect the entire $50,000."[8]

Throughout the 1920s, the newly metropolitan Bronx mushroomed. Each year another four or five thousand buildings sprang up, and the old fields and steep valleys disappeared under the solid rows of modern apartment houses. Yet the borough's wild, rocky topography could not economically be graded, so the streets and new structures deferred to nature. Solid phalanxes of buildings rolled up and down the ridges and inclines, accommodating themselves to the undulating landscape. It was very common to find apartment buildings with their front entrances at one street level and their service entrances several flights below on the back street. The vertical drop between parallel streets was often so dramatic the connecting cross "street" was actually a long, steep, stone staircase, known locally as a step street.

In *Bronx Primitive,* a memoir of her childhood, Kate Simon recalled the neighborhood at 178th and LaFontaine near Crotona Park where her family had moved from Manhattan. Her family, Polish Jews, lived on the fifth floor of a walk-up on a street where unaccented English was a rarity and cause for alarm (it might well be someone official). The young Kate kept a close and protective watch on her varied East Tremont neighbors. "I was the queen of my block. No one but I knew it and I knew it well, each morning making a royal progress on my empty street, among my big garbage cans, my limp window curtains, my sheet of newspaper slowly turning and skidding in the gutter, my morning glory on Mrs. Roberti's porch vine, my waiting stoops fronting my sleeping houses; my hat factory on the corner of 179th, resting from its hours of blowing pink and blue and purple dye smoke; my Kleins, my Rizzos, my Petrides, my Clancys safely in bed, guarded by my strength and will.

"Early one July morning, the sidewalk already soft and steamy like the bed I had left, I made my usual surveillance. . . . All was well: the DeSantis garage door was locked; the factory door was locked. . . . The oldest DeSantis boy, still chewing on a breakfast roll, came out of his stucco house to set a chair on the porch for his grandmother. Annie's father in his working cap, carrying a brown paper lunch bag, ran down the stairs of their house and turned briskly in the direction of the El station. Windows and doors shot open, the trickle of voices thickened and the legs of the fathers on their way to work became a jumble of zigzags on the sidewalk. I watched my show, contented with its expectedness, hoping a little for the unexpected. Maybe Mr. Kaplan would be wearing his new hat to work, like the gentleman and hero he was. Two Sundays ago he had shouted up at a towering goy who wouldn't let him sit on a nearby park bench. 'Because I'm a Jew and you're a Christian I should kiss your ass? You can kiss my ass.' If not Mr. Kaplan's hat, maybe Mrs. Santini would come out on her porch, chewing yesterday's spaghetti and pushing it into the mouth of her new baby, like what birds did, and then nurse it with a pale flood of breast."[9]

The world of the old Bronx neighborhood was a simple one. The fathers, wearing loose somber suits, white starched shirts, dark ties and caps, went off to work, usually in factories or sweatshops in downtown Manhattan, while the mothers stayed home and cleaned the house, did the marketing, washed the clothes, and brought up the children. During the day when the husbands were gone, the peddlers, or better yet, the street singers, made their rounds. The women at their chores would suddenly hear a rich baritone serenading below. Young, brawny, and handsome, the street singer displayed his fine form with an open tieless shirt and rolled-up sleeves. J. Jacobs wrote in his memoir, *Bronx Cheer:* "He would swagger up to the front of the building and with all his heart in stentorian volume, sing such songs as:

> *My Wild Irish Rose*
> *The dearest flower that grows*
> *You may search everywhere*
> *But none can compare*
> *To my beautiful Wild Irish Rose*

"The fact that all his listeners were Jewish was of no consequence. The enraptured hausfraus forgot their cares and called down requests. The housewives paid homage by throwing down a flurry of small white packages which looked like strange snow on the hot sunny street. The packages contained coins which the Side Walk Serenader would pick up, then kiss his hand upward and intone, 'Thank you, dear ladies.' "

The children attended school, did their homework, or played in the street. For the Jews, Friday night was the Sabbath. Saturday was movie day, a matinee at the local theater, or for very special occasions a trip to such fantastic picture palaces as Loew's Paradise on the Grand Concourse. For the Catholics, Sunday meant mass and a big afternoon feast. The days and weeks followed a simple, predictable, and pleasurable pattern. From time to time a relative right off the boat — a greenhorn — would come to stay, sleeping on a cot in the living room until he or she was paired up, married off, and settled in a job and apartment.

Al Smith, the popular governor of New York, was himself the child of immigrants and a boy of the streets. He was the "hero of the cities," the champion of the newest Americans — the Irish, the Jews, and the Italians. Entertainer Eddie Cantor, who campaigned for the governor, wrote, "I can never forget the picture of this young and handsome Mr. Al coming among the ragged, hairy, bearded people of the abyss, extending a hand of welcome and friendship to all of them, as if the lady of the Statue of Liberty had sent her own son to receive these poor, bewildered immigrants on her behalf."[10]

In 1928 Al Smith at last captured the Democratic presidential nomination that had so thoroughly eluded him four years earlier. He gave great thought to who should replace him as governor, and he believed it should be Franklin Delano Roosevelt. Before leaving to campaign in the West, Governor Smith delegated Edward J. Flynn, boss of the Bronx, to persuade Roosevelt to run. Adamantly opposed at first, Roosevelt began to relent with each successive phone call from Flynn. Finally, the only roadblock was financial, for Roosevelt had put a great deal of his own money into the Warm Springs Foundation and was concerned that the health resort be properly managed. Flynn and Smith got John J. Raskob, a wealthy industrialist and at that time chairman of the Democratic National Committee, to agree to underwrite Roosevelt's financial obligations, thus freeing him for political service.

Roosevelt devoted most of his campaign efforts to the up-state counties, but the Saturday before the 1928 general election found him and the rest of the Democratic slate, with the exception of Smith, before the Ladies' Luncheon at the Concourse Plaza Hotel. The air was electric with anticipation, and the lady leaders had to thread their way through a packed entryway to get to the ballroom. Roosevelt and his son James, who had come down from Harvard to escort his father, entered the ballroom, its walls draped in red, white, and blue bunting. All eighteen hundred women rose in a fifteen-minute ovation. Roosevelt exhorted the ladies of the Bronx to make sure their county had "the largest Democratic majority in any borough in the city. This is not only just my hope, but it is your promise to me and to Alfred E. Smith."[11] Bronx voters, spurred on by the Flynn organization, more than fulfilled that promise, but voters elsewhere in the state and nation did not. Alfred E. Smith, bitterly disappointed as the returns rolled in, was roundly rejected not only throughout the country, but in his very own state. Herbert Hoover was the new president.

Flynn and other party stalwarts who gathered at Roosevelt's headquarters for the presidential and gubernatorial returns were shocked. "Gloom and disappointment were everywhere. In fact, the newspapers announced that Franklin D. Roosevelt had been defeated and that his opponent, Albert Ottinger, had been elected Governor . . . Louis Howe was heartbroken. Roosevelt, with his usual good nature, took what he considered his defeat philosophically, and went home."[12]

Flynn, perhaps remembering his mentor Murphy's line, "I have allowed them to cut off my right arm. I have allowed them to cut off my left arm. But I have always outwaited them," sat chain-smoking and analyzing the upstate returns, which were coming in fitfully.[13] He became convinced that Roosevelt had actually won and telephoned to tell him so. A sleepy Roosevelt told Flynn he was "wrong and crazy to wake him up." Undeterred, Flynn called a press conference at two

o'clock in the morning and announced to the assembled reporters that the extreme delay in reporting upstate returns
indicated fraud was afoot and that the Democratic State Committee was sending up one hundred lawyers by train the next
morning to stave off further skulduggery. It was a complete
bluff, but the upstate votes started rolling in, providing the
twenty-five thousand vote margin that made Roosevelt governor. As dawn broke, a triumphant Flynn appeared at Roosevelt's brownstone on East 65th Street to crow over the results. Roosevelt, still in bed, "received the good news with
undisguised astonishment."[14]

The Bronx was accorded new political respect, for Boss
Flynn had played a major role in electing the City's mayor,
Jimmy Walker, and the state's new governor, Franklin Delano
Roosevelt. Political pundits were suitably impressed, but they
assumed Flynn had probably reached a natural and permanent
plateau of power. There was little precedent for an Irish county
boss to do much more than pull local strings. So when Roosevelt took office in 1929 and persuaded Flynn to become
secretary of state, replacing Robert Moses, there was astonishment in the political ranks and speculation that Flynn might
have political ambitions of his own.

5

"Hard Hit by the Depression"
1929–1932

IN late October 1929 the stock market took a final and furious crash. The *New York Times* reported that it "largely affected rich men, institutions, investment trusts and others who participate in the stock market on a broad and intelligent scale. . . . They went overboard with no more consideration than the little trader who was swept out on the first day of the market's upheaval, whose prices, even at their lowest last Thursday, now look high in comparison."[1] With each passing week the ripples from the crash gathered strength. President Hoover, trying to avoid the harsh, old-fashioned label of "panic," eventually coined the kinder term "depression."

All over the country, people lost their jobs as businesses failed or cut back. By the next February Bowery bread lines were drawing two thousand men daily. Families put off buying, and the economic spiral widened. April 27, 1930, was deemed Unemployment Sunday, and Rabbi Beckhardt of Beth Israel Temple in the Bronx declared "work a blessing and unemployment a crime." National income plunged from $81 billion the year of the crash to $68 billion in 1930. The Protestant churches joined together to form an Emergency Work Bureau, which gave married men with two children work three days a week at five dollars a day. The Methodist Church on Mott Avenue opened its work bureau, and every day and night hundreds of men came seeking jobs, armed with the required letters testifying to their desperate need. The chaplain, A. Hamilton Nesbitt, tried to place them all, "a task so stupendous as to be almost heartbreaking. They were not looking for charity but a chance to get back on their feet."[2]

Shortly after the work bureau opened, it was supplemented by a soup kitchen serving sixty-five hundred meals a month at long, wooden refectory tables. The men poured in, tired, hungry, and discouraged, but always respectably attired in white shirt, vested suit, and tie. The churches were financially exhausted, and when it seemed the soup kitchen would have nothing to feed its men, desperate appeals went out to the business community, pleading for money.

The week of October 19, 1930, the Lions Club in the Bronx and elsewhere in the nation celebrated Business Confidence Week, trying to boost morale and the economy. By November six thousand out-of-work men were selling apples from make-shift stands for a nickel apiece on the sidewalks of New York. They so cluttered certain sections of midtown that apple sellers were banned from some streets altogether.

One woman's parents were living in very comfortable re-tirement at the Concourse Plaza, her father having sold his dye works in West Farms to Consolidated Laundries during the boom years. Now Consolidated Laundries wanted to shut his former business. "My father took it back," she remembers, "and he used the fortune he had amassed to try to keep it going and to keep his employees employed. There were forty or fifty of them, and some of them had been there forty years. There was no unemployment, no welfare, and if they were out of a job, they were out of a job. Finally he had used up all his money and he had to close the place." In February 1933, financially ruined, the parents moved out of the Concourse Plaza into their daughter's home in Riverdale.

Families doubled up. Vacant apartments proliferated in the Bronx, and anxious landlords offered two and three months' free rent to new tenants. On May 1, the traditional moving day, thousands of families loaded their households onto large carts, leaving one perfectly good apartment to move to an-other and save a few months' rent. It was a real estate merry-go-round.

The Depression was the worst of times for many, but for one young Jewish matron who lived on the elegant Grand Concourse with her husband and two children, 1929 was her lucky year. An aspiring radio writer and actress, Gertrude Berg had submitted a sample script called "The Rise of the Goldbergs," about the ups and downs of the immigrants Jake and Molly and their Americanized son and daughter. NBC radio, still in its infancy, liked the fifteen-minute show and signed up Gertrude to play her own creation, Molly, launching the Goldberg family on a twenty-year career on the public airwaves, first on radio and later on CBS television. Jake, a cutter in a dress business, and Molly, the housewife, had the thick Yiddish accents of the Bronx. Molly was a bit wacky, but ever wise and kind, and she specialized in delivering delightfully muddled nonnative phrases spiced with absurdly high-toned pronouncements. After a summer vacation in a Catskills resort, she burbled happily to her neighbors across the air-shaft, "The cuisine was incomparable. . . . Everybody was a somebody . . . and one lady told us of her son the legal luminous light."[3] Jake was a good husband and father who was consistently taken advantage of. In the course of the show the kids grew up, went to college, married, and aged like a normal family. The daily travails of the Goldbergs were warm and simple and their fans legion. For millions of people, the Goldbergs *were* the Bronx.

During the Depression, the City was gripped by not only economic but political turmoil. Both Governor Roosevelt and Jimmy Walker, the City's charming, high-living mayor, had been easily reelected in the fall of 1930. Before the campaign, revelations of unsavory doings in the lower courts led Governor Roosevelt to appoint Judge Samuel Seabury to investigate, and as the months passed, Seabury's thorough inquiries widened, encompassing City Hall. By 1932 the mayor himself was suspect. Beau James had allowed his numerous "friends" to enrich themselves at the City's expense, and many wondered, "Had the mayor done the same?" Dramatic hearings took place in Albany. As Roosevelt pondered what action to take, Jimmy Walker resigned on September 1, 1932, and embarked quickly for Europe. It was a great relief to Roosevelt, who was running for the presidency on the Democratic ticket

Edward J. Flynn, the Bronx County Democratic chairman known as Boss Flynn (right), shares a laugh with President Franklin D. Roosevelt, Mayor Fiorello LaGuardia, and Eleanor Roosevelt as they head off to open the 1939 World's Fair. Flynn, the fair's commissioner, was a close friend of Roosevelt.

and did not want further scandal to weaken the party in his own state.

The boss of the Bronx was examined many times. Years later Flynn was to say that it was not Walker who interested Seabury, but Flynn. "He felt that if he could dispose of me, he could dispose of Roosevelt. Way back in Seabury's mind was the fact that he thought he really could become a candidate for the presidency. He searched my records from the time I was born — not only my own records but all of my family's bank accounts, my children's trust funds. He found nothing and he would never admit he found nothing."[4]

While Seabury investigated the City, Roosevelt's presidential campaign geared up under the aegis of Jim Farley and Flynn, and the economic situation got worse. By 1932 national income had dropped to $41 billion, or half its 1922 level. As governor, Roosevelt had established a Department of Welfare, but state finances were straining under the burden. New York City bankers raised a million dollars and lent it to the City to distribute to impoverished families, but the City's Department of Welfare did not even have the money for postage stamps to send out the checks. And the sums handed out were pitifully small, as low as $2.39 a week in 1932 for a family. All over the City shantytowns arose, filled with jobless, despairing men. In the Bronx the local Hooverville appeared on the Harlem River, not far from Highbridge, along the railroad track at the end of Burnside Avenue. Each day its ragged army of poor emerged to seek work or scrounge through garbage cans, trying somehow to survive the collapse of the booming, frenetic, prosperous world that had been America in the Roaring Twenties.

With the Depression so bad and no sign of a recovery — despite constant optimistic pronouncements by Republicans and business leaders — Roosevelt was virtually assured election. His cheery style and self-confident manner were a breath of fresh air after four years of the dour, stuffy Hoover. Although Roosevelt was a wealthy man — a mark against him — he was also a man who had suffered from polio, recovered, and valiantly reentered public life. Neither Roosevelt's candidacy nor his election had been a sure bet when Farley and Flynn launched his campaign, but their political efforts, the dead economy, and Roosevelt's great personal charisma made both men optimistic. From the start, when Roosevelt called Flynn up to Albany in November 1930 and told him, "Eddie, I believe I can be nominated for the presidency in 1932 on the Democratic ticket," Flynn was busy behind the scenes, marshaling funds and votes, and generally assessing what he always called "conditions."[5]

As the presidential campaign reached its final days, Roosevelt went to the Concourse Plaza for the Ladies' Luncheon. The hotel ballroom was magnificently swathed in the traditional red, white, and blue bunting and huge posters of the candidates lined the walls, but — a sign of the hard economic times — attendance was down by a third. A phalanx of City and state policemen swept into the ballroom, Governor Roosevelt in their midst. When the roar of applause subsided, Roosevelt began. "Not long after the Democratic convention at Chicago, at which I was nominated, your leader Edward J. Flynn told me I had a date in the Bronx on November 5. It was the first date that I made as a presidential candidate, and I made up my mind to keep that appointment." The roar welled up and drowned him out again as eleven hundred women Democrats of the Bronx stood and cheered. Through the noisy wall of enthusiasm, Roosevelt praised the progressive tradition of the Democrats and then exhorted the ladies to set another voting record worthy of "Admiral" Flynn, who so wisely "commanded his voting fleet." As speaker after speaker rose to praise Flynn and his mighty organization, the ladies realized they were witnessing an extraordinary tribute, a paean to their leader from the country's highest Democrats, culminating with James Farley, chairman of the National Democratic Committee. "I have met a lot of leaders in political life in my time, but never have I met a man with keener political judgment and with finer and more perfect acumen on political affairs than your leader."[6]

While the rank and file revered and feared Flynn, he was the least bossy of bosses to his elected officials. He rarely ordered anyone to do anything, preferring to make suggestions. The number of registered Democrats had tripled in Flynn's decade as county leader. By 1932 there were 325,269 Bronx Democrats out of 426,978 registered voters. It was not surprising that few elected Bronx officials had to be told to vote one way or another. As one said, "You didn't have to be told, you knew. You followed the party platform." In eight years in Albany as an assemblyman, Christopher McGrath, later a congressman and then a surrogate court judge, says he only once got a call from Flynn asking a favor, which was to hold up a bill for forty-eight hours.

Having so thoroughly adopted his mentor Murphy's style of least-said-the-better, when Flynn did say something it carried great weight. Anyone who failed to take Flynn's "suggestions" seriously did so at his or her own political peril. A Democratic county boss like Flynn, who could guarantee a solid block of at least three hundred thousand votes in a general election, was a powerful personage.

A story is told that one of Flynn's nephews was having a cocktail at the Concourse Plaza's bar when his companion, a prominent citizen, got up to use the men's room located in the hotel lobby. Somehow the companion lost his balance and fell and hit his head on the marble floor of the lobby. The nephew grabbed a beer pitcher full of water and, as he poured water on the unconscious friend, "baptized" him. Shortly thereafter the nephew was summoned by his uncle to Flynn's plush penthouse on a secluded drive in the Riverdale section. Dubbed "Ed's Gothic Aerie," it had thirteen rooms, seven porches, a solarium overlooking the Hudson River, a private elevator, and a separate street entrance, giving Flynn complete privacy. Few politicians were ever invited there. Uncle Ed quietly expressed his displeasure at the unseemly public behavior. He indicated that if his nephew's drinking didn't dry up, his political prospects would. For some time thereafter, the chastened nephew could be seen at social-political functions with a six-pack of club soda.

* * *

With his friend Roosevelt in the White House, Flynn's prestige and importance took a quantum leap. Only he, of all the City's bosses, had backed Roosevelt from the very beginning. He was not only a close political adviser to Roosevelt, but a member of the charmed inner circle of personal friends, in a way that even Jim Farley never was. For many years Flynn owned a country place in Lake Mahopac, Putnam County, and he and his family often motored over to Hyde Park to visit the Roosevelts. Flynn told of sitting on the vast lawn one day with the elder Mrs. Roosevelt watching a handiwork demonstration by some earnest craftsmen. The old woman turned to Flynn and "asked in her stentorian whisper, '*Where* does Eleanor get all these people?' "[7]

Flynn often went down to Washington to visit the White House and check up on "conditions." As Roosevelt's tenure progressed, the president came to value Flynn for his candor and his contact with the world outside of politics.

Eleanor Roosevelt, who was always close to Flynn, said he told FDR "the truth as he saw it and argued fearlessly." According to another Roosevelt confederate, "Ed was like no one else with him. I've heard Ed say to the Boss, 'Come off it, you old son of a bitch, I know when you're faking. Stop lying and tell me the truth.' The President would laugh and laugh and he'd always tell Ed whatever it was he wanted to know."[8] Yet Flynn's charm for FDR was, above all, his ability to put aside politics and talk of other matters. Brain truster Raymond Moley wrote that Flynn, "who always seemed bored with politics, had read widely and could amuse Roosevelt with items far from statecraft."[9]

Once, when Flynn was laid up feeling poorly, Roosevelt sent a telegram: "Drs. Hopkins and Roosevelt suggest new diet of minced marshals alternating with juicy judges. It will kill or cure, with odds on the former, but this is a desperate case. Further advice rendered on request without fee. FDR." The two friends also had a running joke about the political value of motherhood, with Flynn always reminding the president that saying something nice about mothers had a surefire appeal when addressing the electorate. "Everybody has them,

Mr. President," Flynn often grinned, "and you ought to be for them."[10]

Nonetheless, Flynn was prey to two weaknesses thought to be typically Irish — melancholy and drink. Richard Rovere, the *New Yorker*'s political correspondent, found Flynn, "despite his suave and at times cocky manner, an introspective, almost melancholy man who loathes crowds and conducts as much of his political business as possible from a distance."[11] Occasionally Flynn dropped from sight altogether, and it was at first rumored and then later known that Flynn was temporarily afflicted with the "curse of the Irish."

Above all, Flynn was the consummate political boss. Much of his fabled political ability came from simply having time to observe and think. "Flynn was far ahead of most political leaders in detecting the liberal trend among American voters," wrote Raymond Moley in his book *The First New Deal.* "It was on the basis of this appraisal that he advised Roosevelt in 1935 to alter the philosophy and direction of Democratic policies. He described to me at the time this shift of emphasis in the Roosevelt policies from the agricultural areas to the cities. He said, 'There are two or three million more dedicated Republicans in the United States than there are Democrats. The population, however, is drifting into the urban areas. The election of 1932 was not normal. To remain in power we must attract some millions, perhaps seven million, who are hostile or indifferent to both parties. They believe the Republican Party to be controlled by big business and the Democratic Party by the conservative South. These millions are mostly in the cities. They include racial and religious minorities and labor people. We must attract them by radical programs of social and economic reform.' Flynn was thus responsible along with Roosevelt for a profound change in the Democratic party and in national policies, a change the results of which we are continuing to witness today. I personally regretted this change, but Flynn was a realist, and his strategy, whatever one may think of its consequences, meant a new life for the Democratic Party."[12]

While Moley attributed Flynn's assessment to observations

made on long peregrinations into the heartlands, in truth his own county and city offered potent lessons. The people who lived in the Bronx at that time were those Flynn saw as natural members of a revamped, more radical Democratic party — Catholics, Jews, unionists, immigrants, and the children of immigrants. About 1,265,000 people lived in the Bronx of 1930. Fully 70 percent were either foreign-born or children of foreign-born — 97,000 Irish; 106,574 Germans; 464,608 Polish, Austrian, and Russian Jews; and 165,004 Italians. For the most part they were working class and heavily unionized. Of the 412,572 working men recorded in the 1930 census, 40 percent were listed in the category of manufacturing and mechanical industries, meaning carpenters, brickmasons, house painters, tailors, and garment makers; another 25 percent were in trade as store clerks, deliverymen, porters, small shop-owners, and salesmen. There were twenty thousand truck drivers, four thousand policemen, a thousand garbage men, and fifteen hundred firemen. The Bronx working class were almost without exception renters, not property owners. They voted as a block, and they were generally devoted Democrats because their experience told them that the party was a reliable agent for personal service and, on a bigger scale, for social improvement and justice. It was government that had finally outlawed the tenement with windowless inner rooms, ensured pure drinking water with the High Bridge aqueduct, now ran the formerly private subway system, offered free college education at the City's colleges, and maintained the parks and playgrounds. When the Depression deepened, these people turned to the Democrats for help, as they had to Tammany when they or their parents got off the boat. They were looking for more than the Tammany-style personal favor, however. They were coming to see that only structural changes in society would significantly improve their positions. The union men knew from their own struggles that the workers could, if united, wrest better conditions from the upper classes who ran the country. Socialism appealed to these men by advocating a governmental restructuring of society that would share the wealth.

The Depression profoundly altered long-cherished free-enterprise notions of how the world worked. Too many good family men simply could not find jobs. The building boom in Bronx County had collapsed. From almost six thousand new buildings a year in 1926, pumping $210 million into the local economy, new construction had plummeted by the early 1930s to seventeen hundred new starts worth $49 million. The winter of 1933 was particularly harsh. The New Deal had barely taken effect, many families were facing their third year of hard times, and their resources — material and spiritual — were almost gone. The National Recovery Act and the agencies mandated to carry out its mission were wrestling to set themselves up and get relief and jobs out to the suffering. Evictions throughout New York City had tripled from 420 families the year before to 1,257, and many of those unfortunates were relief families who had no money to pay rent. Everywhere journalist Lorena Hickock, Eleanor Roosevelt's friend, found terrible misery, families "skating along on thin ice, barely existing, undernourished, in rags, constantly threatened with eviction from their homes, utterly wretched and hopeless, their nerves taut, their morale breaking down. . . . The magnitude of the relief job in New York City and its complexities are breathtaking. One city block may contain almost 200 families on the relief rolls."[13] Remembers Judge David Ross, who grew up in the working class Third Assembly District: "People were very hard hit by the Depression. When I was in junior high school it was a daily occurrence to see people being evicted into the streets, with their four pieces of furniture, for nonpayment of rent. Women would be sitting in the street with infants in their arms and it would be raining. Neighbors came down with umbrellas and held them over them while trying to figure out where they were going to sleep that night."[14]

Roosevelt appointed Flynn regional administrator of public works for New York, New Jersey, and Pennsylvania, with control of the $3.3 billion allocated by Congress. Flynn now had at his disposal a huge reservoir of new patronage positions to consolidate Roosevelt's — and thereby Flynn's — influence. With its share of the money, New York City hoped to

Women shop the stalls of Bathgate Avenue around 172nd Street, long a bustling Jewish market. In this photograph, taken by Arnold Rothstein in 1934, customers examine socks at one store, while another shopper exits the "strictly kosher" chicken market.

put tens of thousands of men to work completing subway lines; building hospitals, incinerators, and disposal plants; installing new sewers; and regrading and paving the streets.

As the New Deal programs went into effect, and the economy slowly revived, Flynn foresaw the enormous power of government to change people's material lives. Flynn came to believe that if the Democrats didn't pursue this ideal as a national policy, the party's future would be limited. This was a radical philosophy for the time. When Socialist Norman Thomas ran for president in 1932, his planks advocating unemployment insurance, minimum wages, low-cost housing, civil rights, and a five-day work week were all considered utopian. Yet Flynn believed the Democrats must move left and usurp that position, or lose a large and growing natural constituency — the workers of America and the minorities — to socialism or some other leftist party. In the 1932 presidential election returns in the Bronx, 31,247 people had voted for the Socialist candidate Norman Thomas, three times the number of registered Socialists. Another 10,000 voted the even more radical Communist ticket. That was a very significant portion of the non-Republican vote, which totaled 322,577.

6

The New Deal Years
1933–1939

FLYNN was a frequent visitor to the White House, but he did not let business go untended in the Bronx. In 1933 Henry Bruckner, borough president of the Bronx since 1918, relinquished his post, making way for a new candidate. Flynn decided, in light of the Seabury investigation, to select someone with no prior political experience and no old scandals waiting to be unearthed. He lit upon James J. Lyons, a highly successful shoe salesman and Bronx businessman. Lyons had apparently come to Flynn's attention as president of the Grand Jurors Association, whose members were serving or had once served as grand jurors in the county courts. Flynn, always shrewd in his assessments of public feeling, decided to offer voters a strapping, handsome fellow with a genial manner, impressive business credentials, and fortune to prove it.

When Flynn broached the post to Lyons, the borough presidency was a job of tremendous importance. All local power emanated from Borough Hall, a graceful, yellow-brick Italianate building with tall, gently arched windows, and a long, terraced approach on the edge of Crotona Park. It was here that basic municipal services were provided, that street cleaning and repair contracts were issued, insurance policies assigned, and all the other daily, dull business that kept the borough operating smoothly went on, while coincidentally rewarding faithful Democrats. The borough president was also a voting member of the Board of Estimate, the body that approved every penny of spending in New York City's budget.

No one was more surprised by Flynn's selection than Lyons, and he asked for a few days to consider this astonishing proposal. Lyons had completed the eighth grade before going to work as a three-dollar-a-week office boy in the leather company, where his genius for salesmanship soon propelled him into its upper echelons. It was an uneventful, if financially rewarding, job that revolved around his absolute conviction that good salesmanship could sell anything — in his case, four million pairs of ladies' shoes in the depths of the Depression. He agreed to run, a mere formality in Boss Flynn's Bronx.

As he grew comfortable in his new role as elected official, Lyons began to apply his salesmanship to the Bronx. He relished all the stunts he dreamed up to bring his county before the public. The Bronx image was in need of improvement, for it had become known, reported no less an authority than the *New York Times*, "principally through the Bronx cocktail, a concoction of gin and orange juice, and the Bronx cheer, an emphatic labial form of disapprobation. As a result of cruel jibes at the borough's expense by vaudeville comics, the mere mention of its name became enough to evoke mysterious chuckles and bring to mind the distorted picture of a far-off province, tawdry tenements, desolate bluffs, chopped chicken livers, and subway trains fighting their way to the surface for air."[1] As Ogden Nash wrote, "The Bronx? No Thonx."

One of the first official acts Lyons undertook was to christen the Bronx the "borough of universities, cultural influences, comfortable dwellings, healthful climate and low tax rate," which came to be shortened to Borough of Universities. He was a press agent for the county, and he buried the local newspapermen in an incessant blizzard of press releases. He was a peripatetic ambassador of goodwill, appearing nightly at eight to ten political and fraternal dinners or gatherings where he always ended his speech with the ringing declaration that the Bronx was "the greatest county in the greatest city in the greatest country in the world!"

Despite the late hours and overimbibing such a schedule imposed, President Lyons arrived each morning at his office impeccably tailored and looking fresh and alert. He always stopped en route for a shave and trim, his black hair patent-leather slick, parted crisply in the middle and elegantly combed back. His wardrobe was the subject of some comment, for aside from his hundred-dollar suits, which were conservative in cut and color, he always favored rainbow-hued ties (he had a collection of fifty in every imaginable shade and pattern) and finely crafted goatskin shoes (twleve pairs).

As borough president, he presided over all the public works during the Depression. Private construction in the Bronx had ceased. Thousands of apartments stood vacant. Few businesses were in any shape to expand. Empty lots, at one time envisioned as sites for apartment buildings or small factories, remained vacant. As the New Deal set up work relief projects all over the borough, however, men paid first by the CWA (Civilian Works Administration) and then the WPA (Works Progress Administration) could be seen wielding shovels, wheelbarrows, ladders, and paintbrushes. The scope and size of the public works was huge. In the Bronx alone, from 1935 to 1937, almost $58 million was spent for dozens of projects: "a great modern bathing resort" at Orchard Beach, a pool and playgrounds at Crotona Park, tracks and playing fields in McCombs Dam Park behind Yankee Stadium, a new maternity ward building at Lincoln Hospital, nineteen new playgrounds scattered through the county (some with handball courts, wading fountains, and roller-skating tracks), new sewers, 119 miles of regraded roads and highways, remodeled buildings — including the reptile house in the Bronx Zoo, which got a new terrazzo floor — as well as fifteen miles of rebuilt walkways at the Botanical Garden, newly shored walls, and three miles of weatherstripping in the main building. Over near the Jerome Park Reservoir (formerly the elegant Jerome Park racetrack), the swamps that had been used for a City dump were transformed by crews of WPA workers into the sylvan Bronx campus of Hunter College.

While these WPA works made life more pleasant for the populace, four major work relief projects significantly changed the Bronx: the new Bronx County Building at 161st Street and Grand Concourse; the Triborough Bridge; the huge Federal Post Office at 149th Street and the Grand Concourse; and the completion of the Eighth Avenue IND subway up through the West Bronx. The two buildings, the largest and most magnificent public edifices in the borough, and the subway physically shifted the center of power from the old East Bronx, which had grown up around the Harlem Railroad and the IRT lines, to the newly developing West Bronx.

The new County Building was the first to be completed; its opening was marked by three days of celebration and pageantry. On Friday, June 15, 1934, Mayor Fiorello LaGuardia led the entire Board of Estimate up to the Bronx, where they were to inaugurate the building by conducting City business from its new marbled chambers. The dazzling white County Building was massive and ponderous, a ten-story limestone box piled atop ascending stairs and terraces. Huge statuary groups in pink marble flanked each pillared portico. A stylized frieze, depicting universal working man toiling in farm and field or battling valorously, encircled the building. Thin vertical windows alternating with copper insets offered a respite from all the white stone.

Lyons, tall, broad-shouldered, every hair in place and gleaming, presented LaGuardia, short, squat, and always a bit disheveled, with a key to the building. Contemplating the granite pile in all its ponderous bulk, Mayor LaGuardia mused tongue in cheek that "the architect had combined the austere simplicity of the Tudor, the softness of the Greek, the allegory of the Roman sculpture and modernized it so as to make it thoroughly American."[2] (When it was discovered that LaGuardia's key was not purely ceremonial, but in fact would open the door for the courthouse detention room, the mayor kindly sent it back.)

Two years later the cornerstone was laid for the Bronx Central Post Office at 149th Street and Grand Concourse. The Bronx had been browbeating postmasters general since 1903 to get its own main post office. Now, thanks to the Roosevelt administration (and no doubt to Flynn's friendship with Jim Farley), work was finally beginning. Postmaster General Farley, surrounded by officials soaked by rain while marching in a parade to the site, slopped the first trowel of cement over the cornerstone. There lay a sealed metal box with photographs of President Roosevelt, Farley, Lyons, a history of the campaign to secure the post office, and various decrees from the borough's civic organizations.

In 1936 Roosevelt was running for his second term amidst impassioned charges that the then-revolutionary policies of the New Deal were "communistic" and "unAmerican." These were the very policies Flynn had urged on Roosevelt to retain the loyalties of the common man, and they had been spectacularly successful in that regard. The upper classes despised Roosevelt with a venomous hatred, but the president and his party were riding a great crest of popularity. The laying of the cornerstone gave James A. Farley an opportune event for defending the administration before a friendly audience. As he stood at the edge of the mudhole that would be the new post office, he said: "When I read the howls and moans of the so-called Liberty League, the spokesmen for the special interests, and the Old Guard Republican leaders about how the Roosevelt Administration is 'destroying American institutions' and 'wrecking the American system' and 'establishing despotic dictatorship,' I naturally look around to see what these howls and moans are all about, and to save my life I cannot discover any basis whatsoever. I am forced to conclude that these are the general terms with which they hope to create a bugaboo to frighten the American voters." Farley launched into a litany of the administration's accomplishments: saving the banks, establishing deposit insurance, home mortgage programs, farm programs, social security, relief, CCC camps for the young, new labor laws, and lowered trade barriers. Farley looked out at the crowd, which was ignoring the drizzle as best it could, and declared, in ringing tones: "Many of these critics seem to regard special privileges and indifference to the welfare of the people generally as the American system. If this is the case, the quicker we substitute a real American system, the better."[3] The cold, sodden throngs cheered lustily.

A month later, on July 11, 1936, in the midst of a sweltering heat wave, yet another ceremony was held to dedicate the Triborough Bridge, a massive project connecting the three boroughs of Manhattan, Queens, and the Bronx. Work had first begun in 1931, then halted. When Robert Moses took over the Triborough Bridge Authority several years later, he discarded much of the early planning. Marshaling his engineers and lawyers, he forged ahead, securing land and rights-of-way, revamping the designs and organizing the resumption of work under the $44.2 million WPA grant that made this the biggest such project on the eastern seaboard. The gargantuan size and logistics were overwhelming, but Moses, iron-willed and Machiavellian, built the great bridge. President Roosevelt came down from Hyde Park for the dedication. He so disliked Robert Moses, and so feared his growing power, that he had been determined not to attend. As his presidential presence became an issue, he had relented, but only when LaGuardia promised that the sharp-tongued Moses would behave, and that LaGuardia himself would introduce the president.

The Triborough connection with Manhattan and Queens meant that the old neighborhoods of the South Bronx, whose streets and avenues fed into the new bridge, were suddenly flooded with automobiles coming on and off it. It was difficult to mourn the ten blocks of old-law tenements on 134th and 135th streets razed to make way for the approaches and supports, for these had been the earliest tenements, cramped, airless, and often still lacking private toilets, heat, or hot water. But the bumper-to-bumper traffic, spewing fumes and honking impatiently as it wound its way onto the bridge, did nothing to make the adjacent neighborhood more pleasant for residents. And it created new problems of its own that would encourage other measures yet to come.

The new line of the City-built IND subway, surfacing at intervals along the Grand Concourse, had opened on July 1, 1933. Much of the boulevard was still graced with old-fashioned turreted Victorian homes with wraparound front porches, cheery striped awnings, spacious front lawns, and clipped hedges, but with the new subway and the quicker commute into Manhattan, real estate speculation took off. For each family that sold out, others followed suit, unwilling to be overshadowed by big new structures. The large apartment houses that rose along the broad, curving avenue complemented it with their extravagant façades, art deco designs, and grandeur of scale. The art deco buildings boasted spare, curved lines, ornamented with wide swathes of elegant bottle glass, or gleaming colored tiles. More conventional buildings were embellished lovingly with gargoyles, inner courts, crenellated roofs, coats of arms, and all variety of whimsy. The Grand Concourse became the borough's most elegant residential thoroughfare, a Park Avenue of the Bronx. The blocks just north of the Concourse Plaza Hotel and the new courthouse were dubbed "the Gold Coast," for here lived the borough's leading citizens, wealthy businessmen, judges, and professionals, where every building had a doorman and a lavish lobby.

7

War Fever
1939–1945

THE headlines out of Europe grew ominous. In both Spain and Italy the Fascists were taking control. In the Bronx, filled with Italians, Jews, Germans, and immigrants from every European country, the defeats, victories, and oppressions became events of personal and historic importance. Many still had relatives or elderly parents in the old country. Ethnic and religious differences divided neighbors and neighborhoods: "real" Americans reviled more recent immigrants, particularly Jews, as less than worthy, perhaps even communistic. Urged on by the bigoted Father Coughlin and those of his ilk, fanaticism and anti-Semitism flourished. For those Jews who had survived and escaped the pogroms of Russia and Poland, it must have seemed chillingly familiar.

The better citizens of the Bronx felt compelled to speak up, and in June 1939 the Bronx Board of Trade initiated a three-part radio broadcast on "tolerance." President Roderick Stephens invoked the Constitution and the Bill of Rights to remind his listeners that this was America and not Nazi Germany. He was obviously outraged at the susceptibility of some of his fellow Bronxites to the hatemongers: "Intolerance has reared its ugly head in our own borough, and advocates of hatred are spreading their vicious doctrines in meeting halls, at street corner assemblages, and by a whispering campaign. Ostensibly these meetings are intended to combat Communism, but the second phase of this propaganda is to identify the Jew with the Communist, and the stage is now set for the following false conclusion — all Jews are Communists. Next, these advocates of hatred urge as a means of protection against

Communism that we boycott the Jews in business and seg-
regate them, or worse, in our social contacts. The polite word,
as the Nazis use it, is to 'liquidate' the Jews. Fortunately, we
know what that word means. It means everything bestial and
brutal and un-Christian and un-American."[1] The broadcast
must have been a bitter duty, for no one was publicly prouder
of the Bronx than the Board of Trade, those professional
boosters.

By 1940, with America on the eve of entering the second
global war, Flynn had become almost indispensable to FDR,
for Farley had quit early in the year as chairman of the National Democratic Committee to protest Roosevelt's bid for
a third term. Flynn disliked no one more than those he dis-
dainfully termed "amateur politicians," and — awkward for
the president — Flynn classed all the New Dealers in that
category. One of the basic conditions Flynn laid down for
running the National Committee and campaign was that the
New Dealers could not be involved, for to him the two were
like "oil and water." They would have to have a separate
committee and keep out of Flynn's hair. Roosevelt acceded
to that demand, but time and again he infuriated Flynn by
doling out patronage to nonorganization people when Flynn
had insisted that patronage must come through the professionals, for that was the grease that kept the political machines
running smoothly.

"There's no sense interviewing me," Flynn once told a reporter. "I don't have opinions on anything — politics or anything. That's why you never see me quoted. That's why I'm
the lousiest guy in the world to interview." The reporter,
delighted to have such an expansive statement, reported it in
full.[2] Flynn was virtually unknown outside New York, and
the national press found him rather intriguing — a cultured
and seemingly honest boss from the Bronx. *Time* magazine,
amused by his taste in wild ties and his unlikely habit of
chewing gum, put him on its cover. Flynn, however, ever the
astute politician, was afraid that the Republican candidate,
Wendell Willkie, would win the presidency.

Alarmed by the prospect of defeat, Roosevelt swept out

onto the campaign trail that fall. On a cool, blustery October day he made his usual pilgrimage up to the Bronx, a comfortingly Democratic stronghold, in a motorcade, with the president sitting in a big open coupe with Ed Flynn. Thick crowds built up all along the route, bursting into cheers as the cars were sighted. Higher up in the buildings, many families clustered in apartment windows and on fire escapes and roofs. At 465 East Tremont Avenue two women seeking a better view stepped out onto the tar roof, where they saw a local boy, eighteen years old and known to be a bit odd, looking down the street. One realized he had a pistol and cried, "What are you doing with that gun?" as he shot her and then her stunned companion. At that moment, the president and his motorcade roared up the avenue and turned onto Tremont. The boy ran down the stairs and sprinted for several blocks before darting into another apartment house, where he was cornered on the roof by police. There he turned the gun on himself "and took with him into oblivion the dreadful purpose which may have evolved in his brooding mind."[3] The two women both recovered, the potential assassination was hushed up, and the shootings were reported as freak attacks on the two neighbors (in their apartments) by a deranged boy. It remained a local secret until reported in *Bronxboro* in 1960.

By the Saturday before the general election, when the traditional Ladies' Luncheon was held at the Concourse Plaza, Flynn seemed more confident, but he certainly did not want to mislead the twelve hundred women arrayed before him into thinking President Roosevelt was a shoo-in for reelection. Every machine was only as good as its members' determination to get out the vote. Roosevelt, immersed in preparing the nation for its inevitable entry into the war in Europe, had too little time for electioneering, and so Mrs. Roosevelt came in his stead. Tall, and comfortably dowdy in appearance, Eleanor had become a familiar and beloved figure to her legions of fans. That day she made only a few short and perfunctory remarks before slipping out through the rain to her waiting car. Then Flynn, in his new, more public role, arose to give the main speech. After telling the ladies, his own troops, how glad he was to be home in the Bronx, he warned them that the Republicans were spending unprecedented amounts of money to oust FDR. It had been a very rough campaign and a crucial one for the Democrats. On election day, Bronxites turned out in record numbers. Ninety-seven percent of the registered voters, or 634,697 people, went to the polls. The Democrats delivered 333,013 votes to Roosevelt, and the specially created American Labor party line provided him with another 85,918 votes, making for a 66 percent Roosevelt landslide in Bronx County.

When America declared war, Bronx County was second to none in its patriotism. More than two hundred thousand men went off to fight, as reflected in the precipitous drop in registered voters (one of the borough's most precious natural resources) from 1940 to 1942 — 650,688 to 424,414. In his nostalgic reminiscence, *The Beautiful Bronx*, Lloyd Ultan described the exodus and intense borough pride. "Almost overnight, the Bronx was transformed. Young men could be seen walking about in khaki uniforms, and there were tearful farewells as loved ones bid the family good-bye for overseas duty. The only ones left at home were school children, older men, those who had some disability, and those involved with work vital to the war. During the war, the Bronx was dominated by women in the streets, most of whom anxiously awaited the arrival of the mailman each morning and afternoon for a precious letter from a man in uniform. Most of the time, such letters were in the form of V-mail, a photographic reproduction of the actual letter reduced in size for easier delivery."[4]

This patriotism and determination to wipe out the evil of nazism was fostered daily by the voice of the borough since 1907, the *Bronx Home News*. Each afternoon this paper arrived in Bronx homes blaring of new battles and renewed will to win. A year after Pearl Harbor, a huge, double-decker banner headline proclaimed, "GERMAN TARGETS BLASTED IN NEW AIR SWEEP; ALLIES PAVE WAY FOR MAJOR DRIVE IN TUNISIA." Immediately below was a photograph of some old train tracks under the rather baffling headline, "To Make Them Remember Pearl Harbor!" and then the exhortatory caption, "With a grim determination to overlook no slightest cache of precious metals that may be forged into fighting machines, the Bronx gives up another of its links of steel 'ribbon' to be sent into the hoppers that will help to make the little yellow men of Japan and their unholy partners in crime long remember the unparalleled treachery of December 7 at Pearl Harbor."[5]

In the midst of the war fever in 1943, Roosevelt nominated Bronx Boss Edward J. Flynn to be minister to Australia and ambassador-at-large for the South Pacific. Always an enthusiastic and wide-ranging traveler, Flynn was very pleased by the honor and the prospect of serving his country in the war. Of all the political posts offered him, it seems the only one that ever held any allure. Neither he nor FDR, however, anticipated the nomination's reception on Capitol Hill and the resurrection of the "paving block" scandal. Several years earlier Flynn had contracted to have an outdoor parking courtyard installed at his new Lake Mahopac estate, Orchard Hill. At the time Flynn was dashing around the country running Roosevelt's campaign. When he came home he discovered the Borough president's office had dispatched the men and materials to do the work. When he made inquiries about how to repay, word got out and a small scandal ensued. A grand jury investigation exonerated Flynn of any wrongdoing. He repaid the costs ($88 for Belgian paving blocks and $780 for labor) and forgot about it. Roosevelt's enemies seized on it and portrayed Flynn, who prided himself on his honesty, as a petty grafter of the lowest ilk.

As the furor grew, Flynn presented his side of the story and, once his nomination was voted favorably out of the Senate Foreign Relations Committee, he withdrew his name. He felt the whole situation had been turned into a political debacle, a source of division when the country most needed to be united. Flynn had already resigned as national chairman when his ambassadorial nomination went up to the Senate, and he did not resume the chairmanship thereafter, but he continued to play a major role among Democrats as the national committeeman from New York. Flynn had been concerned about Roosevelt's obviously deteriorating health and had strongly advised his friend not to run again. Once it became obvious Roosevelt was going for a fourth term, Flynn then concentrated on finding a running mate who would be acceptable, which meant someone less liberal than Henry A. Wallace, the incumbent. Flynn believed Senator Harry S. Truman filled the bill and oversaw his nomination in 1944.

In January 1945 Flynn left with Roosevelt on the historic mission to Yalta, an invitation that was seen as a small consolation prize for his humiliating treatment in the Senate. The Bronx boss stayed strictly in the background during Roosevelt's conferences with Stalin and Churchill, emerging only to participate in the dinners and informal get-togethers. During the conference Roosevelt told Stalin that he would like Flynn to visit Russia to take up the issue of freedom of religion for Catholics. Stalin agreed, and Flynn embarked on a secret tour to Russia, where he met church leaders and visited schools and orphanages, day nurseries, and the Women's Anti-Fascist League. On his way home he conferred twice with Pope Pius XII at the Vatican before repairing to London, where he met up with Prime Minister Churchill and two unofficial Roosevelt envoys, Bernard Baruch and Samuel Rosenman. Flynn did write later about his "secret" mission, but he never revealed what, if anything, came of it.

The evening of April 12, 1945, just after Flynn had gone to sleep in London, he was awakened and informed that the president was dead. "It was as if one of my own family had died."[6] The newspaper photographs of the mourners at FDR's funeral at Hyde Park show a somber Ed Flynn standing next to the grave as the final rites were read and taps played.

8

The Diaspora after the War
1946–1953

NEW YORK in the wake of World War II was a city on the verge of momentous changes — economic, social, and political. For almost a century it had been a preeminent manufacturing and port city, absorbing the unskilled millions who flocked there from Europe and yielded great fortunes for the astute and daring. The Depression had exacted a terrible toll, and leaders conferred anxiously on how to avoid a repetition of those doleful days as the war economy wound down. The City intended to resume its interrupted program of capital works, with visions of eradicating the slums and speeding eversnarled traffic. The Bronx expected to be a major beneficiary, and borough President Jim Lyons, in his usual overblown way, declared brightly that "When the post-war program is finally executed, the Bronx will be utopia itself."[1]

Even before the war, experts had been cautioning New York that it was losing industry and business to other locales. A 1939 study showed the City's percentage of wage earners down in fifty-eight industries. The situation in commercial printing, traditionally one of New York's great industries, was typical. At the turn of the century Manhattan had dominated, accounting for a quarter of all such work performed in the country. By 1937 the share was down to 16 percent. Printing companies were steadily folding up or fleeing the City.

Wages, complained businessmen, were too high, making New York uncompetitive. Once European immigration had ended after World War I, cutting off the flow of cheap labor, New York City unions successfully pressed their demands for better pay, working conditions, and benefits. This buttressed

James Lyons (left), Bronx borough president for thirty years, escorts President Harry Truman into the Concourse Plaza Hotel in 1948

the precarious existence of the working man, but it forced new costs on an industry that was competing with shops all over the country. There were great incentives for a unionized company in New York City to consider relocating, say, to nearby Elizabeth or Paterson, New Jersey. There a firm could leave the union behind and pay its employees $1.05 an hour, instead of $1.36.

The garment industry faced the same problem as the printers. During the war New York City contained 40 percent of the country's clothing manufacturing capacity, yet the Army and Navy gave it few uniform contracts, preferring the cheap labor and newer plants of the southern states. Clothing executives took the military's cue and began scouting out new locales. The postwar story was a steady hemorrhage of garment work. In 1948 there were 354,000 jobs in the garment industry. Two years later that figure was 340,700. By 1960 it would shrink to 267,400, and by 1984 to 150,000.

The great port of New York remained the largest general cargo port in the country and the second largest in the world, deferring only to Rotterdam. Week in and week out forty thousand longshoremen worked the ninety-six piers encircling Manhattan and the eighty lining the Brooklyn waterfront, manually loading and unloading sixteen million tons a year. Hundreds of tugs and barges plied the harbor and nearby rivers, guiding the big ships to their berths and ferrying cargo. Looking ahead, the new Port Authority of New York cleared forty old piers in Brooklyn and replaced them with fourteen spacious, modern piers, the best in the world.

In the mid-1950s Malcolm McLean of Winston-Salem invented a method of shipping that was to revolutionize cargo ports and make the new piers obsolete. His brainchild was the truck-sized sealed containers that slashed loading and unloading time to almost nothing. A small crew of men could use cranes to load the gargantuan containers, filling a ship twenty times faster than the old gangs grappling with crates, boxes, and bales. The impregnable containers guaranteed against waterfront theft or breakage, eliminating altogether the dockside pilferage that previously had consumed up to 15 percent of some cargoes. Ships that had traditionally spent a week in port could now finish their loading in a day.

The new containers required huge storing areas, far larger than were available in either Manhattan or Brooklyn. When the City of New York proposed modernizing its East River piers to handle containers, the Port Authority said it would have to clear all the land from the river to Third Avenue to do so. Each berth for a ship carrying containers of cargo needed fifty acres of surrounding land, compared to an old-fashioned berth of 195,000 square feet. The Port Authority erected container ports at Port Newark and Port Elizabeth, New Jersey, with their vast stretches of empty land. The old piers of Manhattan and Brooklyn languished — rotting, deserted white elephants. The ranks of the longshoremen, once forty thousand strong, dwindled to nine thousand. In the new technical, mechanized world of container shipping, man-hours fell from 40 million man-hours after the war to 13.5 million in 1983.

The whole postwar economy of New York was in the throes of quiet, but dramatic, changes. The traditional strongholds of manufacturing and printing contracted again and again. In the 1960s, six hundred thousand manufacturing jobs left New York. The new kinds of work were in services, government, finance, insurance, real estate, and contract construction, jobs that called for education and training. Manual labor and rote work, sources of employment for the poor and unschooled who had long come to New York, were disappearing.

Until the Depression, which severely curtailed virtually all housing construction, New York had been perpetually expanding. One decade's desirable neighborhood could be the next decade's slum, so quickly did the wealthy move on to more fashionable climes. Once the long, lean years of the Depression had been survived and the war against Germany and Japan decisively won, prosperity returned, and the mad frenzy of building that historically had characterized New York was unleashed once more. Hundreds of thousands of war veterans were returning home from the battlefields ready to settle down, but instead the country's young heroes found themselves camped out in cars, parks, subways, and Quonset huts with their new brides. The Bronx spokesman for the Jewish War Veterans decried the plight of the unhoused veterans, who deserved better after living so long "in a foxhole with nothing but the sky for a roof and flak for a ceiling."[2] The nation clamored for a more fitting homecoming. The solution was "homes for heroes," and legislation was passed entitling every honorably discharged serviceman to a 4 percent mortgage backed by the Veterans Administration.

Builders rushed to throw up huge tracts of houses and, like the developers who had built the Bronx, this new generation of housing moguls looked for wide-open areas with cheap acreage. They found it not in the Bronx but in certain sections of Queens and in still-rural Long Island and New Jersey. The quintessence of this phenomenon was Levittown, Long Island, where in 1948 a new house cost eight thousand dollars and the monthly charge over the thirty-year mortgage was thirty-eight dollars. Any family with the money to buy a car could drive out to these new settlements, pay nothing down, sign a mortgage, and become the proud owner of a brand new home and yard. The suburbs previously had been almost the exclusive preserve of the wealthy. Now they were open to virtually all, thanks to the generosity of a grateful government and the zeal of developers, who constructed thousands of reasonably priced houses at a stroke.

Another postwar privilege offered the ex-GIs was four years of full college tuition and a modest living allowance. The millions of young men who had never been out of their hometowns until the war were now more seasoned and sophisticated, and they were quick to take advantage of this provision of the GI Bill of Rights. Those who might never have attended college or who could not have afforded it swelled the academic ranks — 7.5 million nationwide. In New York City so many soldiers-turned-students enrolled that when the fledgling United Nations vacated its temporary home at Hunter College in the Bronx, the school could not revert to its previous all-female status. Most of these scholars were the first in their families to attend college, and their working-class fathers and mothers urged them to get that diploma, for opportunities were shrinking for the unskilled and semiskilled workers of New York.

While the millions of veterans were reclaiming their places in society, two great internal migrations were also gathering force. Just as in earlier eras when the immigrant groups came in pairs — the Irish and Germans, the Italians and Jews — so now two new groups were making New York City their destination. These immigrants were not aliens, but Americans — poor rural blacks, displaced by automation in the cotton fields of the South, and Puerto Ricans, whose small, overpopulated, and long-exploited tropical commonwealth was now just a cheap airplane flight away.

There have always been blacks living in New York City, whether as "free persons of color" or, before slavery was outlawed in New York State, as slaves. Following the Civil War, when many emancipated southern blacks began to find their way to New York City, the Negro population doubled to ninety thousand, but by 1890 this still constituted only 2 percent of the citizenry.

Slavery may have been abolished, but its legacy was pervasive, foremost in the widely held belief that Negroes were innately inferior. In other societies where slavery was an institution, slaves were allowed to marry, acquire education, and most important, secure their freedom or their children's freedom. In some Caribbean islands slaves had their own homes, plots of ground on which to grow food, and even their own businesses. In the ancient civilizations of Greece and Rome, slaves were regarded as unlucky in their fate, not as subhumans. Yet in America, with its proud tradition of liberty and equality, the enslaving of black Africans and their children unto perpetuity was justified and rationalized by classing them as chattels and denying their humanity.

Following the Civil War, thwarted and humiliated at every turn by Jim Crow laws, the blacks began to leave the South. In the 1920s alone, 750,000 blacks emigrated. The enfeeblement of the cotton industry, the war boom, and the end of foreign immigration all made the northern and midwestern cities look increasingly more attractive to laborers and share-croppers. Moreover, Negro parents who wished their children to have a good education saw little opportunity in their southern home states, a fact reflected by illiteracy rates and educational expenditure. In 1925 almost 30 percent of the blacks in Mississippi were illiterate, as compared to only 3.6 percent of the whites. The reasons were obvious: Mississippi devoted $9.38 per capita each year to educate black children, versus $42.17 for white children. In South Carolina it was $4.40 for blacks, $45.45 for whites. In 1926 Georgia had only one accredited public high school for black students in the entire state.

Blacks sank their roots in the New York neighborhood known as Harlem, just north of rolling Central Park. Originally settled by the Dutch, Harlem was an attractive quarter that had been peopled mainly by Jews before they started moving over into the Bronx in the first part of this century. "Negro Harlem covers one of the most beautiful and healthful sites in the whole city," wrote black writer James Weldon Johnson in 1930. "It is not a fringe, it is not a slum, nor is it a quarter consisting of delapidated tenements. It is a section of new-law apartment houses and handsome dwellings, with streets as well-paved, as well-lighted, and as well-kept as any in the city."[3]

Not only southern blacks, but blacks from the West Indies, flocked to New York City to revel in the black renaissance flowering in exciting Harlem, home to writers, artists, wealthy businessmen, dynamic preachers, and famous entertainers. This black cultural and spiritual oasis was to suffer acutely from the economic bad times of the Depression, however. Almost 60 percent of the black population in New York ended up on relief. Not until World War II did New York blacks begin to recoup, but even as they did, larger numbers of blacks arrived to swell their ranks.

After World War II the mechanization of the cotton farms in the South eliminated the need for large pools of unskilled labor, and the southern black diaspora began in earnest. Each decade another million dirt-poor blacks from the Deep South caught trains and buses to new lives in the North. The black population of New York grew from 450,000 before the war to 800,000 after it, and traditional black neighborhoods began to burst at their seams. Citified blacks and whites found the newcomers uneducated, unskilled, vulgar, and completely unfamiliar with urban ways. In *Manchild in the Promised Land,* Claude Brown laments: "They were trying to bring the down-home life up to Harlem. They had done it. But it just wasn't working. . . . Liquor, religion, sex, and violence — this was all that life had been about to them. And a prayer that the right number would come out. . . ."[4]

Jobs were hard to come by. The remaining settlement houses and other charitable agencies were insufficient to serve this new wave. Two hundred years of American-style slavery, and another near-century of legislated oppression, had kept Negroes from developing the habits and outlooks that resulted in success. Claude Brown's mother chastised him for wanting to be a psychologist. "You were supposed to just want to work in fields or be happy to be a janitor."[5]

The West Indian blacks, however, whose slave heritage was relatively humane, seemed to possess the characteristics associated with success — thriftiness, hard work, investment, and education — and succeed they did, despite their black skins. Before migrating they had lived in island societies where blacks were not despised as subhumans and where they were entitled to marry, raise families, pursue learning and scholarship, and run businesses like anyone else. The West Indians and the American descendants of "free persons of color" came to dominate the black society of New York, emerging as its leaders and most talented businessmen, politicians, and artists.

All the alcoholism, drug use, violence, and family strife that had plagued the old immigrant neighborhoods at their worst reappeared in the mushrooming black slums. The changing economy of the City worked against the latest wave. Unions made up of whites fought to prevent blacks from making inroads on their dwindling supply of unskilled jobs.

Arriving in New York at the same time as the blacks were

the Puerto Ricans. Their small lush island, one hundred miles long and thirty-five miles wide, lay a thousand miles southeast of Florida in the Caribbean, farther away from the American mainland than Cuba or Haiti. The Jones Act of 1917 made Puerto Ricans U.S. citizens but gave them no right to rule their own island or to vote in national elections. Throughout the 1920s, adventurous Puerto Ricans sailed to New York City (long the destination of trading vessels from San Juan), and settled in East Harlem. Luis Munoz Marin, the island's greatest political leader, developed many important friendships during his stay, and an indispensable understanding of Americans and their form of government. The Depression interrupted the steady migration, but it slowly picked up again. At the outbreak of World War II, 61,500 Puerto Ricans lived in New York City.

Little attention was directed at this new group, aside from a couple of studies by sociologists. They were just another among the polyglot multitudes of New York City. Bobby Garcia, later a congressman, remembers growing up in the 1930s and 1940s on Brook Avenue and 138th Street in Mott Haven, the Irish neighborhood in the Bronx. He was not categorized as a Puerto Rican. He was just another one of the kids, playing stickball all evening, tossing footballs fashioned from newspapers and string, or heading to the Bronx Opera to catch the Jimmy Dorsey Band at a dime a ticket.

During World War II, migration from the island halted. The end of the war brought not only new shipping, but an innovation in island-to-mainland travel. Former pilots in the U.S. services bought up surplus military planes from the War Assets Administration and began offering cheap, quick flights to New York. A voyage that once had taken almost a week was now accomplished in six to eight hours. And with the plethora of competition (up to twenty-seven airlines at one point), fares rarely rose above fifty dollars. During fare wars they dropped as low as thirty dollars. The backlog of migrants who had been put off first by the Depression and then the war filled plane after plane flying over the Caribbean and into the airfields of Idlewild, Newark, Teterboro, and LaGuardia.

In 1947 a three-part series in the *New York World-Telegram* described "perhaps the greatest mass migration in modern history — from poverty-stricken Puerto Rico to lush America, land of hope." The newspaper promised a "penetrating" look at the "explosive problems raised by this unparalleled movement.

"Like the immutable flow of lava from an erupting volcano, thousands of these migrants descend on this city each month, seeking a richer life,but finding themselves too often doomed to disappointment, misery and economic misfortune.

"Suffering acutely themselves they disrupt the economy and customs of their newly adopted home city and find themselves victims of a vicious cycle of discrimination, class hatred and oppression."[6]

The *World-Telegram* told of Puerto Ricans swarming off the planes with less-than-forty-dollar nest eggs, little knowledge of English, and few skills. In areas where they clustered (Spanish Harlem, Simpson Street in the Bronx, and Manhattan Valley) relief costs had jumped 54 percent.

Each year through the late 1940s, another twenty thousand Puerto Ricans flooded into New York City. Spanish Harlem was bursting its borders. Puerto Ricans migrated to smaller enclaves in other boroughs. In the Bronx, Puerto Ricans jousted with Negroes for apartments in such districts as Mott Haven and Hunt's Point. Streets that once had resounded to Irish brogues and Yiddish hummed with Spanish voices. When Oscar Collazo was arrested in the Bronx in 1950 for attempting to assassinate President Truman, the *New York Times* described his Brook Avenue neighborhood as a "squalid Puerto Rican quarter" of "solid grimy, five-story tenements facing equally grimy five-story brick tenements. . . . There were people thick as flies on the fire escapes. Every window was crowded with men, women and children and the sidewalks were thronged."[7]

Puerto Rican migration in 1953 hit an all-time high of fifty-two thousand, bringing the total number of Puerto Rican migrants in New York City close to the half-million mark. In the Bronx alone, by 1950 more than sixty thousand islanders

Puerto Rican families arrive at New Jersey's Teterboro Air Terminal in 1947, part of the enormous postwar migration of Puerto Ricans from their impoverished tropical island to New York City packed into those blocks and streets where they had established strongholds. Airport surveys showed that half those coming to New York had no work experience at all, while 18 percent had been farm laborers, 10 percent factory workers, and the remaining 20 percent clerks, salesmen, or professionals and managers. At a time when one in two New Yorkers had finished high school, only one in ten Puerto Rican migrants had. Seventy percent had not completed the ninth grade. Not surprisingly, they found themselves in the worst jobs.

Many of the earlier Puerto Rican migrants had long since achieved the status of *perfumadas* (sweet-smelling ones). Having embarked for New York in earlier decades when sea passage was costly and long, these Puerto Ricans tended to have started out more ambitious and better educated, with middle-class characteristics that ensured some success. They had come to this country and fulfilled the classic American Dream of working hard, moving ahead, and then watching their children equal or outdistance their own accomplishments. They had approached assimilation, like the German Jews half a century before.

The postwar influx of demobilized vets, blacks, and Puerto Ricans forced New York City to wrestle once more with its perennial housing problems. Where were all these families to live? Upwardly mobile white families were moving to the suburbs. As the offspring of the European immigrants decamped, the Puerto Ricans and blacks snapped up their vacated apartments. Overcrowding, and the newcomers' sheer poverty, transformed decent neighborhoods into slums, and as the new slums spread into larger areas, the solution seemed obvious to City officials — public housing.

New York City had always been the pioneer in public housing. Its enthusiasm dated back to Mayor Fiorello LaGuardia, a foe of slums who yearned to eradicate them forever from his city. "Let in the sunlight" was his battle cry. In 1934, after Congress had passed the National Housing Act and New York State had enacted a Municipal Housing Authorities Law, Mayor LaGuardia had seized the chance to set up the country's first public housing authority. The City borrowed money from Bernard Baruch and bought dilapidated old-law tenements at the Lower East Side's Third Street and Avenue A from Vincent Astor. Dispatching WPA labor and materials, the Housing Authority demolished every third building to let in more light and air and then used the cleared ground for small parks and playgrounds. All the apartments were renovated. Named First Houses, it marked the City's inaugural effort in better housing for the poor. Although First Houses contained only 120 apartments, it proved to many that the City could successfully undertake a real estate venture. Proclaimed a jubilant Langdon Post, first chairman of the Housing Authority, "With First Houses we have moved from the realm of debate into the realm of fact."[8]

Far more ambitious projects rapidly followed First Houses: Harlem River Houses and Williamsburg Houses, each set on twenty-five acres, built by the WPA and leased back to the Housing Authority. The City's objective of eliminating slums was adopted as a national policy in 1937 when Congress passed the U.S. Housing Act, which provided subsidies to local authorities to build and operate housing for low-income families. Subsequently, the New York state legislature enacted the Public Housing Law of 1939, with the declared goal of eliminating "insanitary and substandard housing in New York." This laid the legislative groundwork for the first state-aided public housing program in the country. In New York City an occupancy tax on commercial renters guaranteed a financial base for the necessary rent subsidies.

The city's second major action in the field of housing was to retain the rent controls that had come in 1943 as a national wartime measure to combat inflation. When the federal controls lapsed in 1950, New York State enacted a rent-control program to thwart "speculative, unwarranted and abnormal" rent hikes or evictions during what was termed a housing emergency in New York City. The state exempted all New York City apartment buildings constructed after 1947 from rent control in order to fend off the combined wrath of the building industry, the construction unions, and the banks that depended on mortgage business. The state presented rent control as a temporary measure needed until "normal conditions" returned.

Any student of politics, however, could have predicted the impossibility of ever lifting such controls in New York City, where renters wildly outnumbered the landlords, and which contained more than a million apartments, each housing one or two (or even three or four) prospective voters. What New York City politician, or even an upstate politician running for statewide office and hoping for a substantial vote from New York City, could possibly advocate dropping rent controls? Jaundiced tenants listened to the landlords complain that they couldn't make a profit or maintain their properties and then protested heartily when the state permitted a 15 percent rent increase in 1953, the first in ten years.

9

"There Was No Standing Still"
1952–1953

IN the years immediately following the war, Bronx County retained much of its air of bourgeois and working-class stolidity. There was no sense of impending doom as the same old-boy network of Irish and Jews prevailed in the worlds of business, society, and politics, making deals over an endless round of dinners and luncheons at the Concourse Plaza Hotel. On the last day of 1944 hotel manager Frank Kridel, together with various partners, had bought the hotel from the Central Savings Bank, which had foreclosed in the spring of 1939. Kridel's acquisition was excellent timing. In New York City during the war a hotel room was a valuable commodity. Even Kridel's best customers had to beg to book a room for friends or clients coming to town.

Kridel, a tall, handsome man with dark hair and deep-set brown eyes, foresaw a "great post-war future for this unique hotel in its strategically located neighborhood," near Yankee Stadium, just down the hill.[1] By catering even more assiduously than before to the athletes and fans, Kridel intended to restore the glamour that had faded. Americans were sports mad, and, once the war was won, baseball, football, and the big fights would all be in full swing again. A hotel that pampered the players and their enthusiastic followers would reap the rewards. As a sports fiend himself, Kridel's enthusiasm was completely genuine, and so the Concourse Plaza, which had always considered itself "the business and social center of the Bronx," now geared up also to be the "home of champions."

With Kridel at the helm, the hotel entered its heyday. Paula

Levison, a young newlywed who moved into the hotel during the war with her attorney husband, Stuart, remembers how very deluxe the rejuvenated hotel was, and how glamorous. The marble floor of the lobby was buffed to a high sheen and covered with Oriental rugs; lush plants surrounded the plump sofas and chairs arranged discreetly among the lobby pillars. Liveried bellhops in crimsom uniforms, white spats, and white gloves moved swiftly down the lobby stairs to aid arriving guests. Even permanent tenants had maid service seven days a week. "Every day we had fresh bathroom towels," recalls Mrs. Levison. "Oh, it was marvelous. I was the envy of all my friends."[2] Hotel life was so pleasant that the Levisons elected to stay on after the war and live at the Concourse Plaza. They were joined by numerous judges and doctors, the former finding it convenient to the courthouse across the way, the latter finding it a prestigious and well-located spot for professional offices.

Kridel successfully endeared himself to the ball clubs and managers and athletes. Usually a dozen Yankees — Yogi Berra, Elston Howard, and Frank Crosetti, to name a few — lived there in season, as did the football Giants and the visiting teams coming through. One permanent guest remembered the hulking footballers and their families well. "The wives were mainly southern cracker girls. They'd run through the halls in bare feet, very outré. And they'd take their kids down to the park, some of them, with nothing on. The men were huge. My best recollection is being in an elevator with four or five and being absolutely dwarfed. They were very big, but always nice."

The Yankees proclaimed the hotel their official headquarters, and in 1950 Kridel inaugurated Welcome Home Yankee dinners in the Grand Ballroom. The ballplayers sat up on a double dais like so many gods while their worshipful Bronx fans stretched out before them at long rows of tables, feted them, and wished for yet another glorious season of victory. After dessert, the young boys, grasping baseballs and photographs and special books, lined up to have them autographed.

The good times and prosperity enveloping the Concourse Plaza and Yankee Stadium did not mask the fact that the Bronx as a whole was on the move. The most public symptom was the gradual disappearance of the *Bronx Home News,* the borough's perennial, personable daily newspaper, which had come into being in 1907 and quickly established itself as the paper of true Bronxites. Delivered each afternoon by battalions of Bronx boys, the paper's forte was neighborhood news. (On Thanksgiving Day the *Home News* printed three full pages of names, and "What They Are Grateful For.") The newspaper presented a sumptuous amount of information in its spacious, eight-column spread, peppered with lots of small items — everything from "Subway Cheater Faces Trial in Special Sessions" to "Short Circuit Damages Bronxite's Parked Auto."

"No downtown newspaper ever established the cozy, intimate rapport that existed between the *Bronx Home News* and its readers ('100,000 Daily Guaranteed')," declared Gilbert Chambers, an editor. "This intimate affection and trust showed in the number, variety, and most of all, the uniqueness of Letters to the Editor we received.

"One I have somewhere came from a Hunt's Point reader who delightedly enclosed a harbinger of spring. Telling how he found it in his icebox (of all places), he had glued to the upper right hand corner of his letter the first mosquito of the spring in the Bronx."[3]

Chambers also remembered those determined Bronxites who came to the city room bearing news. Typical was "Mrs. Dobinsky who spoke English in the Bronx idiom and who had never finished elementary school in her native Russia. She had gathered some neighbors into the 'Bronx Browning Literary Society' and they were pursuing culture relentlessly every Tuesday on University Heights." The Society members wanted coverage in the *Home News.* After receiving numerous visits in the city room, Chambers broke down and wrote a story so sarcastic he thought the ladies would never be seen again. They were fervently grateful, however, and Mrs. Dobinsky became — to his dismay — a regular contributor.

In 1945 the *New York Post* bought the *Home News,* but
the *Post* could not make it profitable. On February 16, 1948,
the *Bronx Home News* was folded into a tabloid hybrid called
the *New York Post–Bronx Home News.* That lasted only about
a year before the *Post* removed *Home News* from its masthead
and settled for a Bronx edition with just a few pages devoted
to the Bronx. Leading Bronxites lost their main source of
local information, and reports of ordinary folk with their small
tragedies and triumphs disappeared from sight altogether. It
was like losing an old friend.

The demise of the old *Bronx Home News* went virtually
unnoticed outside the borough, but the unexpected outcome
of a special congressional election in early 1948 gained wide
attention throughout the country. To the acute professional
embarrassment of Boss Ed Flynn, the Bronx Democrats not
only lost their regular congressional seat, but were trounced.
A virtual neophyte named Leo Isacson, a young lawyer on
the American Labor party ticket, beat Flynn's man by 22,697
to 12,578. *Time* magazine reported the upset as a near left-
wing coup, a Henry Wallace victory engineered by zealous
Communists or "fellow-travelers" harping to Jewish voters on
Truman's Palestine policies.

This unexpected rebellion in the well-bossed Bronx so surprised political writer Samuel Lubell that he visited the district
to have a look. He found what he believed was a significant
and profound change in the old "tenement trail" of American
cities, or the movement from neighborhood to neighborhood
in the eternal struggle for upward mobility. This change was
the arrival of the Puerto Ricans and the southern blacks. In
his 1952 classic, *The Future of American Politics,* he wrote:
"Through the Negro . . . two of the greatest of American
social conflicts are being fused — the battle to liquidate the
heritage of slavery, and the immigrant striving to become
Americanized and assimilated. It is the mixture of these two
conflicts — once quite distinct — which is boiling the civil rights
melting pot so furiously. . . ."[4] From the time impoverished
Europeans flooded the great cities of the East and Midwest, the struggle had always been to succeed and escape

the slums. Families who failed risked losing their sons to street gangs and crime and watching their daughters marry into poverty.

"The rhythm of the urban frontier, in short, has been the rhythm of the crowd running away from itself, with neighborhoods booming and declining in a regular cycle as the masses chased through them. At their heels, as each group struggled upward, could always be felt the pressure of the next climbing group threatening to overtake and engulf them. There was no standing still. Either one climbed or one fell victim to the pursuing slum."[5] Yet this cycle had been slowed or stopped in the Bronx, as elsewhere, by the Depression and then the war.

With the coming of peace and prosperity, the march upward resumed, joined now by the blacks and Puerto Ricans. And their mere presence then in a city neighborhood whipped up "the already existing fears of being engulfed in a slum." The lower Bronx, with its walk-up tenements and blind-walled factories, had been host first to the Irish and then to the Jews. By 1948 Lubell found it a "dying Jewish neighborhood where the chill of being trapped penetrates everywhere." Lubell diagnosed Isacson's congressional victory as a rebellious and angry message from the new "economically depressed, transitional racial zones."[6]

The Bronx Democrats quickly regained their lost face in the fall of 1948 when they carried the county handily, rolling up solid votes for Harry S. Truman against Henry A. Wallace and Thomas Dewey, and defeating the short-lived Congressman Leo Isacson, but the racial transition described by Lubell became the leitmotif of the East Bronx. The steady influx of blacks and Puerto Ricans was transforming the old neighborhoods. The young expressed the hostility most forcefully. Gangs of teenagers gathered to challenge the "spics," not just in the Bronx but all over the City. (A heavily romanticized version of gang warfare, *West Side Story,* would later captivate the world and send even the most middle-class of boys into imitations of the Sharks and Jets.)

*   *   *

Bob Munoz, a New York–born Puerto Rican, lived on Fox Street. A big, beefy man, he prided himself on being a "tough bastard." He had managed a number of bars, and in 1958 he bought Bob's Bar at 139th and Morris Avenue, the heart of Mott Haven. He remembers the clashes vividly. "The Irish used to come over from McSherry's Bar anytime they had sufficient beers to get themselves riled up over the Spics. It was a wild free-for-all, and the whole place would be busted to bits by the time the cops got there to break up the fights. Everytime, they just wrecked the place. Then these blacks wanted to buy me out, but the landlords wouldn't rent to them. Finally, I went bankrupt and let it go deep-six. I couldn't afford to fix all those broken mirrors and chairs anymore."[7]

Despite this hostility, the Puerto Ricans continued to pour in, fueled by the miserable life of the jibaros, or Puerto Rican farmers. First they moved into the slums of San Juan, and, finding no steady work there, sold their meager belongings and gambled on New York. This migration pattern was encouraged by Puerto Rico's industrialization plan, Operation Bootstrap, since there was no hope that all the surplus workers could ever be employed. Like the Irish immigrants a century before, the Puerto Ricans were mainly peasants with no schooling or skills, but they faced far greater handicaps than the first wave of Irish: they did not speak English, and a strong back was no longer a sufficient job qualification.

New Yorkers had not seen such widespread misery for more than a generation, and they were not at all happy about it. In an unconscious reprise of Jacob Riis, reporters described three and four families sharing cramped cold-water flats. The old immigrant "hot bed" system was reinstituted, with people taking turns sleeping in the same bed: those on the night shift came home each morning to collapse in a just-vacated bunk, while the nighttime occupant trudged off to his day job. Two Puerto Rican brothers even shared a "hot suit." Like every immigrant group before them, the Puerto Ricans were alternately reviled and pitied. And, warned the *World-Telegram*, there was no letup in sight: "Officials on the island point to a birth rate, equaled in few places in the world, which annually adds 55,000 to the two and a quarter million persons already crammed into a subtropical island."[8]

In the first decades of this migration when the Puerto Ricans disembarked from the airplane they had headed to the tenements of Spanish Harlem. There the fiery Italian politician Vito Marcantonio became their champion. Some people accused him of encouraging Puerto Ricans to migrate to New York and fill his district by sending free tickets or arranging jobs in advance. "That is so much eye wash," snorted one welfare department official at the time. "This migration is larger than any one man. It is a great movement of people on the march towards dreams that have no foundation. He is the one they turn to and it gives him great strength at the polls."[9]

Marcantonio, who ran as a Republican-Fusionist for his ally Fiorello LaGuardia's old congressional seat, quickly tapped into the vast resources of the social welfare programs, steering his constituents through the labyrinth of rules and forms. "The pressure he puts on our welfare centers in his section is terrific and continuous," said a welfare official. "He urges our workers to step up relief for the Puerto Ricans, as he does for the others, too, and it pays off." With his seven-day-a-week headquarters and his appreciation of the New Deal programs, Marcantonio was shrewdly adjusting the oldtime politics to the newly evolving social welfare state.

Puerto Rico had never, until now, had a voting representative in Congress. When Marcantonio's district turned into a Little Puerto Rico, he filled that role by default. He was infuriated by the many press stories about the Puerto Rican "problem" that failed to explain, to his satisfaction, the origins of the migration: dire poverty. "Rice, beans, and dried codfish. A few clothes. A shack. This is the life of the Puerto Rican worker."[10]

Given the choice, most landlords preferred Puerto Rican tenants to blacks. "Despite the fact Hispanics had lower standards of living — after all, many of them had lived in shacks with no plumbing or anything — they were considered more desirable when they moved in because they were not black," explained one Bronx realtor. "They didn't elicit a reaction in the neighborhood as they moved in." *Bodegas* selling fleshy yellow plantains replaced Jewish mom-and-pop grocery stores. Catholic churches began offering Spanish masses, though they were often held in the cold church basements. Elementary school classrooms had rows of young children who spoke only Spanish. Men sat on the sidewalks playing dominoes for hours in the evenings. Spiritualist shops (*botanicas*) offered gaudy statues of saints, as well as herbs and potions for special occasions. Movie marquees advertised Spanish films, and small record stores blared Spanish songs.

The actual number of residents in some buildings and blocks doubled and tripled. Landlords began cutting up large apartments, making their buildings into rooming houses and cramming them with Puerto Ricans. One Bronx building inspector remembers the advent of these instant slums: "In sense of actual crowding, I'd never seen anything like it. On one floor you'd have ten families, young couples with small children. They had community kitchens with six women. What a tough way that was to live." Large families took in friends and relatives, and the Puerto Ricans, used to living outdoors all the time, spilled out onto fire escapes, stoops, sidewalks, and streets.

The original Irish immigrants with whom the Puerto Ricans were compared had had the further advantage of arriving with their own church and priests. The hundreds of Catholic churches and schools all over New York testified to the great accumulated influence and wealth of the Archdioceses of both New York and Brooklyn. The Puerto Ricans, while nominally Catholic, did not have their own clergy, nor were they particularly devoted parishioners. The church in Puerto Rico had always been associated with the Spanish and colonialism. Many Puerto Ricans practiced spiritualism or found solace in the holy-roller Pentecostal sects.

The tiny upper class in Puerto Rico cherished its Castilian-white skin, but the lower classes had long intermarried and intermingled with both the surviving native Indians and the freed black slaves who lived on the island. In many families the children differed markedly in color, from white to toffee to mahogany. On the island, color discrimination had been discreet and subtle. In New York, to the Puerto Ricans' dismay and humiliation, discrimination was more blatant. Racism in the North was nowhere as institutionalized as it was in the American South, one of the major reasons Puerto Ricans avoided that region, even though it was physically closer to their island and far more similar in climate. Nonetheless, prejudice in New York was a painful shock to Puerto Ricans with brown skin. In *Down These Mean Streets,* Piri Thomas, a dark-skinned Puerto Rican, lamented: "I ain't never been down South, but the same crap's happening up here. So they don't hang you by your neck. But they slip an invisible rope around your balls and hang you with nice smiles and 'If we need you, we'll call you.' "[11]

Puerto Rican family structure did not lend itself to the buffetings of New York immigrant life. Consensual marriage was so common — one in four unions was not legitimized on the island — that many women had a series of common-law husbands fathering their large broods. In New York these mothers turned to welfare, and welfare rules hardly encouraged the next mate to declare his paternal attachment. The Spanish macho culture honored the man who had conquered many women, leaving in his wake children as physical proof of his victories, in stark contrast to the Jews or other Europeans, who condemned such loose arrangements.

Although the tradition of devoted godparents provided Puerto Rican children with almost a second set of parents and a strong buffer to breakdowns in the immediate family, the new circumstances of New York warped all the old relationships. Puerto Rican men of some substance in their hometowns on the island were traumatized by their sudden fall from respect. The wives were off working, making equal or greater sums of money, the children picked up English quickly and seemed lost to the strange new city, and the world-at-large condescended to the Puerto Ricans. Some found it too much to bear and retreated to Puerto Rico. In Nicholasa Mohr's novella "Uncle Claudio," one of the characters does just this.

"At home, when he walks down the street he is Don Claudio. But here, in New York City, he is Don Nobody, that's what he said. He doesn't get no respect here."[12] The return migration was huge, rivaling only that of the Italians.

Those who stayed and filled the old working-class enclaves of the Bronx found neighborhoods simmering with racial and class tensions. Father Banome, a Catholic priest at Saint Joseph's Church in Tremont, arrived in the Bronx from East Harlem at the tail end of this tense transition. No doubt the appearance in a Bronx parish of a Spanish-speaking priest must have carried a most unwelcome message to the Irish. "I was just amazed at the struggle between them, the absolute hatred and disregard," says Father Banome. "It manifested itself mainly in gang fights. The Irish saw the Hispanics as dirty, uncaring, allowing their children to run on the streets at all hours of the night, coming just for welfare. They looked on them as unproductive. All the Irish here disliked me intensely, too. It was strange to me that children out of such religious homes could be so full of hate. They were unwilling to compromise. If this neighborhood could not be like they wanted it, they moved."[13]

Despite waning health, Ed Flynn was still a political powerhouse in New York City and the undisputed boss of the Bronx after 1948. (In 1952 he had let it be known that the party needed young blood, and that the ideal candidate for any vacant assembly seat would not be more than thirty-two years old.) In 1953 Flynn intended to back the candidacy of Manhattan borough President Robert Wagner for mayor against incumbent Vincent Impelliteri, thereby splitting with the more conservative wing of the party under James A. Farley.

Edward J. Flynn died of a heart attack, however, in Saint Vincent's Hospital in Dublin while on vacation with his wife and his daughter, Sheila. He was sixty-one years old and had been boss of the Bronx for thirty years. It was left to Congressman Charles A. Buckley, Flynn's successor, to make the public announcement on August 18, 1953. The *New York Times* ran the obituary on the front page. Herbert H. Lehman, then U.S. senator and a longtime ally of Flynn's, commented sadly: "His death is another mark of the passing of an era. The first great knell was sounded by the death of Ed Flynn's great friend and mine, Franklin Roosevelt."[14]

The funeral was held on Saturday, August 23, in the dog days of summer. Flynn had lived in Riverdale, a fancy suburb in the north Bronx, for the whole of his adult life, but his funeral was held in the church of his childhood, Saint Jerome's. It was an ornate, cupolaed church near the Alexander Avenue brownstone he had once shared with his brother Dr. Fred Flynn. The blocks surrounding the church would soon be swept away, all the old tenements and walk-ups, to be replaced by utilitarian brick housing towers in their patchy greenswards.

Two thousand mourners had gathered outside Saint Jerome's behind police barricades. When the hearse swung up, the crowd stood hushed and expectant, many crossing themselves. Flynn's widow, dressed in black, flanked by a son and a daughter, followed the pallbearers into the burnished green-gold gloom of the cavernous church. Built at the turn of the century by the first Irish to settle in the Bronx, it had a gorgeous interior: a high gilded dome with the saints arching heavenward and richly veined green-marble pillars with deeply carved capitals. A thousand people squeezed into the church — friends, relatives, and the political associates from Flynn's thirty-year tenure in local, state, and national politics. Flynn left an estate of almost a million dollars. His legacy to the American language was the phrase "in like Flynn," which became a popular slang expression. If you were "in like Flynn," you had it made.

With the demise of such Bronx institutions as Ed Flynn and the *Home News,* there could be no doubt that the Bronx of the old days was passing. Even the Goldbergs, the quintessential Bronx family, were now off the air. The radio show had made a successful transition to the new medium, television. After its first season on CBS, Gertrude Berg was told that if actor Phil Loeb, who played her husband, Jake, stayed on, then the show would be canceled. CBS hinted that Loeb was a Communist, but his crime was more properly union activism, for he was one of the founders of Actors' Equity. Says Gertrude Berg's son, Cherney: "My mother told them to go to hell, and the show was canceled. It's a monstrous story, because as a result of that and family pressures Phil committed suicide. Three or four years later, as McCarthyism subsided, the show went back on the air."[15]

"Moses Thinks He's God"
1954–1959

B^Y the late 1950s the postwar Bronx was in the throes of a massive rebuilding program. Monumental housing and highway projects had been launched, despite the questions and protests of anxious and bewildered longtime residents. The sheer scale of these public endeavors was altering the physical appearance of the borough, scarring and obliterating whole neighborhoods.

Throughout the county's lower reaches apartment buildings and surviving one-family houses were demolished and cleared to make way for huge, ambitious public housing projects: Forest Houses, Saint Mary's Park, Melrose, Patterson, tall towers massed in the razed blocks. This was in emulation of the highly regarded "towers in gardens" international style of architecture made popular by Le Corbusier, the French architect who dreamed of leveling old Paris and erecting sleek, clean skyscrapers. The French successfully resisted this purist notion of wholesale clearing of their old neighborhoods, but New Yorkers didn't (at first). America still worshiped the cult of "new and improved." All over the East and South Bronx, block after block was slated for demolition to make way for public housing towers.

The City touted the stolid high rises as a better standard of life, but the neighbors in the nearby streets disagreed. They were intimidated by these cold, dominating monstrosities. Clara Rodriguez, who grew up around 138th Street and Brook Avenue where Milbrook Houses rose, remembers that "they were huge; they were ugly; and they were, most importantly, unsafe. Few of the old tenants became the new tenants. People in the projects were afraid. It was an unfriendly place. Playing space was at a premium, and kids were a surplus commodity. Tensions were high. We felt sorry for the people in the projects. Sure, they didn't have roaches, but what about the quality of their life?"[1]

Outsiders might see the streets of the old Bronx with their dingy walk-ups as slums, but the people who lived there saw them as home. They had practical advantages over the projects. No matter how new and modern a project was, a mother on the thirteenth floor could not possibly keep an eye on her kids playing outside. Nor could a child who had to pee just bound up a couple of flights in the project and be home. It was no surprise, then, that the project elevators often reeked of urine. The projects also lacked neighborliness. There were no stoops to sit on and no corner stores to pop into for a loaf of bread and the latest gossip. Nor could you bring in your relatives to live nearby: When the City was the landlord it was hard to put in a friendly word. As each project was completed, it altered the old neighborhood surrounding it. And would any self-respecting street singer serenade beneath project towers?

The New York City Housing Authority embarked on its first projects in the lower Bronx as soon as the war was over, and, proceeding at a steady pace, constructed the largest concentration of public housing anywhere in the country. There was nothing deliberate or intentional about this; it was the consequence of New York City politics. One participant points out that "though it seems so ancient and out of touch today, in those days you had political parties, and the officials who were elected under the auspices of the parties tended to adhere to the party positions. At that time it was city, state, and federal party position to build public housing." Warren Moscow, who became New York City Housing Authority executive director under Mayor Wagner in the spring of 1955, remembers that there was already significant resistance to public housing then, because much of it was all-black. During Moscow's first discussions with the five borough presidents it quickly became apparent that the only two presidents amenable to public housing were those running Manhattan and the Bronx. As the Housing Authority selected potential sites in the Bronx, Moscow would submit them to borough President Jim Lyons for approval. "He'd say, 'Well, I don't much like public housing, but it's better than what's there,' " remembers Moscow. "There was no grand design in the Bronx, no special planning, no evil thought, but one thing and another we wound up with a solid phalanx of public housing along Washington Avenue and that area. It was a mistake because we ghettoized too many poor people together. You had a feeling you were building the wrong thing, but everything was in the pipeline."[2] Ultimately, ninety-six public housing buildings were raised in the lower Bronx for a total of 12,486 apartments.

Most extraordinary was Robert Moses's building of the Cross-Bronx Expressway, gouging a wide swath through the very heart and guts of the Bronx. From the moment Moses announced his plan in 1944, no one in the street took it seriously. The notion that that many miles of solid, tenanted apartment houses could be swept off the earth for a road seemed absurd, and — more to the point — unfeasible. On the park benches, the kibitzers repeated one wag's reassuring line, "Moses thinks he's God, but he's only Moses."

Planning for new highways had begun during World War II, at which time City Construction Coordinator Robert Moses had them designated necessary for national defense. As such they would be paid for almost entirely by the federal government and the state. The first formal notice to the Bronx of these monumentally disruptive undertakings appears to be an article by Moses in the February–March 1944 issue of *Bronxboro*, the magazine of the Bronx Board of Trade. Writing about the postwar Bronx, Moses gave particular emphasis to the Cross-Bronx Expressway. He conceded the "difficult topography and cost of right-of-way" but said a preliminary plan had been prepared by borough President Lyons's office. The Cross-Bronx would connect the Bronx-Whitestone Bridge in the east with the George Washington Bridge spanning the Harlem River on the west.

A year later, in 1945, again writing in *Bronxboro,* Robert Moses reported that a route had been selected for the Cross-Bronx and "it is being worked out with the wholehearted cooperation of the City, State and Federal officials. It has, I believe, the support of business, civic and other organizations of The Bronx." Prophetically, he wrote that "its effects on the Borough will be enormous, and few people outside the public officials involved can visualize the future which these and other postwar improvements will usher in."[3]

No other roads in New York City could come close to rivaling the extraordinary engineering demanded by the construction of the Cross-Bronx Expressway, a seven-mile-long, six-lane-wide ditch hacked through one solid Bronx neighborhood after another. In Robert Caro's biography of Robert Moses, *The Power Broker,* he describes the immensity of the task as first grasped by General Thomas F. Farrell, a Moses consultant who had overseen the building of the legendary Burma Road in World War II. "Stepping out of his limousine at a high spot on Jesup Avenue to look out over a half-mile valley to the east, the general saw that apartment houses crammed that valley solid — a staggering panorama of massed brick and mortar and iron and steel. Looking down at the map Moses had given him, he saw that the Coordinator was preparing to gouge the huge trench of the expressway straight across the valley's heart. But what staggered Farrell most was not what was in the valley but what was on the other side of it, glaring down at him from the high ridge on its far side, a ridge even higher than the one on which he was standing." General Farrell was looking at the Grand Boulevard and Concourse, with its stately apartment buildings, steady stream of traffic, and, rumbling below in the Fordham gneiss, the IND line of the subway. But, as Caro says, "The ridge and valley, in fact, were only a microcosm of the physical difficulties in the way of the Cross-Bronx Expressway. The path of the great road lay across 113 streets, avenues and boulevards; sewers and water and utility mains numbering in the hundreds; one subway and three railroads, five elevated rapid transit lines, and seven other expressways or parkways, some of which were being built by Moses simultaneously."[4]

Bronxites were worried about housing, and in early 1946 thirty-one civic, religious, and veterans organizations banded together into the Cross-Bronx Citizens' Protective Association to oppose a road that would displace tens of thousands of families when that many veterans were still homeless. "Housing before Highways," they cried and protested vociferously when the first tenements were vacated and perfectly good apartments sat empty. "Instead of homes, our public officials are cramming highways down the throats of our veterans," said the head of the Bronx County Veterans Co-ordinating Council. "The basic need is for shelter." Ignoring the outcry of these little people, Moses forged onward, unruffled and determined. The first section, 2.3 miles on the far eastern edge of the county, was proceeding without much trouble, and preparations for the far westerly section starting at the George Washington Bridge were also going forward.

For those who had the misfortune to live in the path of this behemoth road, which would enable passers-through to traverse Bronx County in fifteen minutes, it all seemed surreal. In his book on modernism, *All That Is Solid Melts into Air*, Marshall Berman, a Bronxite, remembers it well: "At first we couldn't believe it; it seemed to come from another world. First of all, hardly any of us owned cars; the neighborhood itself, and the subways leading downtown, defined the flow of our lives. Besides, even if the city needed the road — or was it the state that needed the road? (in Moses operations, the location of power and authority was never clear, except for Moses himself) — they surely couldn't mean what the stories seemed to say: that the road would be blasted directly through a dozen solid, settled, densely populated neighborhoods like our own; that something like 60,000 working- and lower-middle-class people, mostly Jews, but with many Italians, Irish and blacks thrown in, would be thrown out of our homes. The Jews of the Bronx were nonplussed: could a fellow-Jew really want to do this to us (We had little idea of what kind of Jew he was, or of how much we were all an obstruction in his path). And even if he really did want to do it, we were sure it couldn't happen here, not in America. We were still basking in the afterglow of the New Deal: the government was our government, and it would come through to protect us in the end. And yet, before we knew it, steam shovels and bulldozers were there, and people were getting notice that they better clear out fast. They looked numbly at the wreckers, at the disappearing streets, at each other, and they went. Moses was coming through and no temporal or spiritual power could block his way."[5]

In fact, all the powers of Bronx County stood firmly behind the Cross-Bronx Expressway. Borough President Lyons was a steadfast champion, as was the important Bronx Board of Trade. They believed the Bronx would be a better place because of the expressway — more accessible, more attractive to business. And so, block by block, the sturdy apartment buildings in its way were emptied, as were the multitude of small businesses. For all the promises of easy relocation, few families could find nice apartments at comparable rents. People were scared at the thought of having to move when housing was so tight, and then while they searched, they endured the noise, dirt, and disarray of the advancing highway.

In 1953 one East Tremont neighborhood slated to be wiped off the map rebelled. In his chapter "One Mile," Caro tells the story of their valiant fight to persuade the coordinator and Board of Estimate to swerve the highway along the top of Crotona Park to save their homes. Ultimately, concludes Caro, they were betrayed by Jim Lyons. While it was painful for those who had to move, it was also painful for those who could stay. The demolition and ensuing excavation for the roadbed generated tremendous chaos in the contiguous streets. There were mountains of debris crawling with rats and roaches. By day (and often by night) powerful dynamite blasts shook the nearby buildings, showering them with fine dust and grit. The emptied buildings attracted vagrants and winos, who scared the longtime residents. Unsealed vacated stores and disemboweled buildings adrift in rubbish and broken glass became play spots for local children.

Bronxites watched in amazement and horror. Marshall Berman saw "the center of the Bronx pounded and blasted and smashed. My friends and I would stand on the parapet of the Grand Concourse, where 174th Street had been, and survey the work's progress — the immense steam shovels and bulldozers and timber and steel beams, the hundreds of workers in their variously colored hard hats, the giant cranes reaching far above the Bronx's tallest roofs, the dynamite blasts and tremors, the wild, jagged crags of rock newly torn, the vistas of devastation reaching for miles to the east and west as far as the eye could see — and marvel to see our ordinary nice neighborhood transformed into sublime, spectacular ruins. . . . Indeed, when construction was done, the real ruin of the Bronx had just begun. Miles of street alongside the road were choked with dust and fumes and deafening noise — most strikingly, the roar of trucks of a size and power the Bronx had never seen, hauling heavy cargoes through the city, bound for Long Island or New England, for New Jersey and all points south, all through the day and night. Apartment houses that had been settled and stable for twenty years emptied out."[6]

As the Cross-Bronx was built, other big expressways were readied to plough around the edges of the Bronx and up into the cool suburbs of Westchester, bringing noise and fumes to the Bronx and a quick, easy escape from the City for commuters in automobiles. The Major Deegan Expressway, opened in 1955, swung along the western edge of the county, up the Harlem River.

Then Coordinator Moses proposed yet another major expressway for the Bronx, a sixteen-mile, $23 million elevated structure flowing above Bruckner Boulevard that would connect the Major Deegan and the Cross-Bronx to Moses's Triborough Bridge.

The local merchants were astonished at such a suggestion and immediately made their intense displeasure known to President Lyons. Bruckner Boulevard was a major commer-

The Cross-Bronx Expressway gouged through one Bronx neighborhood after another, displacing tens of thousands of families. Demolition and construction, shown here in this 1962 photograph, dragged on for years.

cial corridor, lively with shoppers and business. If there was to be a road, let it tunnel below grade, not tower over the street, throwing off deep shadow, thunderous noise, and a permanent fine rain of dirt and dust. Lyons told Moses his merchants — important men in the borough, not just working-class tenants — were wrathfully opposed to his elevated highway, and he demanded a tunnel. The autocratic Moses announced that the ungrateful Lyons and his unworthy borough would lose the road altogether. "If Mr. Lyons does not change his tactics," warned Moses, "he would forfeit all other highway projects for the Bronx as well."[7]

Faced with alienating and angering the coordinator, the most powerful man in New York, Lyons caved in. "Almost anyone who understood or had a vision of the Democratic process understood that Bob Moses ad nauseam was destructive," says one observer. "Moses paid no bit of attention to the public, nor to a consensus. He just rode roughshod over the political system. He demolished it or contributed in great part to its demolition."

Nowhere had this been more starkly illustrated than in Moses's Title I slum clearance projects on Manhattan's Upper West Side. Known as Manhattantown, the $54 million project proposed to clear the six square blocks bounded by Central Park West, Amsterdam Avenue, and 97th and 100th streets. Moses had promised to relocate all the poor families — mainly black and Puerto Rican — into decent apartments. Yet the truth was, no such homes were available, certainly not at comparable rents. Instead of relocating families, throughout the early 1950s Moses created refugees.

These refugees, the thousands evicted from the most depressed and troubled neighborhoods of Manhattan, streamed into the old South Bronx, seeking shelter with friends and family, living in apartments honeycombed into cubbyholes. In order to build middle-class housing, Coordinator Moses pushed the poor out of Manhattan into other boroughs. "The Bronx was almost an innocent bystander," says one official. "The idea always was to bypass Manhattan with the ugliness as much as possible. You had public housing and highways in the South Bronx, and then, on top of both of those, which were destabilizing enough, you added a deliberate program of slum clearance to displace the worst. You were then at the point that it all started to go downhill. There was no way you could handle it unless you had much more omniscience than anybody had, because everything was going on at once."

11

The New Boss
1959–1963

CHARLES A. BUCKLEY had been designated by Flynn as his successor, and yet it would be hard to imagine two less similar men. Flynn was an urbane, intellectual boss who had run the Bronx almost by remote control; Buckley was a scrappy, street-smart leader who was always available to his boys, whether in his North End Democratic clubhouse or his modest frame house in Fordham. Flynn was a tall, suave lawyer; Buckley was a short, crude, high school dropout who got rich in the contracting business. Both had come to politics in the days of Arthur Murphy, and each was a talented politician, who recognized the other's gift. Buckley was among those district leaders who had voted young Edward J. Flynn into the leadership.

Buckley, like many an Irishman of his time, worshiped the Democratic party for the power and opportunities it had bestowed on the struggling immigrants. He saw the vote as the sacrament; without it, the Democratic organization would fall quickly from grace. When a *New York Post* reporter went to profile Boss Buckley in 1958 he found that the only decoration in the main room at county headquarters was a framed two-year-old newspaper column: "The Precinct Vote: It Wins the Elections." The columnist had figured out that Governor Averell Harriman had won that year by getting one extra vote in each precinct in the state. That paragraph was circled with thick red crayon and next to it someone had scrawled, "Every single vote counts."

A bricklayer and amateur boxer in his youth, Buckley had risen quickly through the political ranks: city alderman, state

tax appraiser, city chamberlain or treasurer (after Flynn relinquished that job to become New York secretary of state),
and then, in 1934, congressman from the northwest Bronx.
His longevity in the House of Representatives earned him in
1950 the powerful post of chairman of the Public Works Committee, which controlled the purse strings of all government
construction projects. It was said that during Buckley's tenure,
255 federal building projects were funneled into New York
City and State. Congressman Buckley never much cared for
Washington, however, and frequently was absent.

The Bronx Democratic machine in the Buckley years lived
off its momentum, almost automatically producing candidates,
jobs, judgeships, and votes. Yet the postwar changes took
their toll, and Boss Buckley ruled under circumstances far
different from those of Boss Flynn. For one thing, the Jews
were increasingly dissatisfied with their portion of the political
pie. Flynn had always appeased the Jews in the old days with
judgeships, but now they were the dominant group in the
borough. The Irish were most reluctant to relinquish their
long-standing hold, and the young Jews were becoming restive.

Far more corrosive and insoluble were the societal changes.
The New Deal, so ardently supported by the Bronx organization, had eliminated many of the machine's longtime functions. People in need turned less often to the clubhouses; they
now looked to government agencies. There was less patronage
to entice new membership, for civil service exams were required for most City and state jobs. Inflation, although mild,
had whittled away the government salaries that once seemed
so attractive. Ambitious young lawyers no longer flocked to
the clubhouses to provide free legal services to voters as an
investment in their own budding careers.

As all this was being prophesied, Buckley enjoyed one last
glorious hurrah. In 1958 he was invited by former Ambassador
Joseph Kennedy to a luncheon at the plush Brook Club in
Manhattan, the topic being the possible presidential candidacy
of Joe's son Senator John F. Kennedy. Buckley, as an Irish
Catholic, liked the idea and quietly let it be known to upstate

Congressman Charles Buckley (left), Bronx County Democratic
chairman for fourteen years, meets President John F. Kennedy in the
White House in 1962. Buckley was an early, enthusiastic supporter
of Kennedy's presidential aspirations.

leaders that he favored young Kennedy. Most of them were Irish Catholics just like Buckley. Was it possible that before they departed this earth they might see one of their own kind ascend to the greatest office in the land? Slowly and quietly they lined up behind Kennedy.

The climax was the annual Bronx County Democratic dinner on May 12, 1960, at the Waldorf-Astoria, where the huge ballroom could accommodate the legions of contractors, union leaders, builders, and anyone else who did business thanks to the Public Works Committee. That night Charlie Buckley virtually delivered New York State to Kennedy before forty of the sixty-two county leaders. Boss Buckley introduced Senator Kennedy as the Democratic Man o' War. "He can run in any state and win," he told the fifteen hundred cheering diners.

Buckley's dinner and endorsement, in tandem with the triumphant West Virginia primary victory, launched Kennedy toward the presidential nomination. It was a great moment for Buckley, for just as Flynn could claim to have helped launch Roosevelt, so Buckley could claim the title of kingmaker to Kennedy.

On November 5, 1960, John F. Kennedy came to the Bronx, just like all the Democratic presidents and hopefuls before him, to woo the Bronx Ladies at the Concourse Plaza Hotel. After dazzling a mob of twenty-five thousand up at Fordham Road and the Grand Concourse on a brief campaign stop, JFK, young, handsome, and as charming as the old FDR, arrived at the hotel, smiling and shaking hands as he squeezed through the crowds. Inside, the Grand Ballroom was covered with bunting and huge campaign posters. Above the round tables bobbed placards declaring "The Home of the Bagel Knows Big Jack Is Able," or "The Home of the Knishes Thinks Jack Is Delicious." The ladies were delirious and, when Kennedy told them, "I come to the Bronx as an old Bronx boy — I used to live in Riverdale," they drowned him out with a joyous roar.[1] When he finally finished and left, there were so many people waiting outside that the candidate had to stand on a car to wave and be seen. He would be the last Democratic presidential candidate to make the requisite pilgrimage to the Ladies' Luncheon.

After the election the newspapers rediscovered the Bronx boss, and they lionized the short, scrappy man who was looking more and more like an old snapping turtle, his unfiltered cigarette clasped in his jowly beak. The reporters wrote long and flattering profiles about the crude-talking boss, but they also took note of Buckley's vulnerability in his own congressional district. The young men who had come home from the war anxious to dive into politics and change the world had started to set up reform clubs. Richard Flynn, son of the great Boss Flynn, was among the first to challenge the machine in 1957. In his countywide race for councilman-at-large he was demolished at the polls, but in 1960 some of the minor Bronx reform candidates did very well, considering that they were facing the famous and supposedly invincible Bronx machine. They didn't win, but for the first time they posed a threat.

On their own, the reformers might not have gotten very far. But Mayor Robert Wagner, who owed his election to early support from the Bronx Democrats, had a falling-out with the county leaders. They deemed him unworthy of a third term in 1961, and he went his own way. Selecting his own running mates, Wagner dumped Lawrence Gerosa, a Bronxite and Buckley man, as comptroller. Buckley could not tolerate this affront to his organization. Of even greater import was Wagner's determination to change the City's charter, stripping the borough presidents of the last vestiges of control over local public works. When Jim Lyons had become borough president during the Depression, the county still ran its own affairs to a great extent, dispensing contracts for snow removal, road work, insurance, and local construction. As the complexity, cost, and scope of public works expanded, however, succeeding levels of government took control — first the City, then the state, and increasingly, after the war, the federal government. Contracts with the United States flowed out of City Hall, not the County Building.

The proposed charter change formalized this power shift,

but in New York City it emasculated the outer boroughs, making them de facto vassals of Manhattan. And it effectively quashed the growing resistance to massive public works. "If you go back," says one official, "you see the criticism was that the borough presidents were too powerful. They didn't want public housing in their boroughs, they didn't want these highway improvements. Therefore, they had to be replaced with a central core of authority in Manhattan, which really knew what was best for the City of New York. The new charter was in effect repudiation of the borough concept of government. Manhattan Island would end up running the whole shebang." It was just this that the Democratic county leaders wanted to stop, and so they lined up against Wagner.

Wagner responded by fashioning a new coalition consisting of liberal Jews and reformers, along with the new immigrants to New York, the Negroes and the Puerto Ricans. The Democratic leaders put up their own ticket to challenge the mayor, and they went down in solid defeat on primary day, September 7, 1961. The longtime Irish Catholic domination of New York politics was dramatically ended. Shortly thereafter, the last shreds of borough autonomy were legislated over to City Hall and Manhattan.

In the Bronx, a Wagner-backed reformer named Bernard Manheimer defeated a Buckley incumbent for assembly. Even more amazing, the organization lost the Bronx borough presidency to a Republican-liberal, Joseph Periconi, in November. Jim Lyons had finally retired after thirty-four years in the post, and John Sullivan, a loyal but lackluster machine minion, had been put up for the job. Mayor Wagner managed to install his own leaders everywhere but in the Bronx. A glowering Buckley growled and champed on his cigarette, "If he wants to get me, let 'em come up and fight."[2]

Emboldened by their unexpected good showing, born-again reformers materialized all over the Bronx, ready to take on the Buckley machine. The early groundwork was laid diligently by young men and women who had cut their teeth on reform politics in Manhattan and were now sent north to dispatch the Bronx dinosaurs. The rallying issue for these

"young turks," (mainly Jews) was greater grassroots participation in the party. The young did not approve of the autocratic methods of the old Irishmen, and they also decried
paying off faithful party hacks with judgeships.

In the same year, 1961, Eleanor Roosevelt and former Governor and U.S. Senator Herbert H. Lehman broke ranks with
the regular Democrats and became the patron saints, along
with Thomas K. Finletter, of the reform movement in New
York City. They brought tremendous prestige and credibility
to the fledgling reformers and got them a great deal of press
coverage. In the Bronx, David Levy, a lawyer and young Navy
veteran, was among the first reformers to launch a club. The
regulars were unimpressed, but after the unexpected success
of the 1960 election and Wagner's triumph over the bosses in
1961, the reformers realized that 1962 would be a watershed
year. David Levy was selected to run for Boss Buckley's seat.
Buckley had been a congressman for thirty-two years; Levy,
a tall, fresh-faced lawyer, had done nothing politically except
organize reform clubs and challenge the machine. He was
young and bright, however, and believed earnestly in what
he was doing. The issues were straightforward: Buckley was
a political throwback who failed to vote a third of the time
in Congress and ran the party for the benefit of the few and
not the all.

Young Levy discovered the political clout of television quite
by accident. On August 7, the morning after his youngest
child was born, a tired Levy got a phone call at home informing
him that his law office was filled with impatient reporters.
President Kennedy had just endorsed Buckley for reelection,
and Levy was taken over the coals by reporters asking how
it felt to run against the president of the United States. As
the last reporters trooped out the phone rang. It was Senator
Lehman calling to say he was telegraphing his endorsement
of Levy at two o'clock. Levy called another press conference,
released the endorsement, and made the television news all
over New York City, killing the earlier press conference.

The next day he went up, as planned, to a handshaking
campaign stop outside Alexander's Department Store on

Fordham Road. "We arrived with Polaroid cameras so as to take pictures of the voters with me and give them to the voters. After only a few minutes we had an incredible line," remembers Levy. "We knew then that TV worked, because the day before no one had known who I was."[3]

Charlie Buckley had routinely shunned publicity. Once a year he let loose at the Democratic county dinner. Political reporters relished these evenings because they could count on the curmudgeonly Buckley to lace into someone — one year he went so far as to say nasty things about Mrs. Roosevelt. Buckley believed that getting elected depended on running the clubhouses right and hauling out the voters on election day. He could not believe that a political nobody like Levy, a pipsqueak with almost no apparatus supporting his candidacy, could be getting all this attention.

By primary night Levy had been endorsed for Congress not only by Senator Lehman, but by Mrs. Roosevelt and Mayor Wagner. Buckley's mood was as foul as his language when he arrived at county headquarters on Courtlandt Avenue after the polls closed. Finally, at half past midnight, with 16,400 votes to Levy's 14,400, Buckley descended and positioned himself in front of the television cameras. Looking rumpled and wrinkled in the blazing lights, he peered through his thick, black-rimmed glasses and claimed his victory. "Will you run again?" "This is definitely my last term of office. I've had enough." The old man tolerated a few more questions and left.

By the time the next election rolled around, the reformers had gathered new strength and resources, and no one was ignoring them anymore, certainly not Buckley. Despite a dozen vows to retire, the congressman was running against Jonathan Bingham. At first glance Bingham looked like easy competition. He was a WASP running in the most ethnic of counties, and he had few roots in the Bronx. Buckley, cranky and irritable as ever, lashed out at the impudent candidate daring to challenge him. "Jonathan — now what kind of name is that for the Bronx? And look at his middle name — Brewster —

isn't that pathetic?"[4] Tall, silver-haired, the scion of a wealthy Connecticut family, Bingham had been a member of the Buckley organization. Once he broke with the machine, the patrician Bingham gave no quarter. While Buckley informed reporters, "I don't campaign, I don't shake hands. I don't go around slapping backs," Bingham was out barnstorming the Bronx, constantly angling for air time on the nightly television news.[5] Buckley's loyal protégé, Jack Kennedy, was dead of an assassin's bullet, and President Johnson's semiendorsement carried little clout in the Bronx.

Running scared, Buckley resorted to a whisper campaign to destroy his opponent. "What the Buckley people did was to have the Bronx DA issue invitations to the Jewish leaders, rabbis, and presidents of synagogues, to discuss what they called a matter of urgent community importance," remembers Bingham. In the county courthouse the Buckley people presented details of the purported anti-Semitism of candidate Jonathan Bingham. "It got no press coverage because it was done as a whispering campaign. We decided to go public in order to refute it. I was tremendously grateful to the TV, believe me, for the coverage they gave that press conference. We went down the charges point by point."[6]

On primary night the reporters once again gathered at Bronx Democratic headquarters to await the results of this unlikely contest. Suddenly a flying wedge of uniformed private guards shoved through the crowd, clearing a path for an angry Buckley. The guards stood in front of Buckley's offices, where Jack Kennedy's portrait was still hung with black. When the extent of the disaster became apparent some of the pols began to leave. At ten minutes before midnight, when it was obvious that Bingham had beaten Buckley badly — twenty-six thousand to twenty-two thousand — Buckley's private guards pushed aside the wall of reporters while Buckley went out the back door. Pursuing reporters were treated to a choice barrage of obscenities before the old man's car zoomed off.

Boss Buckley had lost touch with the new realities of his own county and the postwar City of New York. His vision was too parochial to see beyond the comfortable sameness of the Bronx clubhouses. Edward J. Flynn, as Bronx boss and adviser to FDR, had thought deeply about what the country needed to prosper anew. His solutions centered on jobs and economic security, but the problems troubling Bronx County in the early 1960s were not just material. They also were the more elusive, complex issues of justice and spirit.

12

"Horse Was the New Thing"
1960

BY the early 1960s poverty and crowding had created sprawling ghettos, breeding grounds for despair, drug addiction, and crime. These two evils were in no way new to New York — the immigrant slums of early New York had spawned addicts and criminals aplenty. But the problems that had so bedeviled the City in its formative years declined when millions of European immigrants prospered and established themselves, and as federal drug laws made narcotics illegal and largely unavailable. New Yorkers had virtually forgotten those long-ago dangerous days.

In fact, at the height of the Irish and German immigration to New York in the nineteenth century, crime had been rampant. "Probably in no city in the civilized world is life so fearfully insecure, . . ." Englishwoman Isabella Bird declared in 1840. "Terrible outrages and murderous assaults are matters of such nightly occurrence as to be thought hardly worth notice."[1] In his book *Gangs of New York,* Herbert Asbury wrote of Manhattan's Fourth Ward: "By 1845, the whole area had become a hotbed of crime. No human life was safe, and a well-dressed man venturing into the district was commonly set upon and murdered or robbed, or both, before he had gone a block."[2]

A large and shadowy underclass had subsisted in the dank, airless warrens of the tenement districts or in the charity wards. Their offspring formed teenage gangs that terrorized the City, and fought pitched battles with the police. "The gang is an institution in New York," wrote Jacob Riis at the turn of the century. "The police deny its existence while nursing the bruises received in nightly battles with it that tax their utmost resources."[3] When newspapers reported in one week six "murderous" assaults by gangs upon innocent citizens traveling the public streets, Riis wondered what the real weekly toll was, in light of police inclination to hush up such outrages.

When the Italians and Jews arrived, their children provided new fodder for the gangs, and both groups produced some of New York's most notorious gangsters. The pages of the *Jewish Daily Forward* rang with the anguished cries of law-abiding parents made desperate by their sons' descent into criminality, but crime was a powerful and seductive alternative to the hard grind to survive honestly in dull, low-paying jobs. Monk Eastman, a "nice" Jewish boy, became one of the Lower East Side's most celebrated thugs at the turn of the century. He was a ferocious-looking brawler, with a bullet head, cauliflower ears, mashed nose, and the scars of battle all over his body. He adored cats and birds and often made the rounds of his turf with a couple of felines tucked under his powerful arms, while several more trailed behind him. He and his gang had interests in prostitution, gambling dens, and the protection rackets. He bragged that he had so many bullets lodged in his battle-scarred body that he had to take them into account when weighing himself. Monk was a favorite of the Tammany politicians, who gave him protection until his gang's wars got out of hand.

By the 1920s peace descended upon New York. The City's population was seven- or eightfold what it had been in the crime-ridden 1850s, but the murder rate (the most reliable barometer of violent crime) still averaged about three hundred homicides a year. It fluctuated up and down within that range for the next three decades, an unusually peaceable time in the City's history, unmarked by any significant influx of poor people. In the late 1950s, as poor blacks and Puerto Ricans filled the spreading slums, crime exploded. Within the decade the annual homicide rate topped one thousand murders, a swift and spectacular rise that reflected the explosion of violence of all kinds. And the problem was as acute in the Bronx as in every other borough with minority slums.

Along with gangs and thugs, drugs came back in the 1950s to haunt the City. They, too, were not a novel scourge. Opium derivatives had been popular and legal medications in nineteenth-century America. In 1870 Americans consumed half a million pounds of opium, mostly in the form of morphine-based patent medicines and medical cures. At a time when doctors lacked the wherewithal to diagnose and treat most diseases, these drugs were truly miraculous in their ability to stave off pain.

It was several decades before doctors conceded that they had unwittingly addicted many of their patients. Morphine addiction was widespread among Civil War veterans treated for battle wounds and was sadly referred to as "the soldier's disease." All those who worked in the immigrant slums were familiar with the ravages of drugs. Social worker Jane Addams of Chicago lamented the unregulated sale of cocaine to minors and infuriated local druggists by her campaign to halt such sales.

As the twentieth century dawned, a State Department employee named Hamilton Wright thought to curry favor with the Chinese — and thereby win important trade concessions — by advocating the outlawing of opium. For ten years Wright plugged away at his cause, and on February 14, 1914, he successfully fathered the Harrison Narcotic Act. The medical and pharmaceutical professions endorsed the law only because they understood it to preserve their right to prescribe morphine-based medications and cocaine "in good faith" as deemed necessary. They did not anticipate the zeal of the Treasury's Narcotic Bureau, which defined "good faith" as prescribing ever-reduced amounts of drugs until the patient was drug-free. Next the Treasury Department decreed that no banned drugs could be prescribed except in jails or institutional settings. Treasury agents swooped down on doctors' offices, pharmacies, and clinics. Between 1914 and 1924, twenty-five thousand doctors and druggists were arrested. Few went to jail, but many were ruined professionally. By the time a Seattle physician battled the issue to the Supreme Court and won in 1925, the medical community had gotten the government's message. All respectable physicians shunned addicted patients and refused to prescribe any morphine-based drugs. Another fifty thousand people, mostly addicts, had been arrested in those ten years for possessing morphine and cocaine. They swelled the federal prisons to overflowing, making up one-third of the inmates.

Developed in 1898 by Heinrich Dreser of the German pharmaceutical company Friedrich Bayer and Company, heroin was viewed at first as highly potent aspirin — good for common colds and more serious ailments like asthma, bronchitis, and one of the era's deadliest diseases, tuberculosis. When opium, morphine, and cocaine were outlawed, heroin use boomed.

Heroin had remained completely legal under the Harrison Act, a nonprescription drug available in any drugstore and widely sold by street vendors. Aghast at the situation, Congressman Stephen Porter of Pennsylvania moved to block the importation of opium for the purpose of making heroin. Throughout the hearings New York City provided a goodly portion of his ammunition. A New York doctor sent a written statement declaring heroin the drug of choice in the City's underworld. The U.S. surgeon general stated firmly that heroin use caused insanity. Drug addiction nationwide was set at figures ranging from two hundred thousand to a million. The lower figure was considered more realistic, while the higher figure was favored by those out to alarm the public.

The unanimous passage of Porter's bill in 1924 and the relentless Treasury Holy War were effective against heroin, and the scourge of drug-taking gradually died down, except in the most debauched circles. In 1930 the New York Police Department reported that "the youth of today is not addicted to the drug habit as much as the youth of nine or ten years ago." In subsequent years, figures for narcotics arrests were deemed too insignficant to be included in yearly arrest totals. The government proclaimed its campaign to eliminate the drug menace largely successful. Narcotics use had been driven deep underground and only the most daring, depraved, and bohemian used drugs. This small, select market — estimated at twenty thousand nationwide — was supplied by small-time criminals.

After World War II the small, haphazard drug trade once more became a major industry. Who can forget the powerful scene in *The Godfather* when Don Corleone, whose refusal to condone narcotics trafficking had sparked a major gang war, relented and gave his approval? One Don reassured his peers that his men would sell only to "the colored. Let them lose their souls with drugs." And with the capital, organization, and political protection provided by the mobsters, the drug trade boomed. Narcotics use was most popular in the burgeoning black urban ghettos, a fact highly publicized by the travails of such big jazz stars as Billie Holiday and Charlie Parker. Claude Brown writes in *Manchild in the Promised Land* that by the early 1950s, "horse [heroin] was the new thing, not only in our neighborhood but in Brooklyn, the Bronx, and every place I went, uptown and downtown. It was like horse had just taken over. Everybody was talking about it. All the hip people were using it and snorting it and getting this new high. To know what was going on and to be in on things, you had to do that."[4]

Like an epidemic, drug addiction spread throughout New York City. For many in the ghettos, pushing drugs became the most lucrative endeavor they could possibly engage in. The profit to be made from smuggling illicit drugs into the country and selling them was breathtaking: a kilogram of pure opium bought in Turkey for twenty-five dollars, then processed into heroin, was worth $1 million on the streets of New York. Big-time dealers, lugging their cash earnings around in garbage bags, could not calculate its value before weighing it. There was just too much to count.

In 1946, 623 people were arrested in New York City for narcotics misdemeanors, 56 for felonies; in 1950, the numbers were 1,770 and 191. In the first half of 1951, the total had already grown to 1,294 misdemeanor narcotics arrests and 251 felony arrests. The trade continued to flourish and spread in all the five boroughs. "It seemed to be a kind of plague," wrote Claude Brown. "Every time I went uptown somebody else was hooked, somebody else was strung out. People talked about them as if they were dead."[5] Addiction rates in central Harlem almost doubled, from 22.1 per 10,000 in 1955 to 40.1 in 1961.

The New York City police, with a long tradition of taking bribes and payoffs, looked the other way. Some officers actively joined in the trafficking.

The Knapp Commission, which investigated and exposed widespread corruption among New York City police in the late 1960s, reported that it was commonplace for cops — especially those in the Narcotics Division — to steal money from pushers and to keep confiscated drugs. The commission found "that corruption in narcotics law enforcement goes beyond the Police Department and involves prosecutors, attorneys, bondsmen, and allegedly certain judges. While this fact does not excuse the illegal conduct of policemen who accept bribes, it does serve to illustrate the demoralizing environment in which police are expected to enforce narcotics laws."[6]

The federal government reacted to the rampant drug trade by enacting even harsher laws. Although a few people proposed returning treatment of narcotics addicts to the medical profession, the lawmen were convinced they could prevail, if only given the tools. Congress amended the Harrison Act with the Boggs Act of 1951, which instituted draconian sentences for dope dealers. Heroin's reputation as evil incarnate was solidly established. In truth there were far more people who used heroin recreationally, occasionally, than there were addicts who required a daily fix. Even today the National Council on Drug Abuse estimates that there are five hundred thousand addicts and three and a half million occasional heroin users.

In a city surfeited with poverty, drudgery, and frustration, the euphoria of heroin was a lovely escape. In *Down These Mean Streets*, Piri Thomas describes his own addiction. "Yet there is something about dogie — heroin — it's a super-duper tranquilizer. All your troubles become a bunch of bleary blurred memories when you're in a nod of your own special dimension. And it was only when my messed-up system became a screaming want for the next fix did I really know just how short an escape from reality it really brought. The shivering, [the] nose-running, [the] crawling damp, ice-cold skin it produced were just the next worse step of — like my guts were gonna blow up and muscles in my body becoming so tight I could almost hear them snapping.

"I could make a choice of stealing or pushing to support my new love. I picked pushing."[7]

13

The New "Other Half"
1962–1966

IT was Michael Harrington who first focused attention on the new pool of poor who had been ghettoized while America grew wealthy in the 1950s. His book, *The Other America* (1962), had thrust upon a sanguine nation a disturbing portrait. "The millions who are poor in the United States," he wrote, "tend to become increasingly invisible. Here is a great mass of people, yet it takes an effort of the intellect and will even to see them."[1] When the book first came out, it had a small audience, but a long, thoughtful article in the *New Yorker* in January 1963 called the book to general attention. President Kennedy read Harrington's work and was duly impressed.

Harrington focused on the minorities, the unemployed and underemployed, the citizens of depressed regions, and the aging. As his book became widely read, activists and academics moved with alacrity to rally around the issue. By the fall of 1963 the Kennedy administration was already considering a concerted assault on poverty, a comprehensive program that would imbue the poor with the power to take action and effect change, a popular movement that would truly propel whole groups and neighborhoods out of the mire of longtime poverty. John F. Kennedy's assassination and Lyndon Johnson's assumption of the presidency did not alter the plans.

When the Eighty-ninth Congress convened on January 8, 1964, President Lyndon Johnson declared war on American poverty. "It must be won in the field, in every private home, in every public office, from the court house to the White House," he declaimed to the senators and state respresentatives before him in the marbled chamber. "Our aim is not only to relieve the symptoms of poverty, but to cure it, and above all, to prevent it. And this Administration today, here and now, declares unconditional war on poverty in America, and I urge this Congress and all Americans to join with me in that effort."[2]

Michael Harrington was among those invited to Washington to lay the battle plans. "The important thing was not just that the President was going to commit money to the war on poverty," wrote Harrington. "More than that, the enormous moral and political power which the White House can summon was channeled into this undertaking. There was a sense of excitement, of social passion, in the capitol. Friends of mine in the Government phoned to say they would work at reduced pay and rank if only they could become part of this crusade."[3] The poverty warriors donned the mantle once worn by the New Dealers. Young and talented idealists were enthralled by the prospect of finally eradicating poverty. It was a crusade that dovetailed perfectly with another historic movement, the fight for civil rights, for many of the poor were black.

While Sargent Shriver and his New Frontiersmen were fashioning (in record time) the Economic Opportunity Act of 1964, New York City was preparing to present its case for a major portion of the battle funds. Ten days after President Johnson delivered his first salvo, Mayor Wagner assembled the New York City Council and all thirty-five agency and department heads in the ornate council chamber at City Hall for a special New York declaration of war on poverty. City agencies were directed to mobilize their forces and vanquish the costly blight of poverty. The Republicans were not terribly impressed. "The problem of poverty and sub-standard living in our town is certainly nothing new," said Councilman-at-large Richard S. Aldrich, cousin of Governor Nelson Rockefeller, "yet the mayor, in his sudden desire to lead the attack, naively makes it appear that it has just come to his attention."[4] In fact, Julius Edelstein, a top Wagner aide at the time, says City Hall was not even yet aware of the true dimensions of the problem, nor how rapidly the unskilled poor who depended upon public resources were multiplying.

The City's newspapers, taking up this new battle with relish, sent out commando-reporters to reconnoiter the spreading precincts of poverty. They found a new and yet familiar misery, tended now by an army of professional social workers employed by the government. Poverty in New York City, in 1964, was not worse than it had been in Jacob Riis's time, but far more complex. The end of an impassioned six-part series on poverty in New York by the *New York Post* read: "Today in a dual society, half rich, half forgotten, the boundaries are blurred by television antennas and electric can openers. But in New York the other half has become the subject of intense discussion. Half a dozen committees have been called into emergency session to deal with the poor. Recommendations are pouring in. Endless conferences are scheduled. The time seemed ripe for a beginning."[5]

A *Daily News* article by Kitty Hanson focused on two new phenomena that probably had been insigificant in Jacob Riis's day, but now seemed major problems: households without fathers and young men who did not attend school or work at jobs. In 1964 she wrote: "Death and divorce, desertion and illegitimacy have created a new kind of family in America — families headed by women alone. Nearly a fourth of all the families living below the poverty line are families without fathers."[6] There were sixty-seven thousand women on the welfare rolls in New York City whose children were supported completely by the government's Aid to Dependent Children.

Then Ms. Hanson looked at the army of idle school dropouts who had no role in the City's economy. In Jacob Riis's day even young children were wanted for work, so much so that child labor laws had to be passed to free them from exploitation in the factories and sweatshops, but modern machinery and technology had eliminated much of the backbreaking work and rote labor that once employed the unskilled. Grave-digging machines could excavate in half an hour a coffin-sized hole, a task that once had taken two brawny shovelers ten hours. Push-button elevators, wafting piped-in music, made obsolescent almost forty thousand elevator operators. In the old days, when snow blanketed the City, thousands of men had turned out with shovels to clear the streets.

In New York City the presence of powerful unions contributed to that disappearance of eager hands, because many employers found it far easier to relocate outside the City than to accommodate the demands of the workers. For unskilled, unschooled kids, the job outlook was bleak. Of 571,300 youths between the ages of fourteen and twenty-four and out of school, a core of 73,000 were unemployed or getting by with part-time jobs. "The city that does not provide them with a means to solve their job problems today will be caring for them in prisons, mental hospitals and on the welfare rolls tomorrow," Ms. Hanson's article warned.[7]

Before the City got much further with its antipoverty campaign, Harlem launched its own war. On a hot Saturday night, July 18, 1964, demonstrators gathered in front of the police precinct house to protest the killing of a fifteen-year-old black boy by a white policeman. Police pushed the angry crowd back across the street. A bottle twirled through the air as the police hauled a kid inside. The distraught marchers dashed through the streets telling crowds pouring out of the Apollo Theater and the subway that the police had seized a young black boy and were beating him.

Incensed, the crowds flooded 125th Street, filling the wide shopping avenue. Whenever police appeared, the air sang with flying bottles and trash-can covers. The mob mushroomed. A store window was smashed, trash baskets were set ablaze, and convoys of police cars careened up the avenues. Harlem was rioting. As the hot night deepened, the melee swelled, the crowds always eluding the cops and taunting them. By the early hours of the morning, police had regained control of the streets, littered with the debris of the first riot in New York City since 1943. (That time Harlem had taken to the streets in a fury when a Negro soldier was shot by a white policeman. It was a far more ferocious affair, with five dead and five hundred injured.)

The aftermath of the 1964 Harlem riot was a few dozen arrests and injuries, and even more pressure than before to get the poverty programs going. Within the fortnight Martin

Luther King was at City Hall huddling with Mayor Wagner and his aides, who emerged to announce that the City's war on poverty would move into high gear and scare up twenty thousand jobs for disadvantaged youth. More than one hundred top City administrators were told to develop programs and jobs. The mayor flew to Washington to meet with the president and see how big a cut New York City would be getting of the federal war on poverty. With the Harlem riot a fresh memory, the ante would surely be upped.

On August 20 President Johnson signed the Economic Opportunity Act into law in the Rose Garden of the White House. It had moved through Congress with the speed of many of FDR's first New Deal initiatives, and Lyndon Johnson declared the signing a historic moment. "Today for the first time in the history of the human race, a great nation is able to make and is willing to make a commitment to eradicate poverty among its people."[8]

In December the first $5 million began to flow into New York City. Mobilization for "Youth" and "Haryou-Act," both Manhattan-based antipoverty programs, were slated for big chunks of that money, but the Bronx was not left out. The Albert Einstein College of Medicine, part of Yeshiva University, was granted $289,652 to set up four "first aid" centers for emergency psychological help in the East Bronx. The hospital would train neighborhood people, who in turn would staff storefront offices. Mayor Wagner said he had "great hopes" for the project, which was a model for the "maximum feasible participation" of the poor mandated by the Economic Opportunity Act.

Throughout the winter of 1964–1965 the Wagner administration continued to announce new antipoverty initiatives: an emergency repair program for slum housing, jobs for dropouts through the neighborhood youth corps. As the money trickled down to the community groups, it attracted new activists who saw that the rhetoric was finally translating into tangible dollars. Yet the arrival of the bucks and the realization that the federal spigot was just beginning to open led to the first skirmish over who would control that money when it came: The

self-proclaimed leaders of the poor and the poor, whose in-
clusion was mandated by the soon-to-be-famous "maximum
feasible participation" clause? Or the traditional power apparatus of the cities — the mayor and his City agencies?

Everyone jumped into the fray — politicians, blacks, and
private charities, for there was too much money on the way
to sit back calmly while others determined how it would be
divvied up. By May 1965 a beleaguered Wagner proposed a
compromise. The boards set up when Wagner first declared
his war on poverty would be transformed into a new New
York City Council Against Poverty, replete with members
(eventually) from the poor neighborhoods where six community progress centers were to be established. The council
would have as many as one hundred people, perhaps thereby
co-opting virtually every group in New York with a gripe
about it. There would also be an administrative arm called
the Economic Opportunity Corporation.

It was certainly not politics-as-usual during the summer of
1965 in New York City. Mayor Wagner, after so handily
trouncing the bosses four years earlier, had failed to sustain
his energy through a third term, especially after the illness
and death of his wife, Susan, in 1964. He seemed to fade into
the old woodwork of City Hall, emerging occasionally for such
dramatic declarations as his war on poverty. In contrast to
the spirit of the New Frontier, and then the Great Society,
Wagner seemed tired and washed out. Perhaps twelve years
as mayor of New York would have exhausted the most ebul-
lient leader. Wagner bowed out of the race for a fourth term.

In the ensuing mayoral free-for-all, Comptroller Abraham
Beame, a man even more lackluster than Wagner, won the
Democratic nomination. John V. Lindsay, a tall, handsome
congressman from Manhattan's "Silk Stocking" district, came
from behind to capture the Republican and liberal lines. Lindsay had an excellent reputation as a congressman, and he was
right in the Kennedy mold: liberal, concerned, well-educated
(Choate, Yale, Yale Law), and equipped with an attractive,
smart wife and charming children. As he strode through the

City on May 13, 1965, going from borough to borough proclaiming his candidacy (including a stop at the Concourse Plaza Hotel in the Bronx), he inspired a great deal of enthusiasm and excitement. A newcomer to City politics, he had no organization to speak of, whereas Beame could call on the Democratic apparatus entrenched in all five boroughs. The old machines were tired, however, and on election day the dynamic Lindsay squeaked through with a slender 102,407-vote margin.

The new mayor, launching himself into his new job with vehemence on January 2, 1966, was immediately confronted with the first transit strike in the history of New York. It slowed his blast-off, but not much. Scores of young men and women, the best and brightest of the urban scene, were recruited to City Hall to take over New York City. Their mission? To overhaul the byzantine, doddering bureaucracy, to blunt the machinations of power brokers, to inject new vitality and pride and life into a city that needed to regain its spirit. Action was the word for this new era. The Lindsay administration seemed to care more about becoming the antithesis of its predecessor than about anything else. Nothing would remain unscrutinized; everything would be revamped, recast, or obliterated, as necessary, to create a new, much-improved, dynamic New York City. Mayor Lindsay minced no words in announcing this to the world. The young and idealistic flocked to City Hall, and the cynical and sardonic sat back to watch. Wrote *Daily News* columnist Pete Hamill, "The sluggish years of Robert (Captain Easy) Wagner were over; under John (Captain Marvel) Lindsay a brave new world of vigor, freshness and style would be upon us."

In keeping with the vision of a new, streamlined New York, the poverty boards and committees had been consolidated into one sixty-two-member Council Against Poverty, which continued to seek out suitable poor people for membership and maximum feasible participation. The controversial community progress centers had finally been set up, key outposts in the war on poverty. Lindsay commissioned Mitchell Sviridoff, an expert urbanist from New Haven, to study the City's poverty programs and devise a better way for the new administration.

While he studied and devised, everything ground to a halt, several extended budget deadlines were missed. Lindsayites muttered about holdover antipoverty officials from Wagner's day and Kafkaesque bureaucracies. But the "underlying reason for the delay was too scandalous to tell the press," wrote Woody Klein in *Lindsay's Promise*. "For the first five months of our Administration, literally nothing had been accomplished — except perhaps some hearings in ghetto communities — and everything stood still while we awaited the Sviridoff report."[9]

In late June the report was unveiled. It proposed consoldiating all the social service agencies and antipoverty programs into a "super-agency" to be known as the Human Resources Administration. The "progress centers" would be transformed into "community corporations," and from them would emanate the local leadership and important programs that would eradicate the poverty of New York City. The young mayor hired Sviridoff to oversee this consolidation. Sviridoff in turn raided the Office of Economic Opportunity in Washington for various aides. This good news coincided with the embarrassing revelation that the City had failed to use half its $20 million antipoverty budget in the time allotted, and Washington took back $10 million amidst much publicity.

Some saw the war on poverty as nothing more than a legal, sophisticated form of bribery. "In New York at that time the antipoverty money was given out in place of sandbags and barbed wire as a defense against minority rioting," Jimmy Breslin wrote. "The record shows the money was well-spent. At a time when poor neighborhoods were beginning to stir crankily, when they were given to believe there was a chance that things would change, the openings for misunderstandings and violence were constant. In New York, where the loss of life would have been staggering, there was no major outbreak. Bribery worked."[10]

If the establishment wanted to buy off the restive poor with a war on poverty, the most enterprising of the poor were delighted to serve. Government service had always been a reliable path out of the ranks of the penurious, but the blacks and Puerto Ricans had found little room or welcome so far in the traditional City agencies. The Irish owned the police and fire, the Italians ran sanitation, the Jews had a lock on the schools and civil service. A change in the law in 1960 had allowed the white working class and middle class to live outside New York and still hold City jobs.

So while the earlier immigrants ceded many of their neighborhoods to the minorities (albeit with great bitterness), they certainly were not ceding their government jobs. They became commuters, but this left scant foothold for the newcomers. The poverty programs opened up a whole new world of jobs that offered good pay, prestige within the community, and the prospect of participating in the Great Society. The imminent arrival of all those jobs, the mere rumor of that kind of money, with no substantive plan for its expenditure, guaranteed colossal battles — between individuals, between factions, and between races.

14

The Pondiac's Last Hurrah
1961–1967

EVEN before his 1962 congressional defeat Charlie Buckley had made an effort to rejuvenate the old machine, bringing in blacks and Puerto Ricans in recognition of their growing numbers in the borough. The passage of the Voting Rights Act in 1965 would enfranchise thousands of minorities. If the machine didn't offer something to the Hispanics and Negroes, they would ally themselves with the reformers. Political Puerto Ricans in the southeast Bronx found their way inevitably to the Pondiac Club next to the El on Westchester Avenue.

The Pondiac was the one clubhouse in the South Bronx that had always been cordial to the Puerto Ricans, and as early as 1952 a significant number of Puerto Rican members belonged. The thick 124-page journal for that year's annual dinner-dance at the Concourse Plaza ballroom listed a Pagan, a Gonzalez, and an Ortiz among the Lehmans, Klines, and O'Reagans in the program, and had a number of ads from Hispanic businesses.

The stout, blonde Pondiac leader Clara Gompers was almost a political immortal. One of the district leaders who elected Flynn boss in 1922, she had been "in like Flynn" ever after. She didn't bother to live in her district anymore, but made her home at the Concourse Plaza. The head telephone operator at the hotel marveled at Clara's power in the Bronx. "She was the top banana. I seen myself buy a vacuum cleaner and I couldn't afford that vacuum cleaner no how. I was a little upset over it one day and I was telling Clara that I thought he was going to take me to court. She said 'Let him take you to court.' The windup was — and if I hadn't seen this myself

I wouldn't never have believed it — we're in the courtroom and all of a sudden I see Clara Gompers come out of the door from the chambers and step up onto the stand where the judge was and whisper in his ear. Then she went back out the same door into the chambers. The judge was after him to tear up that contract. Do you know, he did it, he tore up that contract. I tell you, I had never seen anything like that."[1]

It was these sorts of small favors that attracted constituents, and before long the club had established a special service to help Spanish-speaking club members. In 1953, when young Assemblyman Dave Ross became city councilman in a special election, Felipe Torres was the Pondiac Club's successful candidate for the state assembly. For the Puerto Ricans of the Bronx, it was the first acknowledgment of their presence and political importance.

Shortly after Mayor Wagner's 1961 victory over the borough bosses, Assemblyman Torres, long established in the firmament of the Pondiac Club, had infuriated Boss Buckley by sending a warm congratulatory telegram to the mayor, as did many other organization Democrats. Pondiac leader Ed Gilhooley rebuked the assemblyman and barred his son Frank from the special Spanish room without explanation. This was an unbearable insult. The neighborhood was now almost three-fourths Puerto Rican, but the Irish were still running the club. Though the rules said club members had to live in the district, most of the Irish didn't even make a pretense of doing so.

The older Torres resigned to accept a family court judgeship, and promoted Frank, a reserved, young lawyer who had organized his own reform club, for the assembly seat. The Torres family began to round up a campaign staff, tapping their widespread network of friends and relatives. Among the recruits was the husband of Frank's half sister, a young engineer and active scoutmaster named Bobby Garcia. Garcia, a personable guy with thick black hair and a ready, charmingly crooked smile, knew nothing about politics but agreed to take around petitions. He discovered that he had a great talent for things political. "I used to love it. I qualified ten election districts by myself, I swear to God. There I was talking to people, telling them, 'I need your signatures,' then up over the rooftops where the junkies were shooting up and I would stop and say, 'Excuse me, I need your signatures,' and then back down again, like a sine wave in constant motion. I did a lot of petition gathering and I loved it."[2]

The Torres family having seceded in 1961, the Pondiac club needed a new candidate to back for the elder Torres's seat. Into this breach strode Eugene Rodriguez, a hearty, back-slapping attorney who was known in Puerto Rican circles as "the fellow who had a tryout with the New York Yankees." Rodriguez had been born in East Harlem in 1929 and had grown up there. Following his discharge from the Army after the Korean War, he set up a law practice in the southeast Bronx. Once the word flew through the Puerto Rican community that the Torreses had declared war on the Pondiac, Rodriguez presented himself at the club. A jovial, bearlike man, Rodriguez became the main problem-solver for Puerto Ricans at the club and he was duly rewarded with the organization's designation as its assembly candidate, but, for the first time in its forty-year history, the club fielded a loser. Frank Torres won by fifty-two votes and went to Albany to represent the Fourth District in the Bronx.

The Torres reformers rapidly fell to squabbling among themselves, however. While they indulged in silly quarrels and back-stabbing, the Pondiac worked in the next election to recoup its humiliating loss. On primary day in 1964, and in the general election, Rodriguez won handily.

Another Puerto Rican reformer and Wagner ally had done splendidly. In 1964, Herman Badillo, the undisputed hero of the Hispanic community in New York, had been elected borough president of Bronx County. Herman was the antithesis of every Puerto Rican stereotype. He was tall, so handsome he was likened to a Bronzino nobleman, and very articulate in English. Above all, he had come to the United States as an orphan with nothing and had excelled at the American game of achievement and success.

Born in Caguas, Puerto Rico, in 1929, Badillo was just a year old when he lost his father, an intellectual and schoolteacher, in a tuberculosis epidemic. Four years later his mother died from the same disease, leaving him orphaned. Landing in America at age eleven, he moved from family to family in New York, Chicago, California, and back finally to New York. He attended Haaren High School and all the while he worked, first as a dishwasher, a cook, and then a pinboy in a bowling alley. He graduated magna cum laude from City College in 1951, joined Ferro, Berdon and Company as a certified public accountant, studied nights at Brooklyn Law School, and graduated valedictorian of his class in 1954. He set up his own law firm and became active in East Harlem politics.

In 1960 he distinguished himself by organizing the East Harlem for Kennedy for President Committee, which delivered 80 percent of the district vote for JFK, and he backed Mayor Wagner's successful 1961 revolt against the bosses. Shortly thereafter, Wagner made him an assistant commissioner in the Department of Real Estate, with responsibility for relocating poor families from the controversial Upper West Side urban renewal project in Manhattan. Within the year Badillo was appointed the first Puerto Rican commissioner in the history of New York City, head of the new Department of Relocation.

Reporters found the new commissioner fascinating, and Herman enjoyed that thoroughly. He reveled in displaying his intelligence and touting his considerable, hard-won accomplishments. From the moment he came to public notice he was being spoken of as a future mayor, and Herman did nothing to discourage such speculation. He just gave an enigmatic smile and said things like "People aren't used to the idea of a Puerto Rican intellectual who is 6-foot-1, has a college degree and was graduated with honors."[3]

Badillo says he gave the Bronx no special consideration, but he moved to Riverdale shortly after he became commissioner and established what he referred to as "voting clubs" around the Bronx. He also was active in visiting other clubs and organizations. He began eyeing the borough president's office in the Bronx, for incumbent Joseph Periconi was viewed as a Republican-Fusionist fluke who could be knocked off by

Herman Badillo, Bronx borough president and later a congressman,
during a 1973 campaign stop

any good Democratic candidate. Although Badillo laughs it off as absurd, it is still widely believed in the Bronx that during this period he deliberately relocated many Puerto Ricans from Manhattan's West Side to the South Bronx, thereby strengthening his political base there.

When Mayor Wagner decided not to run in 1965, and his longtime aide and ally Paul Screvane, city council president, entered the primary against Abe Beame, Badillo was offered a place on the Screvane ticket as the candidate for Bronx borough president.

Herman Badillo and his campaign manager, Walter Diamond, were a Bronx version of the odd couple. Badillo always looked lithe, elegantly dressed, a bit removed from the tumult of daily politics; Diamond was a disheveled bear of a man whose shirttail was always half out and who had the disconcerting habit of clacking his false teeth while he cogitated. He was a master of political minutiae who joyfully immersed himself in politicking. He spent hours parsing the opposition petitions or figuring out where the registered voters were, what their ethnicity was, and how best to woo them. Diamond made sure every Jew in the Bronx knew that Herman was married to a Jew and had not one but *two* professional degrees. In the Italian neighborhoods Diamond outdid himself with a giveaway of Brillo pads with the little slogan: "Brillo for Badillo," leading the Italians to think Herman was an Italian Puerto Rican, or some such hybrid. In deference to the new realities Boss Buckley had designated black district leader Ivan Warner to run against Badillo.

Badillo and Diamond had extreme good fortune in the passage of the Voting Rights Act that summer, for it suddenly opened up whole new realms of Puerto Rican voters, previously exempted because of illiteracy or lack of formal schooling beyond the sixth grade. On primary night Badillo won by a mere 155 votes, 58,234 to 58,079. In November these new voters gave him a 2,086 margin over Periconi, 198,499 to 196,413. When a three-judge federal court in Washington struck down the sixth-grade provision in the new Voting Rights Act, Periconi called for a new election, claiming that 4,023 of Badillo's votes came from these invalidated voters. But in December a New York state court upheld Badillo's victory, making the issue moot.

Once he was elected Bronx borough president, Badillo barely bothered to mask his ultimate goal: mayor of New York City. In an interview about a year after he had been in office, Badillo told Arthur Greenspan of the *New York Post* that he was "personally aiming to go as far as I can politcally. And there's certainly no limit, but I must do so in a way that I can show new approaches to old ideas here in the Bronx, which has gone gradually downhill for years. I don't want to run for mayor if it will be a disaster. So I must find new approaches. I'm testing in the Bronx — testing myself and new ways of governing."[4]

Politically, things were looking very bright for Hispanics in the Bronx. By 1966, the year Badillo was sworn in as borough president, Eugene Rodriguez, in tandem with Councilman David Ross, had accomplished an amiable takeover of the Pondiac Club from the Irish old-timers. Assemblyman Rodriguez, thirty-six, the successful lawyer, was the first Puerto Rican district leader in the Buckley organization. One term in the state assembly had already given him a more polished demeanor. Now Rodriguez sat back in the big leader's office at the club that had been occupied by generations of Irishmen, and when people came for favors, he dispensed them.

Councilman Dave Ross, a short, red-haired man with a foghorn voice, wry smile, and fiery temper, was Rodriguez's mentor. Ross had recruited a coterie of bright young lawyers who provided the core of the club's constitutent service. Having grown up in a one-bedroom apartment behind his parents' Fox Street bakery, he had a powerful empathy for the struggling immigrants of the district, whether they were Jews like himself or Puerto Ricans like Rodriguez. "Since the beginning the primary problems at the club were welfare assistance, rent and landlord problems, and the kid that got arrested," he says. "The only thing that changed was the ethnicity of the district. Poor Jews have the same problems as poor blacks and Puerto Ricans."[5] There was, he conceded, one major additional complaint in later years, and that was drugs. It became increasingly common for distraught parents or local residents to come to the club looking for help in ridding their building or block of a pusher.

Eugene Rodriguez was making a swift ascent in the organization. "He had the world by the tail," remembers Judge Ross. Already Gene was running for state senate, and he intended, it was rumored, to be county leader in the not-so-distant future. In June 1966 Rodriguez won a four-way primary, and in September he was elected state senator from the Twenty-ninth District, covering the southern Bronx and a slice of northern Manhattan. He was the first Puerto Rican in New York State — probably the whole country — to reach such high legislative office. Bobby Garcia, the onetime Boy Scout leader, had also entered politics and had won an assembly seat in Mott Haven.

On the morning of December 10, 1966, however, Judge George M. Carney entered his mahogany-paneled courtroom on the seventh floor of the Bronx County Building. At the defendant's table, looking confident, sat state Senator-elect Eugene Rodriguez, charged with attempted extortion, perjury, and misconduct as a lawyer.

As the charges were elaborated upon and the evidence presented, reporters and political types from all over the City swarmed into the court. It was a juicy melodrama of the sordid and absurd, and it grew more so with each passing week. Prosecutor Burton Roberts, his face flaming as red as his hair, strode back and forth in front of the jury box, telling the mesmerized courtroom that Senator-elect Rodriguez had kept appointments with ex-con Louis Fess Taylor (who had served six prison terms for various narcotics offenses and manslaughter), in which Taylor, wired for sound, asked for help in quashing yet another narcotics charge. The first taped meeting was in Eugene's law office, the second in his office at the Pondiac Club. And there were subsequent telephone chats. Roberts accused Rodriguez of offering to fix the narcotics charge for fifty thousand or a hundred thousand dollars and accepting a down payment of two hundred dollars from Taylor at the Pondiac Club. ("Just enough to invest in a campaign suit," joked Rodriguez at the time.[6]) District leader Rodriguez indicated that he would, through contacts, help dispose of a kilo of heroin for the drug pusher so Taylor cound finance this large payment. The final twist, explained Roberts, was that Rodriguez never had any intention of helping Taylor; he was just conning him and pulling a big rip-off. The spectators sat incredulous, while the newsmen madly scribbled notes. It was the most sensational "political" trial anyone could remember in the history of the Bronx. The public and Rodriguez's many friends and supporters stood in line for hours waiting for a spot in the hundred-seat courtroom.

Rodriguez, smooth and pleasant, was to explain it all in well-modulated tones. He had simply been discussing a lawyer's fee for representing Taylor in what might well prove to be years of trials and appeals. He said that his enemies were trying to frame him for political reasons. At stake was his Senate seat and his political career, for a convicted felon cannot serve in the legislature of New York State. Undaunted, Rodriguez signed his oath of office and sent it off to Albany, where he was listed among the incoming legislators.

But when court adjourned one day in January, Rodriguez was led away in handcuffs. His bail was revoked, and he was sent to the county jail. Burton Roberts left flanked by two detectives, also a new precaution. What had happened to bring on such measures? DEATH THREATS! blared the papers the next morning. The newsmen, who had managed to overhear goodly portions of a private conference at Judge Carney's bench, reported that the furious prosecutor had told the judge that Rodriguez had put out a contract on both Fess Taylor and Roberts, "that damn red-haired bastard." Rodriguez's chauffeur, Antonio Maldonada, and a crony had been designated the hit men. Maldonada and another sidekick had already been banned from the courtroom for sitting in the back benches and making slashing motions across their throats while Taylor testified.

On January 13 the jury found Rodriguez guilty on all counts.

He faced a potential sentence of 101 years in jail. Outside the courtroom, in a corridor, a hysterical Carmelotta Rodriguez, his wife, wept and waited. Her friends steered her downstairs to evade the reporters and photographers. During sentencing later in Bronx Supreme Court, the judge said the defendant had "certainly let his people down." Rodriguez stood quietly, staring at the floor.

At the Pondiac Club, the membership felt abandoned and humiliated. Not only had the club been besmirched before the entire City with the conviction of its new leader, but they had lost Councilman Dave Ross, their power broker, for the duration of the case. Ross, who had groomed Rodriguez and pushed his candidacies in the club and district, was horrified. His protégé, the Puerto-Rican-who-could-have-been-anything, had turned out to be "the biggest blot on the history of the club." Lamented Judge Ross, "There was no reason for him to do what he did. It was disgraceful."[7]

The Pondiac Club had to rally round a new state Senate candidate. The candidate had to be someone Puerto Rican who could redress the damage inflicted by Rodriguez, someone impeccable. They could think of no one more impeccable than the former scout leader and newly elected state Assemblyman Bobby Garcia. The club backed this new candidate, and Bobby Garcia became the first Puerto Rican to be seated in the New York State Senate.

The Pondiac Club never truly recovered from the betrayal of Eugene Rodriguez. He was to have been the transition figure from the Irish to the Puerto Ricans, a symbol of the ability of the old system to adapt and absorb new citizens with new needs.

Dave Ross returned, but the club was never to flourish as it had. To Iris Rivera, a devoted Pondiac member since 1945, it was all very sad. "The Johnny-come-latelys took over. Many people moved as the neighborhood changed and the crime began. The club was not that serious anymore. It used to be when you belonged to the club, you felt proud. With the new leaders there was no discipline anymore. They thought it was a social club. Before, everything that was to be done they contacted headquarters. After, everyone did their own thing. At headquarters they knew they were getting stabbed in the back. These new people were interested only in themselves."[8]

Throughout the scandalous revelations of the trial, Bronx County Democratic Chairman Charles A. Buckley lay dying of lung cancer. After a short stay at Montefiore Hospital he had come home to Fordham, down to one hundred pounds but still lucid. And so he lay, waiting for death and receiving the pilgrimages of the party faithful. Stubborn to the last, he died at home on Sunday, January 22, 1967, without designating a successor. He was seventy-six years old.

The wake at the Fox Funeral Home on the Grand Concourse was like a scene from *The Last Hurrah,* remembers David Levy. No longer active in reform politics, Levy had enjoyed an unlikely friendship with Buckley in the leader's waning last years. At the funeral parlor Levy watched as the clubhouse men came to pay their respects. "You had this feeling as they went up to the coffin to pay tribute that they were looking closely, to convince themselves he was really dead."[9] Like Flynn, Buckley merited a front-page obituary in the *New York Times*. The photograph showed a relaxed Congressman Buckley at the White House with JFK, who was seated in his trademark rocking chair. The *Times* quoted Senator Robert Kennedy's statement that Charlie Buckley was one of the "three or four men most responsible for President Kennedy being President."[10] His death marked with finality the end of an era for the old, white-ethnic, working-class Bronx.

15

The Puerto Rican and the Priest
1962–1967

As the old-time political clubs grew weak, local blacks and Puerto Ricans grasped the most obvious new means to power — the antipoverty programs. "The real action, the only game in town, was the Great Society programs," remembers Michael Nunez, a member of the Pondiac Club. "The Great Society paid people to do all the things the clubs used to provide for free. So that's what people did. They didn't need the clubs anymore."[1]

The early plums of the antipoverty programs were doled out mainly to blacks. The directors of the community progress centers in Mott Haven, Hunt's Point, and Morrisania were all Negroes. Of course, there was a sprinkling of Puerto Ricans, but blacks cornered the big titles and the big salaries. From time to time the Puerto Ricans rallied among themselves and complained to City Hall that they were not getting their fair share. The City made placating noises, but nothing changed much. There were many differences of opinion as to who truly constituted "leadership" in these poor neighborhoods. The few Puerto Rican politicians in the Bronx — Borough President Herman Badillo, State Senator Bobby Garcia — preferred to steer clear of the programs. They did not want to get embroiled in challenging the blacks, nor did they want to be tarred by any petty scandals. This left the opportunities open to those who could most convincingly assert themselves on the local level.

Ramon Velez, a short, corpulent man with a sensual baby face and radiant smile, was very much at ease among the large "jibaro" population of Puerto Rican New York. He, like most of them, had grown up in a shack (in Hormigueros, a small village where his father had an eight-acre farm), had arrived in New York without knowing any English, and was underestimated because his style rendered him a bit ridiculous, a caricature of the macho Latin male.

Ramon was passionate in his pursuit of stature for himself and his people. The intensity of his ambition impressed people and scared them, for they wondered how an overweight Puerto Rican with terrible English was going to become someone important and influential in New York City. Although it might have seemed strange to some that Velez was making New York the arena for his ambitions, in fact it was a very clever and reasonable move. By the early 1960s New York had a bigger Puerto Rican population than San Juan. Just as important, all federal monies to Puerto Rico were channeled through the New York regional offices of the federal government. Because of the peculiarities of the commonwealth, a Puerto Rican elected from New York City could go to Washington and become the spokesman by default not only for New Yoricans (the local term for Spanish-speaking New Yorkers), but for islanders, too. Finally, the merry-go-round of Puerto Rican migration meant that a big reputation in New York would travel well to the island.

Velez had always been a leader no matter where he found himself. In his childhood village he organized all the other kids and became president of the local 4-H Club. In 1955, after serving in the U.S. Army in both Korea and Panama, Velez enrolled at the InterAmerican University in Puerto Rico. He quickly established himself as a student leader in the anti-Trujillo movement, and helped stop a surprise tuition hike. The young college student Velez was enough of a rabble-rouser to warrant a swift once-over by the FBI and the opening of a file that was to grow steadily over the years. When he completed university, Velez worked as a high school teacher for a couple of years before going to Salamanca, Spain, to study law. By this time he was married and had two young children. He simply could not manage both to study law and support his family, so he quit Salamanca and made plans to return to Puerto Rico.

On his way home in 1962 he stopped in New York to visit. He says he had no intention of staying, but discovered he could get a job as a welfare caseworker — and so it was that Ramon Velez arrived in the South Bronx. His social services beat was Fox Street in Hunt's Point. For two years Velez lumbered up and down the shabby walk-ups, surprisingly mobile, a member of the army of social workers ministering to the poor of the Bronx. It was there, in the stifling hot summers and freezing, unheated winters, that he got his "Ph.D. in human relations."

During his free time Ramon Velez plunged into fledgling New York Latino politics. He worked on the New Jersey Puerto Rican Day parade, a yearly demonstration of pride. Ever the organizer, he pulled together the National Association of Puerto Rican Affairs (NAPRA) to defend the rights of Puerto Rican migrant workers. He worked briefly at the New York office of the Commonwealth of Puerto Rico before moving on to the all-Spanish radio station WHOM, which he used shamelessly as an electronic forum to advance his own interests.

For all his brashness and blatant grabs for power, Velez could be a charming populist — he was a mesmerizing public speaker (in Spanish). His need for new work coincided with the Wagner administration's search for community activists to run the antipoverty programs. In 1964 Ramon Velez was given a job by his friend Monserrate Flores as head of the South Bronx Neighborhood Orientation Center, whose stated mission was to help residents with housing, consumer fraud, and drug addiction, and whose unstated mission soon clearly became the self-promotion of Velez into local leadership. Within two years the small paid staff of four had doubled to eight and the yearly budget was seventy-five thousand dollars. Velez claimed 350 volunteers. Early in 1966, scandal struck: one staffer was caught embezzling money, and as the Bronx grand jury drew up his indictment, the aide fled. Shortly thereafter

Velez's funding was cut and his agency collapsed — not, however, before he had been elected to the board of the Hunt's Point Community Progress Center.

Velez had an admirer working at the progress center, a young man named Mike Nunez. "When I first met Ramon he barely spoke English, but I heard him make a speech in Spanish and he had a magic. He almost hypnotized the throng. I said, 'This is a natural leader.' " At the progress center, Nunez worked and chafed under the black president, Helen Mitchell. "One day she gave me a document describing a new multi-service concept. I saw five federal agencies would be feeding into this one local agency. I showed it to Monserrate Flores."[2] Flores and Nunez realized this could be a promising base for Puerto Rican control. Community based and run, the multi-service center was to provide decent health care to the poor, a first step in cracking the ugly cycle of poverty. The original plan was to establish a center in every poor neighborhood in America. The new South Bronx agency was one of fourteen set up as a pilot project. The Hunt's Point neighborhood (specifically City health districts 41 and 42) was to be graced with this mutli-service center, and the Hunt's Point Community Corporation would oversee its establishment. The director would have to be someone bilingual, from the community, and with qualifications. And so, in 1967 Ramon Velez was resurrected, to resume his campaign for power and respect in New York City.

Velez's soon-to-be legendary organizing talents were unleashed with great success at "Multi-Service," (as it became known). On October 5, 1967, he called together a conference of a thousand people. With these recruits, helped by the ubiquitous consultants of the antipoverty programs, he set up thirty-two workshops to establish agendas of need. Within a year Velez had opened a family day-care center, a parent-child center, a health center, manpower training, and a housing office. He and his consultants said the right words and phrases, tapped the right connections, and the money came rolling in directly from the federal coffers in Washington, circumventing City Hall altogether.

From his initial fifty-five-thousand-dollar base, smaller even than the deceased South Bronx Neighborhood Orientation Center, Velez expanded with remarkable speed. Within three years he had constructed the largest antipoverty empire in the City. He controlled one thousand jobs and $12 million in poverty funds. Jobs, patronage, and favors for the giving — these were the traditional means of power. Velez was determined to see Puerto Ricans (especially him) get their rightful share, as had immigrants before them. The blacks "had" Harlem and Brooklyn, and the Puerto Ricans would "have" the South Bronx.

The South Bronx that Ramon Velez desired to make his power base fifteen years ago bore no resemblance to the bombed-out South Bronx we know today, desolate and deserted for blocks on end. If anything, it was overpopulated. "The South Bronx" in 1967 was a smallish area bounded by 161st Street on the north and Third Avenue and Boston Road on the West. (For unknown reasons, the name South Bronx was already being applied to encompass whatever formerly respectable Bronx neighborhoods became minority slums. When the slums spread, the name went along with them.)

When writer Peter Beagle walked through the South Bronx in 1964, he observed that "the streets of the South Bronx have a limping, lopsided look to them these days, because there is a great deal of demolition and construction going on. To be scrupulously fair to the city housing authorities, they are tearing down what they believe to be slums. The huge, red buildings loom most righteously over the crumbling tenements across the street; they seem, indeed, to have come stomping out of heaven, crushing the doomed houses, the greedy landlords, the rats, the cockroaches, hunger, injustice, insult, and possibly the mad Dr. Sivana into official powder. This may well be, of course, but I doubt it. A ghetto is a ghetto, and you know when you're in it."[3]

Ramon Velez was not the only aspirant for power and prestige in the South Bronx. Father Louis Gigante, a priest with the power inherent in the pulpit, had arrived at Saint Athanasius Church in Hunt's Point in 1962 at the same time that Velez embarked on his two-year stint as a welfare worker on nearby Fox Street. Father Gigante was a very handsome young man, with thick, wavy black hair going prematurely grey, an athletic body, and striking eyes emphasized by dark eyebrows and heavy-framed glasses. He was a charismatic priest who came to the parish with a reputation as street-smart but compassionate.

The youngest son in a close Italian family from Greenwich Village, Louis was the first to attend college, Georgetown University. There he was a star basketball player and captain of the team. Following his ordination Gigante had been selected by the Catholic church to study in Puerto Rico. Upon his return, fluent in Spanish, he was assigned to the lower Manhattan quarter known as Two Bridges. At the Saint James parish Gigante threw himself into working with teenagers. He was soon making the newspapers for his apparently miraculous ability to face down and disperse two hundred youthful rumblers wielding clubs and broken bottles, and then laugh it all off afterward. The kids admired his easy mastery of the playing courts and his fearlessness when it came to heading off trouble in the streets. Just before he was transferred to the Bronx, the *World-Telegram* ran an admiring profile of this fine young priest. The only hitch was the headline: "Priest's Good Works Atone for Brother Who Went Wrong."

In fact, three of Father Gigante's brothers were said by police to be connected to organized crime. As Father Gigante gained fame in his own right as a neighborhood organizer and power broker, he became frustrated and infuriated by the press's fascination with his brothers. He interpreted stories about him that mentioned them as deliberate smears on all Italians and on his family in particular. "My brothers are street people, ordinary people involved in gambling," he would say. He conceded their work was illegal, but "as innocuous to me as smoking this cigar."[4]

In the South Bronx, where toughness was a paramount virtue, the universal perception that Father Gigante was a tough, charismatic guy who had come out of the mean streets of Little Italy was very much to his advantage. In fact, he cultivated this reputation as a "street" priest. In a neighborhood like Hunt's Point, even a priest had to have moxie. If he was going to promote his vision of a people's church and help the poor he would need that respect, for without it he would not accomplish much.

In later years, however, Father Gigante believed he could never fully pursue his political ambitions, which were considerable, because any such effort would bring the press down upon his family like so many harpies. To the dedicated priest, it seemed monumentally unfair. His accomplishments, his talents, were totally separate from whatever his brothers did, and yet they were inevitably brought up.

As on the Lower East Side the young assistant pastor Father Gigante focused first on the local teenagers. He got his South Bronx parish involved in the church's Summer in the City program, offering kids an alternative to hanging around and getting into trouble. There were sports and social events for boys and girls, presented with that special brio of Father G. "G brought a great deal of love to that area, no doubt about it," remembers one young man. Moving to take advantage of the fledgling antipoverty programs, Gigante set up the Simpson Street Development Association. Like all the other storefront operations popping up in the slums, this served up a potpourri of social services.

The dynamic Father G and the ambitious Ramon Velez were by no means the only ones jockeying for position while the antipoverty apparatus was being installed in the South Bronx. Numerous blacks wrangled for precedence and recognition as the spokesmen for their community. The new young black militants constantly challenged and humiliated the established black leadership, attacking them at public forums and sneering at their old-fashioned notions and methods. This internal split greatly weakened the blacks, and the cost of the infighting was felt immediately.

The Hunt's Point Multi-Service Center was one of the biggest projects to come to the South Bronx. Its potential as a source of jobs and programs seemed limitless, for five federal agencies were involved. When Velez convened his mammoth convention in October 1967 to apply for monies and programs, many blacks were among the committee members. One was Reverend Kenneth Folkes, a Jamaican minister who had lived in the Bronx since 1945 and was deeply immersed in community affairs. Once the preliminary work was done and the actual appointments to the multi-services jobs were being made, Velez informed Reverend Folkes that he was ineligible to be on the board; he did not live in either of the "target" areas — health districts 41 and 42. "I felt I had been slapped in the face," remembers Reverend Folkes, his voice cadenced with the singsong lilt of Jamaica. "I called our congressman, Jack Gilbert. He said, 'Kenneth, when you can tell me who is the black leader I can deal with, I will do so. In the Puerto Rican community, I know I can deal with Ramon Velez.' Those were his words. It gave me food for thought and told me more than he realized. He was saying you black folks get together."[5]

Velez's successful capture of the multi-services program for the Puerto Ricans was just the opening, brilliant skirmish in a brutal war to wrest everything in the South Bronx from the blacks and all other rivals. From his burgeoning base at the Multi-Service Center, Ramon directed and personally led a ruthless, single-minded campaign to obliterate any other leader who would not defer to his authority. From Velez's perspective the war on poverty could not have been more aptly named, for he says he drew on his military service to devise his strategies and tactics. "How to assault a problem?" he asks. "I apply my Army experience."[6] Velez assembled loyal guerrilla squads (some called them goons) that amassed weapons, while planting spies in "enemy" camps and arranging secret hideouts for meetings.

Other local leaders might have been content to secure one or two small antipoverty projects in a shabby storefront with its de rigueur posters and limp houseplants, but not Ramon. He drove himself hard, working from seven in the morning to midnight seven days a week, pursuing new programs, consolidating those in place, hiring people, always expanding his network and plotting new conquests. He was often surrounded

Ramon Velez, head of the Hunt's Point Multi-Service Corporation, leaves the polls in 1974 after voting

by burly sidekicks whose clothes showed telltale bulges. Ramon did nothing to dispel the aura of intimidation by his frequent and seemingly casual threats of physical violence to those who impeded his progress. Rivals who couldn't be intimidated would be discredited through whisper campaigns. No one knew quite how to take all this. The South Bronx, like all ghettos, was filled with hustlers, and at first people assumed Ramon was just another hustler, out for a few antipoverty programs that could put him on the map and take care of his friends and followers. His ambitions, however, were far grander than a storefront and a job-training contract.

He wanted to run the whole South Bronx, and he intended to share that power with no one. His dream was to be the first Puerto Rican representative to the U.S. Congress. Just as Adam Clayton Powell dominated Harlem and all black politics, so Ramon Velez would rule the South Bronx and preside over the up-and-coming political force in American politics, the Hispanics. Then, in a blaze of glory, he would return to Puerto Rico and run for governor. His vehicle was to be the antipoverty programs.

The Irish of Tammany had once seized control of the electoral apparatus and then used the jobs, patronage, and myriad favors of City government to maintain power. Similarly, Velez planned to create a parallel political apparatus based on jobs and favors of the antipoverty programs. If the old-fashioned politicians secured loyalty by finding a friend a job in the courts or a City contract, Velez could do the same with a spot at Multi-Services. Of course, people who approached Velez for a job could expect to be asked whether they thought they might have time to work in politics. Those who said no found that there were no jobs for them. Velez was taking a political shortcut with the help of the federal government.

While pursuing the Hunt's Point Multi-Service Center in the fall of 1967, Velez also set out to gain control of the Hunt's Point Community Progress Center, now about to be transformed into "a community corporation" as a result of Mayor Lindsay's reorganization. The community corporations, which actually ran the antipoverty efforts — job training, drug detoxification, and so forth — were also a desirable prize. The reorganization gave them semiautonomous status, the power to handle their own funds, sign contracts, and prepare the payroll; a typical yearly budget was four hundred thousand dollars. Velez's takeover plan was very simple and based on elementary politics: get the Puerto Ricans registered, and, when the election for the board of the community corporation comes around, make sure the Latinos turn out at at the polls.

The day after the 1967 election the blacks went into shock. The Puerto Ricans had won twenty-one of the twenty-four seats in Hunt's Point; the blacks, one, and the Anglos, two. It was a humiliating tromping. Despite their legitimate defeat, the blacks were not about to cede power. They appealed downtown to the black-dominated Council Against Poverty. In January the council ordered the community corporation to appoint thirteen blacks "to bring about ethnic balance." Using tried and true civil rights tactics, 150 Puerto Ricans marched in an angry mass on City Hall, hoisting high a flower-decked coffin with the sign "Poverty Council Buries Puerto Rican Civil Rights." Borough President Herman Badillo, who usually stayed far away from antipoverty matters, was on hand, as were former Assemblyman Salvador Almeida, and, naturally, Ramon Velez. City Council Majority Leader Dave Ross of the South Bronx (and the Pondiac Club) persuaded Mayor Lindsay to see the malcontents. When the Latinos emerged they carried his carefully worded criticism of the council's order. It was a signal victory for the Puerto Ricans.

16

Mau-mauing the City
1967

THE backdrop of the Puerto Rican struggle to emancipate themselves from black domination was always the U.S. government's Model Cities program. (Originally called the Demonstration Cities and Metropolitan Development Act when passed by Congress in 1966, it was renamed Model Cities following the 1967 riots in Watts, Newark, and Detroit, to discourage any notion that demonstrations or confrontation politics would yield bigger bucks to the applicants.) Funded by the Office of Economic Opportunity, Model Cities' stated purpose was "to help cities plan, administer, and carry out coordinated physical and social programs to improve the environment and general welfare of people living in slum and blighted areas."[1] It was straightforwardly billed as a five-year experiment, in which Congress hoped the residents of these slums "could offer penetrating insights" into how this could be done.

While the simple name — Model Cities — made it sound like a sweeping program to create new, shiny cities, in fact it created yet another layer of bureaucracy to dream up a whole range of uplifting programs, and, as the bureaucrats liked to say, "implement" them. But this bureaucracy would have to be native to the neighborhood. Model Cities was to address not only the physical rebuilding — as had the now-discredited urban renewal — but also social needs. What good was a new apartment if the husband had no job?

The truth was that no one knew quite what to do about the cities. Their social ills had been accumulating ever since the postwar migrations. Desperate to appear as if it were doing something, Congress enacted the Model Cities program and hoped that it would help.

At first it was assumed New York would get one Model Cities program, and naturally it would go to the City's most celebrated slum, Harlem. But the administrators at New York's Housing and Development Authority Agency decided to be ambitious and push for Harlem and Brooklyn. Borough President Herman Badillo, who sat on the Board of Estimate, demanded a Bronx program, too.

The boundaries for the three "target" neighborhoods were set by feeding information into a City computer and using it to carve out the three worst sections. So many parts of the City were in such sorry straits that Eugenia Flatow, the executive director, remembers it as being "a cruel choice." The feds, however, were offering only $65 million for nine hundred thousand people, and among the wide swaths of slums the City had to lop off block after block until it got down to the allotted nine-hundred-thousand figure.

Model Cities made its debut in 1967 and 1968 at a strange and chaotic time in the City's history. New York was on the cutting edge of the anger and anarchy fermenting throughout the country. College students were staging a rebellion against the Vietnam War. Blacks and an array of other emerging minorities were demanding more power. These groups had little patience for accommodation or compromise. Only the most flamboyant acts seemed to elicit any response or satisfy the need to protest. What Tom Wolfe labeled "mau-mauing" was much in vogue. The essence of this technique was to "scare the shit" out of your opponents — whether another dude or emissaries from City Hall — so they would recognize you as a spokesman and a genuine leader and grant all your "nonnegotiable" demands. And so everyone, it seemed, took to sit-ins, marches, and near-riots.

The college-bred militancy, fashionable in the middle class, percolated downward very quickly, and the once-quiescent poor were quick to join in. Certainly one of the most extraordinary of these campaigns to unfold in New York was the "welfare rights movement," which mixed radicalized white liberals with the poorest Americans — deserted single mothers, whether black or Hispanic. As unskilled work evaporated and families crumbled, these women had been marooned in the slums with their flocks of children born to successive, absent fathers. These were the new poor: women and children supported exclusively by checks from the program called Aid to Dependent Children.

When it had been incorporated into the Social Security Act of 1935, ADC was offered as a stopgap arrangement for those unfortunate families whose male breadwinner was unable to work or had died. Private charities and settlement houses, which had hitherto helped such families, had been overwhelmed by the Depression. ADC had certainly not been envisioned as the mainstay for families from generation to generation. Yet by the early 1960s, teenage girls who had been daughters in ADC families were now having their own out-of-wedlock babies and embarking on a second generation of ADC life. Black illegitimacy in this period rose from 17 percent of all black births to 24 percent, reaching as high as 30 percent in the cities. (The rate was to double once again in the succeeding decade to 70 percent, fulfilling the direst visions of Daniel Patrick Moynihan's 1965 report on the black family.)

The whole system of welfare seemed oppressive and inhumane to many of the antipoverty workers, who had come to believe that, in a land as prosperous as America, the real solution to poverty was a guaranteed annual income. Some militants even viewed welfare as a government buy-off of the potentially restive poor. Among those who held this belief were Richard A. Cloward and Frances Fox Piven of the Columbia School of Social Work, both active in the Mobilization for Youth in the Lower East Side.

In the May 2, 1966, issue of the *Nation* they outlined "A Strategy to End Poverty" that called for "a massive drive to recruit the poor onto the welfare rolls" with the goal of so overloading and overwhelming state and local government programs that they would collapse, forcing the national Democratic administration to "advance a federal solution to poverty . . . and wipe out poverty by establishing a guaranteed annual income." It was a bold, perverse idea, but it struck an immediate chord. By that summer the National Welfare Rights Organization was born. In tandem with Legal Services lawyers, its leaders challenged welfare regulations and worked to obtain every penny allowed welfare clients. By forcing the bureaucracy to adhere to its own voluminous rules, they hoped to sink it.

Nowhere was the welfare rights movement stronger than in New York City. Half the national membership lived there. The Catholic Charities funded sessions on tactics, and many welfare caseworkers were ardent supporters. In all five boroughs antipoverty workers started by organizing the local welfare mothers, who soon produced their own leaders. The rewards sought were immediate and tangible: an end to "midnight raids" looking for visiting boyfriends; broader eligibility; quicker service; and — most significant — bigger grants and extra money for such purchases as winter coats, new furniture, and camp for the kids.

New York City welfare centers entered a state of siege. Hundreds of welfare clients invaded social service centers and installed themselves, refusing to budge from the offices and hallways until their demands for more were met. In some cases the centers were stormed and ransacked by marauding mothers. New welfare clients were recruited, enrolled, and quickly inducted into the welfare rights brigades.

Before 1967, when the campaign took off in earnest, there had been half a million people dependent upon welfare in New York City at a cost to the City of a thousand dollars per dependent. By late 1968 the number of citizens on welfare had doubled. Increased grants threatened to send the annual New York City bill over $1.5 billion, at an average per capita cost of fifteen hundred dollars. The welfare rights campaign, racking up an additional $8–10 million a month for its participants, parlayed the individualized grants into larger and larger sums.

"I was the Bronx chairman and we had five hundred members," remembers Carmen Arroya, who broke into community work in the South Bronx as a welfare rights organizer. "We found that welfare people were entitled to more than just the monthly check. We were allowed money for clothing, furniture. We studied and went all through the book and we prepared forms for every itemized thing. So you'd say, 'I need panties at fifty cents each' and so on, all down the list. The first time I submitted to the department we went, forty of us, and we all got money."[2] This initial success inspired more effort and more recruits, but the greater the success of the movement, the greater the public resentment. There was little sympathy for the unruly tactics, especially when they resulted in more and more families on the dole.

As anticipated, New York City and New York State reeled under the chaos and mounting costs. At this point, however, the scenario diverged from that envisioned by the welfare rights movement's gurus. New York State, instead of collapsing in a heap and forcing the federal government to step in with some such alternative as guaranteed income, defused the entire campaign by withdrawing its most potent offensive weapon — the negotiable individualized grants. In the spring of 1969 the New York State legislature imposed a flat-grant system that left no room for negotiating. Every family would get the same basic sum of money, with additions only for each extra child. The most militant mothers, who had been getting bigger and bigger grants for their efforts, would now get exactly the same as others who had supinely accepted the status quo. The movement and its supporters protested angrily over the next few months, taking their case to the courts and City Hall and even down Park Avenue; but when the state was upheld, the movement lost its momentum and eventually died out. (Ironically, it was Richard Nixon, a Republican president, advised by Daniel Patrick Moynihan, who most seriously contemplated the guaranteed income, but Nixon failed to persuade the Democratic Congress.)

The welfare rights movement produced greatly enlarged welfare rolls in New York City and virtually immobilized the welfare bureaucracy. Yet the New York movement was just the most vocal, visible symptom of a national phenomenon —

burgeoning numbers of families dependent on public assistance. No one has figured out exactly why the numbers swelled
so dramatically when they did. Perhaps it was just the inevitable result of the movement of the rural poor into the cities,
or, as Charles R. Morris posits in his book *The Cost of Good
Intentions,* it was perhaps the simple reflection of more liberal
attitudes toward welfare among legislators, administrators,
and the clients themselves. Ultimately, the rest of the country
caught up with New York, which today has a lower percentage
of people on welfare than half a dozen other American cities.

The New York welfare department in 1969 was also faced
with housing its many new clients, most of whom were black
and Puerto Rican, for whom the South Bronx continued to
be a principal destination. Angry complaints from Bronx citizens and politicians that the City was "dumping" welfare
people in disproportionate numbers fell on indifferent ears.
After all, borough President Badillo and his successor, Bob
Abrams, were barely on speaking terms with City Hall, and
Bronx politicians in general had little power, so the City found
it easy to ignore their protests about "welfare dumping," and
it began to offer higher-than-market rents to landlords who
took in welfare clients.

Militant tactics, like those of the welfare rights movement,
became common among antipoverty groups. When the bright
young Lindsay people (who were to coordinate Model Cities
plans between the neighborhoods and the agencies) went out
into the field to discuss Model Cities, they were subject to
intense mau-mauing, yelling, swearing, and glowering gazes
from hulking goons. When "the kids" returned to Manhattan
suggesting all the great things the City could do, the long-
entrenched agency bureaucrats smiled skeptically. The old-
line bureaucrats were happy neither with the Lindsay administration, which was constantly ridiculing them, nor with the
unruly minorities who were getting all the attention and the
tax dollars.

The whiz kids, brimming with enthusiasm at first, saw soon
enough what the situation was. "We were the good guys who

thought government should serve the people," remembers one wistfully. "We wanted to serve the community and they [the community] didn't want us. We were really hurt. We thought we were their staff, but then they wanted their own staff. We saw them as frequently hiring less competent people, and then we got into a sham where we did stuff for them and they espoused it as their own work, which is hard to live with. And as for the agencies, you knew *they* didn't like the program. No one believed in it, and no one helped us. Why should they have to do what we wanted, when they never did it before? The attitude of serving the people didn't seem there. We felt we were fighting both the community and the City agencies."

17

Who Will Be Caudillo?
1968–1969

IF the Model Cities program was intended to smooth the roiling waters of poor neighborhoods and calm down the community activists, in the South Bronx it did not get off to an auspicious start. In February 1967 a small advance guard came from the Housing and Development Agency to reconnoiter and set up another new project, known as the Mott Haven Plan Committee. Its mission was to get new housing built, as the first stage in the impending Model Cities program. The wholesale destruction of neighborhoods for urban renewal had now begun to fall into disfavor. Martin Anderson's book *The Federal Bulldozer* had skewered the entire urban renewal program as a disaster, whereas Jane Jacobs, in her classic work *The Death and Life of Great American Cities*, had championed the very kinds of neighborhoods urban renewal set out to replace. She hated the oversized, sterile towers that arose in what had been intimate, manageable neighborhoods. The new trend being touted by the HDA was "vest pocketing." This summoned visions of small, attractive apartment buildings snuggled here and there, without overwhelming either the nearby streets or the families who would live in them.

To longtime veterans of the City's housing department, this new approach was ridiculous. "Mott Haven became a vast laboratory," said one HDA official, "because they didn't test the validity of the approach before committing the entire program to vest pocketing. From my experience it didn't make a helluva lot of sense, because by the time the vest pocket construction is done, the undone portions are falling apart."

He went on: "Planners are notoriously fickle. The first housing project in the city was First Houses, rehabbed tenements that blended in with the neighborhood. That was criticized because it perpetuated 'faults' such as no open space and no setback from the street. Then public housing became towers in park-like settings with no commercial enterprises. Then the planners said that was too impersonal, it isolated the poor in obvious ways. So then we were back to what we started with. Planners are like Seventh Avenue dress designers. How can you take them seriously?"

The Mott Haven Plan Committee was directed to eschew the discredited bulldozer approach to "community renewal" and draw up a suitable housing plan to revive the South Bronx. Long before any plans were complete, however, the HDA's "community liaison" had fled, driven out by the hostility of the neighborhood power brokers, who were cranky and churlish, given to writing petulant memos detailing each slight experienced at the hands of the HDA. They noted every missed meeting, the inadequate office space, and the poor mimeographing services, and accused the City of "mere lip service" to community planning, predicting that "the city will continue to impose plans on our community without obtaining either our participation or approval."[1]

The fact of the matter was, Model Cities promised to provide an enormous cornucopia of goodies, beside which the community action programs and community corporations already looked like small change. No community corporation controlled more than four hundred thousand dollars a year in funds; Ramon Velez's Multi-Service Center at Hunt's Point never pulled in more than $12 million a year; but the Bronx Model Cities program would have a first-year budget of $21.5 million, with prospects of even greater sums later! As one observer said many years later, "People who had been fighting over crumbs now had a chance to fight for a whole bakery." And Ramon Velez, for all his tough talk, his hulking goons, and his Napoleonic manner, had failed to clear the field of his rivals. The local feuding escalated.

In the first round Ramon outmaneuvered his enemies by

engineering the appointment in March 1968, as Model Cities'
neighborhood director, of a mild-mannered former professor
and social worker named Anibal Asencio. An angular-faced
man given to wearing pert bow ties, this quiet academic knew
the rhetoric. In one statement he declared: "I am a grass roots
person, a member of a minority group. I am ready, willing,
and able to fight for the rights of our community . . . I know
what it means to wake up at midnight in order to protect my
children from rats and roaches."[2] The anti-Velez faction was
not impressed, and they were soon complaining to Model
Cities Executive Secretary Eugenia Flatow that Anibal was
just a puppet for Velez, who provided "a ventriloquist for
Mr. Asencio, putting words in his mouth, prompting him and
propping him up at meetings."[3]

There were many factions competing for the eighteen elected
seats on the all-important South Bronx Model Cities Policy
Committee (another five were to be filled by appointment),
and throughout the long, hot summer of 1968 the struggle
intensified. Nothing gave Ramon Velez more pleasure than
performing a personal favor for a desperate constituent. He
was in his element when rescuing wayward sons with bail
money at two in the morning. When he told these stories he
would proudly allow tears to gather and roll down his baby
face. It was a matter of honor and demonic ambition for
Ramon to seize the South Bronx. Years later he would still
aver that "it was our job — the Puerto Ricans — to acquire
the power and deliver to our people, not to accept missionaries
like Father Gigante as if we were people without brains."[4]

Unfortunately for Ramon, his rivals were not very accommodating. Father Gigante refused to acknowledge Ramon as
the Puerto Rican spokesman for the South Bronx, for he was
determined to retain control over what happened in his parish.
Gigante says they fell out completely after a public contre-
temps in which Ramon called Father G a "maricon" (fag)
and got punched in the face by the priest himself. Other Puerto
Rican factions were led by Salvador Almeida, a former assemblyman, and Ralph Alvarado, director of the Mott Haven
Plan Committee. Among the blacks the leaders were Al

Goodman, head of the storefront East 163rd Street Improvement Association and an old-line NAACP man; the militant Black Muslim Lateef Ali; and the moderate militant Richard Weekes.

After the October 12, 1968, election of the unwieldy twenty-three-person Model Cities Policy Committee, no one person or faction emerged supreme. The unresolved question remained, who would be caudillo of the South Bronx? In the months following the fall election, jockeying for power continued unabated. There were lots of late-night powwows, clashes, near-clashes, and ugly threats hurled back and forth. The warriors, packing "pieces" and knives, wheeled and dealed as they vied for votes and influence. Each meeting in the community corporations, and in the dozens of storefront offices dotting the exhausted streets, was dissected for its implications. Violence was always in the air. Ralph Alvarado, who always liked a nice memo or letter, wrote indignantly to a colleague that one member of the policy committee had summoned another to step outside. "Very loud voices started emanating from that room. One of the voices was telling Mr. Scott to mind his own business because otherwise it may be more trouble for him. . . . Upon resumption of our meeting Mr. Scott, visibly concerned, expressed thoughts of resigning, stating that his life has been threatened."[5] The meek Asencio seemed slightly puzzled by the major league egos clashing around him. Try as he might, he could not quiet the warriors long enough for any policy to emerge from the policy committee.

By the summer of 1969 the stalemate in the policy committee had persisted so long, and City Hall was becoming so impatient, that it was obvious some deals would have to be cut. Everyone watched everyone else warily, sensitive to any sign of shifting allegiances. The Model Cities headquarters for the Bronx was in an old supermarket at 161st Street and Third Avenue, right under the El and across from the ornate Beaux-Arts Criminal Courthouse. The office retained some of the ambience of a supermarket, bathed as it was in perpetual fluorescent light. There was a sea of battered desks occupied by people, all ostensibly doing something. Mainly they gossiped and talked about the hypothetical programs, since the high-level feuding made it impossible for anything substantive to happen. There were always plenty of meetings to go to — downtown, "out in the field," or in the main office. Time passed easily enough. And there were all the hangers-on, who spouted the appropriate rhetoric and clothing (dashikis for blacks, battle fatigues or Che Guevera berets for hip Hispanics) and hustled themselves and their ideas for saving the neighborhood.

On Wednesday, August 6, 1969, a policy committee meeting was scheduled for eight o'clock, but it seemed some members were not informed, including Salvador Almeida. With his inevitable retinue of strongmen, Almeida set off to the committee office to see why he had been left out. As Velez's main rival in the Puerto Rican community, Almeida had been very active in the Pondiac Club and had served two terms in the state assembly. Now he had established his own storefront, serving up consumer education programs with antipoverty money. Almeida was a popular man in the South Bronx, an established figure in Puerto Rican politics, and a force within the Hunt's Point Community Corporation; and all of this brought him into continual conflict with Ramon Velez.

Almeida and his contingent stalked into the Model Cities office around six o'clock, when the vast front office was empty. In one of the conference rooms Ramon Velez was meeting with George Rodriguez (his right-hand man), Ralph Alvarado, and other factionalists. It looked as though the long-awaited deal was being cut then and there over a map of the South Bronx. An Almeida sidekick, a big monster of a man named Jack Ramos, came up and slapped Ramon. Velez stood there stunned, while Alvarado ran to his parked car in the lot next door. Then Jack Ramos slugged another man and turned on Alvarado, but Alvarado grabbed a thick chain from the parking lot gate and slammed it into Jack Ramos's face. The Velez group fled to their cars and made a quick escape. As they roared off, an infuriated Velez shrieked, "We'll be back you bastards, we'll break your fucking ass."[6]

The eight o'clock policy committee meeting was not canceled or postponed. Those committee members in the Velez and Almeida groups were boiling with rage, but others who attended that night's meeting sensed nothing untoward. They recall it as an average meeting with the usual committee reports. Father Gigante remembers arriving, only to hear that the meeting was canceled. Others remember its ending in yelling and shouting when George Rodriguez, his usual spiffy self with a pomaded do, sharkskin suit, and diamond pinkie rings, abruptly declared it adjourned.

The Almeida men walked disgustedly out into an evening gentle with light rain to find Velez's men and a squadron of cars gathered along a curb under the El. Edwin Rivera, an Almeida loyalist, stepped onto the sidewalk. He was carrying a cane and ready for trouble. In moments a melee erupted. Everyone was yelling, and Father Gigante and Georgie Rodriguez rushed out and screamed at the men to stop fighting. In the shifting shadows of the El, Rivera was turning grey as one assailant choked him hard. Then someone slammed a board over the attacker's head and he sank to the pavement. Rivera's friend kept beating the attacker's unconscious hulk. Rivera staggered off.

A car engine was revving up and suddenly roared into action. A brown Pontiac Firebird smashed straight into Rivera. He crumpled, and the car continued right over him, snagging his body and dragging it for a block before it came loose. Rivera's face was pulp, his clothes shredded and filthy, and his body deeply lacerated. Shrieking and crying rent the light drizzle, and people yelled for someone to chase the car. Police cars screeched up the avenue, and people tumbled out of the offices and nearby apartment houses. Father Gigante pushed through the gathering crowd and fell to his knees on the wet street beside the writhing Rivera. He began softly chanting the last rites.

Hours after Rivera's death the rumors began to circulate: Ramon was responsible. Everyone knew Almeida was standing in Ramon's way. Whatever the truth of the matter, Almeida himself soon disappeared from the Bronx, allegedly with forty-five thousand dollars in antipoverty money in a suitcase. Most of his followers drifted away, too. No one will ever know who killed Edwin Rivera, or whether it was a premeditated murder or a crime committed in the heat and fury of battle. Various people were subsequently arrested, but the investigation came to nothing. The proximate beneficiary was certainly Ramon Velez. "After that incident," remembers one of the main participants, "people were very intimidated." The constant threats hurled by Ramon were no longer taken lightly. People feared that he was capable of anything.

Rivera's brutal murder was followed by a period of simmering truce, necessitated in part by the nearing deadline for submitting the South Bronx Model Cities program proposals to New York City. Everyone still wanted to dominate the proposals, but there was so much money coming — $21.5 million — that it was decided to try and share. A consulting firm, Community Affairs Associates, was called in to pull it together. One of the consultants, William Salinger, a former regional manager in the antipoverty programs, knew Velez well. (The antipoverty programs were awash with consultants, who advised and validated. Their fees were exceedingly handsome.) Salinger worked with the warriors, setting up committees, and meeting night and day for months to get the documents pulled together, and they emerged with a plan to carve up the Model Cities neighborhood into six fiefdoms with six multi-service centers, to each of which the federal goodies could flow directly.

New York City's Model Cities Executive Secretary Eugenia Flatow took one look and said, "Forget it." There was going to be no more circumventing of City Hall with direct funding or further Balkanization with more multi-service centers. With the federal deadline looming, she hammered out another proposal, listing some twenty acceptable programs, each of which would wash with the feds and would also be overseen by established City agencies. When the South Bronx warriors realized what had been done, they rebelled and, gathering their forces, stormed downtown to besiege Mrs. Flatow and vigorously voice their grievances. There was some heavy mau-mauing (including the usual threats about blood in the streets this summer), but City Hall's patience was exhausted. No concessions were made. Defeated and furious, the poverticians trooped back to the South Bronx to recoup and reconsider.

In the midst of this power struggle between downtown bureaucracy and the community people, the long-standing feud between Puerto Ricans and blacks erupted anew over the Hispanics' successful takeover of the South Bronx Community Corporation. Once again the Puerto Ricans hotly insisted they had won fair and square and denounced the blacks as crybabies for appealing to the black-controlled Council Against Poverty, which sanctimoniously put the disputed corporation in trusteeship.

Mayor Lindsay returned at the end of November 1969 from his postreelection vacation to be confronted by this ugly mess. He quickly appointed a panel to resolve all the bitter complaints. Throughout, Ramon portrayed himself as the innocent, long-suffering man of the people with no aspirations beyond helping them. "I plan to quit in two years," declared Velez in one interview, "and return to Puerto Rico to persuade college graduates and professionals to come to New York to help the Puerto Rican masses."[7]

Not to be outdone, Father Gigante now thrust himself into the media limelight. On December 15 the young parish priest gathered three hundred neighborhood residents onto East 163rd Street between Fox and Tiffany in Hunt's Point and directed them to haul boards and old furniture out of the nearby abandoned buildings. Everything combustible was crammed into ten trash barrels, planted in the middle of the street, and set ablaze. As the soaring flames devoured the refuse, Father Gigante and his bundled-up parishioners marched up and down the block. Their faces reflecting the yellow of the flames, they chanted their grievances: They were without heat, without hot water. They were sick unto death of rats. They were tired of all the junkies. They wanted the City to make emergency repairs and provide fuel, they wanted the federal government to buy the worst buildings and let Model Cities fix them. They wanted action and they wanted it now.

City Hall was thoroughly fed up. Rivera's killing had been a horrible embarrassment. Then there had been the Bronx's blatant refusal to submit a proper program and the subsequent besieging of Mrs. Flatow. The public face-off between the Puerto Ricans and blacks for power and the constant angling for media attention were the coups de grace. A crackdown, long in preparation, was readied. With Mayor Lindsay safely reelected, City Hall moved to reestablish its authority and impose a veneer, if nothing else, of civility in the South Bronx.

Bronx Model Cities Director Anibal Asencio, the ineffectual professor, was ousted. The Model Cities Policy Committee was ordered to propose five candidates for director and was informed that Mayor Lindsay, and not they, would make the final selection. City Hall was anxious, among other things, to present a better face to President Richard M. Nixon's new Republican administration in Washington, D.C. The South Bronx was put on notice to shape up.

Undaunted, the poverty warriors went their merry way. On January 27, 1970, the Hunt's Points Community Corporation at 1463 Southern Boulevard was firebombed and badly damaged, dispossessing twenty-six families who had taken shelter there while Bob Munoz, Ramon's burly director, sought to restore heat and hot water to their apartments in nearby buildings. That blaze erupted just hours after the torching of 1444 Charlotte Street, the office of a rival, feuding subagency, the Neighborhood Counseling Center. Two men were seen on the roof of the Charlotte Street building at 1:38 A.M. pouring out gallon cans of some kind of liquid. The whole building went up so fast and in such a ball of flame that only a gutted shell was left.

Father Gigante, meanwhile, relentlessly pursued his own campaign to publicize the atrocious conditions in his parish. "Our middle-class Hispanics were moving out. Drugs really took a toll. Crime really took a toll. Abandonment of people began. Then there was the heat and hot water problem. People froze terribly."[8] Several weeks after his dramatic street bonfire-demonstration, which had resulted in some meetings with public officials, but nothing else, Gigante sallied to the New York City Council chambers in lower Manhattan. Observing the proceedings from the ornate visitors' balcony, the handsome priest suddenly jumped up and began yelling at the astonished councilmen and women below. Shaking his fist for emphasis, he berated them for ignoring the disastrous conditions in Hunt's Point. Quickly, two guards appeared behind him and started edging him roughly out to the nearest stairwell. Father Gigante told reporters he wanted his neighborhood declared "a disaster area." "We had addicts up the ass," he remembers. "They were like roaches. And pushers everyplace."[9]

A few days later Father Gigante was back down at the council chambers, this time with an invitation to speak to the council leaders. Gigante's public outbursts were the follow-up to a barrage of petitions from local schoolteachers asking the City to do something about the slums that housed their pupils. Heat and hot water had become rarities, and children were constantly ill. When the City failed to respond with so much as a letter, Gigante went the direct action route. The council agreed to come and see for themselves how wretched conditions were. On March 2 they picked their way through the fetid gutters and past the vandalized buildings reeking of urine to talk to families living in freezing flats. The very walls were "weeping" from the cold. The apartments were permeated by the sickly sweet aroma of gas, for ovens were on and open to keep at least one room warm in the frigid weather. The local legions of junkies, taken aback by the unusual sight of men in three-piece suits, made themselves scarce.

Not to be outdone by his rival, Ramon Velez held a public hearing on the drug epidemic at the fire-ravaged Hunt's Point Community Corporation. His followers cheering him on, the corpulent leader called for a war on dope in the South Bronx. Ramon complained that "nobody paid attention when it was just poor people on drugs,"[10] a true enough statement. Narcotics was big business, and the ghetto market (as this hearing indicated) was saturated. It was inevitable that those who traded in illicit drugs would expand into the lucrative middle-class market. The rebellious, disaffected mood of the country made it ready for such illegal, defiant behavior. One ex-junkie stood up and begged the police to put the pushers behind bars.

A little more than a week later, on March 16, 1970, Ramon Velez declared himself a candidate for the U.S. Congress in the Twenty-first District, a new seat created by reapportionment. Ramon, now thirty-six, could certainly congratulate himself on having come a very long way in a very short while. He and his credentials for this honorable office were treated respectfully by no less an establishment organ than the *New York Times*.

One of Lindsay's aides, a young Yale Law School graduate named Victor Marrero, aspired to the job of neighborhood director in the South Bronx Model Cities program. Marrero's family was among the thousands of Puerto Ricans who had been uprooted from East Harlem and relocated to the South Bronx. A graduate of the elite Bronx High School of Science and the Bronx campus of New York University, Marrero was from a family so poor that they had moved out of Saint Mary's public housing because the rent was too steep. A slender man with a controlled, ascetic air, Marrero had spent two years in England after Yale Law School as a Fulbright scholar studying immigration problems before coming to City Hall.

For a borough boy there was something tremendously alluring about having millions in Model Cities money to resurrect his old turf. So Marrero journeyed up to the ever-raucous Bronx Model Cities office, a prematurely balding, scholarly-looking young man with bottle-thick spectacles threading his way through the dudes and bloods and chiquitas at the old supermarket-office space. He submitted himself to the committee, knowing full well that they knew he was the mayor's man, an emissary and (perhaps) enemy from downtown sent up to bring pacification to the feuding South Bronx. They played the charade, put Marrero on the list, and acted delighted when he was named the new neighborhood director of the City's largest antipoverty program. Ramon Velez called up the director-to-be, all of twenty-eight years old, and assured him in his most charming way that Victor had been his top choice and that he had pushed hard to get him selected.

As neighborhood director, Marrero would oversee a Model Cities kingdom of fifteen hundred acres, or six percent of Bronx County. More than three hundred thousand people lived there, more than in any New York State city except Buffalo. Aside from the vest pocket housing moving forward under the Mott Haven plan, virtually nothing had been accomplished by South Bronx Model Cities in its year and a half of vaunted existence.

Marrero's first order of business when he arrived in late March 1970 was to get the office out of the dumpy fluorescent supermarket — it smacked too much of storefronts and unprofessionalism — and he finally convinced all the leaders to move into conventional, respectable offices down at the 149th Street Hub.

On the conventional political front, the congressional race for the new Twenty-first District was heating up. On April 9, 1970, former borough President Herman Badillo, who had given up that job for an unsuccessful run in the Democratic primary for mayor, announced his candidacy for the House of Representatives. In his mayoral effort Badillo had placed a respectable third: he remained the best known and most respected Puerto Rican politician in New York City. Whether he or Velez won, it would be a historic moment — the election of the first Puerto Rican congressman in the nation. Unfortunately, the contest pitted the two leaders against one another and created a schism where none had existed.

Within a week Father Louis Gigante, the fighting priest of Saint Athanasius, had also joined the race. On a rotten, rainy day he staked himself out in front of a Hunt's Point lot strewn with cannibalized cars and old garbage and declared his own candidacy, thereby becoming the first priest in New York State to run for Congress. He denounced the City's apparent abandonment of the South Bronx, where drug addicts were "running rampant" and crime, slums, and garbage were the norm. Clearly dissatisfied with the council's response to this continuing disaster, Father G was taking matters into his own hands.

The fourth candidate was a Queens lawyer named Peter Vallone, and rounding out the slate were two other minor candidates. The Democratic primary promised to be a furious free-for-all, the kind of political anarchy that would have had Boss Flynn spinning in his grave. It was just further illustration of the once-mighty Bronx machine's sorry state. In the slum districts the Democratic machine was just about dead. The very boundary lines drawn for the new Twenty-first District proclaimed the county's diminishing political might. The redrawn Bronx districts now often incorporated chunks of other counties, leaving the Bronx prey to interloping politicians or beholden to voters in Manhattan or Queens. As one Board of Election professional observed, "When you have no political muscle, you become the carrion to be picked clean by the vultures and hyenas."

While these preliminaries were going on, Marrero began to firm up the Model Cities programs that were to improve the South Bronx. Marrero decided the end result had to be highly visible and make a tangible difference in people's lives. For him, a scion of the slums, that meant one thing — housing. A place to live would have far greater repercussions "than four or five people sitting in a storefront doing social outreach."[11] He kept the "social action" programs limited.

Jobs were high on the agenda of New York City Model Cities Administrator Judge Joseph Williams, who took over at the City level shortly after Marrero went to work in the Bronx. The judge began figuring out how to crack open low-level government jobs for the poor minorities, though the City unions were determined to protect this valuable turf from outsiders. Model Cities sought a back door by setting up entry-level traineeships with the fire department, sanitation, police, and the Housing Authority. The judge's goal was to have these trainees gradually absorbed into the regular City de-

Father Louis Gigante, head of the South East Bronx Community
Organization, stands at a large lot in Hunt's Point that has been
cleared of abandoned buildings to allow new construction

partments, thereby circumventing the usual tests and lists. This special access was fought tooth and nail in the courts by the labor unions, and they ultimately prevailed.

The social action programs Marrero set up were training for health careers and clerical work, around-the-clock schools for adult education, youth tutors, English language instruction, and scholarships for college students. Kids were lured off the streets with summer outings and camping, addicts with drug-abuse centers. Released prisoners were assigned to a work release center. Stafffing these fourteen programs involved the usual balancing of blacks, Puerto Ricans, and faction protégés. And then there were the unexpected challenges like the two youth directors who dreamed up a "cultural heritage" safari to Africa and Latin America for thirty-four exceptional children, all to be immortalized in a book and movie. The tab would be picked up, of course, by Model Cities. Wincing, Marrero "promoted" the two into slots that left less to their vivid imaginations. Marrero's real concern remained housing — building new units or rehabilitating the old ones.

Marrero's first stroke of good fortune was Velez's complete annihilation at the polls in the June primary election. It was a dismal, humiliating defeat. In a field of six, Ramon had limped in fourth. Badillo won, beating Queens candidate Peter Vallone 7,732 to 7,145. Father Gigante acquitted himself quite honorably, placing third with 5,621. Although Velez strode through the streets with his retinue, bestowing handshakes, huffing and puffing up and down the walk-ups and the housing projects and exhorting his people to come out and vote for him, his vaunted organizational talents had turned out only 2,644 votes. Clearly, the Puerto Rican votes preferred Badillo.

The Hunt's Point Multi-Service Center promptly became the target of a combined federal and city audit. It was widely assumed that the victorious Badillo was responsible for the government's sudden interest. The investigation began very quietly the month after the primary election. Quite simply, the books were a shambles. Velez's major source of funding, the federal Department of Health, Education and Welfare, decided to discontinue paying salaries at the center while it sorted through the mess. "Somehow," remembers Marrero, "the decision was made to pick it up out of Model Cities funds. The implication was that Ramon had to come to me. It didn't have to be stated, but he knew ultimately that I signed his payroll."[12] As can be imagined, Ramon became far more cooperative.

In the late spring Marrero had signed on George Batista as his deputy director and legal counselor. Another Yale Law School graduate, in his late twenties, Batista had the job of negotiating with the City agencies that by law administered the Model Cities programs. The City agencies were, of course, very covetous of the huge sums slated for Model Cities in the Bronx. Batista remembers: "I was met with tremendous resistance and rejection by the City agencies. They were absolutely unyielding and unreasonable."[13] Negotiations advanced slowly, and the programs got off the ground, but there was still no vehicle for building the housing that was Marrero's major goal.

It was during this time, in the summer of 1970, that Victor Marrero first met Dennis Allee, an aide to Senator Jacob Javits. Marrero saw in Allee a potentially powerful ally. Allee explained that Senator Javits had in mind establishing a South Bronx version of the well-known Bedford Stuyvesant Restoration Corporation in Brooklyn. There, Senator Robert F. Kennedy and the rest of the Camelot clan had joined up with the local black leaders to strengthen a slum with new vigor and economic muscle. The Bed-Stuy board of directors glittered with important New York City people. Senator Javits wished to embark on a similar endeavor in the Puerto Rican South Bronx, using his considerable prestige to attract heavy hitters to the board.

Marrero was delighted. "We agreed to work together, and what I thought we would do is create this corporation and channel all the housing money into it. We mapped out a strategy to have a board of directors including neighborhood and outside people to give the entity credibility and to give potential to raise private money, to attract jobs, commerce, and do housing development."[14] Marrero planned to put $7 million into what was christened the South Bronx Community Housing Corporation, and use it for an array of housing.

There was a major hitch to all this. It was made plain to Marrero that Senator Javits, who was the centerpiece of the plan, would refuse to sit on the housing corporation's board of directors if it included Ramon Velez. Ramon was humbled momentarily by his primary defeat and hounded by the daily invasion of auditors, but as a matter of course he expected to have a major voice. He was not at all amenable to staying off the board for Senator Javits's sake.

Marrero reassured Velez that he could have Georgie Rodriguez as his man on the board and appealed to his sense of patriotism. Velez finally agreed, and by December the South Bronx Community Housing Corporation was born. George Batista was named president. A well-regarded lawyer, John Zuccotti, yet another Yale man, was brought in by Allee to provide specialized housing advice. Marrero was chairman of the board, which was gratifyingly studded with semi-important people, starting with Senator Javits and followed by John G. Heiman (senior vice-president at Warburg, Pincus and Company), builder John Tishman, banker Michael Gill, banker William Panitz, investment banker Henry Loeb, and department store owner Richard Sachs. All the local power brokers were also appointed. Marrero and Batista were now firmly in charge of their own fiefdom with a treasury of $7 million in seed money. The South Bronx Housing Corporation was to be the outstanding legacy of the faltering Model Cities program.

Well intentioned as all the programs and their patrons were, no one could have envisioned how irrelevant they would all soon become. The South Bronx was on the verge of spectacular collapse and conflagration.

18

"The Whole Place Was Caving In"
1969–1970

THE early warnings signs hadn't gone unnoticed. The 1969 New York City master plan deemed one-quarter of the Bronx's rental units either "dilapidated or deteriorating." By the fall of the same year, experts in the field of housing were sounding ominous alarms. At a November 6 hearing in City Hall, Frank S. Kristof of the state's Urban Development Corporation testified that the total stock of housing in New York City was diminishing for the first time in a century. Landlords abandoned their properties. Almost one hundred thousand apartments were already "boarded up, vandalized, burnt-out or otherwise unfit for occupancy." Kristof largely blamed rent control, stating that owners who couldn't make a reasonable profit would continue to bail out, but subsequent experience would reveal a more complicated explanation.

Who, with the exception of a few perspicacious scholars, could have imagined that entire neighborhoods, one after another, would soon come to resemble wartime ruins? There was simply no precedent. That the City's landlords would abandon their properties, en masse, to be burned and gutted was nothing less than unthinkable.

Robert Esnard, later a deputy mayor, remembers vividly his first glimpse of abandonment in 1966 when he was still a graduate student. On a housing tour of Bedford-Stuyvesant in Brooklyn, his guide pointed to a block with empty, vandalized buildings. This, he announced, was "disinvestment." "We were all amazed," recalls Esnard, a native Bronxite. "We had never seen such a thing. No one had ever heard of a property in New York City that no one wanted."[1]

When Esnard went to work in the South Bronx two years later, he saw neighborhoods bursting with people and activity — poor people and troubled activity, but very much alive. The housing shortage was so severe that anyone moving out of an apartment could still "sell" the right to move in to a new tenant. Yet slowly but surely, quietly and steadily, even in the South Bronx the landlords, the merchants, and the residents were leaving, abandoning their buildings and businesses. Planners and officials who noticed telltale empty buildings here and there felt no special alarm, for the streets and surrounding buildings were crowded and cacophonous.

The unseen truth was that the great changes — political, social, and economic — that had convulsed New York City in the twenty years since World War II had finally seeped all the way down to the basic unit of city life, the neighborhood and the block. In the South Bronx, the old neighborhoods were on the point of death, buffeted by extreme poverty, crime, and a state of affairs that made it more profitable to abandon or destroy than to preserve and maintain.

By late 1969 and throughout 1970 officials and housing experts in the Bronx were all singing dirges. City leaders listened politely, but did nothing. The hatred for landlords in New York City was so ingrained and deep that it would be political suicide for any legislator or official to propose ways to keep landlords in the housing business, by giving them more income.

The landlords mounted a mighty lobbying campaign, issuing press releases and brochures, writing letters, taking out full-page ads in the newspapers, and testifying to anyone who would listen. They shrieked when the City's much-admired Housing Authority announced rent increases in its own buildings of almost 50 percent in May 1969 (the chairman cited a rise in operating costs of 125 percent between 1952 and 1967), just days after private landlords were kept to 10 and 15 percent increases. When rents began to rise more rapidly on the four hundred thousand apartments excluded from any rent laws (those built after 1947), the City officials extended rent stabilization laws to these, too.

The Lindsay administration had long since exhibited its antipathy to the owners of the City's aging apartment houses. Its first building commissioner was a young go-getter who burst upon the scene declaring, "This Administration just will not tolerate slumlords! That's all there is to it."[2] In a constant whirl, trailed by bemused reporters, Charles G. Moerdler charged around town inspecting buildings and inaugurating new programs. (He ended up denouncing his own in-laws as slumlords!) Moerdler's policy was to step up building inspections and compel landlords to clean up their accumulated violations. In the Bronx he unleashed three times the normal number of inspectors, with instructions to write up every possible violation, for he had aspirations to run for district attorney in the county. Bronx landlords were outraged at this special attention, but to no avail. Years later he would say, "Oh, they thought I was a son-of-a-bitch. But I was offering the carrot-and-the-stick approach, and that was something new and they didn't like it."[3]

Moerdler descended upon the legislature and got a bill passed in 1966 that allowed tenants of buildings with so much as a single violation to pay only one dollar-a-month rent until such time as the landlord cleared the violations. A building violation could be anything from a scuffed wall to a broken boiler: if wanted, violations can always be found. Poor people suddenly discovered they did not have to pay the rent. The antipoverty workers, who had become professional community organizers, responded to the commissioner's crusade with enthusiasm. Newly savvy tenants learned to ferret out violations, and rent rolls soon dropped dramatically. It made life far more difficult for landlords: rather than raise rents, they now had to go to court to reinstate previous rent levels.

One Bronx community activist, whose first experience was in organizing tenants at this time, sees it all now as self-defeating. "The cost of everything was going up, and the landlord couldn't survive. The City's housing policy was a process in futility. They came up with a couple of Mickey Mouse programs while the whole place was caving in." Landlords who had been limping along were crippled by newly militant tenants adhering to their right to pay a dollar a month in rent. This new law was enforced only briefly, but no one seems to know whether the law remains on the books today. That includes its originator, Moerdler.

By the spring of 1969 unpaid, delinquent property taxes hit an all-time high of $140 million. In a city where 85 percent of the citizens lived in rental housing, New York leaders did nothing. What would happen if private landlords should desert the housing market? If tenants were unable or unwilling to pay the true cost of their housing, then who should foot the bill? Since World War II the City had, by virtue of rent controls, said, "Let the private landlord." And the landlords had done so, underwriting tenants with $20 billion over the years. But they were clearly about to stop. The City chose to ignore this threat. It continued to play by the old rules, even though the landlords began to drop out in droves, for there was no law that could make a landlord keep an unprofitable building. And so, while the City played coy, the old neighborhoods were falling into their death throes, their decay the visible manifestation of a wrecked system.

Even to be included in a Model Cities neighborhood offered no special salvation, as was sadly demonstrated in the case of an ordinary, residential thoroughfare. A side street in the East Bronx, Charlotte Street ran one brief block south from verdant Crotona Park across bustling Boston Road, down a second long block to the intersection of Seabury Place and 170th Street, before it flowed, a third and final block, into the exuberant Jennings Street Market. To the east, beyond Seabury and Minford Place, roared Southern Boulevard, a wide avenue overshadowed by the heavy structure of the elevated trains and their constant din. People who lived in the walk-ups on Charlotte Street could catch the El by walking along Boston Road several blocks to the 174th Street station. Or they could go west to Wilkins Avenue, with its shops and stores, and walk along Southern Boulevard to the Freeman Street station, one stop closer to Manhattan.

This triangular configuration of residential and shopping streets (bounded on the east by Seabury Place, on the west by broad Wilkins Avenue, and sliced off at an angle at the top by northbound Boston Road) distinguished itself in a small way by forming the northernmost piece of the South Bronx Model Cities area. Otherwise, Charlotte Street was just another side street.

Virtually no official attention was directed to this remote outpost of Model Cities until the local school board, Twelfth District, began searching in 1968 for sites for new schools. Public School 61, a venerable red-brick elementary school on the corner of Charlotte Street facing Crotona Park, was overflowing with kids, the offspring of the Puerto Ricans and blacks who had been moving in steadily since after the war. Most of PS 61's small blacktop playground had filled up with temporary Quonset hut–classrooms. An additional school was needed desperately.

In the fall of 1968 district Superintendent Edythe J. Gaines suggested that the new edifice, PS 202, be built on the block bounded by Charlotte Street, Boston Road, Wilkins Avenue, and 170th Street. When an official from the Board of Education visited the proposed site in March 1970 he found it satisfactory and noted: "The block presently has seven or eight burned-out buildings and two vacant lots. This entire area has high density housing that is in fair condition."[4] The downtown school bureaucracy, where New York City public schools are planned, approved, and built at a glacial pace, worried that the crowded site could entail too much relocation — a dreaded prospect for any public agency. Plans were "laid over for further study."

While the Board of Education dithered, the Model Cities program entered the picture, proposing that the Model Cities site be expanded to include the east side of Charlotte Street, so that three hundred units of housing could be built along with the new school. This was agreed to, as well as a plan to close off Charlotte Street to traffic, thereby enlarging the site still further. Next, a new junior high, IS 207, was proposed in lieu of the housing. In early October 1970 emissaries from the Board of Education sallied forth once again to inspect the Charlotte Street site. They were surprised to find that "the overall condition of the area has deteriorated rather considerably since our visit of last June 1970. Many multiple dwellings now stand abandoned that were previously still occupied."[5]

19

Interlude: Sweet Days
on Charlotte Street
1925–1951

To outside observers it was a puzzling and disturbing phenomenon. Despite a dire housing shortage, what had been perfectly decent apartment buildings were going to rack and ruin. True, it became fashionable to write off these dying neighborhoods as longtime dumps and the apartment houses as almost-slums. The story of Charlotte Street, however — an average block in an old Bronx working-class neighborhood — belies that simple, conscience-salving dismissal. For Charlotte Street had been built with pride and had sheltered hard-working families, the quintessence of the American Dream. There was nothing in the neighborhood's early, placid history to prefigure its grim demise.

The names of the streets reflected the earliest days of the rural Bronx and the county's settlement by well-to-do families, such as Quaker William Fox. Charlotte Street traversed his former estate and honored his wife, Charlotte Leggett, who married him in 1808. Jennings Street took its name from a venerable Bronx family whose sons had served in all the American conflicts from the Revolution to the Civil War. Minford Place recalled the Minford clan and their estate. Seabury Place immortalized one of their wives, Amelia Seabury. Wilkins Avenue was a misspelled tribute to the Wilkens family, who had owned an estate farther west and claimed a relative in the court of King George III.

Just half a mile east of the Fox estate flowed the Bronx River, once crystal clear and lively. Various mills, particularly woolen mills, had sprouted along the banks in colonial days to avail themselves of the river's natural power and highly regarded cleansing qualities. Where Boston Road crossed its waters stood the village of West Farms, a name that came to encompass the nearby estates.

In 1899 Fox, president of the first gas company of America, sold his eighty-six-acre estate for $1 million to the American Real Estate Company. Within the month it was announced that the elevated subway would follow Southern Boulevard out to West Farms. There ensued years of blasting and clearing as sewers and streets and sidewalks were imposed upon the former countryside, transforming it into part of the growing city.

New York had already acquired nearby Crotona Park, 154 acres just north of Charlotte Street, from the Bathgate family. Alexander Bathgate, a Scotsman, had come to the Bronx in the early nineteenth century to work as the foreman for the first Gouverneur Morris. Eventually he saved enough to purchase the land from the second Gouverneur. When the Parks Commission bought the property in 1895, it was assumed that it would be known as Bathgate Park, after the former owner. A dispute with the family embittered a commission engineer, however, who retaliated by naming the park Crotona. This was an ancient Greek city in southern Italy that was home to the philosopher Pythagoras and many famous athletic teams. Perhaps the commissioners envisioned the rambling greensward, the large lake, many ball fields, and playing courts, as a haven for both philosophers and brawny athletes.

With the large park just north and the El just east, the triangle of streets bisected by Charlotte Street was situated ideally for development. All through the first two decades of this century, the new apartment buildings, all brick walk-ups, rose on the side streets. On the corners of the avenue they built more grandiose elevator buildings. Even in the walk-ups, Italian craftsmen lovingly installed Carrara marble foyers, mosaic tile floors on each landing, solid brass fixtures, and carved stone cornices that overhung the street.

The new tenants — almost all Eastern European Jews —

Skaters throng Indian Lake in Crotona Park around 1910. The handsome building in the background is the old Borough Hall, now gone.

had escaped from the jammed streets and fetid noisy tenements of the Lower East Side of Manhattan, or else they were leaving Harlem to the blacks. This new Bronx neighborhood had everything a family could want in the early twentieth century — a park, good public schools, convenient subways, synagogues, movie theaters, and excellent shopping. The Jennings Street Market, spilling over into the sidewalk and street, was a cornucopia for the kosher housewife. There were hardware stores, clothing shops, shoe merchants enough, but dozens of food stores: poultry shops where the owners blew on the bird's feathers to show it was truly fresh, fish stores where customers could choose that night's meal as it swam in a tank, delicatessens that prided themselves on the piquancy of their pickled herring, dairy stores with tempting arrays of gleaming white cream cheeses, and bakeries with pungent rye breads and glossy, twisted challahs for the sabbath dinner.

Most unforgettably, there was Jake the Pickle Man, his shop set back in a cool alleyway behind iron-grill gates. In huge wooden barrels filled with brine this local food maestro transformed humble cucumbers into sublime pickles. He had a stormy, artistic temperment. He refused to sell to some customers and threw their proferred coins on the ground and sneered. He was most partial to children and men. Many housewives, having suffered Jake's abuse, delegated other family members to buy the prized pickles. One woman had her husband come home early on Friday just to buy pickles.

Throughout the 1920s the neighborhood grew, although even then a few minuscule farms with cows and chickens survived. Albert Irving* moved in with his new bride, her sister, and her mother in 1925. A recent immigrant from Minsk, Albert had married his good friend Jack's sister. Once part of the family, he had secured a job as a "nailer" in the Marty Abrams Fur Company on West 25th Street in Manhattan. A member of the Joint Council of Furriers union, Albert earned twenty-five dollars a week, a decent salary. Like him, his neighbors were Jews, union men working in the fur trade, in

* Not his real name.

the garmenty industry, or as house painters. Other neighbors owned small local businesses — the candy store, a tailor shop, a deli.

Each weekday morning the men headed off to the subway station. The Seventh Avenue Express was always jammed for their hour-long ride, but it traveled directly to midtown Manhattan and its factories. Most of the jobs there were tough and monotonous. For Albert Irving, summers were the worst. "There was no air conditioning, no fans, nothing, and when you worked with all those furs [his job was to "nail" and stretch the skins] it was just like standing under a shower it was so hot." The union gave these family men dignity, decent wages, better hours and conditions. In 1926 Irving spent seventeen long, bitter weeks on strike to wrest a five-day week from management. And then he used those free Saturdays getting extra work, for he and his wife were starting a family.

Once the menfolk set off to the subway, the wives would embark on their daily chores. No self-respecting married woman worked at a job, for there was more than enough to keep her perpetually busy at home in this era before labor-saving devices and convenience foods: daily marketing, then meals made from scratch, and the dishes to be washed and dried by hand. The mothers scrubbed the clothes and strung them out on the lines. When they were dry, they ironed them. Sarah Irving* remembers her mother, wearing the neat housecoat that was the uniform of the good Jewish housewife, perennially toiling away at her unending round of chores. "She used to say, 'Always I'm working like a slave — from morning to night, so much to do.' She always sang a song in Yiddish, 'I crept in, how do I creep out?' "

In reality, there was no out. In this world, the men were the sole breadwinners. The women were the homemakers and childbearers. There was much marrying in haste after quick courtships, and repenting at leisure as husbands and wives discovered their many differences, always exacerbated by trying to raise a family with never quite enough money. And yet,

---

* Not her real name.

no matter how bitterly the couples might quarrel, or however leaden the silences between them, they persevered in their marriages. There was no possibility of separation, much less divorce. It was not socially acceptable. Think of the children, think of the shame.

It was not economically possible, either. Tellingly, the one divorced mother in the neighborhood had been married to a man who became wealthy and could easily support separate domiciles, but no other man in the neighborhood could possibly underwrite two households. A man who left his family did so knowing they would end up as wards of charity. There was no welfare or relief system for them to fall back on, and they would suffer a most shameful fate. In the Jewish culture the family was too cherished to be easily cast aside.

Ultimately, everything was for the children. These immigrant-parents had no illusions that their own lives would ever transcend the unremitting struggle to provide. Very few had even a high school education, much less complete command of that mysterious language, English. Yiddish was the mother tongue of Charlotte Street. Some women attended special evening classes to learn English, but it was hard to wrestle with such strange words after an exhausting day of children, making meals, and cleaning the house.

The powerful energy and will of these Jewish immigrants, especially the mothers, was channeled into the next generation. The women hoarded their nickels and dimes and opened secret savings account to pay for special lessons or anything else that would enrich their children's lives. Sarah Irving's mother, oppressed by the drudgery of her own life, managed to buy her daughter a broken-down piano and send her to group lessons (each child had a brief session at the keyboard) at Starlight Studios on Bathgate Avenue. "She wanted me to achieve," says Sarah. "She always said, 'You can do anything with your life. You can do it.' "

And the children flourished in the protective cocoon spun by their families, their neighbors, and their schools. Each morning the boys and girls donned neat white shirts and dark trousers or skirts and headed off to Public School 61, the elementary school on the corner facing Crotona Park. The students were expected to have completed their homework, to act respectfully to their teachers (who often lived in the neighborhood, too) and to show enthusiasm and spirit in their class work. No child could fail to know the importance of school and that one's future depended on getting an education. Absorbing this credo that reflected the Jewish reverence for scholarship, the students felt sorry for those who didn't excel academically. After regular school there was often Hebrew school, where the traditions and language of the Jews were taught to these little Americans.

As soon as all the schools were over, the children pulled on their play clothes and rushed down to the blissful freedom of the street. Shortly, they'd bawl up, "Ma, I'm hungry." She'd lower hot corn on the cob or toss a penny on the pavement, which opened up a world of tasty possibilities. There was that lovely elixir, the egg cream, a foamy drink of restorative properties imbibed at the soda fountain. Warm days brought round the ices man with his syrupy confections. On nippy afternoons there were jelly apples or hot sweet potatoes. Or one could run down through Jennings Street to Jake the Pickle Man, who indulged the children, the treasure of the neighborhood. His wife often fished out the best pickles herself, her diamond rings gleaming through the turbid brine. Perhaps most delicious were the "mickeys," potatoes roasted whole in the glowing coals of a small fire in a lot or by the curb.

Games and pastimes changed with the seasons: jacks, jump rope, stickball, baseball cards, handball, sledding, skating, cycling, roller-skating, swimming, tag, and marbles. Whatever couldn't be played in the streets was available in Crotona Park. Indian Lake was packed with rented rowboats in summer; in winter ice skaters glided round and round or formed chains to crack the whip. On Deadman's Hill kids dared one another to make the descent on their sleds (sometimes nothing more than the porcelain drainboard from the sink). The handball courts resounded to the furious grunts and groans of long-running, epic rivalries. Indian Rock, a tall boulder, was a favorite destination for clambering and adventure.

The park's curved wooden benches were the province of the men. Here they relaxed from their jobs and the long commute. Some brought out musical instruments and, in the cool of the summer evening, as the trees turned into dark shadows, played and sang Yiddish songs. But most talked politics, vehemently discussing world events and local situations. "If you wanted to argue or agree, you'd know where to go," remembers one man. "Indian Lake was where the anarchists argued. I'd go with my father. There were anarchists, there were communists, there were miscellaneous socialists, there were Zionists. And if you weren't interested in politics, you might be interested in religion. And if you weren't interested in either one, then you were probably interested in making money. Those were the basic distinctions."[1]

Families congregated in the park for picnics, carrying out blankets, baskets of deli food, and cards onto the wide lawn. On hot summer nights, many even brought their sheets and pillows and slept on the grass under the trees to escape the ovenlike heat of the apartment buildings. Young couples ambled its paths, seeking privacy to kiss and neck, and sometimes more, as the used condoms thrown in bushes and behind benches testified. It never occurred to anyone to be wary of muggers or rapists. Such people didn't exist.

The most companionable activity of all was hanging around the block. There was always something going on, something to watch or do. There was the milkman and his horse and cart, a marvel to behold, for the horse knew the route so perfectly that it zigzagged on its own from one building to the next. There was coal delivery in the winter, the gleaming chunks roaring down the chute leaving a cloud of fine black dust. And then there was the I Cash Clothes man, yelling his trade and haggling with the housewives.

After supper, when the dishes were washed, the mothers and fathers descended with their folding chairs or empty crates to sit by the front stoop. The whole block would be lined with families sitting out, chattering a mixture of Yiddish and English, watching the tumult of children playing in the street, or taking brief excursions to the candy store for a soda pop, a newspaper, or a phone call. Once everyone drifted inside to bed, those teenagers who lingered too long talking would soon hear from above, "Vaddya vant? Hot or cold?" and a torrent of water would inform them it was time to find another stoop or go on home.

With so many families living in such close quarters certain strict protocols had to be observed. Those who flouted them felt the intense displeasure of their neighbors. Garbage was neatly packaged and sent down the dumbwaiter to the super after dinner. Kitchens and bathrooms were spotless, for a slobby neighbor could become the central breeding point for the roaches every housewife abhorred — not to mention, God forbid, mice; or, horror of horrors, rats. Cleanliness was almost a second religion with these women, who had known the ground-in filth of the Lower East Side and the vermin and diseases it could breed.

The landlord came round at the beginning of every month to collect the rent. The rents of twenty-five or thirty-five dollars were paid in cash. Those who did not pay punctiliously found themselves seriously threatened with eviction. The landlords, like their tenants, were mainly Jews. Some families maintained friendly relations over the years with the man to whom they paid their largest single monthly outlay. Others despised the landlord, on principle, as a capitalist.

As for the proper behavior of children, the neighborhood had shared values and goals. When boys and girls showed signs of unruliness or incipient delinquency the adults did not tolerate it. People who grew up around Charlotte Street in that era can barely think of anyone who committed the two greatest sins in the world — dropping out of school or getting knocked up. In a world ordered and supervised so closely, it was hard for a kid to get started on the road to perdition.

Being "bad" meant sneaking cigarettes, wearing lipstick, or going drinking at the Zombie Bar on Boston Road. Truant officers and principals enforced school attendance. Mothers guarded the home front, and people who had known you for years filled the busy nearby streets and parks. The policeman on the beat was a feared friend. One woman remembered their cop as "an overseer to the kids. Anyone misbehaving, like shooting dice, was taken care of by him. The kids loved him and tried to do very little to cross him."

Courtship (and possible seduction) was pursued in Crotona Park, the back rows of movie theaters, and apartment foyers. No one had a car. One man who is happily married to his neighborhood sweetheart groaned, "Sex on Charlotte Street meant five years of foreplay." He could think of only one girl who had gotten pregnant, and she had quickly married her boyfriend. The neighborhood cared intensely what happened to its young, for they were a legacy, the vindication of the years of toil and sacrifice.

When the Depression struck, this neighborhood knew it. The Bank of the United States at Freeman Street and Southern Boulevard was one of the first to collapse. Seven thousand depositors besieged that branch to withdraw their savings, and Mr. Irving lost fifteen hundred dollars, saved up from his job of "nailing" furs. As businesses folded some men were reduced to making an uncertain living from pushcarts. Most managed to keep working at their trades, but erratically and for lower wages. The sense of struggle intensified. "It was a hard time," says Irving. His daughter remembers her mother pressing her father over money, for clothes or food for their three children. Her father always shrugged helplessly. "I'm working with my ten fingers as hard as I can."

Sheila Shapiro moved to Charlotte Street in 1936 when Roosevelt was running for his second term. Times were still tough. Sheila's father was grateful for his job as an elevator operator. Buffeted as they were by the Depression, these families idolized FDR. "We were all for Roosevelt. We were brought up with him as a god," remembers Mrs. Shapiro. When Roosevelt came up Boston Road in a motorcade and passed Charlotte Street people talked about nothing else for weeks. They might talk of socialism or anarchism, but in the elections they voted for Roosevelt.

Throughout the 1930s, these families scrimped to get by, and every dime counted. In his *New York Times Magazine* article "The Glory That Was Charlotte Street," Ira Rosen tells of "my grandfather, Harry Biglaiser, kicking a quarter down Charlotte Street during the Depression. The day was Saturday, Shabbat, when Orthodox Jews are not permitted to work or to touch money. So, he didn't touch the coin. He kicked it. And he kicked it for five blocks until he reached the front of the house. He spent all Saturday afternoon by the window, to make sure that no one would touch the quarter that he had covered with leaves. Before he went to afternoon services, he told grandmother to watch the coin. She didn't; she thought he was crazy for not simply picking the coin up, since he'd already touched it with his shoe. When he returned, after sundown, he went to the gutter where he had hidden the coin. It was gone. And he didn't sleep all that night."[2]

The children never saw themselves as poor or deprived, however. (The exceptions were those few on relief, a horrid embarrassment. One man still recalls the daily shame of having to wear government-issued knickers when all the other boys had graduated to long pants.) Remembers Sheila Shapiro, "Everyone I knew had no more than I did. When I grew up I thought you had to be poor to go to summer camp — like the Fresh Air Fund or whatever, so I knew we weren't because I didn't go." They had no way of knowing. There was no television as yet, and radio served a steady diet of pleasurable, escapist fare. The movies about rich men and women were clearly fantasies.

One Charlotte Street boy discovered existence outside the Bronx only when his father got him a job as a delivery boy for Berkley's Deli on 34th Street in Manhattan. "Having that job changed my life," he says. "It gave me exposure to an affluent, sophisticated world," an exposure that widened when he became an after-school delivery boy for a swank Upper East Side dry cleaner. He got glimpses of elegant apartments with thick rugs, oil paintings on the walls, and large vases of cut flowers. It was a revelation.

Adolescence meant entry into Herman Ridder Junior High School on Boston Road, an imposing grey limestone art deco building topped with a tower. Named for the philanthropist publisher of the New York *Staats-Zeitung* (one of the ancestors of the Knight-Ridder chain) and opened in 1931, Ridder prided itself on being a model, progressive school that offered its students rigorous courses and every kind of extracurricular activity. "The happy experiences shared by its students and the people of the community have made Herman Ridder not just a school but a legend," proclaimed one yearbook.[3] It was a pioneer in student government, its drama shows were renowned, and its publications regularly won prizes. Students continued on to such high schools as Morris, James Monroe, De Witt Clinton, Stuyvesant, or Bronx Science.

These public schools molded full-fledged Americans who were not intimidated by the outside world as their immigrant mothers and fathers had been. Now the teenagers began to take the subway into Manhattan to visit the museums, walk the avenues, and marvel at the books in the 42nd Street library, or at the opulence of the stores. Older brothers (and a few older sisters) were attending City College. Writer Vivian Gornick, who lived some blocks north, remembers the euphoria of her escape into that whole new universe. She "grew drunk on words, books, ideas; and indeed, it was exactly like some great escaping high. There were dozens like me; we sat talking in the basement cafeteria at City as late as possible, and then took an hour to walk to the subway at 145th Street because no one wanted to go home — to the Bronx. Talk, talk, talk. We couldn't get enough of it."[4]

All these stirrings became irrelevant when World War II arrived. The older boys began to enlist in the military. They strolled along Charlotte Street in the splendor of their new uniforms and then shipped out. In almost every apartment house stars hung in windows telling of that family's personal, human contribution to the war. Some windows had several stars. The fathers debated even more ferociously in the park;

anxious mothers and girlfriends sent off letters and care packages. The younger brothers and sisters foraged relentlessly for scrap metal, accumulating balls of aluminum foil and clanking collections of pots and pans that were given in at the police station. And everyone listened to the radio or gathered round the newspaper to follow the course of the latest offensives and battles.

There was a special poignancy to the war in this Jewish neighborhood. Long before most Americans realized how systematically the Nazi regime was persecuting European Jews, the Jews on Charlotte Street knew, for reports and stories had filtered back. Husbands and wives tried frantically to extricate their relatives before the Nazis got them. Many failed. Families gathered in the Minford Place synagogue on Friday nights for the service and prayed. It was a terrible time. And when the longed-for victory finally came, the revelation of the concentration camps and the organized murder of six million Jews surpassed anyone's worst imaginings.

The neighborhood was grateful that nearly all their sons came home alive. The block celebrated joyously with raucous parties, dancing in the street, and barrels of beer. The war had at least boosted the economy, and these working-class people were enjoying a flush period. After the war, the rationing, and the constant worry, the neighborhood wanted to get back to how things had been before the war. But it was not to be.

The boys who had left to fight came back men of the world. They had traveled to foreign lands and fought side by side with men from every class and region of the country. They were not about to settle for the world of their fathers. They did not want to work in the garment district, commute an hour in a crammed train, and trudge up several flights to an apartment. They wanted something more. The GI Bill gave them that chance, an almost-free ticket to a college education, and the boys of Charlotte Street, who knew the value of a degree, grabbed the ticket and enrolled in City College. The excellent training they had gotten in the public schools in the Bronx served them well.

The families on and around Charlotte Street prospered in the postwar world. The couple of dozen Charlotte Street families who had had listings in the 1940 telephone book swelled to two hundred in the 1949 book. Shiny cars parked along the curb, delighting the young boys, but interfering with their stickball boundaries. A few families bought televisions, and neighbors crowded in to watch the Milton Berle show. With all these new diversions, the whole block no longer turned out evenings to sit around and socialize.

As the young men finished college, got jobs, and married, they moved to the West Bronx, with its more elegant elevator buildings, or they opted for a house in Queens or the suburbs. With a VA mortgage, the cost of buying a house was the same as or cheaper than renting an apartment in the Bronx. People began to feel that families with a future would move on.

20

Charlotte Street: It Was Not a "Good" Neighborhood
1951–1961

As the Jewish families moved, they were replaced by the new immigrants, blacks and Puerto Ricans. The first Puerto Rican family had arrived on Charlotte Street just before the war started and was accepted as an oddity — Spanish people in a Jewish neighborhood — but they made friends and settled in. Then, when coal was replaced by oil after the war, dozens of former coal bins were cleaned out and made into basement apartments. Blacks and Puerto Ricans, desperate to escape the slums of East Harlem and Harlem, gladly moved in.

The arrival of Puerto Ricans and blacks in discernible numbers made the old residents of the neighborhood notably nervous, for the newcomers were generally poorer and less educated. Their ways were different. The Puerto Ricans didn't speak English, much less Yiddish. Some white residents declared forthrightly that these were not people one wanted to live around, much less associate with — they were inferior. One Hispanic woman remembers some of her Jewish neighbors muttering at her. One even spat at her. Others just moved. A 1946 survey of the East Bronx read: "Many of the white people in the area are anxious to move out, and are held back only by the critical housing shortage. Since they are on the threshold of leaving, they are indifferent to efforts at amelioration."[1]

As the neighborhoods directly south of Charlotte Street filled with more blacks and Puerto Ricans, apprehension grew. Sheila Shapiro remembers her parents making sure she went to James Monroe High School, rather than Morris High School a mile south on Boston Road. When she went out to dances and social events and came home on the El her father insisted she get off at 174th Street, rather than Freeman Street four blocks south, and he always met her and walked her home. These precautions were warranted.

One night in 1951 a man with a knife had followed a young woman up the stairs of her Charlotte Street building. Terrified, she resisted, and the man fled. The incident was recounted again and again throughout the neighborhood. Sheila knew from the way new friends at Monroe reacted to her address that she did not live in a "good" neighborhood.

Mejias Brothers opened a grocery in the Jennings Street Market, and produce stands began to stock exotic-looking Caribbean fruits. By 1957 a third of the Charlotte Street names listed in the phone book were Spanish, such as Cruz, Bermudez, and Alama.

In 1957, when the public schools began keeping records of ethnicity (in response to the 1954 landmark desegregation case, *Brown v. Board of Education of Topeka*), PS 61 on Charlotte Street had 48 percent Puerto Ricans, 15 percent blacks, and 35 percent whites. Herman Ridder Junior High School, several blocks away, was still mainly white. It had 27 percent Puerto Rican, 16 percent black, and 57 percent white. The children of the new families were young.

By 1960 PS 61 had become 62 percent Puerto Rican, 21 percent black, and 17 percent white. Herman Ridder was 43 percent Puerto Rican, 15 percent black, and 42 percent white. The next five years saw the completion of the white departure. By 1965 PS 61 was 66 percent Puerto Rican, 27 percent black, and 5 percent white, while Herman Ridder was nearly the same: 67 percent Puerto Rican, 27 percent black, and 6 percent white. Meanwhile total enrollments had risen about one-third, jamming the classrooms and corridors.

The apartment buildings on Charlotte Street were by this time forty and fifty years old, and all their systems were worn out, as the natural lifetime of the electrical wiring, plumbing, and heating systems was coming to an end. Many of the original landlords were reluctant to make the big investments of a complete overhaul. The income from rents didn't justify it. In 1940 median rent for an apartment in the Bronx had been $38.80, higher than any other borough except Queens. By 1950 median rent had increased to $45.20, compared to $53.91 for Queens and $56.22 for Manhattan. By 1960, when it rose to $68, it lagged far behind Manhattan, with $85, and Queens, with $87. And yet to operate a building cost the same in every borough. Furthermore, since many of the Charlotte Street apartments were rent controlled, rents had not kept pace at all with increased City taxes and other expenses.

The new tenants had more children per capita than the Jews. In the years from 1960 to 1970 the number of youngsters in the Bronx rose 63 percent, from 314,100 to 512,807. This naturally put far greater wear and tear on the buildings. Aging plumbing succumbed to debris thrown into the toilets, windows broke as boys roughhoused, walls were defaced by scrawling infants, grease fires flashed in heavily used stoves. There were many small disasters, all of which cost the landlord money. Men who had been landlords for decades and for whom these buildings had been a good investment, a regular, trouble-free source of income, began to sell. The buyers, the new landlords, were either inexperienced, unscrupulous, or both.

Carmen Rodriguez,* who moved to Charlotte Street in 1952 after her father deserted the family, watched the steady exodus of longtime residents. "The neighbors were nice and said, 'Hi,' but kept to themselves. It was very clean then, so clean you could eat off the streets and sidewalks, that's how clean it was." Her best friend was a Jewish girl, and it hurt to see how her Jewish neighbors acted with each new Puerto Rican family. "They were afraid when they saw Spanish people, and they just moved."[2]

By 1960 the turnover was almost complete, and the old-timers were gone. The 1960 census for tract 153, encompassing

* Not her real name.

Charlotte Street, shows that of 4,537 families only about 11 percent had lived there since before the war. Almost 60 percent, or 2,666 families, had moved in during the previous five years!

The Jews moved because what they saw in these new families scared them: the symptoms of poverty and social disintegration that they had struggled so hard to escape from on the Lower East Side and to avoid in their own lives on Charlotte Street. They saw families like Carmen's where there were no fathers. They saw men standing around the streets drinking and gambling. They saw families with too many children crammed into too small a space. They encountered housewives who didn't understand the neighborhood codes about garbage disposal. They saw sons and daughters growing up too much on the streets without supervision. They saw casual attitudes toward sex, procreation, and marriage. They saw men without steady, decent jobs. They saw a people who often didn't want to be in New York at all, who resented having to come so far for the lousy jobs they did find. And the Jews disapproved, because, for all their own struggles, they believed New York and America had been a *mitzvah,* a blessing. Just as the earlier immigrants had looked down on the Jews, the Jews looked down on the Puerto Ricans. And as more and more Puerto Rican families fell back on welfare, it only confirmed the Jews' low opinion.

The Jews left Charlotte Street peaceably, some willingly because they wanted better-quality housing, some reluctantly but feeling they had to, because their neighborhood was now Spanish and alien to them. There were no Jewish gangs or confrontations. The long history of Judaism was one of movement and displacement. It was easier just to move again than to struggle. They left quickly and quietly.

Not so the Italians and Irish who lived on the far side of Crotona Park. They were anything but passive in their response to what they viewed as an unwanted invasion. The young men, picking up the hostility of their parents to the "niggers and spics," joined gangs and challenged the newcomers. Carmen vividly remembers the summer night when the white gangs stalked through Crotona Park and faced the Puerto Rican gangs on Charlotte Street. The young men ploughed into one another, screaming and beating with bats and chains. "There was blood all over," says Carmen. "All the white people left then." The Jews shook their heads in wonder at these crazy people and fled to safer precincts.

When Father William Smith arrived in 1961 at the Catholic parish of Saint John Chrysostom that served Charlotte Street (as did the Church of Saint Thomas Aquinas farther north), he was the fourth Spanish-speaking priest to be assigned there. He found a Puerto Rican community that was very poor, ill-educated, and highly ambivalent about being in New York. "They were people with one foot in Puerto Rico and one foot here. They had no burning necessity or desire to learn English."[3]

The Puerto Ricans lacked many of the qualities that had helped the Jews establish themselves. The Puerto Ricans were poor and traditionally terrified of authority. They had no history of organizing or standing up for themselves. They were disenfranchised politically by their lack of education and English (although this would change after 1965 with the Voting Rights Act). The family structure was frail. Serial monogamy was common.

The change in Charlotte Street soon manifested itself in such simple things as garbage and litter. The street, which had once been "so clean you could eat off it," was filthy. Tenants were changing so fast that old-timers could not enforce the old protocols. Garbage was left in the halls, and, worse yet, garbage was strewn on the streets and sidewalks, chicken bones buried in clumps of coffee grinds. With the garbage came rats. One Jewish housewife who couldn't bring herself to leave did so at last when she found her husband's shirts gnawed by rodents. During the 1950s a million whites moved out of New York City, including 200,000 from the Bronx. In the 1960s, when the number of whites leaving New York City stabilized, the number leaving the Bronx rose by a quarter, to 256,000.

And many of the first wave of Puerto Rican and black families were moving from Charlotte Street, too, following their Jewish neighbors to more middle-class climes. Middle-class Puerto Ricans moved out, and poor Puerto Ricans moved in. As they assessed their prospects — the lack of jobs, the crowded living conditions, society's indifference — they were attracted to the lovely oblivion of narcotics.

21

Charlotte Street:
"What a Madhouse It Was"
1961–1968

"ON Charlotte and Minford they sold drugs like they were groceries," remembers one resident. "They used to carry the drugs upstairs in a baby carriage." As early as 1961 those streets entered the preserve of the pushers. Soon after his arrival Father Smith got involved in counseling addicts and trying to get them off heroin. "There was no place for drug addicts, no rehabilitation centers except Manhattan General Hospital [now known as Beth Israel]. The only other place was Lexington, Kentucky. Every family, practically, suffered with a member on drugs or suffered from burglaries. It was a terrible, terrible problem with no support from anyone in political life or the institutional church. That came later, when it spread outside the ghettos. I learned it didn't help to give them money to buy drugs, even if they were begging for it."[1]

The crime and misery spawned by narcotics was extraordinary. Junkies worked up habits that cost them fifty to a hundred dollars a day. No addict had a job lucrative enough, and satisfying a full-blown heroin addiction became a full-time, desperate occupation. Those who became pushers recruited their near and dear, widening the circle of addiction. Those who chose thievery also preyed on their own families. When their kin kicked them out, they preyed on their relatives and neighbors. A study following 237 addicts in Baltimore over eleven years confirmed what everyone on Charlotte Street knew: Those few addicts had committed five hundred thousand crimes.

One shopkeeper who watched the transformation of the neighborhood with amazement and sorrow was Charles Lefkowitz, who had come to his brother's Wilkins Avenue clothing store in 1922 when he was fifteen and still in knickers. He first noticed the addicts in 1962 and soon became expert at spotting the telltale scratching of the nose and face and the deadness of the eyes. As drugs and crime picked up, he and his wife closed the shop earlier. More and more people were crammed into the neighborhood, and business had never been so good, but the "incidents" were constant. One day a junkie wandered into the small store and Lefkowitz gave him fifty cents "just to get him out of my hair." Later that night, Lefkowitz got a call at home saying this very same junkie had been caught breaking into his business. "I said, 'Why did you pick on me?' and he said, 'Charlie, I was so hopped up I didn't know what I was doing.' But I prosecuted him, and he threatened, 'When I get out I'm coming back to burn your place up.' Sure enough, when he got out, he came back and started a fire in the window. They called me at three in the morning."[2]

As the junkies multiplied, longtime merchants closed their doors for good, including Jake the Pickle Man. He retired after forty-five years as a premier pickle maker, but continued to live on Jennings Street. He who had once been the terror of the housewives was now scared of addict-muggers. One neighbor remembered him calling up his stairs to make sure no one was lurking. On June 10, 1963, Jacob Shertzer was found murdered in his apartment, his hands trussed behind him, the gas on, his mouth stuffed with a rag. Jake's brutal murder sent waves of fear through the nearby street and shops. What kind of animal would kill an old, helpless man like that? In a neighborhood that had never seen a mugging from one year to the next, it now seemed there were vicious killings every two or three weeks. More of the old stores closed on Jennings Street — Rosenblatt's dry goods, Stern's bakery, Weintraub's ladies wear, and Ralph's grocery.

By 1967 when Patrolman Sam Strassfield of the Forty-first Precinct (soon to attain widespread infamy as "Fort Apache") was assigned to the Jennings Street–Charlotte Street foot patrol, the addicts were as bad as a plague of locusts — they swarmed everywhere and were just as destructive. "So many people OD'ed," remembers Strassfield, "we used to get them all the time in the hallways and vacant lots. Who had time to deal with the drugs? Our job was to protect lives and property. The junkies went to the roofs and the cellars to transact their business."[3] (The ranks of the junkies were swollen by the combat veterans back from the escalating war in Vietnam. On tour they had been introduced to heroin, and they brought their habit home with them.) Crime figures reflected the addiction. In 1961 in the Forty-first Precinct there had been 18 murders, 183 robberies, and 667 burglaries, and the citywide homicide total was 390. By 1971 those figures had soared to 102 murders, 2,632 robberies, and 6,443 burglaries in the Forty-first Precinct. The citywide figure for homicide had more than quadrupled to 1,466.

An unwed mother, Carmen Rodriguez lived at home, continued school, and worked part time at an office supply company. One Friday she had been to visit her mother in the hospital, and as she turned onto Charlotte Street she had more than $250 in her pocketbook, including her mother's cashed welfare check, and her own pay. The super was outside. She said hello and passed inside to walk up to her apartment. Out of the shadows lunged a young man, someone new to the neighborhood. He cornered her, grabbed her pocketbook, and tore downstairs. Hearing Carmen's shrieks, a neighbor dashed out with a baseball bat, but it was too late and Carmen sobbed with fear and over the loss of all her money. In time the welfare department replaced the check, and her boss took up a collection at the office, but she no longer felt safe in her own neighborhood. Addicts were so brazen they waited for working people to alight from the subway. One teacher was held up at gunpoint in the entrance of PS 61.

To an outside observer it was a frighteningly chaotic world. Patrolman Strassfield, a nondrinker, found that he sometimes needed to steel himself with a prework snifter. Each afternoon or evening, depending on his shift, the patrolman set out on foot from the stationhouse and headed north toward Jennings Street. (This was before the Lindsay administration put all police into radio cars.) Sometimes, on warm days, Strassfield just stopped and watched. "I just used to think what a madhouse it was. You had to see it to believe it. The market was jammed with people, the stores and their stalls spilling out onto the street, like a Persian bazaar. Every street was jammed and the hydrants always open and running so the sewers would back up and the water would be collecting into lakes. The kids would be swimming in this filthy water, while passing cars were stalling out. We called it Lake Wilkins. There was constant music and fights. People would run down the streets brandishing bats, shrieking and yelling. People would come up to you bleeding.

"There were a tremendous number of kids, just in shorts, with no shirts, and it was like you were in India or Bangladesh. Children were those people's pleasure and their future and there were always terrible tragedies — they were always getting hit by cars, falling off fire escapes and out of windows. There was just a constant clanging of bells. There were police cars running up and down, fire engines roaring back and forth, and ambulances whining through. The kids ran around till all the hours of the night and there were lots of family fights. Ninety percent of these people were decent; it was the other ten percent.

"I can remember two homicides in the same building, one right after another. Who can remember which building? There were so many homicides. I delivered twenty-seven babies, even one set of twins. They sent them home from the hospitals because there was no room for them to wait. Then there was a guy shot with a shotgun and I had to hold his guts in with my bare hands. These people came to better themselves like everyone else. They got welfare and that was better than they had had.

"To work here you had to have a very even temperament. It was like a three-ring circus. There were fellows who after one night took their badge and left it at the desk and quit. We used to have a hundred jobs backed up at times."[4] Occasionally Patrolman Strassfield would be sought out by the few remaining Jewish men around Charlotte Street, for they needed a tenth man to complete the minyan at the Minford Place synagogue. Without ten they could not worship.

Just as the Jews had vanished from Charlotte Street, so had the old landlords. The new ones quickly figured out that it made no economic sense to overhaul their buildings. Even had the landlords wanted to, it is doubtful whether any bank would have lent them the money. (In the still-stable West Bronx, landlords of perfectly maintained buildings tenanted by whites were being turned down flat for improvement loans.) In the Charlotte Street buildings the equipment was constantly being broken, and legions of junkies stole whatever they could get their hands on. At first the landlords had welcomed the steady stream of welfare families, for the Department of Social Services was so desperate to place its ever-growing list of new clients — swelled by the tremendous success of the welfare rights campaign — that it was paying higher-than-market rents and finder fees, which tempted landlords to become slumlords. By 1970, of 3,181 families living in the Charlotte Street neighborhood, 1,467 families, or almost half, were on welfare.

There was a major catch to the landlords' windfall. Welfare families discovered quickly that they could live better if they kept the rent money for themselves. When they were threatened with eviction, the department would often pay the back rent or find the client a new apartment, and the cycle would begin again. No landlord could survive long if even one or two tenants didn't pay rent. Many discovered that the most profitable course was "milking" the building. This strategy entailed providing just enough services and promises of services to collect rent from some of the tenants while no longer paying taxes to the City. Only after they were three years in arrears could the City attach the building. Fires here and there might produce some insurance payments in the meantime.

Once the landlord embarked on this destructive course, it was amazing how doggedly the tenants resisted. They survived winters with almost no heat or even hot water by bundling up in all their clothes and turning on the gas stove. When utility bills soared so high no one could afford them, they were not paid. When the electricity was out, people jerry-rigged wires to tap into the hall currents, or even out to the street lamps. When junkies ripped out the plumbing and there was no running water, families again made do, fetching water from fire hydrants in coffee cans and milk containers. For a shower or bath they visited relatives or friends. As the neighborhood became poorer and crazier with drugs and violence, the abandonment escalated, as did the fires.

22

Charlotte Street: The Fires
1969–1973

JERRY ALBERT came to Engine Company 82, the company that served the Charlotte Street–Jennings Market neighborhood, in 1957. That year the red trucks roared out to fires fifteen hundred times, four or five times a day. Apartments were at a premium, and those damaged by fire would be repaired and rented out again within two weeks. By 1967 the work load at Engine Company 82 had doubled. They were called to three thousand fires a year, making this the busiest firehouse in the City. It was obvious to the firemen in the field that the surge in fires was due to arson, but there were so few fire marshals in the department to investigate arson, a felony, that one or two marshals were given responsibility for entire boroughs. They did not have cars on the job and often did not arrive at the scene of a suspicious fire until a day or two or even several days later.

Moreover, the fire marshals were almost pariahs in their own department. Their duties encompassed not merely arson but collaring firemen up to no good — those accepting bribes from businesses without proper fire exits or those bringing women into the firehouse. The police department, their natural allies in fighting the crime of arson, viewed fire marshals as incompetent interlopers. If arson was a crime, the police believed, the police should have jurisdiction. Cops fought crime, firemen fought fires. The firemen and the cops both focused their hostility on the fire marshals.

Although the Charlotte Street neighborhood was experiencing more fires, there was no official reaction except to increase the number of firemen in the firehouse. All through the 1960s and early 1970s, there was no press coverage, and there were no denunciations by Model Cities officials or expressions of concern by politicians. As the Bronx began to burn, no one said anything.

In particular, no one said anything about arson. Says one fireman with decades of frontline service, "The arson, I would say, was officially ignored. The fire commissioner, the chiefs of department, they just wished this place would go away, that they could sell it to Westchester County and get rid of it. At Charlotte Street there were twelve hundred false alarms in one year. You know how many arrests they made? Zero. It was a very lax attitude all the way up — don't make waves. They got the fire reports downtown every day, they knew the runs and workers and all the suspicious fires. Every fire in a vacant building had to be arson. No one lives there, and yet when we pull up, the fire's out thirty windows. It's a definite case of arson, not lightning or anything else. Officially, we put out the fires and filed reports. We got visits from the big brass telling us what a nice job you're doing here, you want to transfer out you can, you know, stuff like that."[1]

As the arson increased, the firemen began to categorize it. There was arson commissioned by landlords out for their insurance. (A Lloyd's of London syndicate was to lose $45 million on fire insurance written in the South Bronx.) Arson was set by welfare recipients who wanted out of their apartments and into something better (preferably public housing), but knew they could do so only if they got onto a priority list. Large signs in the welfare centers stated very clearly in Spanish and English, THE ONLY WAY TO GET HOUSING PRIORITY IS IF YOU ARE BURNED OUT BY A FIRE. The welfare department also paid two or three thousand dollars to burned-out families for their destroyed goods. Many fires were deliberately set by junkies — and by that new breed of professional, the strippers of buildings, who wanted to clear a building so they could ransack the valuable copper and brass pipes, fixtures, and hardware. A roaring fire in an already-vacant building made their job much easier. Fires were set by firebugs who enjoyed a good blaze and by kids out for kicks. And some were set by those who got their revenge with fire, jilted lovers returning with a can of gasoline and a match to annihilate entire buildings and teach one person a lesson.

Fire and arson became a way of life around Charlotte Street, another variable to be reckoned in. One mother who lived near Engine Company 82 says, "The firehouse was right down the block, and if my kids had any lullaby to go to sleep, it was the fire engines." One fifth-grade teacher at PS 61 remembers her students coming into class smelling like smoke. Sometimes they told her, "We have our suitcases packed. This week is the fire." (The word had been thoughtfully sent around beforehand, so people could escape with little loss of life or property.) When students said this, the teacher knew those kids would indeed soon disappear from the class.

The firemen could never quite get over the scenes they saw again and again: a building consumed by flames and the families to the side, fully dressed and with suitcases and cartons neatly arranged on the sidewalk. Not all arsonists were that thoughtful, however, and the firemen saw other, terrible scenes as the fires burned away the neighborhood. Once they found three boys, paid to burn down the building, trapped in a fire of their own making. Said one man, shaking his head, "One kid was caught in it and he was a crispy critter when we got to him. The other two kids were badly burnt."[2] In that rare instance, the landlord was prosecuted and convicted. Even the local antipoverty agency, the neighborhood's sole governmental presence, was torched.

During 1970 Engine Company 82 made 6,204 runs to 4,246 fires, or eleven fires a day. No one officially recognized that arson was an issue, much less *the* issue. In a long and prophetic memo written March 17, 1970, on fires in the Bronx by Charles F. Kirby, deputy fire chief, to John T. O'Hagan, the chief of the fire department, there is not one mention of arson as the major cause of the escalating incidence of fires. "Between 1964 and 1968 while structural fires in the city rose 42% the Bronx increased 70 percent," wrote Chief Kirby. "In the same period, non-structural fires (trash, brush, cars, etc.) in the city rose 75% while the Bronx increased 95%." He noted that the increase in fires began around the area served by Engine Company 82 and spread first south and then north. He predicted further increases because "there are no physical and sociological changes to warrant a contrary assumption at the present time. . . . The potential of the spread for the 1970s consists of a further intensification of fires in all but the most southern portion and a spread in the central area to Fordham Road."[3]

The spread of devastation by fire could be averted, believed Kirby, but "to do so rehabilitation must move forward at a greater rate than decomposition." He proposed better sanitation programs and sprinklers in all apartment buildings. "There are many more physical and social changes which must be planned to reverse the fire trend. If these are beyond the fiscal capabilities of the City or inequitable with our economic structure it does not relieve us completely of our obligation to point up problems as we see and forecast them. . . . The actual fires and the constant threat of fire must surely be a devastating horror to people required to live in houses in a deteriorating neighborhood." Only obliquely did Chief Kirby hint at arson: "I feel that it can be said that rather than being accidental, fire is largely a social problem and the Bronx has and will have its share of such problems."[4]

In his best-selling book, *Report from Engine Company 82,* fireman Dennis Smith bemoaned the frustration of battling fires when no one seemed to care — from City officials to the people who lived there. When the alarm bells started ringing two, seven, four, three, the firemen knew that box too well, for 2743 is Charlotte Street and 170th. "We go to that intersection more often than any other. It is usually a false alarm, but there is no such thing as 'crying wolf' in this business. . . . Few people even turn to watch us go by. Screaming fire engines and police cars are part of life in the South Bronx, just sounds to which people have adjusted.

"There are three men sitting on milk boxes near the alarm box drinking from cans of beer wrapped in small brown paper bags. Jim Stack and I walk up either side of Charlotte Street looking for smoke or waving people. We have done this a thousand other times, and it now seems to be a dumb ritual.

"The three men are disinterested, and talk among themselves. Captain Albergray looks around and goes to unwind the alarm box. I walk over and ask the men if they saw anyone pull the box. One man, without looking at me, said, 'Yeah, a kid. He went up the street.'

" 'I guess you didn't think of grabbing him,' I said.

" 'That's not my job, man,' he said."[5]

The fires, the false alarms, the drugs, the apathy, and the violence waiting to erupt were constant, day in, day out. The firemen, like the cops, were called upon to staunch the endless flow of disasters besetting this disintegrating world.

The Charlotte Street alarm sounds — 2743 — and Engine Company 82 rushes out. A young woman is there this time.

" 'My husband,' she says, 'he took an OD.'

" 'Where's the address?' Captain Albergray asks.

" '811 Seabury Place, Apartment 6,' she answers.

"The pumper takes off, leaving her to walk the short block to Seabury Place. We reach 811. Someone has painted a sign on the marble wall of the vestibule: NO JUNKIES ALLOWED — ENTER AT YOUR OWN RISK. How ironic. We climb the stairs to the second floor. The door of Apartment 6 is open, and there is a young man and a girl standing over the sprawled body of a handsome Puerto Rican. He is lying on the kitchen floor."[6] The firemen revive him with ice and cold water and wait until an ambulance comes to take him away.

The South Bronx was burning and no one seemed to care. The South Bronx was hooked on drugs and no one seemed to notice. But the generation that was coming of age in this hellhole was about to add new dimensions of misery, terror and brutishness. The new youth gangs were forming.

23

Charlotte Street: The Gangs
1970–1975

IT is hard to say exactly how or why these new gangs got started. Some say for social reasons, for fun, the way all clubs get going. Once a few formed, others followed. Some say they arose from a wish to rid the neighborhood of the heroin pushers. Certainly these teenagers had seen their older brothers and sisters, even their parents, ravaged by "smack." They had come home to apartments burglarized by junkies and listened to tearful tales of muggings. They had seen many die from overdoses.

The gangs imposed upon themselves elaborate rules and rituals and stern codes of "honor." They had fearsome initiations and hierarchies to rule their territories. They adopted uniforms with emblems and colors that identified them. They had devised their own brand of order for their own small world. Every few blocks spawned new gangs. When they walked out together, in their denim jackets emblazoned with warlike names and symbols, they relished the power of the group and the fear they stirred up.

They had no occupation except harassing junkies and pushers, and this was not a full-time pursuit for young men with time on their hands. The gang members attended school sporadically or had dropped out completely. And so the gangs, like third-rate duchies in medieval times, embarked on permanent states of hostility, punctuated by elaborately negotiated, short-lived states of peace. When they were not warring on one another, they mounted intermittent attacks on the authorities and a fearful local populace. A third wave of terror broke in the streets, reinforcing the fires and the drugs.

The new youth gangs subscribed to violence and the macho ethic, the first generation to come of age under television's relentless diet of easy beatings and murders. The gangs acquired arsenals and weaponry that would have impressed any serious guerrilla group. Believing, as youth always has, that all youth is immortal, they plunged into deadly feuds with rival gangs and against the world in general. They cloaked their viciousness in noble rhetoric. Others always describe them as "pathological." One priest remembers, "In the late 1950s, early 1960s, you had gangs, the West Side Story stuff. Those young men came [into the Bronx] with families. They knew us and knew we knew them. If they were having a rumble and you appeared, they'd scatter. They were afraid. The gangs of the 1970s were pathological. They engaged in random violence for no reason."

Charlotte Street's gang was the Turbans, whose most serious rivals were the Royal Javelins on Vyse Avenue just east of Southern Boulevard. The Turbans hung out in a basement on Minford Place. All the clubhouses had the same basic decor: black walls covered with crude Day-Glo paintings portraying violent or obscene themes illuminated by fluorescent lighting, rooms furnished with broken-down armchairs and mattresses salvaged from the streets or burned-out apartments. It was in the clubs that the gangs stashed their arsenals — handguns, shotguns, rifles, even machine guns, grenades, and dynamite.

When every few blocks became turf to yet another youth gang, the mass media discovered the South Bronx. The fires and the drugs had passed almost unnoticed, but the gangs were too flamboyant and self-righteous to ignore, and they made terrific copy. These teenage crusades and vendettas were not subtle. One gang raped and killed a woman they said was running a shooting gallery for addicts in her apartment. Another stabbed two addicts, after the Forty-first Precinct had failed to act upon a gang ultimatum to arrest the junkies. They put a gun to another junkie's head and suggested he join a drug rehabilitation program.

Journalists swarmed into the South Bronx, seeking out the

Youth gangs sprang up all over the South Bronx in the early 1970s, terrorizing the local populace and fighting deadly wars with one another

gangs in their basement lairs. The kids, dressed to kill in their most intimidating outfits — denim jackets sewn with skulls dripping blood and swastikas, studded leather wristbands, heavy belts and boots — were delighted to entertain the reporters. As the *New York Post* told its readers, "There's an intriguing air of unpredictability in their basement clubhouses and on the streets they claim as their own, a mood that can suddenly propel these bored, unsupervised gun-toting youths towards debauchery or violence."[1]

There were pretty teenage girls, sexy in tight jeans and gang jackets, who formed the women's auxiliaries. Their role was to wait on the young warriors, party with them, sleep with them, bear their illegitimate babies, and serve as alluring testimony to their manliness. There was little doubt about the function of the old mattresses in the back rooms of the black-walled clubhouses. Sex and violence — it was a great story.

VOICES OF THE SOUTH BRONX
JIM GELBMAN

A husky man with chestnut hair and blue eyes, Jim Gelbman was born in 1943, in Bronx Hospital, only blocks from Charlotte Street. He grew up in Hunt's Point on Fox Street in a ground-floor apartment. His father was a house painter, his mother a housewife. His childhood was a placid routine of public school, Hebrew school at Hunt's Point Jewish Center, and leisure time playing on the street.

In 1956 Jim was selected by his sixth-grade teacher to complete three years of school in two at Herman Ridder Junior High School on Boston Road. "I was extremely proud and happy," he remembers. There were good science and math courses, four language courses, shop, art, English, history, and a wealth of extracurricular activities. "I was in *Finian's Rainbow*," he recalls with a smile. "We had a great time. The teachers who did this weren't paid extra, by the way. But they were happy to do it."

One day, while still in junior high school, Jim realized his life had changed. "There were very few Jews left on Fox

Street. Very few. But more traumatic than losing the people was losing the trees. Once they were doing something with the water main, and they pulled all the trees out and never replaced them. I really liked the trees in the spring. I always associated the loss of the trees with the loss of the people."

When he became a teacher in 1965, Gelbman was once again commuting from Fox Street to Herman Ridder. "A tremendous change had taken place in the eight years since I had graduated," he says. "There were five or six white kids in the whole school, and the special progress classes I had been in were gone. I wasn't completely fazed by the kids — I had taken my training in Harlem — but I was floored by their lack of ability to read. We're talking about second- or third-grade level, if that much. And I was amazed by their inability to articulate their thoughts. This I had never been trained to deal with. They had no idea how to do homework; they had no study skills."

The Gelbman family continued to live in its Fox Street apartment. "I was never afraid, but I saw so many things," he said, recalling his college days. "I saw people get mugged. There was a shoe store in our building and I saw the place being broken into. I remember studying for the Regents examinations sitting next to a steam radiator that was totally frozen, bundled up in three or four sweaters with the stove going." The year he began teaching, his mother had been mugged on their doorstep. "We felt, okay, we have to start looking for something else. It was not easy because we were paying forty-nine dollars a month in 1964 for that apartment, which was very cheap, and my mother had her marketplace, and the train, both very nearby."

From 1931 to 1964 Herman Ridder had had three principals, each of them strong, demanding leaders. Between 1964 and 1970 there were seven, including one who was absent for twelve months. The teacher turnover ran just as high. "The old-time teachers did not want to teach remedial reading after years of advanced subjects," says Gelbman. The dozens of new teachers, green and inexperienced, were frightened by the school and the neighborhood. "The culture shock wasn't as great to me. I considered myself part of that neighborhood."

Yet even he was shocked "when I found that most of the students — I mean three out of four — did not have two-parent homes. Getting parents in for consultation was difficult because there were other siblings who couldn't be left alone. If the mother worked, and that was unusual, very rare, you would be taking her away from the only job she had. So I went to the homes, and for me it brought back Fox Street, only Fox Street was never like that. We're talking about going up steps where there are no steps. When I got into the homes I could no longer tell them, 'Your child is s son-of-a-bitch.' I was just overwhelmed by the physical surroundings. Then I realized these kids have big, big problems and those problems are coming into the school."

As a teenager, Jim's life had revolved around the Herman Ridder school. His mother, a piece worker in the garment district, was away for long hours. "I resented that," says Jim. "It wasn't a sweatshop, but the boss took advantage of the workers." His father occupied his free time watching television or occasionally playing cards. "I had two parents, but I felt I was on my own. What I had was my school." These kids lacked even that.

Now disintegration of the surrounding streets carried into the school. The student body had doubled, but course selection and after-school activities were cut again and again. The theater groups, glee clubs, school publications, and sports teams that had so enriched Gelbman's wonderful two years at Herman Ridder were gone. In their place reigned chaos and fear. "Drugs were a big, big story. There were kids who lived away from home for days in these so-called social clubs and gang lairs. They preyed upon local stores, which eventually had to close down. There were at least six major gangs at Ridder, but a couple of good deans insisted that the gangs not wear their colors. You couldn't blame the teachers for not wanting to hang around."

As the neighborhood collapsed, Herman Ridder became

nothing more than a way station. "Every day, you got new kids. I'm not exaggerating — every day. And every day you lost kids, though you wouldn't know it until two weeks later. Teaching is nothing more than maintaining order in a classroom and imparting the knowledge and reading skills these kids need. With all that constant change, it became very hard, very demoralizing."

In the late 1960s Jim had married and moved to northern New Jersey. "We were going to move to Co-op City like all the other Jews in the Bronx, but my wife said why not go for a house? Co-op City? The way it was presented was just fantastic — our own generator, our own shopping center. It seemed like it was going to be a secure neighborhood with all the amenities. Once we decided to get a house we didn't even think of looking in the Bronx. We wanted something better. We saw the suburban life and it appealed to us."

Each day he commuted by car to Herman Ridder, but fires had started to eat away the adjacent blocks, and the wail of fire engines was constant. "How did the kids talk about the fires? How do you talk about the weather? A normal occurrence. I'll tell you something more tragic. Kids would come in and talk about their brother being stabbed in the same nonemotional way as if their building had been on fire or as if to say 'We just moved to another apartment.' The same way as 'I lost my books.' The same noncaring attitude as 'What's your next class?' or 'Lend me a dime?' And maybe, on a kid's level, they had no other alternative. Either they accepted it or went crazy.

"They were impressed by violence. I believe they learned a great deal of violence from television. They were impressed by superheroes, and their fantasies were to do something excellently good or excellently bad. They wanted notoriety. They had nothing else. You didn't get in their way because psychologically they'd think nothing of killing you. A lot of teachers were deathly afraid going into that school building." He laughs. "They were also deathly afraid of going out."

The nadir was the early 1970s when the school had twenty-six hundred kids, so many beyond its capacity that an annex

was established on one floor of a nearby high school. Says
Gelbman, "The kids did an effective job of destroying most
of that high school floor physically." Back at Herman Ridder
some classes were totally out of control. "There are obscene
stories of kids masturbating in class, about windows being
broken, fires set, all with the teacher there. People say I'm a
good teacher because I have order in my class. Well, for that
all you have to do is get one gun and set it in front of the
class. That's cheaper than a teacher."

Gelbman could not look at his students without thinking,
"There but for the grace of God go I. Maybe the only difference is I didn't have any junkie friends. I didn't shoot up.
I had school. Maybe that was ingrained in me by my parents.
Maybe those were the values I picked up. Other than that I
don't see why I shouldn't have become a junkie or a gang
member.

"Their problems were compounded by the transiency. They
don't have the neighborhoods like the Jews had. We had a
home base, a social system in the neighborhoods. I went to
one Hebrew school, and those were poor Jews (and I mean
poor), but the center was there and you had a solidifying force
the Hispanics and blacks did not have. I had nothing else *but*
my schooling, which is the reason I did well. These kids either
had their drugs or their gangs. Maybe they thought they were
better off."

Over the years Gelbman would become an active leader in
the local teachers' union. He began working on his Ph.D. at
Fordham University. His thesis topic? A case study of his
school district, District 12. "I saw that decisions were made
not for educational reasons, but for political reasons. This
disturbed me." Many federal programs were funneled into
Ridder. "As far as I could see these programs did not ma-
terially and significantly improve the education of these kids."
He says he regrets his decision to become a teacher. "My
mother, who had no faith in me as a person, suggested I
become a teacher, and I took the easy way out and listened
to her." And yet, he remained at Herman Ridder teaching
into the 1980s, a career of two decades.

The official attitude toward Herman Ridder is perhaps best reflected in the small fact that from 1965 on, the classrooms and halls would not once be painted. Concerned parents steered their children into other junior high schools. As for Ridder's graduates, what befalls them? Says Gelbman, "They become junkies, they become welfare people, they get killed, they go to Riker's Island. They are the people you want to put away and that you don't want to think about. It's a loss, a tremendous loss. It's hard for me to imagine [people] being Jewish and being treated that way."

In the glare of publicity, the gangs used the media to inflate their reputations, portraying themselves as modern-day Robin Hoods. "Why don't the cops take dope out of the neighborhoods?" demanded Turbans' president Manny. "The police department is the biggest gang out here. So we decided to take care of business ourselves."[2] The gangs were the law now. On Minford Place the Turbans claimed they had "banished" all junkies in 1971, making their point by beating up a few and then plastering the block with signs warning JUNKIES KEEP OUT. But most of their energy was devoted to warring with other gangs, especially the neighboring Javelins. The two clashed regularly, and the neighborhood was always the loser. In one encounter on 173rd Street, three innocent bystanders were shot.

The Bronx Boys' Club, in Javelin territory on Hoe Avenue, just parallel to Southern Boulevard, was declared a neutral zone, and the boys would go there to hang out. The only condition was they check their weapons at the door.

In one day, March 8, 1971, the Forty-first Precinct arrested three members of the Savage Nomads for assault. Hours later, the same gang attacked a lone kid and shot him in the hand and leg. That night one member was arrested for having a blackjack. A few days later the Black Spades brazenly attacked a cop. One former Javelins member, Louis Lugo, says, "The cops didn't care. We used to carry rifles in our pant legs, limping along. It was pretty obvious, but the cops didn't stop us. We had bloody battles. In 1970 a gang member, Mr.

Kool, was killed, stabbed in the heart in a brawl at a party in Hunt's Point. He was seventeen.

"We had stationed Mr. Lettle as a lookout in an abandoned building near our basement clubhouse. He got shot by a shot-gun blast and was left lying there. We found him several days later, bloated and stinking so even we could barely recognize him."[3]

Lugo talks about the antidrug crusade and the gangs' own approach. "I caught three guys cooking stuff up on the roof. We took them to the basement and gave them a trial and then whipped them. Using dues money, we bought methadone tablets. Otherwise, we made them quit cold turkey.

"The gangs quickly became a matter of survival," says Lugo. "You had to belong because everyone else did. We had incredible arsenals. We bought this stuff — .45s, Lugers, gas bombs, bow-and-arrow style rifles — mainly from junkies who had got it in burglaries. I didn't have to go to Vietnam to feel like I was a combat veteran. We fought our own war here."[4]

And the press chronicled much of it. "You knew you were famous," he says, "and you had to play up to your name. They overpublicized us and created a lot of static. Geraldo Rivera came around, and I remember his major concern was whether we had a Thompson submachine gun as he had heard. Then he asked, 'Is it true Vietnam Vets trains you?' "[5] A French filmmaker came to live with the gangs and had her videotapes shown at the Whitney Museum. Gang members appeared on the TV news and got their pictures and opinions in newspapers and magazines.

Father Smith was seething over the media glorification. "They made celebrities and heroes out of them. They said they were keeping out junkies, but their real ways came clear when they brutally killed an old black man who hadn't done anything. Much of the violence and killing came out of girls claiming their honor had been smirched, as if those girls had any honor left."[6] He had conducted too many funerals to see the glamour in gangs and violent punks. His fury with the press echoed turn-of-the-century reformer and journalist Jacob Riis, who complained that the press of his day reported the gangs' "doings daily with a sensational minuteness of detail that does its share toward keeping up its evil traditions and inflaming the ambition of its members to be as bad as the worst.''

Elizabeth Martinez, the super (along with her husband) at 1709 Boston Road, was puzzled by the proliferation of the gangs. Late at night as she swept the sidewalk in front of her building she talked to the boys and tried to draw them out. "I said to one of them, 'You're going to get killed.' He said, 'I don't care.' I said, 'Why don't you go home?' and he said, 'There's nothing at home. My mother's a drunk.' I said, 'You don't care if you die?' and he said, 'Nope.' Then I said, 'You haven't begun life yet. You don't know what it's all about.' He said, 'You're a nice lady, that's why we leave your building alone.' They picked buildings to attack. Then I asked 'Why don't you go to school? Become a lawyer, a doctor?' They'd say, 'I don't do good in school. My mother's too dumb to help me. When I ask her something, she doesn't know. Then at school I feel stupid.' "[7]

The more Liz Martinez talked to these teenagers, the more appalled she became at their utter alienation. "It was unbelievable the stories coming out of their mouths. Where were their fathers? One kid we caught breaking into an apartment was wanted for three murders. I remember one night I had finished cleaning and I was putting the garbage out and I noticed old man Kaplan's window was about six inches open because of the heat. I saw a figure in the darkness and I shined my flashlight on him. I saw it was a kid lying on the ledge. I said, 'Hey, what are you doing up there?' Then Kaplan's daughter heard me and ran to her father's room. The kid jumped from the ledge and broke his ankle. I grabbed him and said, 'Why are you up there?' He said 'I'm hungry and I was going to ask him for fifty cents.' Sure, at three in the morning. He would have killed that old man. The cops took him and frisked him and there was a big old Jim Bowie knife in his shoe."[8]

In the fall of 1973 Liz's building was being rehabilitated, one of the very few under repair in the neighborhood. Her huge lobby was full of expensive appliances — stoves and refrigerators — destined for the redone apartments. Before embarking on her usual round of chores, she checked the roof door and found two kids trying to jimmy it. Always fearless, she collared them and hauled them down to the lobby. There in the gloom she and her husband argued over whether to let them go or call the cops.

Unknown to them, a third kid was prowling about the building, a boy they knew named Jimmy. While they argued, Jimmy had secreted himself on the other side of the lobby. When Liz moved toward the front door, Jimmy jumped out and began shooting at her. Liz collapsed instantly, her blood slowly forming dark pools on the marble floor. The boys charged off, leaving Pete to save his wife. She had been struck by all six bullets, her intestines perforated in twenty-two places. "The thing that saved me was my bra wire," she says. "It ricocheted the bullet heading for my heart."[9] Today she still carries three of the bullets around inside her. Jimmy was never caught. His family disappeared along with him.

The gang members killed one another off, fled, or were arrested and jailed for a wide variety of serious crimes. Moreover, ironically, many gangs got heavily involved in drugs. Others, remembers one gang member, became arsonists for hire. "We were tired and exhausted," says Louis Lugo. "There were too many funerals and the neighborhood was going up in flames. The neighborhood was here and then it was gone. It happened so fast." Late at night, Louis, who lived on Southern Boulevard under the El, would go out to walk his German shepherd on the dying streets. As he passed the charred front doors, the lots deep in the rubble of former apartment houses, he dreamed of how it had been when he first moved in in the 1960s. "There had been so much life, so many people and stores. Everything was busy, busy, busy."[10]

24

Charlotte Street: The Collapse
1973–1975

INTO these expiring blocks in March 1973 came John Pratt, a black "streetbanker" sent out by Chemical Bank to figure out whether there was any alternative to closing its branch next to the 174th Street subway station. Employees were terrified. Their cars were being stolen, their lives threatened. Pratt began to work with the few community activists — Genevieve Brooks of the Seabury Day-care Center, Father Smith of Saint John's on 167th Street, Jack Flanagan of the Forty-first Precinct, Ralph Porter of the Hoe Avenue Boys' Club, and Eae James Mitchell of Togetherness Management, Inc., a housing company.

Pratt found the blocks around the bank under the control of the Royal Charmers gang, who had strung up the conventional banner, "PUSHERS STAY OFF THIS BLOCK." Pratt, a soft-spoken man wearing an elegant three-piece suit, says, "It was the strangest situation I've ever been in. You had fear all over the place and no matter what you did, you just weren't acting fast enough. No one seemed able to do anything. When I arrived in 1973 there were only seventy-three businesses who were customers of our bank. Everything was going down the tubes very quickly."[1]

Charlie Lefkowitz was one of those shopkeepers who had fled. "The other merchants pleaded with me not to go, but I had to. I figured my luck was going to end. We had had two holdups in one week and that's when I knew I had to go. Believe me, I cried when I got out. I broke down and cried. I came in knee pants to that store. That was the only thing I did in my life, and here I was leaving at sixty-four years old.

But I was afraid that if I didn't walk out on my own two feet, they'd carry me out after another burglary."[2] And so the merchants left.

"When I would leave work on a Friday," says Pratt, "there might be forty-two businesses. By Monday when I came back up on the subway there would be only twenty-two, thanks to the burnouts and assaults by the Royal Charmers, who figured if they couldn't get jobs they would just help themselves."[3]

By the time of Pratt's arrival, the fire and abandonment had wiped out entire blocks. The Board of Education, which had acquired a Charlotte Street site for the building of PS 202 to handle the overflow of children from PS 61, rescinded the plan because there were no longer enough children in the district to justify a new building. Enrollment at PS 61 had dropped from twenty-six hundred in 1970–1971 (when half the overcrowded students had been attending classes in Quonset huts or other temporary quarters) to twelve hundred children in 1972–1973.

It was about this time in 1973 that the magnitude of the drugs-crime-fire-abandonment-devastation cycle began to elicit some concern. John Pratt, as a representative of Chemical Bank, was an important catalyst to local action. His bank put up two thousand dollars in seed money to fund Genevieve Brooks's new Fire, Safety, and Educational Program. Around this coalesced the local community activists and Captain John Ruffins, a black fireman in charge of the fire cadets program in Model Cities.

Mrs. Brooks, a slender, demure-looking black woman who radiated intelligence and ability, had already attracted the support of Senator Jacob Javits. He had helped set up the Seabury Day-care Center for working mothers, one of his few visible accomplishments in the wake of Javits's "adoption" of the South Bronx. His earlier support had made Chemical Bank willing to back Brooks's new endeavor, which was to force the City to notice that her neighborhood was burning down.

The new pressure group began by asking the fire department to put the area under the surveillance of fire marshals and to tally up the number of fires. The fire and safety group's goal was to focus the spotlight of publicity on the incessant fires eating up the South Bronx. The figures were startling. In one two-week period in August 1973 the blocks immediately around Charlotte Street had fifty-six fires in twenty-two buildings. The group took photographs, did more surveys of the damage, put together their case, and invited everyone in the Bronx and the City who mattered: the local politicians, including Congressman Herman Badillo, Planning Commissioner John Zuccotti, the press, the bankers, the real estate men, the fire department brass, the police department, and the insurance industry. The game plan was to shock their guests with a walking tour. They wanted these powerful people to see and smell the destruction, to understand the scope and seriousness of the fires. They wanted them to digest the terrible loss in housing and commerce.

On February 25, 1974, the invited guests turned out in force. Two hundred bigwigs listened as Mrs. Brooks showed the pictures and charts detailing the collapse of the nearby blocks and explaining the need for changed welfare rules and insurance laws, then ushered them into several buses and had them driven around. They stopped from time to time to stroll along the burned-out streets, peering through the lightly falling snow at broiled mattresses and charred chairs visible beyond the shards of windows and smashed front doors. The cold air was acrid with the smell of fire.

John Pratt trailed along, fascinated. These were the City's power brokers, and he was appalled by their genial indifference. "What you wanted someone to say was, 'Dammit, this isn't going to go another block.' Instead, it was just a lot of cocktail talk about the weather and the mouthing of conventions like, 'Oh, doesn't this remind you of Berlin after World War II?' But the press wasn't at all interested in the abandoned buildings or Gennie Brooks. They were completely absorbed by Herman Badillo, who was running for mayor, and whatever might come out of his mouth."[4]

Gennie Brooks, with her white bullhorn, explained the reasons for the fires as the group stopped at one vandalized empty hulk after another. The impassive faces of the visitors and their polite indifference infuriated dapper Eae James Mitchell. He grabbed the bullhorn and began screaming epithets. Everyone ignored his rantings. As one observer pointed out, "How much surprise could they express? Can they say that something is going on right in the middle of their city and this is the first time they're seeing it? The first time they've heard about it?"

But Mrs. Brooks, usually enthusiastic, was stunned. "No one, but no one, was interested. Everyone thought that because this was a predominantly minority area it was just junkies and welfare folks. No one in authority was trying to combat arson."[5]

There was a follow-up poster campaign aimed at the hearts and minds of the community, an educational effort to explain the consequences of the fires. A thousand copies each of five different posters were distributed. On them local luminaries like Badillo gazed out, exhorting, "Fires are destroying our homes and ruining our businesses. Join with us to save our neighborhood. Prevent fires." There was still no mention of arson, just words about the need "to decrease the number of fires and false alarms and crime by uplifting and renewing pride in Seabury and the South Bronx community."[6]

Although Brooks, Pratt, and everyone else knew perfectly well that arson was the real issue, City officials "still did not want to admit it," she says. On April 7, 1974, when most of Charlotte Street and the surrounding blocks had fallen in ruins, a reporter from the *Daily News* managed to write a story about the poster campaign in the neighborhood without once mentioning arson. The story, entitled "Series of Small Fires Licks a Neighborhood," described the devastation and Brooks's campaign, but it maintained the official line. It read: "Why do fires eat up poor neighborhoods with such intensity and not middle- and high-income areas? The reasons vary, depending on who gives the answers, but the basic causes are generally agreed upon by all. Both fire officials and community leaders cite general apathy and lack of education in fire prevention as a major cause. Many residents frequently leave empty paint or gas cans with rags and garbage in hallways or rear yards. Another point cited is the dire need of repairs in many buildings which have been abandoned by landlords, rather than paying the taxes they owe. Many tenants remain in these buildings. Other landlords have their tenants mail rents to a post office box number. In most cases the superintendent does not even know the name or address of the landlord. In these cases, fire hazards quickly develop in the buildings and are not corrected, it was charged by community residents." The article ended with this sentence: "Firemen tell of people standing in the street, with their luggage, as fire engines pull up to extinguish a blaze in their apartment building."

The concomitant and widespread practice of nonpayment of rent by welfare tenants — and the consequent economic demise of buildings they lived in — represented as serious a problem as arson. Eae James Mitchell waged a fruitless battle to recoup all the unpaid welfare rents in two large buildings he managed. When Mitchell demanded that the welfare department pay $1,195.50 owed by one tenant, who claimed she wasn't getting her housing allowance from the department, an agency director wrote back: "The collection/payment of rent is a landlord/tenant relation. Our agency cannot guarantee payments of rent by a recipient of public assistance. We regret that we are unable to provide you with satisfaction in this matter."[7] Two-party checks sent to the tenant to be turned over to the landlord for rent were a very controversial issue. Their mere existence said that the family could not handle its finances, and it undermined the one piece of leverage the tenant had with the landlord. Very few such checks were issued, and those, too, could be sold by the tenant (rather than paid to the landlord) for about half their face value.

Mitchell discovered that the welfare department itself, when dealing with clients far behind in their rent, was advising that they simply move without paying. When one welfare tenant, evicted after falling $717.15 behind in her rent, inflicted $946 worth of damage to the apartment, Mitchell again wrote to the welfare department. "We wish to find out if there is some

This is the same view of Faile Street, taken in 1984, showing the abandoned apartment buildings. Virtually all the ground-floor windows and doors have been sealed with cement blocks to deter vandals and strippers. The trees that once lined both sides of the block are gone and a trash fire burns unheeded down the street.

This photograph, taken probably in the 1920s, shows Faile Street at 165th Street, looking east toward Westchester Avenue

way of recoupment that we can get for this damage, for we feel that she should be penalized in some manner. This is happening more and more in the Bronx, where tenants flagrantly abuse welfare privileges, destroy and then go on to destroy others. We sincerely hope something can be done in this matter."[8] Nothing was.

(In 1978 a City comptroller's audit found that 80 percent of welfare families in a random sample of City-owned buildings had not paid rent for as long as six months. Unlike Mitchell, City building managers at that time made almost no effort to recoup or dispossess.)

It was becoming obvious that the recurring cycle of drugs, crime, fires, abandonment, and more fires was almost out of control. Urban planners privately reassured worried local officials that the devastation would not leap such major hurdles as the Cross-Bronx Expressway or the large public housing projects farther west and north. Community affairs cop Jack Flanagan remembers meetings with City planners. "They just didn't understand the speed, the scope, the size of it. We dumb cops tried to tell them what was happening, but they had their models and theories and they told us it didn't work that way."[9]

What contributed substantially to the sense of despair was President Nixon's decision in early 1973 to freeze all federal housing monies. This caused a major catastrophe in the South Bronx, where a whole slew of long-planned Model Cities projects were stopped cold. Acres upon acres that had been cleared and readied for new construction — at great cost in disruption to the surrounding blocks — turned into weed lots.

The South Bronx Model Cities program had revved up briefly under Victor Marrero's direction. When he moved on to a bigger job in early 1972, the factions began fighting again over who would control Model Cities. During a year of feuding, only the South Bronx Community Housing Corporation, Marrero's cherished creation, continued to be productive. Eventually, Ramon Velez installed his own man at the helm of Model Cities, a man undistinguished by anything but loyalty to Ramon. "With Velez everything is politicized," explained

one former employee. "He hires people who are not competent, but are willing to play his politics. When he does get
someone good they quit because they cannot lower themselves
to be his puppets. In that way, he destroys everything he
touches." Ramon's control certainly dissipated whatever momentum the program had gained under Marrero, but in a way
it was too late, because the feds had lost interest. Community
block grants would emerge as the device to replace Model
Cities, one that gave equal weight to the suburbs, Republican
constituencies.

Again and again Velez cleverly enlarged his domain by
gaining de facto control of other organizations. As the boards
or officers were elected or appointed, Velez made sure his
loyalists were among them, until he gained a voting majority
and control. Using this quiet method, he soon managed to
seize control of the South Bronx Community Housing Corporation, but Velez had no skill in administration. It fell apart.
The corporation's management of one Bronx housing project
was such a disaster that the Department of Housing and Urban
Development, which held the mortgage, issued an ultimatum
to Velez to get professional managers in or face a total cutoff
of funds. Banks threatened to call in mortgages when payments were missed. The corporation's management of its own
affairs was so feckless that it was ultimately evicted from its
own headquarters for nonpayment of rent. Over the years,
Velez and his agencies weathered endless audits in which "ir-
regularities" and mismanagement were cited, but no one has
ever been indicted. One official who has known Ramon Velez
twenty years says, "Ramon is a complete enigma to me. I
don't know if he's for the community, as he says, or for himself."

As for the opportunities lost in Model Cities, Father Gigante rolls his eyes and groans. "It was stupid, stupid. By
their antics we lost. If we had been good boys, if we had been
able to keep the peace, the City would have let us do what
we wanted to do. We could have done a lot of good."[10] The
three great legacies of the Model Cities era were the South
Bronx Community Housing Corporation (which, before Velez

ruined it, had built or renovated more than two thousand units of housing), the five thousand local students who attended college on Model Cities scholarships, and the raised consciousness that integrated thousands of local residents into "the system." Remembers one veteran: "We found out where City Hall was and how to conduct a meeting with Robert's Rules of Order. Those were major advances."

Some believed that many landlords who had counted on the Model Cities program to buy them out, or to improve their areas, now gave up and turned to arson to solve their financial predicaments. And so the fires raged.

Frustrated and angry, a group of Catholic clergy banded together in mid-1974. Father Neil A. Connolly, vicar of the South Bronx, was the instigator. Other members were Father Gigante, who had recouped from his unsuccessful run for Congress, started his own political club, and been elected the city councilman from his district. Father Smith from Saint John's also joined. Under pressure from the priests, the police department and fire department agreed to look into the fires and arson.

In January 1975 Father Connolly received a one-and-a-half-page report from this new Bronx Arson Task Force about its findings. The report read: "Two fire marshals, two detectives, and one sergeant conducted an intelligence-type investigation to determine whether the fires in vacant buildings in the South Bronx represent an organized conspiracy or are the result of vandalism. Their investigation, conducted from August 12, 1974, through October 8, 1974, indicates that conspiracy is a probable cause of many of the fires.

"During a one-month period, while operating in the South Bronx area, the Task Force interviewed community leaders, interested citizens, tenants in the vicinity of suspicious fires involving vacant buildings, Model Cities employees, gas station owners, members of the service and the Bronx district attorney's office and others in an effort to determine the cause of fires in vacant buildings." The Bronx Arson Task Force concluded that there were significant incentives to arson, and further reported that "nearly all the people felt that many of the fires were started by paid arsonists, but none would give specifics as to who they were or who was paying them." It recommended that investigators be available on a twenty-four-hour basis so they could arrive at the scene of a suspicious fire as it burned. Already, during the Bronx Arson Task Force's brief existence, there had been a marked reduction in fires. "It may be surmised that this had been brought about due to the knowledge of the task force's existence, the many conferences with community leaders, and the frequent surveillance of persons suspected."[11]

The South Bronx Church Coalition decided this situation was serious enough to warrant alerting the Justice Department. Father Connolly was delegated to contact Paul Curran, then the U.S. attorney for the Southern District of New York. Father Connolly wrote on January 29, 1975, and asked if someone from that office could meet with the coalition. Curran declined to get involved, saying it was a matter for the local authorities.

Meanwhile the coalition discovered, to their dismay, that the Bronx Arson Task Force had been disbanded in mid-January. The clergy demanded a meeting with Bronx District Attorney Mario Merola and Borough President Robert Abrams. The clergy threatened, if the meeting was not granted, to hold a press conference denouncing the officials as Neros, who were fiddling while the Bronx burned. Merola and Abrams agreed to meet and invited representatives of the police department, fire, welfare, and housing. The clergy wanted to know why the task force had been disbanded in the wake of its damning report.

The gathering convened on March 13, 1975, in the district attorney's office at the Bronx County Courthouse on the Grand Concourse. Father Connolly led the attack, laying out all the reasons arson had become a lucrative practice in the South Bronx. Government policies actually encouraged arson. The Housing Development Agency's well-known preference for awarding rehab monies to already-vacant buildings meant that an owner could look forward to fire insurance and, once having emptied the building, to receiving a government-backed renovation of the damaged apartment house. (Later one investigator from the district attorney's office calculated that the owner and developer of a two-hundred unit building stood to earn $1 million in profit from combined fire insurance and tax shelter sales to finance its rehabilitation.) The coalition also complained about the welfare department's practice of, in effect, rewarding clients who were burned out.

None of this was new. Most of the people at the meeting had heard Gennie Brooks say the same things more than a year earlier, although by now there was more emphasis on the rehabilitation–tax shelter aspect. Both Bronx Fire Chief Francis Carruthers and Bronx Police Commander Anthony Bouza said they saw no pattern to the fires, nor any point to a task force. Chief Bouza wrote off the fires to social conditions no one could control or affect. (Bouza was an attractive and articulate cop who delighted the press by dubbing his men "an army of occupation of the ghetto" and local gangs "feral youth.") Both Carruthers and Bouza said they saw no reason to reinstate the task force. When the coalition expressed its ire and astonishment, Bouza and Carruthers shrugged their shoulders. If they wanted an arson task force that much, fine, they could have it. (Why did the coalition succeed where Gennie Brooks had failed? Perhaps because a lone black woman with some interesting credentials could not equal the clout of white men, some of them priests vested with the considerable authority of the Catholic church.)

At this point a young assistant district attorney named F. Giles Giovinazzi spoke up to observe that in the whole discussion he had not once heard the officials say they wanted to *stop* the fires. He had researched the arson issue, and he believed the policies of the welfare and housing departments were encouraging arson, in that there was definitely profit to be made by burning buildings and then rehabbing them.

District Attorney Mario Merola, a man with extraordinary winglike eyebrows, declared that a new Bronx Task Force would be formed. He asked the coalition, whose pressure had been the catalyst for official recognition of the fires and arson, to allow him and borough President Abrams to handle the press. Looking back on this years later, Father Connolly laughed cynically. "Abrams and Merola really took us. When they asked about the press we were stupid and said, 'Fine.' We should have controlled it. Merola, who had said when we first came to him, 'Fires? What fires?' came out looking like the great arson battler."[12]

Two weeks later, arson, which had never been so much as mentioned by any official as a problem, suddenly became the great Bronx cause celèbre. The first press release made for ironic reading, for by this time most of the neighborhoods around Hunt's Point and Morrisania had already burned down. Abrams and Merola noted in their release that the "startling increase in destruction of Bronx housing by fire" necessitated the formation of a special task force. "The culprits, whether isolated or part of a concerted effort, must be rooted out, tried and convicted in order to prevent the further destruction of one of our country's most basic resources — housing."[13] It was wonderful how completely officialdom had come to share the concerns raised by the Bronx Church Coalition. (But well they might. Fires in their borough had tripled, from 11,185 in 1960 to 33,465 in 1974.)

When borough officials finally declared war on arson and fires, most of the old East Bronx (by now enclosed in the spread of the South Bronx) had turned into a gutted ruin, devoured and demolished by the angry god of flames. At least, however, from that moment forward the burning Bronx was constantly in the news. The landlord of 1062 Faile Street was arrested after he was spotted at two in the morning with five-gallon gasoline cans just before a second-floor apartment burst into flames. Another group of men was nabbed with an incendiary device in the wee hours just blocks from a group of tenements owned by one of them. Another landlord and his son were seized with five Molotov cocktails in a vacant building they owned. Day after day the fires, completely ignored for the previous seven years, were avidly reported, complete with heartbreaking feature stories on the terrible toll they exacted on their innocent victims: Mrs. Lucy Rodriguez, a $142-a-week warehouse worker, was described numbly sur-

Residents in nightclothes flee their
burning building at 174th Street and
Southern Boulevard in 1974

BOTANICA MERCADO 1A
LA MILAGROSA

Firemen train their hose on an old wooden family
house consumed by flames in a 1972 fire

veying the charred, soggy mess that represented the remains of her worldly goods, for which she had toiled nineteen years.

With the media spotlight suddenly trained on the burning Bronx, the public pressure for results intensified. The churches in particular turned on the heat. Episcopal Bishop Paul Moore, Jr., strongly questioned the City's commitment in an address May 10 to the Episcopal Convention. "It seems incredible that they are unable to stop this rash of fires," he said from the pulpit of the Cathedral of Saint John the Divine. "The investigation seems to have no muscle. The South Bronx seems to have been redlined, chalked off. One day last week there were fourteen fires in the South Bronx alone. There were three hundred a month or more in the City of New York. We challenge the City, the fire marshals, the district attorney, the police, to intensify their investigation. Our city is being burned down in front of our very eyes. What good is it to have the struggling housing programs we try to have growing out of our life together, when each week more houses are burned down than we can build?"[14]

Ten days later Cardinal Terence Cooke, one of the most influential churchmen in the country and a native of the Bronx, spoke out just as strongly, designating May 25 as Stop Fire Sunday. Backing up his priests, who had forced the issue in the first place, the cardinal decried the "alarming situation that confronts us. Nowhere is this tragedy more terrifying than in the South Bronx, where whole areas looked like the burntout ruins of war. . . . The ominous wail of sirens has become a terrifying part of people's lives. There is one building in the Bronx in which families live in constant fear because just last week the building next door was set on fire seven times. . . . If in fact there is a conspiracy, it is a ruthless crime which calls out for punishment."[15]

District Attorney Merola and borough President Abrams responded by stepping up their efforts, writing various federal authorities, including FBI director Clarence Kelley, to ask for assistance. "Last Monday night, the fire problem reached a new high, with an outbreak of forty fires in a three-hour period, eighteen of which were described as major by fire officials. Fighting these fires drained the entire borough of its fire-fighting capability, and even required pulling in sixteen units from the rest of New York City. . . . It seems clear from the pattern of these fires that many are the result of arson."[16] The FBI again declined to get involved, like all the other federal agencies, so the fires blazed night after night, with a now-fascinated press keeping close tabs.

The City stepped up its efforts. The Bronx Arson Task Force (whose cops and firemen were by now no longer speaking to each other) was to be supplemented by a strike force under the aegis of Deputy Mayor Stanley Friedman, a Bronxite who had quietly worked his way up from his early days as a member of the Pondiac Club. The strike force would "establish a computerized arson intelligence system that would use insurance information and other data to identify landlords, tenants and individuals who are cashing in on the fires."[17] Meanwhile the number of arson arrests increased, but so did the fires. Those who might have pondered cashing in were moving swiftly before the crackdown became effective.

In 1974 the energy crisis had struck. The price of oil, once a minor cost in running a building, had tripled. In time it would soar from 6 percent of the total cost to 40 percent. Many landlords who had survived the lean years of rent control, rising taxes, and then Vietnam War inflation, could not absorb the soaring price of oil. More buildings were abandoned, which provided more fuel for the fires.

By mid-June eight more arson indictments were handed down, including one of a man who had collected $125,000 in fire insurance from twenty-one different fires in both the Bronx and Brooklyn. As the antiarson campaign intensified, two fire marshals were shot while tracking a suspect to an apartment. He burst forth, guns blazing, clad only in boxer shorts.

On July 13, 1975, the august *New York Times Magazine* ran a story on arson, "Raking the Ashes of the Epidemic of Flame," detailing the difficulties of gaining convictions in "the fastest growing crime in America." In another story, two Bronx youngsters, ten and fifteen years old, confessed cheerfully to setting forty or fifty fires for as little as three dollars, although they insisted they drew the line at occupied buildings. "For most of Hector's career as an arsonist, he said he never worried about getting caught. But now, Hector said, 'The cops are starting to get warmer, they're starting to get mean. I mean they're starting to work. Before they used to see somebody back inside a building and they'd just keep going. Now, they see anything like that and they come after you.' "[18]

All the incentives to arson remained intact, however. The insurance companies continued to pay out all claims and raise everybody's rates rather than challenge a claimant and risk a lawsuit. The welfare department never questioned even those applicants who had had several suspicious fires. Banks sold foreclosed mortgages for minimal sums to dubious characters. Junkies and vandals still mined empty buildings for their valuable materials. True, some people were apprehended and made an example to society, but the risks were nearly negligible. Arson and the destruction of buildings continued to be extremely lucrative.

Where, one might ask, were the political leaders of the South Bronx while it burned? Why was it the Catholic clergy who had to force the officials into action? Ramon Velez, the great organizer and community activist, says he was powerless to do anything. "I was not connected to City Hall and real estate. I could not get involved because it was a law enforcement situation. I knew it was happening. I walked the street, I got calls. I had emergency shelter in my offices. But you had no control, it was something that hit you from left field."[19]

Ultimately, Ramon did not feel the fires were that important. "The physical destruction is inconsequential," he explains. "I care about my children being able to walk the streets and not be ashamed of their culture and their roots. I'm saying, don't steal my identity. Don't implant your values. I'd rather have no housing than sell my soul."[20]

Mike Nunez, a longtime Velez ally, says: "Somehow, we still saw a lot of people and buildings and we didn't mobilize around it. Before we knew it, we accepted the fires as an everyday occurrence. Then one day, there it was on the World

Series [this was not until October of 1977], Howard Cosell telling the world the Bronx is burning down. That was the shock, when it hit me."[21]

Herman Badillo, borough president and then congressman during these years, says he never conferred with the Bronx's power brokers in banking, insurance, and real estate to talk about how to stop the fires. "Not at all," he says. "Because you see, I was the enemy to them. I was Puerto Rican."[22]

District Attorney Mario Merola, when he did finally launch the antiarson campaign, found the local leaders indifferent. "When we went to the community we ran into tough resistance. They refused to cooperate, to give me the torches. There was such deprivation, they didn't want to help me in the prosecutions. There is not one minority leader that spoke out against the arson [he is obviously forgetting Gennie Brooks here]. The way out of their dilemma was burn, baby, burn. The community leaders all wanted money to be invested the day *after* the fire."[23]

25

The Grand Concourse
1965–1969

As the Charlotte Street neighborhood emptied out, along with the areas to the south and north, its residents began moving west toward the Grand Concourse, an avenue that had always symbolized success. Now it also signified safety, for no one could imagine that the kinds of fires and crime that had wracked the old East Bronx, and finally destroyed it, could possibly be unleashed on that most wonderful of boulevards, with its art deco buildings and rows of shade trees.

This image was dangerously outdated, however, for the Grand Concourse, the pride of the Bronx, was suffering the early stages of the devastation disease. Those who moved onto or near the Grand Concourse in the early 1970s saw the Champs Élysées of the Bronx sadly diminished in splendor.

The downfall was most immediately apparent in the belle of the boulevard, the Concourse Plaza Hotel. Once the home of famous ballplayers and eminent judges, host to presidents and the borough's social elite, the Concourse Plaza's guest roster was now made up almost exclusively of welfare families, who, burned out of their homes in the East Bronx, were housed temporarily in the hotel by the Red Cross and the department of relocation.

On July 11, 1957, Frank Kridel had announced the sale of the Concourse Plaza Hotel to Nassau Management Company. For a couple of years, the tall, handsome "innkeeper" had been talking privately about getting the hell out of the Bronx and into greener pastures. "There was almost a sinister quality to what he was saying," remembers Gerry Doyle, a local weekly newspaper editor, "because the Bronx seemed to be thriving."[1] But Eugene Lynn, Kridel's banquet manager, who departed with him, remembers that the Bronx real estate men had hinted to Kridel that he might think about getting out while the getting was good. The borough's future, in their opinion, did not look bright. Publicly, Kridel said he had sold the Concourse Plaza so he could devote himself full time to renovating and managing the Hotel Manhattan near Times Square. The Concourse Plaza was sold to the Nassau Management Corporation for $1.25 million.

When Kridel left he took his best employees, his athletes, and his glamour with him. He told the *World-Telegram,* in a big feature on his new theater district hotel, "My bookings indicate that already a good number of my teams will follow me here. No matter what time of year you stroll through the lobby, you will see headline athletes."[2] To add insult to injury, Kridel even took the Welcome Home Yankees Dinner downtown. Bronxites, who considered the Yankees their team, felt betrayed and angry. Fathers who had proudly taken their sons to the dinner year after year stayed away to show their displeasure and hurt. "It was a slap in the face," said one.

By late January 1958 the new owners of the Concourse Plaza were already close to bankruptcy. Nassau Management owed thirty-three thousand dollars in unpaid City taxes on the hotel and had failed to meet a seventeen-thousand-dollar mortgage payment in mid-January. At a raucous meeting the 250 small investors who had recently provided the purchase price for the Concourse Plaza elected a steering committee called Interim Operations, Inc., to ensure the hotel's continued operation until a financial rescue could be effected. Renovations then in progress were abandoned, leaving the main entrance without a door. All through the winter, makeshift sheets and boards did little to keep out the freezing winds that swirled up from the river and into the plush lobby.

By late April a new syndicate had stepped in to buy the Concourse Plaza and rescue it from its financial limbo, and by summer these owners, headed by Philip P. Zipes and Charles Fuchs, had arranged a $4.5 million thirty-year lease with a new management group. The new hotel manager was Jack Schmertzler, and the new caterer was Joseph Kahn. The two operations were now totally separate. Although the new management made extensive renovations, they simply did not possess the flair and zealous attention to detail that had distinguished Kridel. Winnie Corbin, Kridel's chief telephone operator, hadn't been able to bring herself to leave the Concourse Plaza. She loved the hotel and, furthermore, it was close to where she lived. To her the difference between the old and the new was simple: "Service was put on the shelf."[3]

In October 1965 the Concourse Plaza Hotel once again changed hands: Charles Fuchs and his partners sold to Joseph Caspi. The new owner was a manufacturer of women's sportswear in the Bronx who wanted to quit the garment business in order to find a less grueling way to make a living. A tall man with silvery hair and a thin Adolph Menjou mustache, Caspi was given to wearing diamond rings and driving Lincoln Continentals. He was a boy from the Bronx who had made good, a genial man who cherished his own memories of going to the beautiful Concourse Plaza for weddings and other big family celebrations. He had never dabbled in real estate at all, and he could not believe his good fortune in acquiring the hotel. "I bought it as an investment," he said years later. "I had nothing to do with running or managing it. The caterer had the ballrooms, and the operator had a thirty-year lease, and the bar and grill was leased to someone else. I bought it subject to the various leases. I just took over the ownership." In the first years of his proprietorship, Caspi would stroll through his domain, admiring the huge hotel that now belonged to him. He says he had no inkling that a precipitous slide was imminent. "When I bought the hotel in 1965 the area was great. Fuchs may have seen the changes taking place, but he was very experienced in real estate and I wasn't. I would never have bought it if I had known the neighborhood would change."[4]

In fact, the Fuchs group had sold the hotel only months after a *New York Times* article appeared on February 2, 1965, about the avenue's declining image. The headline was "Once-Grand Concourse," and the subhead, "The Avenue: A Symbol of Prosperity Has Grown Old and Causes Concern." The story, replete with map and photograph, was gentle and good-natured in tone and quoted lamentations of longtime residents. "Once it was a big achievement to live on the Concourse. It was a big step up in life. When I first came up and saw the Concourse there were trees all over. Oh, it was beautiful. Now it's changed; it's older. It's not so beautiful."[5]

The *Times* story was an affectionate portrayal of Bronx Jewish culture at its height tinged with regret that the old ways were fading. It only hinted at more serious problems. One rabbi was quoted as saying, "We find the windows of the stores smashed in with a little too much frequency now." A woman admitted, "I'm afraid now, why shouldn't I be? You read so much in the papers now. Is the Concourse so different from any other place?" And then, far down in the story, a single paragraph, "Of course, a lot of people moving away are simply afraid of integration. Negroes are moving into the side streets, and a lot of people who aren't admitting it are just plain frightened."

Many longtime residents had already moved out of fear, based not on vague apprehensions or racism but specific incidents. Donald Darcy, president of the North Side Savings Bank, had lived at 940 Grand Concourse, but he moved regretfully to the suburbs in 1965. "What chased most people was crime. I had two sons, both of whom were mugged in Joyce Kilmer Park on the Concourse. I asked one of my sons to go get a bulldog edition of the *Daily News* around the corner at the candy store and he saw two teenage girls thrown to the ground by a black teenage purse snatcher. He chased the kid into the park and caught him with the help of another man. That night my wife said to me she was afraid something was going to happen to our children. Everyone was having experiences of this kind."[6] Crime was usually the decisive factor in the decision to move: the YWHA director whose doorman was murdered, the assemblyman who found his lobby smeared with blood two mornings in a row, the trust fund director whose wife was shoved down some stairs by teenage toughs.

Darcy's service as a grand juror gave him ample opportunity to grasp the overall trend. "I remember at Webster Avenue two women were killed, and so they started tenant patrols and people would keep watch in the lobbies. Then when they saw someone walking down the block they would go and escort them home. But that is a helluva way to live. You can't have a cop on every corner."[7] People moved, even at the cost of giving up cheap apartments and the comfortable world of their block and neighborhood.

On July 21, 1966, the *New York Times* ran a front-page story in the second section, the headline of which read, "Grand Concourse: Hub of the Bronx Is Undergoing Ethnic Changes." The subheads read, "Transition Felt to Be Posing Threat to Stability of Area" (changed in later editions to "Nearby Slums Encroach on Old Prestigious Area") and "City Seeking to Halt the Flight of Whites from the Section." One photograph showed a closed shop, Mrs. Graber's Kosher Home Cooking, with a big sign: "Store For Rent."

Alan V. Davies, whose grandfather J. Clarence Davies had been a major developer of the Bronx, was sitting in the family's Manhattan real estate office with his father when the *Times* arrived. They still had extensive holdings in the Bronx. "I remember it vividly," says Davies. "I had only been in the business a few years and so I didn't understand the power of the press. But my father had spent his life in real estate and he was very astute. When he saw the story he was furious. He had gone to school with Orville Dryfoos, who was then editor of the *Times*. I remember he immediately called Dryfoos and told him the paper had done a terrible thing. I remember him saying, 'Your paper will be responsible for the ruination of this neighborhood with that story.'"[8]

Irma Fleck, a longtime community activist who lived in a penthouse on the Grand Concourse, remembers the awful sinking feeling she had as she read the *Times* story. "Here was the *New York Times* saying the Grand Concourse is going.

It was a self-fulfilling prophecy. Landlords read that article and the real estate market fell immediately. No one wants to live in a neighborhood the *Times* has said is becoming a slum. Everyone wanted to flee."[9]

The 1965 *Times* story about the "changing" Concourse had been affectionate and lighthearted, but the 1966 article told a grim story, a steady drumbeat of doom. It began, "Hands behind his back, Rabbi Theodore Robinson swayed slightly, as Orthodox Jews do when they pray, and watched the traffic on the Grand Concourse. 'The neighborhood is deteriorating, there's no getting away from it,' he said with a shrug. 'We had 140 families seven years ago and now we have 60. Even the big synagogues on the avenue are having trouble.'

"On 167th Street, Hyman Hans leaned on the white enamel counter of his kosher butcher shop and said: 'Three shops closed around here last month. You couldn't buy a single store on this block 10 years ago for any amount of money. Now they'd give it to you.' "

The article went on to say that Co-op City, a gigantic development being built in the far reaches of the northeast Bronx, reported that a sizable number of the first five thousand applications had come from the Concourse.

The young adults of the Concourse had left or were leaving. When their aging parents moved to the suburbs or retired to Florida, there was not a second generation of Jews to fill those vacated apartments. "The landlords decided to accept Negroes rather than vacancies," one real estate man told the *Times*. The arrival of black tenants coincided with a new laxity in services from both the landlords and the City. In a few apartment houses, a new kind of tenant was being installed — the welfare family. "They've started to blockbust some buildings here," said one aide to a local congressman.

Six months later, in February 1967, the *New York Post* ran a story portraying the siege mentality gripping the Concourse. "The fatal stabbing and beating of Philip Lewis of 1155 Walton Ave. by an unidentified Negro thief Monday night sent shock waves through the community," the story reported, and went on to detail the "sad atmosphere of fear and friction in a '6 p.m.' neighborhood whose residents are mostly elderly Jews who live in terror of muggers and thieves, and Negro and Puerto Rican newcomers who feel unwelcome and isolated."[10]

Three weeks later the *New York Post* ran yet another story, "City Fights White Exodus from Grand Concourse," explaining a suggested plan for the City to rent thousands of apartments along the boulevard when they would be emptied by families moving to Co-op City in late 1968. The City would attempt to attract white families and maintain an integrated neighborhood. Nothing came of this unwieldy proposal, nor had anything come of the programs proposed seven months earlier when the *Times* ran its grim story. Borough President Badillo demanded that the South and Central Bronx be included in the Model Cities program and that large areas be designated for rehabilitation and urban renewal. He criticized the City for allowing Co-op City to be built without "first considering its impact on the total Bronx housing picture."[11]

Co-op City was to be the world's largest cooperative apartment complex, housing sixty thousand people. Its 15,375 apartments in thirty-five massive high-rise buildings would be spread out on a former swamp bounded by three expressways. The United Housing Foundation, a nonprofit group of labor unions, civic associations, and other like-minded organizations, was building this colossal new city on the abandoned precincts of Freedomland, a defunct amusement park.

As Co-op City rose, architecture and planning critics vigorously panned it as "fairly hideous" and "a disgrace to humanity." It was so far north and east that not even the subway went there. The purchase price was right, however — $450 down per room, plus a monthly maintenance charge of $35 a room. That added up to $1,575 down on three and a half rooms and $123 a month in maintenance. Buyers lined up by the thousands. When Co-op City prepared to open its first thirty-three hundred apartments in late 1968, it had on file ten thousand applications, including seven thousand from the Bronx. Four thousand were reported to be from the central Bronx and the Grand Concourse.

"A lot of people are trying to escape from something,"

Harold Ostroff, executive vice-president of the United Housing Foundation, told the *Times*. "They are running, as so many have been running, from changing neighborhoods."[12] When word got out that the City was contemplating buying a block of apartments at Co-op City to rerent them to low-income families, hundreds of people deluged the foundation's switchboard with calls. Even though the foundation reassured everyone that it was not participating in any such plan, fifty buyers withdrew their deposits.

In 1965 another large co-op development, Concourse Village, had opened just off the lower Grand Concourse between East 150th and 158th streets. Established Concourse residents viewed this huge complex as an unwanted "bridge" to the bad neighborhoods farther east and south. When a doorman was murdered at 800 Grand Concourse shortly after the "Village" opened, the two events were irrationally but inextricably linked.

Alarmed at the growing panic on the Grand Concourse and the vision of thousands of Jewish residents decamping en masse for Co-op City, the prestigious American Jewish Congress had undertaken its own study, including interviews with more than five hundred people: building superintendents, residents, property owners, real estate brokers, and officials at lending institutions.

Its report, "The Grand Concourse, Promise and Change," issued in November 1967, concluded, "When the data were analyzed, it became clear that the fears, the rumors, and the predictions about the demise of the Concourse had little basis in fact." It found that, contrary to popular notion, 75 percent of the residents were still white, and in buildings facing the Concourse 95 percent of the residents were still white. Those black and Puerto Rican families moving in were small and stable and middle class. The local housing was well maintained. Where it had deteriorated the fault was the landlord's, not the tenants'. The turnover rate of 10 percent belied the reports of white flight, which was also reflected in the low vacancy rate (1 percent). Most important, it said that Co-op City would not "have a significant impact on the Concourse.

In direct contradiction to the report in the *New York Post,*
Co-op City management told us that only 15 percent of the
applicants are from the Concourse area. The fear of a mass
exodus appears totally unfounded."[13]

On the paramount issue of crime, the report said, "Crime
rates, while increasing, are lower in the Concourse area (and
increasing more slowly) than for the city or the Bronx as a
whole." Yet when it amplified this the congress was far more
wishy-washy. "Crime on the Concourse has increased (as it
has throughout the city, state, and nation) but it is not at all
clear why. Whether this increase is due to improved crime
reporting or rising tensions within the society or combinations
of these and other factors is under careful study by many
experts."[14]

The American Jewish Congress felt that the major reason
the Concourse was getting such a poor name was the fact that
four hundred stores were vacant. They had no explanation,
but conceded that these vacancies, so visible and so dreary,
transmitted "a false and depressing feeling about the community."

The "most perplexing phenomenon" on the Concourse was
discussed last of all — the "apparent collapse of the real estate
market." In New York City a prime piece of rental property
traditionally sold for at least five or six times the annual rent
roll. Yet now even on the Concourse no one could command
more than three or four times the annual rent roll. By the
1960s investors were putting their money into something less
aggravating than rental housing. The American Jewish Congress accepted this as a fact. "If it is said frequently enough
and by enough people that an area is turning into a Negro
slum, many persons will believe it. This is being said on the
Concourse. It is believed by potential buyers who are not
interested in becoming slumlords and who have other places
to put their money."[15] In conclusion, the congress proposed
new investment and rehabilitation, organizing residents, putting the vacant stores to some use, increasing garbage collection and police protection, and promoting better racial relations.

Simeon H. F. Goldstein lived on the Grand Concourse and served as chairman of the local community planning board at this time. The congress's study, he remembers, was done "with the best of intentions," but its effect, for all its calm and optimistic tone, was the exact opposite of what the congress had hoped. "It created a panic," says Goldstein. "Here was an organization to which the average Concourse resident could feel much closer than, say, the *New York Times*. But the solutions were of a nature which could not win the confidence of people of average education and experience. In one synagogue alone thirty-six families moved that year."[16]

The borough responded to the report by setting up an organization called A Better Concourse, Inc., or ABC, which worked with the Lindsay administration. The City furnished a lot of fanfare — rallies, newspaper stories, new motorcycle police patrols, high-density street lights, and redesigning of parks to thwart muggers. But those who were active, including Goldstein, can't remember any lasting results. "There may have been one or two things accomplished, but I can't remember a single, permanent thing." By November 1968, with Co-op City set to open in a month, borough President Badillo, who was positioning himself to run for mayor, denounced the Lindsay administration for not doing "a damn thing about the Concourse — they've done absolutely nothing."

Meanwhile, other local politicians were bluntly counseling their own constituents to move out, reported Samuel M. Goodman in his University of Bridgeport 1981 master's thesis on the Bronx, "The Golden Ghetto." One astounded father remembers his state senator telling a parents' association at the junior high school that "those who could afford to should give serious consideration to relocation."[17] Another woman recalls the day a police official told another meeting of concerned residents that there was not much police could do about crime. "I immediately realized it was over," she said. "It was time to move."

*   *   *

Those who had known the bustling vitality and richesse of the Grand Concourse and Boulevard in its heyday could not watch its fall from grace without sorrow. A 1949 *Commentary* article, "By the Waters of the Grand Concourse," had described "a Jewish community as dense, traditional, and possessive as William Faulkner's Yoknapatawpha County, and through it flows a great middle-class river, the Grand Concourse whose waters . . . carry an irrepressible elan, a flood of self-indulgence and bountiful vitality, vulgar and promiscuous, withal, luxuriant and pleasurable."[18] And this was exactly what Louis Risse hoped for when he envisioned the Grand Concourse: a great "boulevard, a promenade, a drive, an avenue of pleasure . . . and endless processions of family parties enjoying the air, beaux and belles."

All the Bronx landmarks that lined the Grand Concourse contributed to its mystique. The Bronx County Courthouse stood near Yankee Stadium with a day long ebb and flow of judges, lawyers, and officials up and down its terraced marble steps. Across the street, the red-brick-and-limestone Concourse Plaza Hotel overlooked the graceful shaded paths and gardens of Joyce Kilmer Park, prime territory for mothers or maids with children, or serious bench sitters. Parks Department gardeners groomed the hedges and lawns and announced the changing of the seasons with their flowerbeds, from brilliant daffodils and tulips in the spring to the somber chrysanthemums of the fall. At the north end of the park stood a tribute to German Jewish writer Heinrich Heine, the white stone Lorelei Fountain.

On the same west side of the avenue, some blocks farther north, stood the Andrew Freedman Home, an Italian renaissance–style palazzo set in a formal garden. This was the philanthropic legacy of a man who made his fortune building the New York subways and who once owned the New York Giants. It was a retirement home aimed at people of culture and former wealth, for its benefactor feared an impecunious old age. The Andrew Freedman was popularly known as the Home for Poor Millionaires. Almost directly across the broad boulevard was the Hebrew Y, a handsome building of pillars and pediments, a palace of athletic fitness and community spirit.

Continuing north, passing the apartment extravaganzas of art deco, with wraparound windows, bold terracotta tile designs, and stylish bottle glass encircling green and silver entryways, one encountered the majesty of the block-square Roosevelt Gardens, with its fountained courtyard. Several long blocks north stood the prestigious Lewis Morris Apartments, renowned as the Medical Building for its impressive roster of resident doctors and dentists. It occupied an entire block, and its battalions of doormen, elevator operators, and maintenance crews worked to keep the marble and brass gleaming and the privileged tenantry happy. (The back half of the building descended an extra six floors to Walton Avenue, so many residents took the elevator down from the Concourse rather than up.) Again, moving north there was the ultimate movie palace, Loew's (pronounced Lo-wee's) Paradise Theater. No one who ever entered this mammoth temple to filmdom could ever forget its sybaritic gorgeousness. But now the *Times* mourned the demise of the wondrous Loew's Paradise Theater. "A lush red light bathes an empty pond where fat goldfish once swam. Most of the French renaissance furniture and the statuary and paintings are gone. The rugs are tattered and worn. And while stars still twinkle on the ceiling inside the darkened theater, the enormous lobby is curiously empty and ravaged, as if waiting an eventual doom."[19]

Those who had the good fortune to live in the precincts of the Grand Concourse always proclaimed it, evoking suitably impressed responses and murmurings. Even to say "I live just off the Concourse" (pronounced *Konkus*) was a declaration of importance. Those who were not so blessed took comfort in merely strolling its shaded walks. At no time was this more in evidence than the Jewish holidays when families outdid themselves in finery. Women donned extravagant hats and suits in rich fabrics and sumptuous textures, topped by a thick fur stole or jacket. They paraded proudly on the arms of their dark-suited husbands, greeting their neighbors and acquaintances, shepherding their children before them.

Now one realized that the holiday strollers were meager in number; there was little sense of a festive crowd. The holiday greetings were likely to be followed by whispered exchanges of the latest news on who had moved or been mugged. It was all so hard to believe, and yet it was true. The Jews were leaving the Concourse.

26

The Hotel and the Concourse
1969–1976

As the Jews left, the institutions that had been pivotal to their world foundered. The Concourse Plaza was one of the first to feel the impact, as many of its longtime clientele disappeared. By 1968, however, the hotel's manager, Jack Schmertzler, found a response to the financial decline. As the fires and arson escalated in the East Bronx, the Third Alarmers, a voluntary organization, escorted homeless families to the hotel every night. Many of these people were welfare clients, and the City, hard-pressed to find them new homes, asked the hotel if they could be put up on a long-term basis. Schmertzler, delighted, began charging for a week's stay what permanent residents had paid for a month. The New York Yankees, who had always lived at the hotel in season, arrived to find their usual suites full of dispossessed families. They drifted off, making arrangements to stay elsewhere. Joseph Caspi, the hotel's owner, says he was most displeased by this turn of events. "When they started bringing in all these welfare people I tried to break the lease. Any dispute had to go to further arbitration, but I had no teeth in my lease. We went to arbitration and we lost. Schmertzler was making a fortune. He was putting up three, four, five, six people in a room and charging per head. They were milking it to the hilt."[1]

With the once-grand Concourse Plaza turning into a welfare hotel, caterer Joseph Kahn found it difficult to keep up his business there. Wedding parties and business meetings in the Gold Room or the Wedgwood Room were a bit taken aback by unsupervised kids dashing in and out. Try as Kahn would, he could not impose order. Valued clients like the Bronx Rotary, which had met at the hotel for fifty years, fled the premises and convened their weekly get-togethers elsewhere. Mary Johnston, a waitress who started working at the hotel in 1947, remembers coming to work one day in July 1970 to find a padlock on the kitchen door: Kahn had declared bankruptcy.

This precipitated a major crisis for hotel owner Caspi. Kahn had paid one hundred thousand dollars a year for his lease, and now he was kaput. "Everything I had was tied up in that hotel," recalls Caspi. "I was really panicked." Caspi took over the banquet rooms, closed the kitchen, and concentrated on booking bingo games and dances to which people brought their own liquor. "It became an all-black thing," says Caspi, "churches or promotional dances, and they would pay me a thousand to fifteen hundred dollars and provide their own entertainment and music. It was fantastic. I ran these things myself and I loved it. For a while everything was going fine, but the remaining white people in the neighborhood were raising hell because all these functions brought in more black faces than ever before, and they did not like that. A lot of judges lived in the neighborhood and they used every tactic imaginable to take my license away. They said the hotel was the cause of muggings."[2]

In the hotel itself, welfare families were filling the rooms and Schmertzler's coffers. By the summer of 1970 one hundred welfare families were in residence and the hotel was charging the city $273 a week for a single room. One woman and her six children, who had been burned out of their apartment by junkies, lived at the hotel for six months waiting for the city to find them somewhere to live. The bill for their room was fifty-one hundred dollars. To encourage this steady source of income, the hotel rented an office in the lobby to the Department of Relocation.

When welfare hotels around the City came in for bad publicity, precipitated by the scandal of welfare clients being lodged at the Waldorf-Astoria, the Concourse Plaza attracted its share of unwelcome attention. By 1971 it was charging $446 a week for a family of eight. In contrast, the elegant New York Hilton billed only $406 a week for two rooms, while a Holiday Inn cost $322. Small fires were a constant problem at the Concourse Plaza, as was theft of anything not nailed or soldered down. One errant Canadian tourist who wandered into the hotel for a two-day stay in July 1971 described it as "the dirtiest I've ever seen."

On the morning of August 20, 1971, Simeon Miller, forty-four, the resident manager of the hotel, dashed upstairs just after eight o'clock to stop a man who was beating a woman. Someone summoned the police, but by the time they arrived at half past eight the man had been ordered out of the hotel. He cursed Miller and vowed he'd be back to get him. No one paid much attention to this sort of bravado, and Miller concentrated on finishing his duties so he could leave on vacation with his wife.

Later in the morning the unruly guest strolled back into the lobby, flashing his key receipt and asking for his two-dollar deposit back. He was given the money and put it in his pocket, then pulled out a .32 caliber gun. The desk clerk dove to the floor for cover as a bullet pierced Miller's left side. The stunned manager whirled and raised his arms instinctively to protect himself as a second bullet ripped into his chest. Schmertzler yanked open his office door, angry that the brats were setting off firecrackers, and scrambled for cover.

Miller crumpled, blood gushing forth, while the assailant dashed through the lobby. Aston Foote, an eighty-year-old bellhop, seized a chair and lunged. The gunman pumped a bullet into Foote's stomach and fled. He jumped into his waiting car and roared up the Grand Concourse, leaving in his wake a clutch of hotel children waiting for the day-camp bus. Miller was dead on arrival at Morrisania Hospital, just off the Concourse. Like so many spur-of-the-moment violent crimes, it went unsolved and unpunished. The bellhop underwent six hours of surgery, which saved his life in more ways than one. "When they opened him up they found he had cancer of the intestines. They figured he wouldn't have lived another six months. As it was, I saw him five years later and he was very fit," said one hotel employee.

Otherwise, the hotel operated as always, putting up a steady stream of welfare burnouts at very remunerative rates. A Red Cross volunteer who first saw the Concourse Plaza in 1972 remembers it as a "terrible hellhole. There was bulletproof glass at the desk, and you transacted business through a small hole in the window. All the hallways and elevators were dimly lit and I remember seeing rodents and bugs slipping into the shadows. Maybe this was just my middle-class reaction, but I couldn't wait to take a shower after being in that hotel. I remember the rooms just had beds, no bureaus or any other furniture. It was a terrible, terrible place."

The City began thinking of ways to use the hotel. There was talk of transforming it into a community college or a high school, but, as Caspi recollects, "Schmertzler and I were not getting along at all. We were feuding and so that never came to pass. I thought I'd be in clover leasing to the City, but then when the City went broke, I was glad it didn't happen."[3]

By early 1972 the hotel was looking even worse, and the City began seeking desperately for some way to buy it up. Officials could no longer delude themselves that the Concourse was not seriously imperiled, and the condition of the hotel was doing nothing to help matters. Caspi continued to run his all-black functions, and in December 1971 his son had opened a successful discotheque in the old Baroque Room. The neighbors complained bitterly to the police about the Tunnel disco and its rowdy customers. In March 1973 the neighbors got the disco closed for operating without a license, and, in an additional coup, closed Caspi's ballrooms. Caspi was furious and charged bigotry, particularly over the revocation of his ballroom license. "We have the finest black and Puerto Rican organizations in the City coming here," he said. "We have the Masons, NAACP, professional groups. Those people don't make trouble."[4] By rallying black support, he was able to reopen his ballrooms, but not the disco. The police had made a few too many arrests for possession and sale of

narcotics, assault, and public intoxication, not to mention issuing thousands of summonses for double-parked cars and
moving violations.

Years later, Caspi was still bitter. "My personal opinion is
that the local politicians were able to bring enough pressure
to stop the blacks being in the hotel, hoping they might retard
change in the neighborhood. I can never prove it, but that's
what I thought. Then the Department of Real Estate of the
City of New York got in touch and said, 'either you sell the
hotel or we'll condemn it.' "5 If he were to sell, Caspi would
have to terminate his lease with Schmertzler and share part
of the sale price. To encourage Schmertzler to terminate his
little gold mine, Caspi says, the City began squeezing off the
steady influx of welfare clients.

The assessed value for the hotel listed by the Bronx Board
of Realtors ranged between $460,000 and $1.7 million. This
tallied with the estimate given by a Helmsley-Spear expert on
hotel sales, who figured that a hotel like the Concourse Plaza
was worth from $2,000 to $4,000 a room (it had 440 rooms),
or a top assessed value of about $1.7 million.

Caspi responded to the City's pressure to sell by continually
raising his price. He had bought the hotel in 1965 from the
Fuchs for $1.7 million. Even though the neighborhood had
declined precipitously, Caspi was now asking $2 million. No
doubt he sensed the City's growing desperation. The price
rose to $2.6 million. In December 1973 Mayor Lindsay and
borough President Abrams announced that the City was buying the hotel for $2.6 million — Caspi's asking price — to
convert it into housing for senior citizens.

Once the City took possession of the Concourse Plaza, the
welfare families were transferred out. Dozens of planned functions, including many weddings, were canceled at short notice.
The City was bombarded by phone calls from furious brides.
There were still dozens of permanent residents to deal with,
many of them elderly. Caspi went through the hotel tacking
up notices announcing that everyone would have to move
because the City was the new owner and it was vacating the
premises. The older tenants feared they would be relegated

to nursing homes. One woman was so distraught she tried twice to commit suicide with pills. Another person, a midget known as the Mayor of the Concourse Plaza, became despondent, and one morning a maid found him in Room 520, hanging dead from a clothes rack, a chair kicked over beneath his dangling legs.

The Concourse Plaza closed down nine months after the other local landmark with which it had always been linked — Yankee Stadium. Both were to be overhauled at taxpayer expense for the good of the neighborhood. The City paid probably almost $1 million over the true value to get its hands on the hotel, but that turned out to be a big bargain compared to the bills for the renovation of Yankee Stadium.

Mayor John V. Lindsay had first announced, on March 3, 1971, the City's intention of buying Yankee Stadium (then owned by CBS) and refurbishing it, for otherwise the Yankees said they were going to take their balls and bats and play somewhere else. The football-playing Giants had shown the way already by planning a move to New Jersey. The total renovation cost of Yankee Stadium would be $24 million, and the City Planning Commission okayed that, together with neighborhood improvement as an urban renewal package. By January 1973, when George Steinbrenner bought the Yankees, the estimates had risen 50 percent to $33 million. After the 1973 season the stadium closed and demolition began.

Meanwhile, the City's great fiscal crisis was approaching. By the spring of 1975 free-spending New York faced grave financial difficulties. City construction projects were to be canceled or cut back. Layoffs of City employees were readied. Plans to transform the Concourse Plaza into senior-citizen housing were scotched — the City could not afford it. The court offices that had moved into the ballroom and function rooms continued to operate, but otherwise the great old hotel went into mothballs. Its sole resident was Adolph Menendez, the superintendent who had worked there for many years. Guards patrolled its silent halls to make sure vandals didn't begin "finishing" this building as they had so many others.

In October 1975, as the bills mounted at Yankee Stadium for such items as VIP boxes with private bars and private bathrooms, air-conditioned dugouts, and wall-to-wall carpeting in the players clubhouse, the City decided that the one way it could save money was to eliminate funds earmarked to improve the surrounding neighborhood. From the beginning, the renovation of Yankee Stadium had been billed as urban renewal. Now, as the cost of renovation soared to $100 million, the city reneged on the one part of the plan that would serve the local residents. In a dazzling display of indifference and insensitivity, part of this $2 million "savings" was then spent to buy the Yankees three hundred thousand dollars' worth of equipment — a new tarpaulin, security devices, supports for the scoreboard. Meanwhile, the stadium's protracted closing had contributed to the demise of twelve local businesses, including the Jerome Cafeteria right across from the ballpark.

When the stadium opened on April 15, in time for the 1976 season, the neighborhood was feeling ill-used. Community groups gathered and marched on the stadium to protest the City's waste at the ballpark when the South Bronx was virtually dying around the corner. Yankees owner George Steinbrenner tried to assuage the angry natives and local churchmen by announcing Neighborhood Project No. 1, a thirty-five-thousand-dollar plan to spruce up the nearby athletic fields of McCombs Dam Park. The fact that the tall lights erected under this project mainly lighted nearby Yankee parking lots is probably coincidence. The Yankees say other work done in the park totaled another thirty thousand dollars. Oh, Steinbrenner himself also gave five thousand dollars to a local athletic organization. It turned out that this five thousand dollars had been raised by selling outdoor advertising space on the surface of the stadium, a stadium owned by New York City.

27

Roosevelt Gardens
1974–1975

B Y the time the new, gilted-edged Yankee Stadium opened, there was no doubt whatsoever that the whole Grand Concourse was in serious straits. Roosevelt Gardens had recently gone vacant after a dramatic and agonizing battle between finishers and besieged tenants. Similar tragedies had been played out in thousands of other Bronx apartment houses, but now the curtain was falling on the county's most prestigious boulevard and Roosevelt Gardens was the first to go. Borough President Abrams was beside himself. "Seeing buildings fall away, then blocks and neighborhoods, it was eating away at my insides. When the first abandonment happened on the Concourse, I couldn't stand it. The people at the Housing Development Administration didn't know what that apartment building was, its significance. You try and get them to act and you get lost in a quagmire. You couldn't allow the Champs-Élysées of the Bronx to fall! It would break the back of whatever confidence there was."[1]

The Theodore Roosevelt Apartments had opened in 1922, just before the Concourse Plaza Hotel. An elegant, white stucco six-story elevator building of "pure southern Spanish architecture," it boasted ornamental Spanish corners and mansard roofs of Spanish tile bedecked with flags. Occupying an entire block, the building formed a rectangle surrounding a large Italian garden, dominated by a massive fifteen-foot stone statue of Theodore Roosevelt contemplating his African discoveries while a lion slept at his feet and a sphinx smiled enigmatically. The Roosevelt statue stood as centerpiece for the courtyard's Fountain of Strength. The builder and proud owner of this luxury apartment was Logan Billingsley, an Oklahoma boy who stormed the Bronx and became one of its most prominent citizens and businessmen. Gardeners cared for the flowers and shrubs in the Italian garden and trimmed hedges in front of the professional offices along the Grand Concourse. A staff of porters maintained the building, polishing brass, washing the marble lobby daily. Doormen guarded the peace and privacy of the many doctors, lawyers, and businessmen who lived there. For three decades, the Theodore Roosevelt was a sedate, classy address.

Then, in the late 1950s, the Wolf Weinreb family bought the apartment house. Gelvin Stevenson, an economics writer at *Business Week* who lives in the Bronx, traced its demise for a 1979 exhibit at the Bronx Museum of the Arts, called "Devastation/Resurrection." He found that service began to decline immediately upon the Weinrebs' accession. The most frequent complaints were inadequate heat and out-of-service elevators. The Weinrebs applied for a hardship increase in their rents and were granted 4 percent. "Cost cutting at Roosevelt Gardens [as it had been renamed after the war] became more evident. The office worker was laid off. One laundry room was closed and the other moved to a cubbyhole so that the owners could rent out all the basement space — to a candy store, a carpentry shop, and a tailor. Dumbwaiters were sealed, and tenants had to take their garbage downstairs, where it was stored in the buildings, creating a deplorable odor."[2]

VOICES OF THE SOUTH BRONX
HELEN JOHNSON

Helen Johnson had moved into Roosevelt Gardens in 1958 with her parents, three brothers, and three sisters. "It was my mother who first realized what has happening and articulated it. That was around 1966. She said no matter whom she spoke to in the building, they all told her the same thing — they were going to Co-op City. She said, 'As soon as Co-op City opens, everything's going down the tubes.' She kept saying, 'Every Jew in this place is going to Co-op City. We'll be left here, the riffraff's going to move in, and the whole thing's going to start all over again.' Because we were off in college, or working, or graduate school, we weren't tuned into it the way my mother was. She had a feeling of impending doom."

The Johnsons had already fled once, from Clay Avenue eight blocks east, where all the children had grown up. "The whole situation was being visited on us again," says Helen, an attorney in the Bronx district attorney's office. She is a big woman, with sandy hair going grey and a soft, low voice. "In my mind everything happened at the same time — everyone left to Co-op City, the Weinrebs bought the building, all the supers were fired, there was no garbage collection, the elevators were never fixed, and the riffraff came. A family moved in above us that lived like barnyard animals. They flooded us out at least once a week. They were filthy and unkempt. The apartment smelled of urine. The garbage was not collected and there came to be a roach problem. Then we started to be afraid again. Even when the elevator was working, you never used it because you were afraid to get in it."

The Johnsons were baffled and embittered by the crumbling of the Bronx they had grown up in and loved. "I knew that it was happening, but I didn't understand why. I did know that people were making an awful lot of money doing it."

The Johnsons had watched an outsider make a fortune destroying their block on Clay Avenue between 166th and 167th streets. "The Man started to buy up the block in 1955 or 1956. There were fifteen walk-ups on each side of the street. He bought the first one and paid people to move out. If he couldn't get anyone to move, he made conditions intolerable. He would flood your apartment and drive you absolutely crazy. People took him to court and fought him; it was a whole saga. You see, once he got an apartment, he would cut it in half. Instead of getting one welfare check, he was getting two. He was specifically moving in welfare people, and the rents he was charging were enormous — several hundred dollars for a chopped-up apartment. At that time we paid about fifty-six dollars. And welfare didn't care what they paid him because they couldn't find apartments for these people.

"His buying of the block took three years. You had to have

someone in your apartment at all times to call the police if they started up through the floor. They came through the closets with pipes so they could install bathrooms in the divided apartments. Once the pipe went through — that was it, you were done. Because then two families moved in upstairs and you had enormous numbers of people in much too small a place. Then the halls became cluttered and dirty. We didn't go through that, but we watched the neighbors go through it. But a great many Puerto Rican people had moved into our building and I can remember being very frightened by them. They were strange, and the men made noises at me when I came in and out of the building. I was afraid of them, and they were always in the hallway.

"When the Man bought our building, we sat down as a family and participated in the decision about what to do. The girls wanted to move, I remember that distinctly. I remember telling my father I was afraid. Then we decided, because we were all still in school, to move to the Concourse, which was fairly near."

Helen had obliterated the Man's name from her memory. Her brother Harry remembers it instantly: "Mr. Barinoff. He used to come around in a Cadillac, but he stopped doing that after he had some bricks thrown at him from one of the roofs. His office was at Finley and 166th Street, and I remember when push came to shove and we had to move, my father went there with me and my brother for a backup. He went into that office, threw open the door, and went right after Barinoff. He put his hands around Barinoff's throat, picked him up, and laid him across the desk. He told him, 'We're gonna move, but you're going to pay us five hundred dollars.' We got the money."

"My mother was devasted when we moved," says Helen. "She sobbed all the way to the Concourse. I guess she never really got over it. By the time we left, all the old shopkeepers had gone; so had all the neighbors." But their paternal grandfather, an electrician who had been apprenticed to Thomas Edison in his youth, refused to leave his apartment on Clay Avenue. Says Harry, "He was the old guy who wouldn't give up, the last white guy. My father was pissed at him, and he was a constant source of fights because he wouldn't move. We all took turns going every day to take him food and visit. He never budged and was there till he died in 1968."

Harry and Helen's parents were second-generation Bronxites, half-Irish, half-German. Their father was a fireman and a devout Catholic, their mother a homemaker. They had moved to their two-bedroom, third-floor walk-up apartment at 1112 Clay Avenue in 1939. Helen was born in Misericordia Hospital on December 18, 1942.

"The block on Clay Avenue defined my world," she says. "The bulk of the Jewish population lived in a very large elevator building on the corner. There was a large German population on the street, and a very small number of Italians and Irish. My mother told me there was ill feeling left over from the war, and so there was a German butcher and a Jewish butcher. Different storekeepers served each group.

"As a young child, I can recall all the supers being out every morning scrubbing the stoops, polishing the brass, fixing the curtains, and taking the fingermarks off any windows. All the windows had awnings, and it was neat and tidy. One never sat on the stoop or loitered in front of the building. That was not permitted. There was one place you were allowed to sit, and after lunch the women brought their wooden folding chairs and met in this spot with their baby carriages. The seats would be arranged more or less in a semicircle and the infants would take naps.

"My mother's sister lived across the street. They had seven children, but they moved to Queens in 1947. My father's parents also lived across the street. My other grandmother, who remained on 134th Street in the Saint Jerome's parish until she died, came up every single day to help my mother. You knew every person on the block, and their grandmother and grandfather, aunts and uncles, and everyone's cars. If there was a stranger on the block, you would know almost instantaneously.

"Mr. Levy, the druggist on the corner, was in charge of everything. That was the only telephone when we were children, so you'd go up there and chat with him and then he'd know everything. If you got something in your eye, you'd go to Mr. Levy, or if you got cut, or if you needed stamps. The Democratic captain of the block was Mr. Whalen, and you went to him with your problems having to do with bus stops, school lunch programs, or getting into a certain school.

"My idol lived in the elevator building — Bluma Gottlieb. First of all, she went to Hunter College, a thing so overwhelming and so incredible. *And* she went to Europe after she graduated from college. *And* she played tennis. She had tennis dates and wore a special dress and white sweater with stripes on the bottom that she threw over her shoulders with the sleeves tied around her neck. Her family had two apartments, not one; they broke the walls through. And they had a maid. Better than Bluma Gottlieb you couldn't be. She was my idol, absolutely.

"People left and people stayed on the block for different reasons. We stayed because my father felt it was the only way we could get our educations. It was rather unusual, my father's aspiration that we all go to college. I went to Saint Angela's, then for high school to the Ursuline Academy on the Grand Concourse until my last year when it was sold and I went up to Mount Saint Ursula. My sisters and I were very religious. We were very close to the nuns, and we went to church twice on Sundays and a number of times during the week.

"My family thought it very odd that I wanted to be a lawyer. They tried to talk me out of it. They knew I would be banging my head against the wall and that I would be terribly hurt. I went to Hunter and had the best law boards. I applied to Fordham Law School in 1964 and was denied. I got all dressed up and went down to see the head of admissions. He said, 'We can't waste a seat on you. You're going to get married.' So I went back to my professor and she said, 'You're going to get no place with Catholics. The only people who can help you are the Jews.' So I went to Brooklyn Law School and they gave me a seat and scholarship money. There was a lot of guilt involved for me, because if I had gone out into the world and taught, like I was supposed to, I could have been helping the ones behind me. I was one of three women in my class. The only place I wanted to work was the Bronx D.A.'s office. I don't know why, that was just it. I applied for a job, as did a number of my male classmates. My application was pending six months, theirs six minutes. I was devastated. After many months of this, my father got outraged. I heard him talking to some man on the telephone, and the next week I had a job.

"I worked in homicide when Fort Apache, around Charlotte Street, was at its worst, and I spent enormous amounts of time over there. I watched the whole place fall apart and all those people move over to the Four-four [Forty-fourth police precinct], the Concourse, Highbridge. I began to see the enormous displacement of people. I didn't understand until I got there that entire neighborhoods moved.

"We all lived at home. In Roosevelt Gardens in the late 1960s, my father came home from work and sat down at the head of the dinner table and looked at all these adults and said, 'Would someone please *move*?' I was an assistant D.A., Harry was in housing. Also at the table was a policeman, a schoolteacher, a fireman, and a secretary. My mother had to put three roast beefs on the table. It was absolutely incredible. Then Agnes, the baby, graduated from school and my father came home one night and said, 'That's it, troop. I've told you time and time again, move out, but nobody wants to move out. So your mother and I are moving out.' They went to Long Beach, where my father had been fixing up a bungalow. We were absolutely flabbergasted. They moved in 1969. All the other terrific people had moved to Co-op City, it seemed." Harry remembers, that "the whole talk along the Concourse became, 'Did you get your notice yet?' People were waiting by their mailboxes to hear from Co-op City. It was crazy."

Within four months of their parents' departure, the siblings went their separate ways. It was not hard to leave Roosevelt Gardens, which was on the skids. Eventually, Helen would marry, move to the suburbs, have two children, and rise to the number three job in the district attorney's office. And yet, her sense of loss and anger did not diminish. She remembers vividly the tranquil summer mornings when the only sound on her block was the harness bells from the fruit and vegetable man's horse. And then it was gone, destroyed. "All I know is, someone made a lot of money ruining the Bronx — the Weinrebs of the world, particularly," says Helen.

In the late 1960s and early 1970s, the Weinrebs began selling Roosevelt Gardens back and forth to various corporations they owned. Back and forth, back and forth, sometimes twice a year. What was the point, Gelvin Stevenson wondered. "One possibility: landlords frequently use buildings as tax shelters. Selling them back and forth lowers taxes by increasing depreciation and thereby decreasing taxable income. These transactions aren't illegal unless they're done to avoid taxes.

"Such buying and selling can also increase the paper value of a building, allowing it to carry a larger mortgage — a lucrative tool because using mortgages to borrow money is cheaper than almost any other sort of loan."[3] Such tactics can also yield increased insurance coverage in the event of fire.

In July 1971 the Weinrebs had borrowed $164,000 for a new boiler and improved heating system. Rents rose two dollars per room in consequence. But "several tenants remember that the heat didn't improve." This coincided with a brief period of what was called vacancy decontrol, meaning that whenever a rent-controlled apartment came on the market it could be rented at the market rate rather than raised some set percentage. In 1972 the Weinrebs began renting to tenants who would pay far more than market rents on the declining Concourse, and whose very presence was guaranteed to empty the remaining rent-controlled apartments. The landlord brought in large welfare families. The welfare department paid a security deposit and finder's fee for each family. Assemblyman Seymour Posner, whose office was three blocks from the apartment house, believed the landlord "decided to make a killing. He rented to 104 relocatees from burnouts without screening one. He absolutely stopped screening tenants."[4]

Weinreb's new policy was a marked success. By late 1973, one year after he had brought in welfare families, virtually every single apartment was emptied of its longtime tenants. The new residents provided more income. Stevenson found that between 1943 and 1973, or thirty years, the rent roll at Roosevelt Gardens increased 80 percent. From 1973 to 1975, two years, it increased 90 percent. In some apartments it rose as much as 182 percent, and the annual rent roll for Roosevelt Gardens had risen to $708,750.

One tenant who moved in 1968 found that by 1973 all pretense of services had disappeared. The basement flooded during Christmas, and "when the phone company came to repair the line, they refused to enter the basement because there were so many rats and water bugs."[5] Incessant calls to the City's Buildings Department produced no improvements. Once, angry tenants surrounded owner Wolf Weinreb when he visited the building. He escaped into his car only when the super hurled water down on the crowd encircling him.

A doctor named Morris Halper berated the black and Hispanic teenagers who hung around the lobby for pestering his patients. The kids smashed the windows of his car. The doctor rushed out and began scuffling with them. Someone punched him and broke his glasses. Infuriated, he stormed into his office, grabbed a gun, and raced after one of the boys, Thomas Franco. When Franco stumbled and fell, Halper shot and killed him.

The Weinrebs began to pull out. In early 1974 they paid their last real estate taxes. They continued to collect rents from those tenants who would still pay, but they did not even go through the motions of operating their building. They repaired nothing, and on October 4 the situation led to a terrible tragedy. "Eight-year-old Missy Holden entered the elevator on the main floor," wrote Stevenson. "Missy pressed six, and the elevator didn't move. She started to crawl through a broken window; the elevator started up, crushing her head. Missy was dead on arrival at Morrisania Hospital." Owner Wolf Weinreb's comment? "The insurance company took care of that."[6]

By June 1975 the Weinrebs owed the City more than $150,000 in unpaid real estate taxes, water bills, and penalties. The building, despite its deplorable condition, was still assessed for $1.1 million. They sold it for eleven thousand dollars to David Teichner, who proceeded to "finish" the building.

Teichner extracted rents from the still-occupied apartments by appearing at the door in the company of a man with a gun. He suggested to Assemblyman Posner, who was trying to organize the tenants, that this activity was not conducive to long life and good health. He settled in to dismantle Roosevelt Gardens piece by piece. Stevenson figured that "the burner of the boiler was worth five thousand dollars. A finisher could earn at least sixty-five hundred dollars from the resale of stoves and refrigerators alone. From the boilers and radiators, six thousand. And from the tons of brass pipe, two thousand."[7] If even a small number of the welfare families could be intimidated into paying rent, Teichner could recoup his eleven thousand dollars at once.

Under this reign of terror, the building actually began to collapse. Summer rains flooded top-floor apartments whose ceilings had gaping holes; one woman referred to her apartment as "Niagara Falls." The Red Cross came to evacuate some apartments. Then the manager's office was broken into and the master keys stolen. Fires were started all over the building. As Teichner's men ripped out the pipes to sell them, leaks and floods inundated whole sections of the building. The water was turned off. The elevators went dead. The remaining tenants had to walk up and down unlit stairs to fetch water from a fire hydrant out front, and use flashlights to see inside the hallways. Everyone was terrified that Teichner might put the place completely to the torch. "We went to bed with our shoes on every night," said one tenant.

Finally, the City took Teichner to court to prevent him from reselling. "It was a critical building. Even though it was too late to stabilize, it was not too late to save what was there," said one official.[8] That done, a vacate order was issued by the City. Despite the primitive and dangerous conditions, 28 of the 273 apartments were still occupied. Stevenson figured that the Weinrebs, in abandoning their building, may have made as much as a half million dollars in clear profit; but Roosevelt

Gardens was sealed by the City with cinder blocks and fenced off, a large eyesore on the borough's most distinguished boulevard.

Abandonment had struck the Grand Concourse and was gnawing past it into the far ridge of the West Bronx, middle-class neighborhoods with the country's largest concentration of art deco buildings. Abandonment was estimated to be consuming six to ten blocks a year and moving northward. And no one in government had any remedy. Peter Magnani, director of the Bronx office of the City Planning Commission, conceded as much to a Columbia journalism student in 1976. "There's no doubt in my mind that the lower Concourse area will become no better than the worst section of the South Bronx in a matter of a few years. There's absolutely no way to stop it that we can see."[9]

Roger Starr, the housing and urban expert, was administrator of the City's housing department. On January 14, 1976, he gave a speech to the real estate industry lodge of the B'nai B'rith, where he astounded his audience by suggesting that the City should "accelerate the drainage" of the worst parts of the South Bronx by what he called "planned shrinkage," or the deliberate emptying out of largely destroyed neighborhoods.[10] Starr said the City, deep in the throes of a financial crunch, should consider closing subway stations, police and firehouses, and hospitals and schools as a means of saving money and consolidating services.

Real Estate Weekly quoted Starr as saying the South Bronx could then be razed and used for a "national park." While he later denied the park suggestion, Starr was absolutely serious about shutting down whole neighborhoods. The City was so broke (except when it came to frills for Yankee Stadium), and the devastation so out of control, that it was grasping wildly for solutions. Robert Moses, author of the Cross-Bronx Expressway, also advocated in 1973 razing the slums of the South Bronx and relocating all the inhabitants into new high rises at Ferry Point Park. Like Starr, he found the South Bronx "beyond rebuilding, tinkering and restoring. The people living there must be moved."

Not surprisingly, Starr's "planned shrinkage" provoked a firestorm of criticism, and the administration of Mayor Abraham Beame, who had taken office in January 1974, disavowed any part of it. Such a discussion could only confirm the darkest suspicions of those who believed that there was an organized goal to the never-ending cycle of drugs, crimes, fires, and abandonment — to push the poor minorities out of New York City and be rid of them. (The flaw to this conspiracy theory is that the poor minorities who were burned out of one neighborhood were pushed farther into white working-class or middle-class neighborhoods in search of new homes.)

The truth was that for many years City officials had responded to the precipitious collapse of neighborhoods like the South Bronx by talking about programs and big bucks that would turn things around. The Nixon White House had turned off the federal spigot, and now New York itself was broke. There could be no more consoling talk about programs. Everyone knew there was barely enough money to pay the cops or the garbage men. Those who had believed the government could save the South Bronx if only it tried began to realize that the public officials had no idea what to do, and no money to do it with.

28

The Grass Roots
1974–1977

As the City government faltered, grassroots groups sprouted. Since no one had yet devised an antidote for crumbling neighborhoods, anyone crazy enough even to try reviving a building or a block commanded the grudging respect accorded doomed idealists. Although the neighborhoods around Charlotte Street were almost completely cleared out by 1976, a few unusual people began to contemplate this urban wasteland in a new light, as a land of opportunity. They reconnoitered the territory and devised their own individual notions of what could be made of the South Bronx.

Irma Fleck was a veteran Bronx activist who spanned the old Jewish Bronx and the new Hispanic Bronx. A short, redhaired go-getter, she had founded and built up several successful community organizations. One day she was attending a meeting at a lovely old Bronx church encircled by empty lots deep in rubble and litter. Joan Davidson, a New York philanthropist, stared at the dreary vista with her. Why, wondered Davidson, didn't they just plant corn and cover all this? Fleck remembered reading a column by Martin Gallent, vicechairman of the City Planning Commission, suggesting something similar, and she thought, "Why not? Why not turn the South Bronx into a garden?"[1] She was tired of reading all those awful newspaper stories about the borough that looked like Dresden after the firebombing. She was going to substitute "amber waves of grain."

It was such a crazy idea that everyone loved it. And it had historical precedent, since, after all, much of the Bronx once had been estates, farms, and gardens. Irma Fleck hooked up with Jack Flanagan, the community affairs cop from the Forty-first Precinct, who looked suitably agrarian with his bushy beard and lumberjack build. They named themselves the Bronx Frontier Development Corporation. Their goal was the greening of the South Bronx. There was now more vacant land in the South Bronx than in the Westchester suburbs — four hundred acres scattered in lots on the avenues and side streets.

A group called the Urban Guerrillas explained the rather daunting economics of even a small garden. The immediate need was going to be topsoil, which at fourteen dollars a cubic yard was just too expensive to buy. Fleck, however, had a brainstorm. Bronx Frontier would make its own, using the refuse thrown away daily at the new, sprawling Hunt's Point Produce Market, the City's wholesale distributing point for fruits and vegetables. This would be composted with leaves, ground-up rubble, and manure from animals at the Bronx Zoo. Spread thickly on cleared lots, it would create gardens, and the gardens in turn would provide healthful food for the poor and the gratification of having grown it themselves.

The short Jewish doctor's wife and the big Irish cop launched themselves, in tireless supplication, upon City and state agencies and friendly foundations. First they needed land for their composting. They wangled three and one-fifth waterfront acres next to a sewage treatment plant on the Hunt's Point peninsula. There they dug a drainage system, put up fences, and set up a trailer to use as an office and laboratory, for the compost had to be sterile when it was all through and ready for spreading. Dr. Curtis Suerth, a Cornell biochemist and plant physiologist, joined up to oversee the composting operation. They tried out a ten-ton compost turner, worth fifty thousand dollars, to be purchased if it did the job. There were plans for a rubble pulverizer. They looked at the endless harsh vista of dead buildings and rubbled lots and imagined them green and bright with red tomatoes and yellow squash and alive with converted gardeners tending their vines and bushes. It was heady stuff.

In Hunt's Point, the community group known as SEBCO

(South East Bronx Community Organization) was flourishing under Father Louis Gigante's leadership. Founded in 1968, SEBCO had put in a housing rehabilitation plan shortly thereafter. Once he saw that Model Cities and the antipoverty programs were going nowhere, however, Father Gigante went on pursuing traditional politics after losing the 1970 congressional primary. He established his own political club on Bruckner Boulevard and built up membership with the tried-and-true method of doing favors and solving problems. He ran for Democratic district leader and polished off the regular candidate fielded by the Pondiac Club, which had been mortally weakened by the fall of Eugene Rodriguez (the district leader and almost-state senator who had gone to prison on a a narcotics case-fixing rap). Gigante's election to district leader was the coup de grace that closed the Pondiac Club after fifty-two years.

In 1973 Father Gigante ran for the New York City Council and won. Then he made his peace with Bronx Democratic leader Pat Cunningham and played power-broker politics with gusto. He relished the horse trading and wheeling-dealing, but above all he delivered results to his ever-diminishing neighborhood. He kept pushing the City, state, and federal governments for his SEBCO housing funds, for as he himself said, "We lost the battle to preserve the neighborhood. Now we hope to rebuild it." He told one interviewer that "the problem wasn't only housing. It was that and drug-related crime. These were the two most pressing problems in the neighborhood. I decided to focus on housing, because otherwise I would have had to be a vigilante. Also with housing there was something to start with."[2]

By the fall of 1976 the first group of 360 SEBCO units were completed in nine buildings on East 163rd Street around the corner from Saint Athanasius Church. "I had a desire to fulfill the Gospel, which is to house those in need, to clothe those in need. Housing was a need here, so we built."[3] Work was to commence on another 615 units in 1976–1977. In this era of rebuilding, Father Gigante truly came into his own. He presided over impressive renovations of dilapidated slums and then ran them with an iron hand. No one could spray graffiti on his walls or "air mail" garbage in his buildings without risking eviction.

On the other hand, Ramon Velez, Gigante's longtime foe, failed to make a similar transition to local developer. No neighborhood looked worse than the "turf" Ramon ruled. The housing he ran fell apart and the premises surrounding his own multi-service center in Hunt's Point were filthy and vandalized.

Not far from Charlotte Street, a small miracle was in the making. A young man named Ramon Rueda, a charismatic radical who affected a navy blue Mao cap with red star, gathered a small crew of workers together to homestead 1186 Washington Avenue, an abandoned five-story apartment house whose basement was knee-deep in putrid mud studded with garbage and the carcasses of dead dogs.

Rueda was a Bronx boy from a sheltered family who had been radicalized during the 1960s while an activist at the state university in Farmingdale, New York. He went underground to avoid the draft in 1971, but was caught by the FBI two years later and given a three-year suspended sentence. Looking for a new direction, he visited the homesteading project of the Harlem Renegades street gang. Intrigued by their example, Rueda signed up for a housing course taught by the New York Urban Coalition. He returned to the Bronx as an Urban Coalition intern to see how apartments were being renovated by the New York City Housing Authority.

Near one of the Housing Authority renovations stood 1186 Washington Avenue, or, as the engraved stone above the entryway read, Venice Hall. The corner buildings already restored by the Housing Authority anchored the block, along with a stucco Evangelical Church of God and half a dozen spacious wooden houses with yards. Washington Avenue was not one of those gutted, abandoned streets. Rueda decided this was the place to do his homesteading, and he and ten others dubbed themselves the People's Development Corporation in December 1974.

They cleared the upper floors of mattresses stinking of urine, dead rats, and old excrement. Then they waded into the
basement and began shoveling out the frozen, stinking mix
of mud and garbage. They worked on the building during the
free time they had from their other jobs, knowing full well
that Venice Hall belonged to the City. They were trespassers
who had no right to be there. In the South Bronx, such niceties
no longer mattered. The idea was that the "sweat" from their
labor would dramatically cut the costs of renovating and count
toward ownership or "equity," and that ultimately — somehow — they would all move into the building and own it as
a cooperative.

Several months into the job, the People's Development
Corporation decided the time had come to find some loans.
It was possible to gut Venice Hall with only their own labor,
but rebuilding required real money. Rueda made some contacts with housing activists, who were most impressed with
this self-generated enthusiasm and accomplishment. They suggested some possible sources of funds, the most promising
being the City of New York.

Using the old mau-mauing tactics of the 1960s, the PDC
descended upon Roger Starr's office at the Housing Development Agency in full working regalia — hard hats, heavy
boots, and dusty overalls. Brandishing their construction tools,
they denounced the City and its indifference to the South
Bronx and proceeded to occupy the agency. One way or another they managed to extract a $311,000 City construction
loan, a $19,000 loan from the Consumer-Farmer Foundation,
and a $22,000 grant from the Criminal Justice Coordinating
Council. Many new people joined, and, as the weather turned
nice, the PDC began to clear an empty corner lot to make
Unity Park. It became a local landmark with its extraordinary,
larger-than-life mural of all the original PDCers, proudly posing in their work clothes with their shovels and brooms. It
bespoke a vibrancy and dedication long absent from the South
Bronx.

Then disaster struck in the form of the New York City fiscal
crisis of 1975. The major construction loan was frozen by the

new Emergency Financial Control Board. The council grant was stalled, too. For the next nine months the PDC just scraped by with the $19,000 Consumer-Farmer loan and hoped the other money would appear.

Rueda occupied himself in part by drawing up even more ambitious plans, with the help of the Pratt Institute Center, to redevelop the entire nine-block sector surrounding 1186. The plan went far beyond mere housing and envisioned a "village" of ten thousand replete with jobs, parks, child care, and health services. "We want to be as self-sufficent as we can," Rueda would explain, a local Messiah in overalls, bushy beard, and frame glasses. "We even want to grow some of our own food on vacant lots. We'll be an extended family of ten thousand people."[4]

Finally, in the summer of 1976, the money logjam broke, and the PDC was soon awash in funds. More people came on — mainly unskilled young men from the nearby blocks — and as they "sweated" they learned construction skills under the tutelage of union men. A solar collector was built on the roof to provide most of the hot water, a food cooperative was started, and Rueda began to lay the groundwork for the larger, long-range dreams of job training, economic development, and energy development that would make the "village" possible.

Rueda and the PDC saw themselves as engaged in developing new modes and models for living, thriving, and reviving within the urban jungle. They were the most prominent and promising outpost seeking a new order. It was all a bit vague, yet they were certain that with time, experience, and plenty of funding this new order would fall into place and the South Bronx would rise again.

By the spring of 1977 the first homesteaders were moving into 1186 Washington Avenue. The interior decor reflected the exuberance of the new residents — the halls were painted with gay stripes and hung with Picasso reproductions. One apartment had snazzy track lighting and a sunken bathroom. The homesteaders felt tremendous pride of workmanship and ownership. The PDC geared up to tackle another five build-

ings. Venice Hall became a showplace for those touring the
South Bronx with government officials or foundations.

On March 22, 1977, CBS television broadcast "The Fire
Next Door," a documentary by Bill Moyers. It was a vivid,
gripping show that offered a horrifying glimpse of the continuing, unchecked collapse of the ever-expanding South Bronx,
for now the plague of fires was eating away at what once had
been known as the West Bronx. The residents seemed besieged and hopeless. Horrors that would have outraged anyone elsewhere had become commonplace here. Moyers could
hardly believe that it had come to this in America, that "we
seem willing to accept this as the natural order of things."[5]
No one who saw the show could forget Bill Moyers's encounter with Mrs. Sullivan, a silver-haired Irish lady retired
from her supervisor's job at the Plaza Hotel, and a resident
of Davidson Avenue in Highbridge for thirty-eight years. When
Moyers interviewed her in front of her house, she was waiting
for the movers. As Moyers gently queried her, she was almost
in tears for sheer terror. Her voice quavered: "I couldn't walk
the stairs alone; I had to get someone to go up with me —
because one kid said he'd cut my throat if he had a knife."
"Cut your throat?" asked a shocked Moyers. "Yes, if he had
a knife," she said. "He said 'she has money and we kill her
someday,' so now I can't stay here. I never slept for a moment
because they watched me when I came in, they followed me
up the stairs, and they threw me down, and then took everything I had. What can I do?"[6]
While Moyers talked to her on the sidewalk before his
cameras, the young punks who had so terrorized her were
upstairs breaking into her apartment, tearing apart her packed
goods, looking for something else to steal. The police had
been called, and as they arrived Moyers and the camera crew
went back up to the apartment with old Mrs. Sullivan. They
captured on film her despair and grief at being violated yet
again. "Oh, oh look what they did. They broke everything
here. Oh, God."[7] She began to weep quietly. It was a small,

poignant glimpse of the tragedy in each empty apartment and vacant building of the spreading South Bronx.

Moyers found one bright spot — the People's Development Corporation. This was nothing less than inspirational. As Moyers took his cameras through and met some of the homesteaders, one told him, "You have this vast wilderness of decaying housing, neglect, everything else, and we've actually come in and decided to reclaim the land, rebuild our homes, and it is very fitting that this year of our nation's bicentennial, you know, maybe we can rekindle a small spark of some of the things that made this country great: people coming in and deciding, 'This is where we're gonna settle down, this is where we're gonna make our home.' "[8]

To Moyers, the PDC offered the best hope there was for the Bronx. "It's time to bet on them," he said in summation. "With capital, jobs, and enough time, they might collectively create from these ruins good neighborhoods to live and grow in. After all, they have nowhere to go; their lives are at stake. For the rest of us, it's a test of whether democratic capitalism will be made to work for the poorest among us — that, and the knowledge that unless we do act, the fires will no longer stop next door."[9]

In July of 1977 the miracle of Washington Avenue was touted nationwide on the cover of the *Saturday Review,* which called the PDC and its accomplishment "one of the most arresting and heartwarming developments to hit the inner city in decades." The author of the article, Roger M. Williams, was bowled over by the audacious daring of idealism in the midst of unremitting misery. "Everywhere in the South Bronx, they say, groups are working to reverse the tide, to resurrect their community, phoenixlike, from its own ashes. The task is so formidable that the PDC, with its one success, has come to symbolize the struggle."[10]

Moyers's show brought the PDC some concrete benefits. The immediate one was the advent of Plenty Commune, an offshoot of the Farm, a large commune founded in 1970 and centered on a 1,750-acre spread near Summertown, Tennessee. For some years, the Farm had been dispatching paramedic teams to Third World countries like Haiti and Bangladesh. After viewing the Moyers piece, there was an instant response (especially from the former Bronxites among the communards) — they felt that the South Bronx needed them as much as any Third World country did. A delegation contacted the PDC, and after a few meetings it was decided to homestead 1157 Fulton Avenue, the edge of the nine-block village-to-be.

The four-story brick tenement on Fulton Avenue had no boiler and no plumbing. The first floor was four feet deep in muck. The second floor had become a lair for a pack of wild dogs. A black family was camped out in the basement, somehow getting by. After truckloads of stinking trash had been carted away and the basics of heat and hot water restored, Plenty communards — fifteen adults and twenty children — moved in.

They were an unlikely group — leftover hippies with long hair, coiffed into braids and held back with headbands, and wearing flower-child garb of tie-dyed T-shirts. But Plenty Commune's people were dynamic and resourceful. They concluded that the best service they could render would be an ambulance corps and a training program to certify local people as emergency medical technicians. Their first vehicle was a donated former hearse. Word-of-mouth was their only advertising. In a neighborhood where the remaining residents usually called the fire department for medical emergencies because they knew the fire trucks would show up, Plenty filled a real need.

If the Moyers show did not hammer home just how far beyond control crime and fires in the South Bronx were, the great blackout of July 13, 1977, did. At 9:35 on that sultry July night all of New York City suddenly went dark. Fifteen minutes later, when it was clear that the lights weren't coming back on for a while, people began pouring out of their apartment buildings to embark on a destructive rampage of looting and burning. In the course of a long night New York businesses lost $150 million in goods and damaged property. (This was in marked contrast to the 1965 blackout, when crime actually went down and the camaraderie became part of the City's folklore.) Lawlessness lurked just below the surface now, and when the lights went, so did all social restraint.

Major shopping streets were quickly attacked by crowds that tore back the grates and bars on the stores, smashed plate-glass windows, and swarmed inside. Looters hit 473 businesses in the Bronx, leaving half of them badly damaged and almost a fifth burned. Mobs broke into automobile dealers (fifty Pontiacs stolen), cleaned out entire stocks of sneakers, and carted off televisions, stereos, and all the material goods Madison Avenue proclaimed necessary for the American good life. During the frenzy and excitement, the Bronx was struck by 307 fires, including three multiple alarms and fourteen "all-hands."

The Grand Concourse turned out a solid mass of people to storm the stores. A Ford Foundation study reported that "one Puerto Rican merchant who protected his sporting goods store with a shotgun, backed up by several armed friends, told us that the crowd extended from one side of the Concourse to the other, across six lanes and two dividers. Another Concourse merchant said again and again, 'You cannot comprehend how many people were out there . . . everyone was out there!' "

No one knows how many businesses never reopened afterward, or how many decided to phase themselves out of the Bronx. The Tru-Form Shoes store at the ground-floor side of the Concourse Plaza Hotel complained to its landlord, the City: "The gates were broken and windows destroyed during the blackout and many thousands of dollars worth of merchandise stolen. The salesmen we employ are afraid to work here. Our manager just gave me notice, and we are at our wits end, as it is impossible to continue to operate this store."[11]

The blackout, the fire and the looting and rioting made the City, already teetering on bankruptcy, look still worse. Mayor Abraham D. Beame, running in a tight primary race, needed some dramatic response, something to emphasize that the City was reimposing order in its neighborhoods. It was too late to crack down on the looters. Those who had been caught would be dragged slowly through the city courts. But fire and arson, well, that was always a good issue. The *New York Times* had just run a long front-page story saying that fires in the City jumped 40 percent in just three years. If New York was burning down, what better time to save it than during an election campaign?

On August 3, 1977, the mayor made his move and announced the creation of a hundred-person Arson Suppression Team, made up half of police, half of fire marshals. The team pushed for stepped-up demolition of abandoned buildings, more seal-ups, and a crackdown on junkyards that would buy scavenged building parts. The City also recommended legislation that would allow it to confiscate fire insurance proceeds paid to landlords in arrears on their taxes. Mayor Beame also declared a long-hoped-for change in welfare rules. Now those persons on welfare suspected of burning themselves out would lose priority on Housing Authority waiting lists, and their two-thousand-dollar grants for lost furniture and goods would not be issued automatically.

Ten days after the new team leaped into action, the Beame administration was ballyhooing its instant effect. In Brooklyn alone, it was credited with reducing suspicious fires by 60 percent. It only made one wonder why it had taken the City so long to try it, which quickly undermined the move as a campaign ploy. Mayor Beame lost the Democratic primary (and for all purposes the election) to Congressman Edward I. Koch.

29

The President's Magic Visit
1977–1978

BY the time President Jimmy Carter came to New York in early October 1977 to visit the United Nations, Mayor Beame was a lame duck. The UN trip was the declared purpose of Carter's presence in beleaguered New York, but he also had a secret itinerary known only to a handful of City officials. The planning for this hush-hush mission had been hurriedly arranged during the previous three weeks.

In mid-September Victor Marrero, now the City's planning commissioner, got a phone call from John Zuccotti, his mentor, who had just resigned as deputy mayor. The two, both Yale Law graduates, had first met when Zuccotti helped Marrero set up the South Bronx Community Housing Corporation in 1970. Zuccotti had some very exciting news. He had heard through his grapevine that President Carter, piqued by postblackout criticisms from Vernon Jordan and other black leaders that he was inattentive to the plight of the urban poor, was planning to visit an inner-city neighborhood. Patricia Harris, Carter's secretary of housing and urban development, was thinking of Bushwick or Bedford-Stuyvesant, but Zuccotti thought it might be possible to steer the tour up to the South Bronx. Marrero would have to act quickly, however, to convince Harris's aides and then secretly prepare an itinerary in advance. A short tour was drawn up, and in late September Alan Weiner, area director for HUD, escorted Mrs. Harris over the proposed route.

On the morning of October 5, 1977, the president asked an astonished Mayor Beame, who had not been let in on the secret, to accompany him up to the South Bronx. No other local officials were invited, or even informed. As the president's motorcade passed the Bronx County Courthouse, borough President Bob Abrams looked out the window and wondered who was traveling through the Bronx in such style.

The cream-colored limousine, flags flying, raced up the Grand Concourse, three helicopters whirring overhead. Startled pedestrians saw that it was the president of the United States and yelled out, "Give us money!" "We want jobs!" The motorcade of officials and media all watched the passing sights — the mothballed Concourse Plaza Hotel, the ever-impeccable Andrew Freedman Home, the fenced-off Roosevelt Gardens. They went east on Tremont Avenue, a major shopping street that had been hit badly during the previous summer's blackout. Some stores were still boarded up.

At the end of his show "The Fire Next Door," Bill Moyers had stood inside a burned-out building and said, "So the vice-president travels to Europe and Japan, the secretary of state to the Middle East and Russia, the UN ambassador to Africa. No one of comparable stature comes here."[1] Well, Jimmy Carter changed all that as his cortege headed south on Washington Avenue. He was seeing firsthand the shattered buildings with only shards left in the dark windows, the broken sinks ripped from the wall and smashed in a hallway, the packs of scrawny strays sniffing at strewn garbage, the quiet of the morning streets where few people had to be up and off to work. It was a glorious fall morning, staining all this wreckage with a luminous glow. The limousine pulled up to Venice Hall, the small miracle of the Bronx wrought by the People's Development Corporation.

Some of the early birds, sitting out enjoying the lovely morning, took the president's arrival in stride. "Hi Jimmy," said one. "I'm glad to see you're in the Bronx checking out conditions." Carter, wearing a dark suit and tie, asked, "How do you think we're making out?" The homesteader nodded, "Fine, we hope to make more progress." Meanwhile, someone bounded upstairs to rouse Ramon Rueda, who dressed hurriedly and came down to the door. It was the answer to his prayer, for the group was in dire need of funds, thanks to all the bureaucratic wrangling and footdragging over their loans. The consequent penury had nourished a lot of bad feelings and tension. Carter said, "We're proud of what you're doing."[2]

Rueda took command. He told the president, "We're proud of you, too. We have a low-interest mortgage, but we need more money, Carter. If you would assist us in getting more CETA money, we could show a serious dent in the South Bronx." They invited the president to see their work, but an aide said there wasn't time. The cavalcade rolled away and Rueda rhapsodized to the reporters, "I feel ecstatic. He seemed completely sincere."[3]

The president now drove up Third Avenue, pocked with burned-out buildings ineffectually tinned up. On many façades he could see the scorch marks where raging flames had licked out windows and seared the brick in an upward flash. The limousines veered east on Claremont Parkway, crossing through Crotona Park, its lovely old trees just beginning to turn golden, its playgrounds smashed, its wooden benches half gone. The pathways glittered with shattered glass. At Boston Road the motorcade went left and came to rest at what was left of Charlotte Street. The limousine door opened and the president emerged, as did Mrs. Harris and the mayor of New York.

The breeze was blowing very gently as reporters piled out of their cars and vans and started hurriedly making radio broadcasts or filming the three officials. There was almost nothing left on Charlotte Street itself. All the walk-ups, even the elevator building on the corner, had been turned into high piles of bricks, a mountain range of failure. Carter began to walk, his hands deep in his pockets, his Secret Service men eyeing the abandoned buildings all around with apprehension. Aside from the squawk of walkie-talkies and the reporters talking steadily into microphones and televison cameras, the place was eerily silent.

The president turned to Mrs. Harris and said, "Most of this occurred in the last five years after Nixon cut off the urban renewal funds?" She said, "Yes," and he instructed, "See which area can still be salvaged. Maybe we can create a rec-

OPPOSITE, ABOVE: President Jimmy Carter at Charlotte Street
in 1977 listens to HUD Secretary Patricia Harris while Mayor
Abraham Beame looks on. Journalists take notes behind the president; Secret Servicemen scan the surrounding abandoned buildings.

OPPOSITE, BELOW: Burned-out buildings on Charlotte Street in the
summer of 1977 just before Carter's visit

ABOVE: A man works on his auto in the midst of the devastation of
Charlotte Street. In the background stands I.S. 98, Herman Ridder
Junior High School.

reation area and turn it around. Get a map of the whole area and show me what could be done."[4]

Around the corner, Assemblymen Louis Nine was standing before his bathroom mirror lathered up and shaving when he heard on the news broadcast that President Carter was visiting Charlotte Street. Soap still clinging to his jaw, the portly businessman dashed downstairs past his small locked liquor store, rounding onto Charlotte Street just as the presidential entourage and trailing press retreated into their cars. He yelled and ran, trying to catch their attention so he could speak to the president, but the convoy was peeling away from the curb, wheeling back to Manhattan.

That night American television watchers saw their president walking through an absolutely extraordinary cityscape of empty lots heaped with bricks, bottles, and old auto carcasses against a backdrop of empty apartment buildings, their windows blank and without panes. An occasional torn curtain or old blind flapped in the breeze. This was, intoned CBS's Bob Schiefer, "perhaps the worst slum in America." But it wasn't all gloom, for here was a shot of Ramon Rueda et al. being praised for refurbishing their building.

No one could remember a president foraying forth with such fanfare into the urban slums. (Nixon had made a little-noticed visit to a Washington block after the 1968 riots there.) The *New York Times* pontificated that a visit to the South Bronx was as "crucial to an understanding of American urban lie as a visit to Auschwitz is crucial to an understanding of Nazism."[5] The president of the United States, the most powerful man in the world, had come to the South Bronx. Local officials were stunned at the boldness of it, furious that they hadn't been included, and thrilled at the largesse they were sure would ensue. Remembers Lloyd Kaplan, a young planner with the mayor's office, "Right after Carter's visit the feeling was euphoric. Maybe we could do sonething about Charlotte Street. For a rare and fleeting moment it had a chance. Everyone all over the country knew about it and people in Sioux City, Iowa, suddenly cared."[6] Overnight, the South Bronx had been vaulted to stardom as the worst place in America, maybe the whole Western world.

Only a week later, during a World Series game at Yankee Stadium, the ABC Sports cameras spotted a ball of flame lighting up the pitch-black sky just blocks from the ballpark. At regular intervals the camera swiveled to focus on the roaring conflagration, and announcer Howard Cosell pronounced in his inimitable nasal twang, "The Bronx is burning." While the Yankees played ball, the Bronx was going up in smoke. The casualness of the episode, displayed to millions in the World Series audience, somehow made it even more painful and humiliating to sensitive Bronxites, past and present, than the Moyers show. One remembers starting to cry. "It was so awful," he said. "Seeing it there and knowing the whole world was watching." The burning building was not, as first supposed, an apartment house, but an elementary school. It took almost five hours to extinguish the fire.

"After Carter's visit the City was crazy to get out a report because Beame, whose term was ending at the turn of the year, wanted very much to be associated with something of national prominence," remembers Lloyd Kaplan, the mayoral aide. "The report got out in December, one of Beame's last acts before his departure." [7] Rebuilding the South Bronx had been postponed for so long that officials came to the meetings with maps and figures originally prepared for the Model Cities program almost a decade earlier.

During the late 1970s the Catholic church quietly emerged as the institution most committed to preserving and resurrecting the benighted South Bronx. Not one church or Catholic school had been closed; the schools still provided good, safe education to legions of young Bronxites. The charismatic Father Gigante was single-handedly rebuilding his Hunt's Point parish. Father Smith was the driving force, along with Gennie Brooks, behind the Mid-Bronx Desperados Development Corporation, which was planning the redevelopment of the Charlotte Street area. Up in the northwest Bronx, the Community and Clergy Coalition had organized what was probably the largest Alinsky-style neighborhood power network in the country to keep its district from being South Bronxed.

The Maryknoll Brothers had moved into a rotting tenement near Saint Rita's parish on College Avenue and had begun working with the poor, performing such traditional acts of charity as visiting the friendless and needy, and the less traditional acts of clearing rubble and escorting battered girlfriends to the hospital. The Maryknoll Brothers had been preceded at Saint Rita's in 1971 by the Missionaries of Charity, an order established by Mother Teresa in Calcutta. A second contingent of the Sisters had been dispatched to the South Bronx to transform a burned-out apartment house into a soup kitchen and refuge for beaten wives. They made their way silently through the desolation of the South Bronx, strange apparitions swathed in blue-bordered saris modestly pulled to cover their heads. Those who had served the poorest of the poor in India found the South Bronx far more trying, for here they were dealing not so much with straightforward material want as with spiritual and emotional deprivation. Some months after President Carter's visit, Mother Teresa came quietly to the South Bronx, her presence unnoticed by any but the church and local parishioners.

When Edward I. Koch was inaugurated as the City's new mayor in 1978, there was still of course no plan for reviving the South Bronx. Koch asked Beame aide Lloyd Kaplan to stay on and coordinate the City agencies. Koch also asked Congressman Herman Badillo (whose third mayoral bid Koch had defeated) to join his administration as deputy mayor. Swallowing his considerable pride, Herman signed on and immediately staked out the South Bronx redevelopment as his turf. (This in turn paved the way for state Senator Bobby Garcia to run for Badillo's congressional seat against Councilman Ramon Velez and win.) Badillo also purged the poverty programs. He scrutinized all the remaining community corporations and dismantled those that could not justify their existence.

Badillo favored quick, splashy results — he wanted to see

housing rise up from the dust stirred by the president's shoes. Says Kaplan: "We were shoveling fog when we talked about doing something dramatic. I thought we should work with the remaining groups to reinforce the existing pockets of strength. Part of Herman's view was to test the national commitment. He wanted to do something major and see a lot of money up front."[8] Kaplan could not reconcile himself to Badillo's big splash theory, and so he resigned.

Badillo, meanwhile, drew up a $1.5 billion plan whose centerpiece was housing. The White House had already said it could make available only $55 million from a variety of federal agencies, and it now reminded the City of this, and also of their request that the City assemble a planning unit to allocate priorites. Badillo recruited Edward J. Logue, a veteran of urban renewal and large-scale building, who had redeveloped New Haven and Boston and had presided over the construction of thirty thousand housing units (including Roosevelt Island) while head of the Urban Development Corporation in New York State. In 1975 Logue had resigned from the UDC under a cloud when the state agency neared bankruptcy. Now Logue was returning to the fray, determined to resurrect his own reputation along with the South Bronx. It was a formidable assignment, and fans and foes had to admire the high-stakes gamble Logue was making.

It was already apparent that the White House (in the person of presidential aide Jack Watson) and City Hall (in the persons of Badillo and Koch) were talking at complete cross purposes: Washington was talking jobs; New York was talking housing. Thomas Glynn, managing editor of the New York Urban Coalition's *Neighborhood* magazine, wrote some time later that "the White House felt the plan was too ambitious, that too much money was involved. Moreover, the White House staff felt that everyone was headed for embarrassment. . . . Watson met Koch and told him he favored realistic projects and solid planning."[9]

Nonetheless, when Mayor Koch and Herman Badillo unveiled their $1.5 billion plan on April 12, 1978, with its emphasis on rebuilding at a City Hall ceremony, Watson introduced the White House's $55 million plan emphasizing economic development. (Carter hadn't heard anyone yelling, "Give us apartments!" He had heard people yelling, "Give us jobs!")

Even without agreement between City Hall and the White House, the South Bronx had become a glamorous cause worth battling for. Grassroots groups found themselves the beneficiaries of a journalistic invasion, and of renewed interest by corporations, foundations, and government agencies.

The most sought-after grassroots group was Ramon Rueda and his People's Development Corporation. Why not? They had been personally endorsed by the president. "Suddenly, in the wake of Carter's 15-minute tour of 1186 Washington Avenue, we were all stars," Steve Katz of the PDC was to write, in the magazine *City Limits*. "Foreign visitors and journalists streamed up to Morrisania. Ramon was on constant call to speak at hearings, conferences and meetings. It was a nice gift, but it certainly turned some people's heads around. And it did nothing to heal the painful internal difficulties or the external restraints."[10]

What it did do was shake loose the loans the PDC had been waiting for and bring in other sources of money. The Louisiana-Pacific Lumber Company gave twenty thousand dollars' worth of materials. When the PDC mentioned wanting to recycle garbage into soil with a worm ranch, Worm World, Inc., of Denver donated half a million red hybrid worms. The PDC quickly went from being a struggling, shoe-string opertion staffed with a couple of dozen idealists to a full-blown $4 million organization that was involved in construction, job training, alternative energy, economic development, and "village" planning. The number of employees increased tenfold to 250, and the work sites expanded from five to twenty.

Ramon reveled in this vindication of all his dreams and travails. "He was Carterized, that's for sure," says Jack Flanagan, the on-leave cop busy with Bronx Frontier and greening the South Bronx. "After Charlotte Street, Ramon and I went downtown for meetings and there were all these guys doing their bureaucratic shuffle and there's Ramon pounding his fist on the table and saying, 'Now, when I was talking to President Carter at my house, he told me not to let the bureaucracy get us bogged down.' After a while I knew his whole spiel. Ramon would say, 'I'll never forget that day. I woke up and heard all these helicopters and the next thing I knew there was Carter.' It changed his whole life."[11]

There were tangible rewards for Bronx Frontier, too. After Carter's visit, Flanagan met up with Tom Fox, a savvy young activist dispatched from the Institute for Local Self-Reliance in Washington, D.C., to see if they could be helpful. Fox set about organizing the Open Space Task Force, which became a "greening" coalition of Bronx Frontier, the PDC, the Green Guerrillas, the New York Botanical Garden, and others. They went after Department of Interior funds never before allocated to cities, and after a mighty effort wrested $1.1 million to transform fifteen garbage-filled lots into miniparks throughout the South Bronx. Bronx Frontier would oversee the development of nine parks, the PDC another five, and another group the remaining one.

Bronx Frontier had an exciting summer in 1978. The Chuck Wagon program, a mobile kitchen in a former bookmobile, roved the streets teaching cooking and nutrition. It was extremely well received and was incorporated as a regular feature at a few local schools. Over on the "ranch" on the Hunt's Point peninsula, the giant compost turner was in its test period. Mountainous piles of vegetable waste were being carted over from the nearby Hunt's Point Produce Market, then laboriously culled of unacceptable debris, then churned and shredded with leaves and zoo manure. (Eventually, this mixture came to be marketed as ZooDoo, although the veggie component was abandoned as too much trouble.) To everyone's vast relief, it worked. By the end of the first summer, two thousand cubic yards of compost (worth twenty-eight thousand dollars) had been created. Some was stored, and the rest was distributed to seven new gardens and three that were in their second season.

Bronx Frontier was now inundated by officials eager to see the notorious South Bronx — visitors from Africa, Japan,

Switzerland, England, and France. The interruptions became so hard to handle that a weekly show-and-tell was put together, including a bus tour through the rubble to the gardens, those little oases of love and pride.

Bronx Frontier decided to purchase a windmill to generate its own power for use in the composting operation. This elegant machine, tall and slender, was to whirl majestically above the ranch, catching the winds whipping across the small promontory. Christened Aeolus after the Greek God of Wind, it was the first windmill to rise in the Bronx since the long-ago days of the Morris family.

The summer of 1978 saw the birth of yet another grassroots group, Bronx 2000. Bronx 2000's sphere of influence was the ten-block area north of Charlotte Street, surrounding East Tremont Avenue, a famous shopping street that had been badly hurt by the 1977 blackout. David Muchnik, a tall, rangy Harvard-trained lawyer who liked to wear cowboy hats, was hired as a consultant to get this new venture off the ground. Muchnik had taught sociology at the New School for Social Research and worked as a congressional liaison for housing. He raised fifty thousand dollars from the Vincent Astor Foundation and thirty-five thousand dollars from the State Division of Housing as seed money, and then went on to raise another $1.25 million. This accomplished, he decided to stick around and make sure the job was done right. Bronx 2000 organized both tenants and merchants, cleared lots to make them into parks, and generally tried to spruce up the neighborhood. They brought in a farmers' market to add a festive air to the weekends and give residents access to better food. They pondered mushroom farming in an abandoned parking garage, or opening an herb nursery in nearby vacant lots. Both foods were delicacies in great demand in Manhattan restaurants.

Yet another group sprouted a couple of blocks west of Father Gigante's turf, with the improbable name of Banana Kelly. In August 1977 residents on the short, curving Kelly Street (hence the banana) had refused to give up their buildings to City demolition crews. They organized and began to redeem the block. Over the next several years they planted a community garden and rehabbed six apartment houses.

Perhaps the most unlikely of the post-Carter benefits was the arrival in the Bronx of Fashion Moda, the "Museum of Science, Art, Invention, Technology and Fantasy," on Third Avenue near 147th Street, just below the 149th Street shopping hub. Founded in 1978 by Austrian artist Stefan Eins, this ultra-alternative space showed "weird amalgams of local, downtown and international culture." Deciding his "alternative space" gallery in Soho was too insular, Eins set his sights on the South Bronx to prove that "quality achievement can happen anywhere." He told the *New Yorker* that he "needed a strong challenge to get my creative focus. I chose the South Bronx partly because of its media image as the worst ghetto in the nation."[12] His gallery became a legitimizing force for graffiti "writers," introducing them into the fashionable downtown art scene.

30

Disenchantment
1979–1980

Back at City Hall, inevitable rumblings surfaced over the grand plan to revive the South Bronx. Neither the White House nor the City was distinguishing itself. Jack Watson, now a frequent visitor to the South Bronx, held a press conference for the weekly Bronx papers, and various local politicians crashed it to complain that they had not been consulted about the plan. The local press was dismayed that Washington could commit so gross an oversight as forgetting to massage indigenous egos.

The White House's Bronx plan featured business loans, a new federal office building, a job corps barracks, a mental-health center, and a renovation of the Claremont Village housing project south of Charlotte Street. "What then is new," queried the *Riverdale Press*, "about this rag bag of recycled WPA, War on Poverty, and outdated urban renewal programs? How does it differ from past failures?

" 'Well, before,' said the President's Secretary in his statement at the Bronx County building, 'we were failing to create critical masses of impact, because we were failing to target our resources well and to leverage them to the greatest extent possible with private sector investment.'

"Only a government that mistakes that kind of language for thought," the *Press* went on, "could mistake this resurrection of discredited programs for the revitalization of the South Bronx."[1]

Herman Badillo's prize package remained 732 low-rise, middle-income apartments smack in the middle of the devastation of Charlotte Street. Badillo was gambling that the presidential election coming up in 1980 would force the White House to capitulate and switch to his plan. On February 8, 1979, the City Board of Estimate met to vote on closing off Charlotte Street. As the debate unfolded, the board members expressed various reservations about yet more housing in a borough where one expensive project after another had gone down the tubes. Who could forget the infamous Fox Street debacle, where a $2.8 million renovation of nine buildings had been abandoned within a year after it was invaded by junkies and set afire? Or the Mott Haven Housing Development Fund disaster, where twenty renovated buildings had been totally trashed?

The other boroughs represented on the Board of Estimate saw no reason to give up money to the Bronx just because the president had alighted there. The Brooklyn borough president said disgustedly, "If President Carter's chauffeur had taken a right turn instead of a left turn, we'd have all the money going to Bushwick now."[2] It seemed the City was being asked to expend all its federal housing monies in the Bronx in the name of Charlotte Street and President Carter. Board members voiced their objections with greater and greater conviction, and voted to quash Badillo's plan.

Years later Badillo was still bitter. "Koch never wanted Charlotte Street to happen because he saw that as creating a constituency for me to run."[3] In the ensuing months Badillo threatened to resign a number of times and finally did, quitting City Hall to engage in the usual pursuits of the politician without a public job — lawyerhood and host of a television talk show called "Urban Journal."

On the other side, Mayor Koch "ate crow," retracted his assertion that without Charlotte Street the whole South Bronx plan was dead, and began anew. Ed Logue had established the South Bronx Development Organization with $3.5 million and was methodically surveying the Bronx, its strengths and its weaknesses. He opened one office in Manhattan and another on Courtlandt Avenue off the 149th Street Hub in the Bronx. (Logue was technically a consultant, and he paid himself a commensurate salary, one hundred thousand a year.)

Logue began the unenviable task of wooing the local leaders, all deeply suspicious of yet another government official promising salvation. Ramon Velez, weakened by Badillo's attacks, shutdowns of his various poverty agencies, and a number of unfruitful investigations of his operations, instinctively opposed Logue as an outside imperialist trying to tell the Puerto Rican South Bronx what to do.

Internecine warfare had erupted even at Venice Hall, in that brightest of Bronx stars, the People's Development Corporation. Serious disputes had led to the departure of one-third of the aspiring homesteaders. In February another group of workers was dismissed. The construction manager found his car windshield bashed in by a baseball bat. Vandalism quickly escalated, and a few days later the main office of the PDC was gutted by arson fire, destroying all financial records and consequently the PDC's credit.

Ramon Rueda's new thirty-thousand-dollar salary and frequent absences to gallivant around the country as a "sweat equity" star at conferences and meetings were heartily resented. Now he returned to mediate the unleashed furies of his workers, but to no avail. The fire was followed by break-ins. The spirit that had carried the original homesteaders through the worst times disappeared in prosperity and was further eroded by the PDC's Hispanic cast in a basically black neighborhood. Homesteaders stopped paying their rents at Venice Hall, and the City repossesed the building for unpaid taxes. Work lagged seriously on the other five apartment houses. In April the main office was torched a second time. The final denouement was the disappearance of Ramon Rueda himself. Perhaps he feared for his own life. The Washington Avenue dream was dead, a victim in a sense of the Carter visit and the excess of money that followed it.

By the summer of 1979 Carter's campaign for reelection was revving up, and the City of New York was milking it for all it was worth. Victor Marrero had joined the Carter administration as an undersecretary of the Department of Housing and Urban Development, where he was pushing hard for Bronx projects. In February 1980 Mayor Koch announced a federally subsidized small-homes program that would yield 250 single-family houses at four sites in the South Bronx. Streets once dense with five- and six-story rental buildings would now be reborn with modest brick houses, driveways, and small front lawns. Planners had been told again and again that Puerto Ricans and blacks from the South and Caribbean islands believed a home was a house with a yard. If working families were to be lured into the worst wildernesses of the South Bronx, this sort of housing would be the most appealing.

A month after Koch's announcement came another. The long-talked-about development of industrial parks was going to be given its debut on Bathgate Avenue. Ed Logue had sold both the mayor and the White House on the idea and then lured the wealthy and powerful New York Port Authority to participate. The City would combine its $3.1 million with the feds' $4.3 million to clear a twenty-one-acre site and construct a large industrial building to be leased to private companies.

In July 1980 Logue's South Bronx Development Organization announced its vision of how to rebuild the borough, calling for the creation of twenty-five thousand new and rehabilitated owner-occupied apartments, five million square-feet of industrial and commercial space, ten thousand new jobs, and 193 recreation spaces and facilities. The price tag was $20 million a year for seven years. As one City Hall official said, "Election years are good times to get commitments." Countered the White House, "The Carter pledge will keep on within the limits of our means."

VOICES OF THE SOUTH BRONX
VERALYNE HAMILTON

"Ed Logue came into town and they were ready to lynch him," says Veralyne Hamilton, a longtime activist who became district manager of Community Planning Board 3, which includes Morrisania and Charlotte Street, in 1981. She is a comely black woman who still speaks with a bit of a southern accent. "I had been through all that burning and now all these people were saying 'I don't want anything built unless I have input into it.' I could see District 3 getting left out altogether because they were bogged down in that debate. That is the reason I became district manager. Ed Logue is who he is, and I respect him because of his knowledge. But his style caused him a hard time. I said, 'Okay, Ed Logue may be a racist, but he knows how to push projects. You see this vacant land around here, ladies and gentlemen? Well, it could be like this forever if you don't hook up with this new situation. This is the story. This is the deal.' "

Mrs. Hamilton had moved to Morrisania in 1957 from Richmond, Virginia, where she had been attending all-black Virginia Union College and supporting herself as a companion and baby-sitter for a minister's family. "When they saw my struggle to pay tuition and manage myself, they recommended I go to New York because certain colleges wouldn't make you pay tuition if you had a good grade average. I came to the Bronx and lived with a woman on Third Avenue and Claremont Parkway. Those buildings aren't there anymore. It was a railroad flat, and the El went right by her bedroom window. Catholic Charities got me a job with a mailing company that sent out magazines."

Originally from Norfolk, Virginia, Mrs. Hamilton had been raised by her grandparents. "My mother had left my father. He was trying to get her to come home, a fight ensued, and she killed him. About eighteen months later her lover killed her, and so I went to live with my grandparents. My grandfather, who was illiterate, had a little grocery store. My grandmother was a housewife. We were too poor to have anything in our house but the Bible. My mother had been a Catholic, and so I went to Saint Joseph's School. When I was fifteen I started doing my own little research about my situation and it bothered me a lot emotionally. I rebelled against the stigma and started playing hooky from school. A black social worker made the determination that it would be best if I was not in Norfolk, and I was transferred to Richmond and lived with foster parents. I finished high school, and my social worker enrolled me in college, but I didn't see how I could afford it.

"Friends and relatives had returned from the City with all these glorious tales of New York. So you were brainwashed about the streets of gold." The South of that time was still rigidly segregated. "In that separate society, you were nothing: you were a non. Whites had the selection to deal with you as they wished. Can you imagine going through life with individual white people having that kind of decision on you?" And so she came north.

Mrs. Hamilton got sidetracked earning a living, however, and then raising a family after she got married in 1958. "For five years I was home having babies, being a housewife, and not knowing anything about New York. We were living at the corner of 167th Street and Stebbins Avenue at my in-laws' house. New York for me at that time was going to the clinic with my kids, shopping, going to Central Park. Wherever you take children, that's where I was." She remembers the Morrisania district in which she raised her four daughters as being packed and lively. "The neighborhood then had a trillion people, sitting on the stoop. That's where I learned to like Spanish music, because it was very Afro-Cuban. Prospect Avenue was a great place with lots of movie theaters, bars, and real church on Sunday. Crotona Park was heavily used with picnics and things. There were still many middle-class people, with jobs in the post office and such." Her own husband worked for the transit authority.

In 1967 she was ready to send her oldest daughter Pam to the elementary school down the block. Her sister-in-law, a teacher, advised her that the little girl would get a better education at PS 105 way up Pelham Parkway. "I said, 'I have moved all the way up here from the South for all these opportunities and here I am having to send my kid off in a bus.' So I came out of the house to find out about the school situation and the whole 1960s thing was there. I went to a local community organization and told them I was interested in bettering the neighborhood and whatnot.

"Everyone was a part of 'the cause' at that time. I got hooked into housing. Who owned a building was often a big mystery. I remember going into Union Avenue — the buildings aren't there any more — and it was cold, so cold, with snow on the ground. It was seven at night and there was no light at all in the building, a walk-up. This elderly man with me had a flashlight. The hallway was tiled, and the water from the broken pipes had formed ice. So we were slip-sliding, going upstairs. I was very green at the time, but I had promised to try and get them heat and I had just found out who the landlord was. We knocked on this woman's door and said, 'We've finally found who the landlord is.' She looked at us and said, 'I don't need to know, my father has died.' He didn't freeze to death, but he was ninety-two years old and he had contracted pneumonia.

"In that same group of buildings we went to knock on another door. There was no light at all, and so when the door opens, you don't see anybody, you just hear this little voice say, 'My momma isn't home.' There was a little boy about this high in an undershirt all dingy and raggedy. He said, 'She said she was going to the store.' When he shut the door I said, 'Can you imagine anyone leaving their child in the dark by themselves?' So there we see her coming up the steps with this bottle under her arm. She said, 'In order to stand this sort of stuff, this cold, I just go out and get me a little drink.' I'm thinking this is the worst woman in the world. Then I thought, you know, if I didn't have my husband helping me, supporting me, I might be the same way. You're not that certain that if it was you, you wouldn't raise the window, throw your kid out, and follow yourself."

When Model Cities came along, Mrs. Hamilton plunged in. "It was a wonderful learning experience. It exposed people who didn't know, like me, to real power. We went down to City Hall with a group of people and we walked right into the Blue Room and we talked to Mayor Lindsay. So I do not say it was thrown away. But if there was any one time when I felt cynical, it was the end of the Model Cities era in 1972. If ever the Bronx was going to do what it was supposed, it should have happened then. The politics were right, the funds were right, but the missing ingredient was commitment by the decision makers, the higher ups."

Mrs. Hamilton had started attending Hunter College nights, while working downtown in the giant realty firm of Cushman and Wakefield. "When the government stopped giving tax shelters for building low-income housing, then my little unit [Construction for Progress] no longer served a purpose." She resigned from Model Cities (but her colleagues refused the resignation), applied for a Model Cities scholarship, and returned full time to college. "On the personal side, what I had begun to do with a career put a heavy weight on my marriage." She and her husband agreed to separate.

Then one day "I came home in 1972 to find my daughter on the stoop talking to some gang members. I called her in and asked what she was doing with them. She told me how they had been on TV the night before. She had told her class she knew some of them and now she was doing a report. She saw those kids as TV celebrities. That night I knew we would have to move, because I could see my daughter had a fascination for these gangs and I was not going to lose her to that. I panicked." When Mrs. Hamilton confided her fears to a woman friend, she offered her a large apartment in upper Manhattan. And so the Hamiltons moved their residence.

After she graduated from college, Mrs. Hamilton returned to work in the Bronx, running a day-care center on Sherman Avenue. She felt terrible about having left her old neighborhood, but she was still active on the local planning board. "The amazing thing in the Bronx was, you were so caught up in your day-to-day struggle, you did not see what was happening. The impact hit me one night when I was watching a documentary on channel 13 and these women were the only ones left in the building and they had these obstacles running down the steps to keep people from pulling out the water pipes. I probably had been in some of those buildings, but the impact didn't hit me until I saw it on film."

As director of the local community board, Mrs. Hamilton had the responsibility of escorting many of the urban disaster tourists after the Carter visit. "Everybody wanted to see Charlotte Street. So I would go with them and they would say, 'You must be very surprised that someone would come from as far as Japan or Norway, but you have to remember that when this scene came on TV we could not believe that in the

United States of America an area looked like this where it had not been declared war.' I would say, 'Yes, I can understand.' Then I got back and the idea popped into my head, 'But a kind of war was declared.' It *was* a war. It was a *war*. It just seemed like everybody went crazy at the same time. You knew the suffering that people had had here, and it made me determined that something was going to happen positively here. I felt guilty for moving, but I elected to stay and work.

"I feel optimistic about the Bronx. The decision makers are familiar with it — 'Oh, this is the internationally known decayed urban area. We don't mind sending some resources to the Bronx.' Life goes on, and where there's life, there's hope."

Charlotte Street and National Politics
1980

CHARLOTTE STREET had become a must for political as-
pirants. Teddy Kennedy made his appearance there in
March 1980, just before the New York presidential primary,
in the company of Herman Badillo, who squired Kennedy
around in the rain, taking him to the very spot where Carter
had stood. With this most dramatic of backdrops — dead
buildings, the famous mountain range of rubble — Badillo
extended his arm and indicted the landscape and the president. "Take a look around you, Senator, and see for yourself
what the Carter promises have done."

Ronald Reagan came for his turn. On August 6, trailed by
reporters and camera crews, the Republican candidate for
president headed north to Charlotte Street after speaking to
the National Urban League conference at the New York Hil-
ton. Various artists had been readying Charlotte Street for
the People's Convention, an alternative to the Democratic
National Convention just days away. In neat, stylized letters
the word DECAY had been stenciled by artist John Fekner in
vivid orange across the side of one empty building. Across
the way an enormous and accusing BROKEN PROMISES covered
yet another gutted wreck. Reagan emerged from his limousine
into the blazing sunlight and stood on Charlotte Street in his
cream-colored suit. He looked and commented, as had so
many before him, that he hadn't "seen anything like this since
London after the Blitz." Then he stepped onto a low platform
and condemned Carter for not keeping his promise, thereupon

Candidate Ronald Reagan came to Charlotte Street
during his 1980 campaign

Following Carter's visit, Charlotte Street became a backdrop for many events, including this parade by Hiroshima survivors in 1978 advocating a "reordering of national priorities" to spend more on poor urban neighborhoods and less on bombs

promising himself to see the South Bronx rebuilt through tax
incentives and private industry. Across the street, a hostile
crowd of sixty or seventy chanted, "You ain't gonna do nothing," and "Go back to California."[1]

Reagan completed his prepared speech and then bravely
headed across the street to confront his hecklers. He told them
earnestly, "If you'll just listen, I'm trying to tell you — I know
now there is no program or policies that a president makes
that the federal government can come in and wave a wand to
do this." Unimpressed, they kept on chanting. Now Reagan
got angry and reprimanded them: "Look, if you will listen —
I can't do a damn thing for you if I don't get elected. It's
awfully easy to make promises. If you'll look at what I did
for eight years as governor of California, you'll find I did these
things." The chanters were unmoved and switched to a new
message as Reagan retreated to his limousine: "We want Kennedy, we want Kennedy." Later, Reagan mulled over the
bleakness of it all to the reporters. "There we were, driving
away, and you think of them back there in all that ugliness
and they have no place to go. All that is before them is to sit
and look at what we just saw."[2] A sobering thought.

VOICES OF THE SOUTH BRONX
MARIA HERNANDEZ*

It looked terrible, but it was home. Maria Hernandez had
moved away from Charlotte Street in 1970 and across Crotona
Park, but she missed her old neighborhood and soon came
back to a place near PS 61 on Crotona Park East. "I was born
in Ponce, Puerto Rico, in 1943. We came to Longfellow Avenue in the Bronx right after the war. My father worked as
a cook in his sister's restaurant, La Dalia, on Westchester
Avenue. Then he died of heart disease and in 1951 we moved
to Apartment 2A at 1517 Charlotte Street, where my mother
became the super. It was a beautiful block. We were the first
Spanish in our building. The landlady, Esther Halprin, and
her sister lived in the building. I remember their apartment

* Not her real name.

was like a dollhouse with small, lacy things, and they were always serving tea and little cakes. My mother did everything for them, the shopping, the cleaning. She took care of them."

Maria and her three sisters slept in bunkbeds in one bedroom, her four brothers in bunkbeds in the other, her mother on a foldout couch in the living room. "Everything was very beautiful then, very strict. When it was very hot we went up on the roof to sleep and we were never afraid. We had picnics up there. I used to go to PS 98, Herman Ridder, wearing tight skirts and lipstick, and those teachers would make you wipe off the makeup and loosen the skirt. In those days, if you played hooky, the truant officer would pick you up and take you to family court. Now, they don't care."

In eighth grade, Maria fell in love with a man named Louis and a year later, when she finished ninth grade at Herman Ridder, they were married. "Living on Charlotte Street was a happy, beautiful life. My mother was very proud when I was married in a big wedding with a white dress and eight bridesmaids. I was sixteen, he was twenty-five, a clerk-manager in a grocery store. Men promise you'll finish school, but it doesn't work out that way. Then they say, 'Why do you want to go to school?' At that time I was Miss America. I wish you could have seen how beautiful I was," she says wistfully. Now she is very heavy and her long hair is drawn plainly back into a bun. "I didn't even know what birth control was and I had four children straight."

In 1964 she discovered her husband had been running around with a married woman with children. "We had a big fight and he destroyed everything in the apartment. He went to Puerto Rico for a while, then I did too before coming back. It was tough, I was a young girl wandering around and I had no place to stay. My mother was very angry with me for breaking up with Louis." She moved in with a neighbor at 1515 Charlotte Street with her four children.

"The burglaries and drugs were everywhere by then. I remember drugs in the streets, the stairs, the house. Then came the gangs. They were supposed to be helping, but they did bad things. My brother was in the Turbans. They made people pay protection, and I knew one place they set on fire because they wouldn't pay up. My brother was on TV. He would hide guns in the house. And he was involved with drugs, too — heroin.

"The way I found out was one day I was looking for him and I saw some of his friends in an empty building on Wilkins Avenue. As I walked in I saw one of his friends sticking a needle in his arm. I remember screaming, 'No, no, no!' Then I took him everywhere for a cure, all kinds of clinics and finally Phoenix House. I went through all this hell with my brother. My mother never knew about his drug addiction. Then once a guy came to shoot him. He was running after him, I jumped on him, and we wrestled to the ground and my brother got away. The things I saw . . . one guy who jumped from the roof and just kept on going."

Irrevocably separated from Louis, Mrs. Hernandez began living with a Charlotte Street neighbor, Ruben. Meanwhile, more and more people were moving out, including Maria's mother. "People were afraid. There were holdups, fires, and people destroying apartments. My mother said the welfare people destroyed the place. She said they don't want to work and they spoil everything. People couldn't go out of the house one minute or the junkies would rob them. Finally, the only Jew left on our block was the old landlady, Esther Halprin. It was terrible what they did to her. A tenant would knock on the door and when she opened it someone would rush in and stick her up. They robbed her many times like this and beat her up. Finally, she had to move away.

"By 1970 everyone was gone from Charlotte Street but us. Everyone had been burned out and ours was the only building looking alive. I was used to the place and I wasn't afraid. We watched the building very good to make sure no one took the pipes. At first we used to collect rents from the remaining tenants and use it to buy fuel oil. Then one tenant, an Italian lady, said she didn't want to give rent anymore. That's when it started getting bad. We had no oil and so no hot water, maybe once in a blue moon. When no one would pay the rent we ran the boiler on old tires and got something like heat. After three winters like that, finally it was just too cold and we decided to move. We made a thousand dollars stripping all the pipes from the building and selling everything we could from it."

When Maria split from her husband, Louis, she had gone on welfare. All through the years that she lived with Ruben and bore him four children she remained on welfare. "Every woman on welfare gets money from some man," she says. "Sometimes Medicaid is more important than the welfare. Once I got off and then got back on because I needed to go to the doctor." She and Ruben argued from time to time about her never getting divorced so they could be married, but nothing changed. They lived together on Crotona Park East, Ruben working as a super, Maria raising the eight children.

The fate of her offsping was a source of deep depression to Mrs. Hernandez. "I feel I had bad luck. My mother did a great job and she was by herself. But I feel very disappointed in my children. None of them finished high school and the older girls all have babies and no husbands. It's been very tough for me. I feel so sick, nervous, and depressed, worrying about everything. All the problems come to my house."

Her oldest son never learned to really read or write. "He gets frustrated, embarrassed, and he can't get a job. I would be the happiest woman on earth if he had a job, but I don't see it. He doesn't use drugs, but selling — yes. He was not out on the street corner, but higher up. He had a gun-possession case in court and he was afraid of going to jail. So he promised, 'If I have to starve I will not go back to selling drugs.' He was making five thousand — ten thousand dollars a day. He blew all the money and now he has nothing. He was riding around in limousines. Women were coming after him from everywhere. They smelled all that money. Oh, and clothes — he threw out one wardrobe and bought a new one. I tell him, save, but he doesn't. He sent his wife for a pregnancy test in a limousine with a TV set. Now he has no money she's not interested. He's been in this business so long he just likes to hang out, have a good time. He can't settle down. I did everything for my son, but I don't know what will become of him."

Three of her four daughters are single mothers on welfare. One has three children, another has two, and a third has one. The fourth daughter has stopped going to high school and stays home to keep house. Mrs. Hernandez sighs bleakly. "Now Sonia's 'husband' is using drugs and has gone from worse to worse. She feels very frightened. At three in the morning he breaks into her apartment and steals everything, even the baby's new clothes. She had a gun and was going to shoot him, but the cartridge was in wrong, thank God. Now all these children ruin my life with all their problems. I could go to school, go to college. Instead, they complicate my life more and more. My husband gives me a hundred dollars to buy myself some clothes, and it ends up being spent on three coats for the babies. They survive because of me. All the girls care about is clothes, like any teenagers. They don't want to wear the same shoes two days in a row. They want money to buy designer jeans."

One of her favorite brothers was stabbed to death in 1983 in a drunken fight over money, his corpse dumped in an abandoned building amidst old garage and debris. Her mother was devastated by his murder. There is a suspect, but he has never been arrested. Maria's brothers and sisters have fared well overall. They all finished high school and some even went to college. "I'm the only one who never finished school," Mrs. Hernandez says disconsolately. "One dream I pray is my son gets himself in shape. I want to go to school. I think there's a lot of things I could do. I'm not afraid of the world. I may not speak perfect English, but there's no book I can't read. If I didn't have all these children. . . ."

She has now lived almost thirty years on and around Charlotte Street. During that time most of it burned down and disappeared. Yet she is not bitter. "I love this neighborhood. I go round at all hours, even through the park. I take a baseball bat. I never even had a holdup here. Everyone knows me. But in order to survive in this neighborhood, you got to be tough. You don't take nothing." She describes a complicated altercation and confrontation at a park playground. "These black kids came out and were jeering and threatening me. They insulted me, called me a fat elephant and said we came on banana boats. I was so mad if I had had a gun I would have used it. Before it was all over the police came. You can't take those insults. You have to fight back. That's how you survive in New York City."

As the Democrats streamed into town for the great party convention of 1980, the circus on Charlotte Street was just getting into full swing. What better place for the Counter Convention of the Coalition for the People's Alternative? Three days after candidate Reagan's visit, five hundred alternate representatives (half the number predicted) arrived at the temporary tent city in the South Bronx. Three small wooden shacks had been erected as embarrassing reminders of Carter's failure to produce. One was draped with a sign, "The White House of Charlotte Street." The organizers of the People's Convention indulged in a lot of grandiose rhetoric and intense powwows. The delegates represented an array of groups aligned against sexism, ageism, racism, and all the other ills of an imperfect society — the African People's Revolutionary Party, the National Association of Neighborhoods, the National Association of Lesbian and Gay Filmmakers, the Gray Panthers, the New Jersey Tenants' Organization, and the National Task Force on Prostitution.

Their encampment did no more for Charlotte Street than the visits of the hundreds of other urban disaster tourists. There had been the Bolshoi Ballet, and then a cluster of visiting Russian officials, escorted to the infamous spot by Councilman Gilbert Gerena-Valentin. The councilman thereupon proposed that the USSR give the South Bronx $5 billion in foreign aid. On another occasion a parade of Hiroshima survivors dressed in Buddhist robes marched down Charlotte Street chanting for peace.

En route to say mass at Yankee Stadium, Pope John Paul II stopped at Morris Avenue and 151st Street to bless the site of two fireproof apartment houses to be built by the local parishes. Reverend Neil A. Connolly, the vicar of the South Bronx who had led the early antiarson efforts, greeted the pontiff: "Your presence here tonight means that we count."[3] The pope in his white raiments mounted a wooden platform and accepted a bouquet of lilies and chrysanthemums.

The lights failed, and Cardinal Cooke had to shine a flashlight while the Pope read his speech. To the delight of his audience, he spoke in Spanish, saying; "I came here because I know the difficult conditions of your existence. I know the sorrow that takes place in your lives. For this reason, you deserve particular attention on the part of the Pope. My presence here signifies an appreciation of what the church has done and continues to do. . . . Do not abandon yourselves to despair, my brothers and friends, but collaborate among yourselves, take those steps that all are possible for your greater dignity and unite your efforts toward moral goals."[4] His listeners were elated as the Pope departed to visit Cardinal Hayes High School and then Yankee Stadium. Exulted one ecstatic woman, "It means that at least God loves us. If the politicians don't care about us, at least God loves us."

The White House continued to pump money into the South Bronx as the 1980 presidential campaign reached its climax. It told the *Christian Science Monitor* that the South Bronx had been the beneficiary of $175 million for programs and $25 million in loan guarantees since Carter's visit. As the campaign moved into its final weeks, Logue's South Bronx Development Organization got another $1.5 million. Father Gigante netted eight hundred thousand dollars to build an elegant Spanish courtyard in front of Saint Athanasius. The American hostages in Iran and runaway inflation had soured the country on Carter however, and he lost badly to Ronald Reagan in November.

In the aftermath of Carter's visit to Charlotte Street, many political professionals were puzzled. Why had he gone to the South Bronx if he didn't know his administration could deliver something? When nothing visible resulted except a lot of squabbling, local officials and residents became embittered

A young boy poses solemnly on his roller skates while two men behind him share a smoke in the Hunt's Point neighborhood

Children joyously playing a game of *leap!* from an abandoned car on Faile Street

and scornful. They had been thrilled when the president of the United States came, but they were deeply disappointed when it all amounted to nothing but a lot of publicity. And it made the South Bronx look like a basket case. If the president comes and can't get anywhere, who can?

But government money alone could never address the fundamental problem of the South Bronx, which was the continuing abandonment and devastation of its neighborhoods. Officialdom had yet to figure out how to preserve a collapsing neighborhood. In the East Bronx, the grassroots groups were rebuilding. But in the northwest Bronx, they faced a far more complex situation, the classic South Bronx cycles of poverty, drugs, crime, fires, and abandonment. Again and again, as neighborhoods were hit, residents organized to stop the crime and the fires, but they always foundered. One had only to look at the streets and blocks and neighborhoods that had fallen like so many dominoes, starting in Mott Haven and Hunt's Point and then traveling relentlessly north, through Morrisania, West Farms, into East Tremont, then heading west and engulfing the Grand Concourse and beyond, into the West Bronx, and the old Irish neighborhood of Highbridge.

As each neighborhood was stricken by this plague, it too came to be known as the South Bronx. Each year, the "South Bronx" expanded.

32

"The Next Part of the South Bronx"
1972–1978

THE great institutions of the northern Bronx had been watching uneasily while the neighborhoods farther south first turned into slums and then burned. They pondered what this presaged for their own futures. Fordham University, the renowned Jesuit institution whose roots in the Bronx dated back to 1846, was sufficiently concerned in the fall of 1970 to appoint seminarian Paul Brant to the new position of community liaison.

Brant came to his job thanks to the great 1969 Christmas blizzard that immobilized New York. Four days after the snowstorm, Queens was still buried, and Queens regarded it as a major scandal. But seven weeks later, the northern Bronx was still not plowed, and no one, except the beleaguered residents, seemed to notice. "I thought there was something wrong with that," Brant recalls.[1] He began to contact various levels of officialdom, to no avail. He soon found himself appointed to the Fordham job.

The young, brash Brant gathered together the Catholic pastors of the northern Bronx and suggested they work with the university to stabilize their neighborhoods. "They were all scared except for one. Some of them didn't think the church should be involved, others were afraid it would incite racial conflict." The one exception was Monsignor John McCarthy of Holy Spirit parish in Morris Heights. With his snowy-white hair and deeply lined visage radiating gentle good humor,

McCarthy was a "stereotypical Irish pastor of the old school," says Brant, "firm and caring, but he had a backbone."[2]

McCarthy and Brant teamed up to form the Morris Heights Neighborhood Improvement Association, but the local situation was already deteriorating. "Between the initial meeting with McCarthy and the time the improvement association started in October of 1972 one year had elapsed, but it was the year Co-op City really opened up and it just siphoned people out of there like a vacuum cleaner," says Brant. "The South Bronx was burning and being abandoned, and welfare people were moving west."[3]

Morris Heights stood on the westernmost ridge of the Bronx, overlooking the Harlem River, just north of the New York University campus with its Hall of Fame. Originally part of the Morris estate, the streets had names that preserved its Revolutionary War heritage: Featherbed Lane where housewives had spread their mattresses to muffle the passage of American soldiers; Popham Avenue, named after one of Washington's officers and owner-by-marriage of the estate. Morris Heights had long been a middle-class neighborhood of apartment houses and single-family homes settled by a mélange of Jews and Irish.

Brant imported two organizers, both of whom had attended seminary with him, although they had dropped out. One was Roger Hayes, twenty-five, trained in Alinsky-style organizing in Chicago and fluent in Spanish from a brief stint in Peru. The other was Jim Mitchell, twenty-five, a quiet, unassuming young man with a background in housing from working with the church-sponsored Brothers Construction, Inc., in Detroit. "Roger had the moxie on the streets and Jim was the genius, though you'd never pick it up, he's so understated," says Brant.[4]

When Hayes and Mitchell began organizing, Morris Heights had become 70 percent black and Hispanic and largely working class. It was assumed that this would be the next part of the South Bronx. There were already pockets of trouble — unemployed men hanging out on the streets drinking, some junkies in evidence, a few buildings with ripped-out mailboxes and graffiti, others without heat or hot water.

There was an earnestness to the young organizers and the parish priests that made them hard to brush off or disappoint. They were from the church, not from a government agency or poverty program. Their message was straightforward and simple — you can gain control of your own lives if you work together. Monsignor McCarthy told of this tenant meeting one night in an apartment lobby. "A man walked through with his dog, which 'littered' as they went through on their way upstairs. The organizer looked at the tenants and said, 'You can't blame that on the landlord.' They were quiet and then three men rose and went up and got the man, who came back down and cleaned up after his dog. You have to have pride of ownership and pride of tenancy, and that was what we tried to promote."[5] Most problems were not resolved that easily.

It was clear to Brant that the system was barely functioning in the northwest Bronx. "We were up against a stagnant bureaucracy and a real estate and banking complex which had written off that part of the Bronx. Their whole philosophy was, 'It's worn out, we'll make as much money as we can until it's abandoned and then we'll pull out, clear it, go back in, and buy the land and develop it.' "[6] Making the system operate as it should was going to entail a series of major and very protracted battles.

At the same time that the Morris Heights campaign got going, a group of Catholic priests who met to discuss bingo and such progressed to more serious topics. One pastor mentioned that he had just lost six families from his parish because of fires. This struck a chord with a number of the clergy, who were similarly losing parishioners. Comparing notes, they realized they were facing potential disaster. "Our problem here," said one priest bluntly, "is survival. If those neighborhoods go up, our parishes go."

These parish priests of the Northwest Bronx Clergy Conference began organizing tenants' associations and battling with the City and with private landlords for proper services. Like many well-meaning volunteers before them, they became discouraged when they came up against the pervasive apathy and labyrinthine ways of modern government in New York City. Monsignor McCarthy introduced them to the young Fordham firebrand, Paul Brant. The pastors, impressed with the charismatic seminarian's success with the intractable City bureaucracies, suggested they make common cause.

No one at first imagined the potential of such a coalition. Founded by sixteen parishes of the Catholic church, an institution with deep roots in the Bronx and possessed of great authority and power, the Clergy Conference, as it was called, summoned up inherent strength. Heretofore, although churchmen like Father Gigante and Father Smith had been involved as individuals, the church had never acted collectively. There had been no coherent strategy or overall alliance to save the parishes. The borough's neighborhoods were the basis of the parishes and thereby the church. Catholics in the Bronx did not move from one neighborhood to another, but from one parish to another. The church's self-interest was engaged.

Brant proposed that the conference transform itself into an ecumenical, nonprofit group encompassing eight parish neighborhoods, each replicating the Morris Heights organizing model. The territory of the new Northwest Bronx Community and Clergy Coalition covered almost a quarter of the county, from the Bronx Zoo and Botanical Garden to the east, Van Cortlandt Park and the City line to the north, the Harlem and Hudson rivers to the west, and the Cross-Bronx Expressway, Webster Avenue, and 180th Street to the south. Their stated goal was "to preserve the northwest Bronx and make it (where it isn't) and keep it (where it is) a decent place to live and raise a family."[7]

The southeasternmost of these parishes were already affected by abandonment. From the start, the coalition stressed that it was not opposed to change as reflected by the moving in of blacks and Hispanics. It wanted to "build a spirit of neighborliness and grass-roots responsibility and leadership through shared decision-making and actions."[8] Full-time organizers would be hired to assume the daily burden of the campaign.

Monsignor McCarthy had been the ever-gentle instigator behind this new group. As the coalition took shape, he and a few other priests recruited the highest-ranking local churchman to their ranks: Bishop Patrick V. Ahern. The pastor of Our Lady of Angels Church, a "country club" parish in Kingsbridge Heights, the bishop had spent a decade as secretary to the powerful Cardinal Spellman, leader of the Archdiocese of New York for almost thirty years. A silver-haired man with a loving manner, Bishop Ahern could see nothing awry in his pleasant parish, but he was convinced to join the group when he saw the concern of the other pastors.

The psychological lift was crucial, but another contribution was more important yet. "The bishop's potential to raise money was magnificent," remembers Jim Mitchell. "He hadn't done it before, but he'd known a lot of people over the years, and he'd never asked any of them for money. He was the linchpin."[9]

In June 1974 the clergy hosted a three-day conference at Fordham University on "Strategies for Ministry in the Urban Struggle." Cardinal Terence Cooke, spiritual leader of the 1.8 million Catholics living in the Archdiocese of New York, gave his blessing to this new activist turn with an impassioned opening address. The parishes, he declared, "are a promise of stability, of permanence in a storm of change, of security that at least one of the major structures of our society, the church, has not pulled out and thrown up its hands in frustration at the appalling convergences of urban crises."[10] Father Gigante came up from Saint Athanasius to give a slide show of his ravaged, burned-out parish, a terrible vision of what was to come if the northwest clergy did not prevail. He made a deep impression.

In the ensuing months, the Northwest Bronx Community and Clergy Coalition was launched. With fifteen thousand dollars from Henry Waltemade, chairman of Dollar Savings Bank, and a thousand or two from other banks and businesses, they hired six full-time organizers. Numerous Fordham students worked for free. The minuscule salaries and office expenses required expansion, though, and the coalition turned to a source unique to the church — the Sunday collection.

Bishop Ahern visited all the parishes and at mass after mass he awed the parishioners with a stirring cry to battle. "If the Bronx dies, then the hopes of a million and a half people for justice and a decent life, here and now, will die with it. We're trying to stop that from happening. . . . And so far as we know, what we're undertaking in 1975 in the northwest Bronx is unique in the American church, both for its scope — and for its challenge. . . . The scope is to renew the neighborhood of the northwest Bronx. . . . The adversity which our life in the city subjects us to can make us bitter or it can make us better. It can destroy cities, or inspire us to renew them."[11] Parishioners of the northwest Bronx gave more than forty thousand dollars in their collection plates for the coalition.

From the start, the coalition distinguished itself by its altruistic, practical-minded devotion. It truly provided a conduit through which neighborhood people could effect changes and improvements. The approach and technique were modeled on Saul Alinsky, the legendary Chicago organizer who believed people could be galvanized to help themselves. "Basic Alinsky," said Hayes, who trained the new recruits, "is finding issues around which you can organize. At the beginning you build confidence and a base by taking on small issues. Then you look for a bigger issue. It's like starting a lot of brushfires and then later on starting a big bonfire."[12] These disciples, however, were contravening one of Alinsky's basic tenets — never try to organize renters. In the northern parishes, where crime was a big issue, the organizers instituted block patrols and meetings with police. In the southern parishes, where the issue was building services — typically heat and hot water — the organizers became adept at summoning building inspectors, leading rent strikes, and battling landlords. "Some of those people were the scum of the earth," remembers one organizer, describing landlords who ruthlessly cut off heat in the most frigid weather. In South Fordham, the tenant as-

sociations became strong enough to go after one awful slumlord with fifteen buildings, wrest them from him in court, get
his real estate broker's license revoked, and then drive him
from Bronx county. ("We hear he's selling used cars in Yon-
kers.")

While organizers at the neighborhood level nurtured these
spreading grass roots, the leaders of the coalition worked
through the wondrous maze of the City, state and federal
agencies, under Paul Brant's leadership. In December 1974
Brant (now chairman of Community Board 5) had written to
John Zuccotti, chairman of the City's Planning Commission,
criticizing the allocation of federal community development
funds. The northwest Bronx was a textbook case: an aging
community that needed renewal, yet not a penny of the millions allotted to New York had trickled into it. Zuccotti suggested that the coalition apply, which they did, and they
began a two-year hegira through the governmental wilderness,
being jerked hither and yon by the bureaucracy.

When the budget hearings were held before the City Council and the Board of Estimate in February 1975, Bishop Ahern
swept down to City Hall to champion the Bronx and the
coalition. He had soon realized that the City's priority should
be preservation of housing. It was the simplest "a stitch in
time saves nine" logic. Where was such a program or approach? asked the bishop. "We do not see the program on
the horizon. . . . We do not have another year to save the
36,000 housing units the HDA estimates will be lost from the
low and moderate (i.e., working class) income housing stock
this year."[13]

This gaping policy gap vis-à-vis preservation was a constant
frustration for the organizers. "There was a total vacuum,"
remembers Hayes. "If the landlord had walked away, the City
usually wouldn't provide emergency services because the landlord owed them so much already."[14] Organizers could and
did resort to the housing court, a nightmarish madhouse located in the basement of the Bronx County Courthouse. They
could perhaps get a judge to appoint an administrator to run
a building. But without money — the rent roll was rarely

sufficient — these administrators could not order repairs to be made. For want of a few thousand for repairs to a front door or a boiler, apartment houses worth hundreds of thousands would soon be ravaged by junkies, scavengers, and finishers.

By 1975 the coalition was functioning at two levels. The bishop and the higher-ups were using their prestige and entrée to press the establishment — the government agencies, big business, and foundations — for money and policy changes. Having set up the basic organizational structure and philosophy, these leaders played a vital role in fund-raising. In July 1975 Paul Brant was sent to Chicago, and Jim Mitchell, quiet and self-effacing, took over as head of the coalition. He and other staff gathered the names of board members of Fortune 500 companies and gave the lists to Bishop Ahern, who had met many of these men in his years with the Cardinal. He would peruse the lists and select those he thought might be sympathetic. When the coalition approached them for funds, the bishop's referral and his attendance at subsequent meetings provided instant credibility. Exxon, for instance, sent along a student intern and then a twenty-five-thousand-dollar check. The Catholic bishops' charity, the Campaign for Human Development, awarded the coalition seventy thousand dollars a year for three years.

Meanwhile, the organizers concentrated on rallying people and developing local leadership. As New York's fiscal crisis deepened, the already abysmal City services actually worsened. The coalition badgered City agencies for more cops, better garbage pickup and street cleaning, but the City continually pleaded poverty as its excuse. When the word got out that Mayor Beame was cutting off funds for a City block security program, two thousand furious Bronx residents turned out to a protest meeting, and were further enraged when none of the invited City officials appeared or even replied. To make sure their ire was known, these same neighborhood people tracked down Deputy Mayor James Cavanaugh at a Fordham University sherry gathering, where he was to lecture on "New

York's Urban Crisis." They hectored Cavanaugh about the cutbacks, whereupon he got up and fled.

The Morris Heights Neighborhood Improvement Association engaged in its own holy war on the City's ineffectual housing department. Bishop Ahern and Monsignor McCarthy alerted Bronx Democratic leader Patrick Cunningham, who in turn dispatched Deputy Mayor Stanley Friedman, a Bronx boy and scion of the moribund Pondiac Club to Morris Heights. In November 1974 the Morris Heights people presented Friedman with a list of fifteen buildings that were without heat and hot water despite repeated calls to the City's Emergency Repair Program (ERP). The organizers criticized the tortuous process one had to go through to get any repairs. Friedman, who looked like an overage Frankie Avalon with a goatee, shocked the assembled residents with his swaggering manner and offensive remarks. He leered at one mother worrying about her children in their icy cold apartment and said, "Don't worry, I'll make sure you warm up."

The upshot of the Friedman meeting was a realization that the contemporary Bronx Democratic machine was impotent to deliver once-commonplace favors. Here was a high City official, deputized by the supposed Bronx Boss Pat Cunningham (later jailed for tax evasion), to help out Bronxites freezing in their apartments. Three months later Deputy Mayor Friedman had managed to restore heat and hot water in only three of the fifteen buildings. When he returned to report this meager accomplishment, one hundred furious tenants threw it at him as final proof that the Emergency Repair Program did not work, since, while he was seeing to it, the list of buildings without heat and hot water had expanded from the original fifteen to fifty.

The political machine had atrophied into a shell of its former self, arrogant and indifferent to the people. "The reform Democrats favored us," remembers Brant, "but reform people found they couldn't deliver any more than the regulars."[15] Organizer Hayes, a veteran of Chicago precincts, says, "After the Chicago machine, I was amazed at the weakness of the politicians in the Bronx. *They* were asking *me* how to get things done."[16] Nothing showed the county's demise as a political force more graphically than the voter registration numbers, down to an anemic 268,139 registered Democrats by 1983, compared to the machine's 1940 heyday of 650,688.

Borough President Abrams, a reformer, seemed friendly and well-intentioned, but he "was always presenting himself as a weakling," remembers one coalition leader. "He'd say things like, 'Would a really stinging letter from me help?' A busful of us went down to the borough president's office once, and we caught Abrams sneaking out the back door. He pleaded his usual impotence when we asked for help. Generally, the local politicians couldn't do anything."

In 1975 the coalition's first year of operation, it organized tenant associations in 350 buildings, got 12,165 housing violations fixed, and improved security in 123 buildings. It instigated twenty-two street cleanups and started five neighborhood patrols. All in all, it was a respectable track record for neophytes. But as the coalition gained experience and confidence, its leaders and members saw that the government institutions that were supposed to serve them, for which they paid taxes, did not do so. Parks looked filthy and shabby, garbage was collected infrequently, police presence declined although crime was worse.

At their annual meeting in December 1975, the coalition created standing committees that would tackle these pervasive, areawide problems. By bringing together activists from all the coalition neighborhoods "people got a sense they'd have more clout," says Mitchell, "and because it was multiracial, people could not dismiss it as either all-white or just minorities. Beame was reducing services, so we decided to do something about that."[17] Thus began the Committees on Housing and City Services.

The Housing Committee immediately targeted the Emergency Repair Program and badgered the City's Housing and Development Administration in an escalating campaign that included almost daily visits to the agency's office to complain. They marched upon Commissioner Roger Starr, who had refused to meet them, when he was talking at Fordham. "They just got a little tired of seeing us," says Hayes with a wry smile, "and finally they agreed to set up this program where we would call in. It was a tremendous organizing tool, because once people found out there was this group that could get you an inspector in twenty-four hours and get your heat back within two days — something that used to take weeks or months — it built a lot of confidence."[18]

In 1976 the coalition's long quest for Community Development funds was denied. Bishop Ahern, beside himself, fired off three scathing letters to City officials, with copies to Cardinal Cooke. "What contempt City government exhibits towards neighborhoods and committees such as ours!" he wrote to Roger Starr at the HDA. "In our view this is only the most recent in a series of evasions, deceptions, broken promises and buck-passing dating back to December, 1974, when we first dared to submit a proposal." He asked John Zuccotti, now deputy mayor, "I would like to be able to understand how you expect communities in desperate and justifiable need of governmental support to stand alone and fight the wave of deterioration that threatens to engulf them, while monies specifically allocated for this purpose are misdirected in the useless patronage of ineffective city agencies?" To Mayor Beame: "Your Honor, our neighborhoods are at a critical stage of transition and every month's delay brings irreparable damage. I ask you once again to reconsider our requests and direct some assistance to this area. Now, before it's too late, is that too much to ask?"[19] Yes, as it turned out, it was.

Anne Devenney and the City Services Committee now hit the warpath over the sorry state of Bronx parks. Chairwoman Devenney was a grandmother and former president of the Altar and Rosary Society of Saint Brendan's parish. A large, stout woman with a grey, bowl-cut hairdo, she had an expressive face that gave her the look of a shrewd medieval monk. She had already been uprooted from one apartment by Robert Moses and his George Washington Bridge, and had no intention of being dislodged again because her neighborhood was being allowed to fall apart. She led twenty-five people down to City Hall, and before anyone could intervene they occupied Deputy Mayor Stanley Friedman's office. In short order, Friedman produced Parks Commissioner Martin Lang. The cornered commissioner had to promise to give Friedman and the committee a written response to its pages-long list of park-by-park complaints and also to tour the parks in the company of Friedman. The deputy mayor took a liking to Devenney, who had a flair for simple sayings. "You only get the government you deserve," she would aver, and then, smiling impishly, "And I know I deserve better." Or, "I'm a senior, but I'm no bingo player. I play for higher stakes."[20]

In the wake of their successes with the Emergency Repair Program and the prospects of progress in the parks, the co-alition began to consider new challenges. The neighborhood organizing was moving ahead, and now those small "fires" could be stoked up in to a "bonfire," a bigger cause. Some of the staff and members had made the pilgrimage to the annual Washington, D.C., meeting of the National People's Action, a major league grassroots power group. There had been much talk about bank redlining. The organizers realized they had often heard decent landlords complaining that they could not get money to fix up their buildings. Community Development funds figured as another big topic and an abiding source of frustration for the coalition. They decided to set up committees to address reinvestment by banks and reinvestment by government.

Bill Frey, a native of Wisconsin and a Fordham grad who had been an organizer in South Fordham, led the research on local savings banks. He was astounded to discover how totally the banks had pulled out of the Bronx. The Home Mortgage Disclosure Act of 1975 made possible the unearthing of some extraordinary statistics. In 1965, 298 new mortgages had been granted in the northwest Bronx; in 1975, only 44 came through. In 1965, Eastern Savings Bank (formerly Bronx Savings Bank) had granted 59 mortgages and refinanced 63. Ten years later, it gave one new mortgage and refinanced two; yet the bulk of its deposits still came from the Bronx.

Research into another bank, North Side Savings, showed

almost $300 million in deposits, 90 percent of that from Bronx depositors, and two-thirds of that in northwest Bronx branches. And yet, in the year 1975, the savings bank had granted only one mortgage (thirty-four thousand dollars) in the northwest Bronx. This paltry investment in its own community was dictated by the bank's revamped mortgage guidelines which excluded from consideration three-family homes, pre–World War II buildings, and apartment houses with less than twenty-five units: in other words 90 percent of the dwellings typical of the northwest Bronx.

Dollar Savings Bank, the fifth-largest savings bank in the country, with $2.4 billion in deposits, had given only 26 mortgages worth $2.2 million in the northwest Bronx in 1975.

The chairman of the coalition's new Reinvestment Committee was Richard Gallagher, a postman who lived in the Mosholu-Woodlawn section and had been active in coalition block security patrols. "When the banks saw all the destruction in the Bronx, they couldn't cope with it," he says. "They just threw up their hands in the air and walked away. It was a shame. We wanted to make them live up to their responsibility."[21] But how to make the intangible and complex issue of banks and money pertinent to tenants who rented apartments? "These people were unfamiliar with mortgages," said Frey. "They only knew leases. So we made it applicable by bringing out the importance of the mortgage's 'good repair clause.' A lot of the responsibility for the decline of the properties had to be laid to the banks."[22]

Although it certainly was important to the tenants that banks grant new mortgages and refinance old ones, the prime issue was how the banks treated their existing real estate portfolios. The Reinvestment Committee was horrified to find that Eastern Savings had sold a $70,000 mortgage on Valentine Avenue and a $150,000 mortgage on East 183rd Street for $100 each to known speculators. How could the bankers moan and groan about the Bronx becoming a slum when their actions delivered buildings into the hands of speculators and slumlords? The committee felt the banks could prevent their properties' downfall by enforcing the "good repair clause." They also asked the banks for lists of all their buildings so embattled tenants could call upon the banks for help to pressure recalcitrant mortgage holders.

These, then, were the issues delineated by the Reinvestment Committtee in late 1976. Eastern Savings Bank, with its alarming track record of dumping buildings, came first. A bank official met with an advance party of the Reinvestment Committee and said he would have to consult with the board and get back to them. He never did. When the committee finally called him, they were told the bank felt no need to respond, then or ever. There would be no further meetings.

Such intransigence left little room for reasoned discussion or negotiation. "Our only leverage was to picket," says Frey, "to do something visible. This was a turning point for Bishop Ahern and Monsignor McCarthy. In effect, we had learned that [the bankers] were destroying the community. And these were people the clergy knew on a different level than they knew City officials. They knew them socially, had attended the same luncheons. The Bishop and McCarthy made the decision not only to be supportive, but to join the Reinvestment Committee. And they put the word out to the rest of the clergy."[23]

On April 1, 1977, 150 Bronxites gathered to picket Eastern's Pelham Parkway and White Plains Road branch. The protesters were an ordinary crowd, people you might see at a parish dinner or a bingo game. The bishop and Monsignor McCarthy were there, old-fashioned churchmen in black cloth and white collars. They marched back and forth in front of the bank, attracting the enthusiatic approval of passersby, who assumed the clergy and their flock were protesting the pornographic movie theater next door. Only when they got up close did they see the signs, "Let's give up Eastern for Lent."

Flustered bank employees rushed outside. One outraged bank officer sputtered at Anne Devenney, "Lady you're a Communist." She rolled her eyeballs, "Oh, mister." She was really enjoying this excursion. "It was fun to take on a bank and let them know — hey, the old days are over. It was like David and Goliath," she said.[24] That same day Eastern management reassured the coalition that it was all a misunderstanding. *Of course,* they would meet.

The new Community Development Committee was researching just where Community Development funds were going, if not to the deserving Bronx. They had been told by the Office of Management and Budget in Washington that $180 million of $343 million allocated New York City had never been spent and that 80 percent of what was spent went for salaries in City agencies. For instance, $150,000 each year went to salaries at the West Tremont Neighborhood Preservation Office in the West Bronx. That office's sole function was to process low-interest loans to fix up buildings, but in three years it had not cleared one loan. (Later, however, in the Koch era, the office would become highly productive.)

As 1976 ended, the coalition had organized another 199 tenant associations and 33 block associations, 128 cleanups, and 7 new civilian patrols. In two years of existence it had drawn 12,747 residents into community activity aimed at stabilizing neighborhoods. Each of the neighborhood associations had a full-time youth organizer, in addition to other full-time organizers. The Youth Development Program ran everything from local football leagues to job placement and general counseling.

The coalition had also introduced a monthly newspaper, *Action,* whose thirty thousand copies were distributed free. No paper could replace the long-defunct *Bronx Home News* with its avid and regular neighborhood coverage. But *Action* was chock-full of information about local events — everything from the long-sought demolition of an abandoned building to a new softball league in need of players.

Despite all these encouraging successes, the coalition had to resign itself to the South Bronxing of a few of its neighborhood, including its own birthplace , Morris Heights. Roger Hayes and several local leaders had organized one hundred apartment buildings on the Heights, almost a third, but they had come in too late. Without money they just could not pull enough buildings back from the brink. The new welfare tenants moving in and replacing the departing working class behaved too passively. "They had much lower expectations since they were often beaten down in dealing with day-to-day survival issues in the South Bronx. And then the housing in Morris Heights was significantly better," said Hayes. "We'd say, 'You haven't had heat for two days' and they'd answer, 'Hey, we didn't have heat for two years where I used to live.'"[25]

When drugs and crime reached epidemic proportions, many of the tenant leaders themselves felt compelled to move. "It had become ridiculous," said Hayes. "They and their kids would have to walk home through junkies nodding out and selling. At some point you have to say, 'Something might happen to my kids and I gotta get out of here.' Multiply that by a hundred people and it really gets tough."[26] As in the South Bronx, fires followed in the wake of the drugs, and buildings began to empty out. In 1974 New York University closed down its University Heights campus, disrupting that community and adding to the threat engulfing the western ridge.

Such deterioration within the coalition's borders brought home more strongly its reason for being. The Reinvestment Committee stepped up expressions of dissatisfaction to various banking and regulatory agencies. Its members met with the Federal Deposit Insurance Corporation and the state Banking Department, laying out their damning research on local redlining. The regulators seemed nonplussed. "They had never dealt with people like us, only bankers," Gallagher remembers. "They weren't used to people coming and asking them questions, putting them on notice that we were going to hold them accountable."[27] The FDIC agreed to launch an investigation.

In 1977 and 1978, the coalition and the banks squared off regularly. Both Eastern Savings Bank and North Side Savings Bank were baldly resentful. The latter was soon hit with a picket line. "Darcy, the president, called up the Chancery and raised holy hell," says Gallagher. "He was really fuming. They said they had no control over us."[28] There ensued a tense and stifling meeting at the bank, where the air conditioning wasn't working. Donald Darcy asked Bishop Ahern to open with a prayer. Then an in-house memo denigrating the committee members somehow surfaced in the paper shuffle. It sneered at the effrontery of Gallagher, a mere postman, or other members, a student, or a teacher, or a messenger. Who were they to question the bankers, and what did the clergy know either? The bishop responded sharply that all institutions, including the church, could expect outside scrutiny. A week later President Darcy informed the committee that the bank's mortgage policies were being revamped.

Dollar Savings Bank was far more adept at fending off the coalition by steadily making small concessions. Chairman Henry Waltemade delegated a top manager to handle it, but Waltemade, like the other bankers, did not acknowledge the Committee directly, writing instead to the bishop. Despite its savvy, Dollar, too, would be picketed, much to Waltemade's chagrin. He found it a supremely ungrateful act, since his largesse had gotten the coalition going. When they picketed Dollar at its Grand Concourse headquarters, the coalition amassed pledge cards from depositors promising to withdraw more than $1 million if Dollar didn't invest more in the Bronx.

The bitter struggle took a decided turn in the coalition's favor when the FDIC announced it was denying Eastern Savings a new branch in Hauppauge, Long Island. The FDIC cited "unfavorable findings on the factors of financial history and condition of the bank and general character of its management."[29] The coalition, which had opposed the branch, was jubilant. "The banks were very surprised we had the ability to get the regulatory agencies involved," says Frey. "Actually, we were surprised as well."[30] In the aftermath the banks began to make more concessions and cooperate a bit.

Despite these accomplishments, the winter of 1977–1978 was a demoralizing one for the coalition. In the fall, the depressing Moyers documentary ran, and the coalition work got no mention at all. The weather turned bitterly cold, and the City was encased in frozen, filthy snow. Each week the depressing news of another evacuation filtered into the coalition's shabby basement offices. More than a hundred buildings were by now empty and vandalized in the blocks south of Fordham Road, the most recently declared northern Maginot Line of the South Bronx. The Women's City Club had conducted a detailed study of abandonment in the Bronx and their grim 1977 report "With Love and Affection" expressed "no doubt about the total ineffectiveness of the City in checking or preventing abandonment."

Furthermore, the coalition, which had besieged the Beame administration officials into reluctant cooperation, now turned to establishing a working rapport with the new administration of Mayor Koch. Despite an inauspicious first meeting, during which the mayor's face never lost its sour expression, the coalition took the mayor's advice and began meeting his commissioners. They found them competent and helpful. "All you got out of Beame's people was reaction," said one now-seasoned organizer. The new commissioners were innovators. The coalition was particularly impressed with Housing Commissioner Nathan Leventhal and Parks Commissioner Gordon Davis.

33

"We're Still Here"
1978–1982

NINETEEN SEVENTY-EIGHT was the watershed year for the coalition. The movement to the suburbs had slowed significantly, rising mortgage rates and suburban housing costs were pricing families out, and rising gasoline prices made commuting expensive. Crime, which had pushed so many to seek safety, had spread everywhere. As Anne Devenney exhorted, "Don't move! Improve!" She also expressed a deeply felt sentiment when she said, "The Bronx: there's so much that is the best in it, the rest of us must reinvest in it."[1]

A crucial factor in the rising, but cautious, optimism was the steadily subsiding fires. The year 1976 had marked the Bronx's worst year for conflagration — 33,465 fires of all kinds: commercial, residential, vacant buildings, cars, and garbage. In 1977 that figure dipped to 29,564, dropping again in 1978 to 25,487. The most important statistic, that for residential structural fires, was as encouraging: a steady decline from 9,201 in 1975 to 7,180 in 1978. All structural fires in the Bronx dropped from 13,672 to 10,054. How many of these fires could be attributed to arson was anybody's guess, but the fire marshals deemed more than a third of them suspicious.

No one could answer with real authority why the fires were dying down. It might seem reasonable to suppose that some of the measures taken by the City were at last having an effect: the City now had second crack (after the first mortgagee) at fire insurance monies paid on properties whose owners were delinquent in city taxes; welfare families were not being "rewarded" for burnouts any longer, and the fire and police departments had cracked down on arsonists. In the Bronx, from 1974 to 1976, only fifty-one people in three years had been convicted for some kind of arson felony. In 1977 alone fifty-seven people were convicted, and in 1978, sixty-one. If, as fire marshals suspected, three thousand fires a year in the county derived from arson, those conviction figures weren't impressive, but they showed improvement.

Just as important, the two traditional insurers of last resort in the Bronx were starting to get tough. The New York Property Insurance Underwriting Association, which administered the Fair Access to Insurance Plan, tightened both its underwriting and claims-paying procedures. It became progressively more willing to challenge and litigate. Lloyd's of London, the unlikely alternative to FAIR, had been thrown into an unprecedented crisis by the profligate and questionable underwriting habits of its shady Sasse syndicate. The London police had been called in to investigate this American syndicate, which had written thousands of fire insurance policies in the South Bronx that would generate the largest single loss ever incurred by a syndicate in Lloyd's history — close to $45 million. The Sasse syndicate and Lloyd's would soon be embroiled in recriminations and lawsuits.

The Koch administration provided the first real tools to fight abandonment and to rehabilitate buildings. The City housing agency, newly renamed the Department of Housing Preservation and Development, took the lead. Housing court judges had long been appointing administrators to run buildings whose owners were milking them or had departed altogether, but time and again buildings worth hundreds of thousands were wrecked for want of ten thousand dollars in repairs. The City finally made modest loan monies available. It also worked up a whole range of low-interest rehabilitation and tax incentive programs to encourage landlords to invest in their aging buildings. The coalition developed numerous creative approaches that mixed expensive private loans with cheap govenment money to stretch resources further. Invoking the "good repair clause" at one hundred large apartment buildings had encouraged better services and security. The coalition, often accused in its early days of being hostile to landlords, now functioned frequently as a conduit for landlords needing bank loans.

The coalition's sense that the tides had turned was dramatically confirmed during the cold weather of 1978–1979. Weeks went by, and then months, and still the buildings held. Organizers and tenant leaders looked at one another and began to hope that they might be seeing the first real fruits of victory. That winter only a handful of buildings were abandoned. "We went from total depression to skepticism," remembers one person. The malignancy that had been eating away one Bronx neighborhood after another seemed to be in remission. "We're not the jet set. We're the get set," Anne Devenney could say with pride. "We get things done."

The coalition then stumbled upon a problem as important as bank redlining for the future of their neighborhoods — insurance redlining. The insurance issue came to their attention when a woman walked into the Fordham-Bedford Neighborhood Association in 1978 and complained that the insurance on her small apartment house had been canceled for no discernible reason. A quick check around turned up other clusters of recent, abrupt cancellations. It was another of those crucial, but totally undramatic, issues. Landlords and homeowners have to have insurance. If traditional insurance was being withdrawn, they would have to pay far higher premiums for government-backed coverage or Lloyd's of London. Anything that diminished an owner's bottom line gave an additional impetus to abandonment.

A number of coalition members began calling insurance brokers to inquire about building insurance in the northwest Bronx. They were always asked their local zip code, and when they gave it, a number of brokers said; "Oh, forget it. That neighborhood's going to be part of the South Bronx soon. The arsonists will be there any day now. We wouldn't touch that with a ten-foot pole." A coalition Insurance Committee went to work.

They immediately contacted the Chicago-based National People's Action, which had been studying insurance redlining. People's Action set up a meeting with Aetna Life and

Casualty Company's chairman, William O. Bailey. The coalition attended. Bailey, who was sympathetic and concerned, wrote a strong memo to all Aetna agents. "We went back to the local brokers," remembers James Buckley, the staff organizer on the Insurance Committee, "and got rejections that were just more sophisticated. The brokers were scared stiff of being canceled by the company if they actually wrote Bronx policies. They figured the memo was written under pressure."[2]

After mulling over the situation, the coalition proposed to Aetna that Bronx policies be submitted to local brokers and to the company at the same time, which would get the brokers off the hook by sharing responsibility with Aetna. By the spring of 1979 Aetna had designated ten Bronx insurance brokers to write policies in the northwest Bronx. This was an immediate boon for fifteen owners who had been canceled by mainstream companies and forced to buy high-risk insurance at three or four times their old rates. When the Aetna brokers discovered that the Bronx was profitable, they wrote hundreds of policies, bucking up the regular insurance industry before it could flee. As Anne Devenney told the insurers, "You used to knock on our doors selling nickel policies to the poor. Now we're knocking on yours."[3]

Encouraged by Aetna's generally receptive attitude, the coalition approached Aetna with the proposal that they actually invest money in the northwest Bronx by making loans for moderate rehabilitation of apartment buildings. Meanwhile, they continued meeting with state insurance department officials and legislators to push for laws against insurance redlining. They encouraged other insurance majors like Travelers to make arrangements similar to those reached with Aetna.

For someone coming to the northwest Bronx from the South Bronx, the accomplishments and style of the coalition were a revelation. Father John Jennick moved north to Our Lady of Refuge parish in 1978 from Saint Thomas Aquinas near Charlotte Street. "I had tried to organize and do something there, but one after another the buildings just disappeared. Then the supermarket burned down and it was a problem for people to even shop for food. We were all amazed at how the fires just ripped through and nothing was done. When I came to Our Lady of Refuge I looked around and I said, 'It's going to happen here.' I saw it creeping across Fordham Road. But the coalition was very savvy and they had expertise and altruism. When buildings were abandoned in the South Bronx, no one protested. When buildings went on Decatur Avenue here, we said we have to do something, and we did."[4]

Jennick, depressed after his defeat at Saint Thomas, came round to believing that the South Bronxing of his new parish was not inevitable. It was just this sort of psychological about-face that the coalition was always striving to promote. Buckley, a big hefty fellow with a bushy beard, said; "I don't know how many people told me, 'This neighborhood's got two years left.' That was probably four years ago. And we're still here."[5] He gives a hearty guffaw.

In 1980, a year when only one building was lost, the coalition marked its sixth anniversary. They had much to be proud of, for they could justly claim credit for slowing the deterioration and waves of arson that had so swiftly consumed the lower reaches of the Bronx. The number of neighborhood associations now under the coalition's umbrella had expanded from the original eight to eleven, and they had organized a total of twelve hundred buildings.

This was not to say that serious problems did not still afflict the northwest Bronx. The travails of 2755–2769 Sedgwick Avenue in Kingsbridge Heights illustrated dramatically the struggles still being waged. The 120-unit building, a pleasant apartment house with front courtyards, stood on the curving main avenue of Bishop Ahern's "country club" parish. Mary McLoughlin and her husband had moved in in 1948 as newlyweds and raised eight children there when the super still scrubbed the stairs and halls every day and neighbors left their front doors unlocked and ajar to catch the breeze.

Then the management closed the carriage room and ceased dumbwaiter service for garbage. Next, a new landlord hired a nasty, lazy super. "Many people moved because the place was dirty and they weren't into being insulted," recalls Mrs.

McLoughlin. Throughout the 1970s the situation deteriorated. The landlord accepted new tenants who stayed up all night playing loud music and defaced the halls with graffiti. He rented part of the basement to a social club. "I was told they was looking for a go-go girl," Mrs. McLoughlin says wryly.[6]

A core of fed-up tenants organized. Then, in August of 1979, the landlord removed the boiler and never bothered to replace it. The new tenants' association went to housing court, and the landlord agreed to reinstall the boiler. The building's back retaining wall collapsed, threatening to undermine the whole structure. The desperate tenants sought a City housing administrator. The case dragged on for more than a year. Worn down and discouraged, the tenants still persevered, attending more than one hundred meetings with City agencies and court hearings, many of which were canceled or postponed. A mysterious fire broke out above Mrs. McLoughlin's apartment.

Only a rare and faithful citizen could hang on through these seemingly fruitless dealings with the housing bureaucracy. Yet the coalition's secret was to persist doggedly in apparently hopeless causes. "The coalition helped us right down the line," says Mrs. McLoughlin, who some called an "unsung saint." "They gave us technical assistance and drove us to court and provided backup." Mrs. McLoughlin wears a neat navy dress with a leaf pattern and has her shoulder-length brown hair pulled back with bobby pins. "I said to myself, 'This is a good building. I am not going to move. I am not going to allow a lousy landlord to deprive me of a place to live.' "[7] And so she continued the struggle. She had what people in the South Bronx had lacked — a larger organization to guide them and give them heart, and, just as important, new City programs that would enable an administrator to restore their buildings.

The annual meeting of the coalition on January 12, 1980, was a joyful occasion. On that frigid afternoon the savings banks and Aetna Casualty and Insurance were invited to pledge to underwrite 200 new investment projects in the northwest Bronx and enforce the "good repair clause," and also pledge to advertise the availability of housing money. Aetna was to designate the northwest Bronx as one of six neighborhoods that would be lent money from a $15 million fund.

The entire first row of the Saint Philip Neri auditorium filled with black-garbed clergy. They had all, from the bishop on down, turned out for this momentous victory. Monsignor McCarthy felt tremendous pride. "The organizers worked for a pittance, but you couldn't possibly buy that quality for any sum. They were so keenly intelligent." He confessed, "I was always afraid that the banks would try to steal our people."[8]

The federal Community Reinvestment Act had passed in 1977, enforcing by law many of the coalition's assertions that banks had a responsibility to lend money where they garnered deposits. By 1979 the rules governing the act were laid in place, giving community groups new means of leverage when opposing redlining.

Everyone wondered if Dollar Savings, the mightiest of the Bronx banks, would be humbled into signing the pledge. Chairman Waltemade was still irate over the coalition's "ingratitude." As Dollar's turn drew nearer, its representative could be heard frantically consulting his superiors on a phone in the hall. Finally, all the other banks and Aetna had signed. Rich Gallagher said into the microphone, "Could someone ask Dollar to come forward?" Mike Durso of Dollar walked up, every inch the banker in a dark suit and striped tie. He gave no clue by his manner as to whether his bank was going to concede. He began to speak, rambling on and on. People began shifting in their seats. When he said, "Now the other institutions have shown Dollar a better way," a takeoff on their slogan, everyone perked up. "Well," he went on, "we're a very proud bank and we'll sign this gladly."[9] The room erupted in wild applause and whoops of approval. The coalition had taken on the banks and won.

They had also achieved notable progress with the ever-elusive Community Development funds. The coalition had continued to harry the various agencies, and slowly money came through. The coalition's turf had been designated a

"Neighborhood Strategy Area," and as the money trickled down, it became visible in spruced-up parks, freshly paved streets planted with trees, and renovated shopping areas. The fight would pay off handsomely in ensuing years, when $22.5 million would be invested in major projects such as sewer construction, subway station makeovers, park renovations, connecting incomplete streets, and redoing Fordham Road, a major shopping street.

The successful forced return of the institutions that had given up — the City agencies, the banks, and the insurance companies — required the coalition to adjust. "We were in the position of having to say, 'What do we do now?' " says Jim Mitchell, the coalition's longtime executive director. "We won all these projects. How do we get the money into the buildings?"[10]

So the organization that had made its name as an *enfant terrible* now became the ally of landlords looking to improve their buildings. To formalize this new role, the coalition spun off nonprofit housing and development corporations, including one new endeavor called BUILD. Mitchell moved over to run it, and James Buckley took over as executive director of the coalition. Having changed the nature of the local housing game, the coalition — or actually its offspring, the housing corporations — became participants in it.

Over subsequent years the coalition would help to attract $37 million for the rehabilitation of seven thousand apartment units. (Among those was Mary McLoughlin's Sedgwick Avenue abode, where the tenants finally won their epic battle in 1981.) Yet none of this happened easily. The savings banks, struggling to survive skyrocketing interest rates and enormous cash outflows, could not fulfill all the commitments they had made. Dollar Savings merged with Dry Dock to become Dollar–Dry Dock, the nation's third largest savings bank. The new managers weren't very interested in the Bronx or promises made there. Despite these setbacks, Bill Frey says the "banks changed their attitude substantially and that's important. They are responsive to things that are brought to them now."[11] The alliance with the insurance companies has been most fruitful, and together they have reliably furnished funds.

All this growth and maturation at the coalition coincided with the early months of the Reagan administration, to which the coalition reacted by encouraging the private sector to take action in their neighborhoods. The Reaganites, drastically scaling back governmental programs, increased that impetus. Never timid, the coalition aimed high — to the pinnacle of the Fortune 500, the powerful giants Chase Manhattan Bank and Exxon Corporation.

And so the coalition found itself gathering for a meeting on April 19, 1983, in the vast white marble lobby of the Chase Manhattan skyscraper in the heart of Wall Street. Outside, it was cold and raining steadily. Inside, guards in powder-blue uniforms and white gloves monitored the ebb and flow of sleek business-suited men and women. The coalition members, bundled up in old sweaters and scruffy parkas, awaited the arrival of the Sisters of Charity, stockholders in the Chase Manhattan Bank. With proxies from the nuns, they were to attend the annual stockholders' meeting of Chase Manhattan to hear if the bank had come through with a $10 million loan fund sought by the coalition. Anne Devenney, now president of the coalition, led her motley troops into the huge auditorium, a sea of pin-striped suits and striped ties.

Chase's board of directors, an impressive array of corporate royalty, radiated power in the first few rows. These twenty-five individuals (all men except for Joan Ganz Cooney of the Children's Television Workshop) included chairmen and chief officers of Exxon, the General Foods Corporation, Macy's, Xerox, the Rockefeller Foundation, Dartmouth College, Standard Oil Company, and Bethlehem Steel.

Ultimately, the meeting rolled around to the stockholder proposals. Sister Eleanor Dougherty of the Sisters of Charity requested in a lovely modulated voice that "whereas Chase began exploring the possibility of offering a weatherization loan program in the spring of 1982 . . . a report be sent to all shareholders during 1983 on the progress made by Chase."[12]

Anne Devenney, her ample self cloaked in a tan knit dress, walked slowly to the aisle and took the microphone. All the Chase directors turned around to look at her. She introduced herself, and the huskiness of her voice betrayed both nerves and deep feeling. "We are from the Bronx," she said. "Everyone has heard of it and its problems. But now, after all the destruction, we are coming back. We are working people and we want to save our neighborhoods. I am unpaid, but I have dedicated my life to working for the neighborhood, for the children and the grandchildren. We are asking you to lend us money to weatherize our buildings. You will not take a loss. The landlords need this. We need this. We are not asking for charity. But we want to bring back the American Dream of being able to live in a safe, good home that is warm and secure. Thank you."[13] She sat down to warm applause. (It was no wonder Monsignor McCarthy referred to Anne as the coalition's secret weapon.)

Chase Chairman William C. Butcher praised the coalition as a "substantial, meaningful" organization. Then the coalition heard what it had been waiting for. Chase President Thomas G. Labrecque announced that just the previous night the bank's management had decided to cooperate with the City's Housing Preservation and Development agency to make available $10 million for weatherization loans.

Delighted as they were to hear this breakthrough announced in such corporate splendor (the stockholder proposal itself was voted down, although it attracted an impressive 6 percent of the total vote), Anne Devenney and Jim Buckley were already concentrating on a second target — Howard C. Kauffman, president of the Exxon Corporation. Thus far the campaign to get Exxon to ante up another $10 million for weatherization loans had included a "birthday greetings" on Exxon's hundredth anniversary that calculated the corporation's current rate of profit at $12 million an hour. Taking up Exxon's own theme of making America energy-independent, the coalition's deluge of greeting cards suggested Exxon "lend us an hour of your time" to "tap a gusher" in the Bronx.

Perplexed Exxon officials, never before broached with such

The Northwest Bronx Community and Clergy Coalition demon-
strates in front of Exxon Corporation as part of its 1983 campaign to
persuade Exxon to put up $10 million for low-interest weateriza-
tion loans. Anne Devenney holds the left-hand side of the sign.

a suggestion, and never by such a group, insisted that this was not their sort of endeavor. They did, however, agree to tour the northwest Bronx. In the summer of 1982, there had been an Adopt-an-Executive program, an attempt to give oil executives deprived of contact with ordinary Bronxites the chance to get to know them and visit their neighborhood. When puzzled Exxon officials said at one meeting that the corporation could not afford what the coalition was asking, the Energy committee said this revealed "unnecessary modesty" on Exxon's part. They had a stockholder proposal brought before the annual meeting, and it lost, as expected. So Exxon had continued to resist, and the coalition had continued firmly but pleasantly to apply their special brand of suasion.

Now, as the Chase meeting broke up, Jim Buckley, Anne, and a third organizer named Lois Harr bore down on Mr. Kauffman, a short, slight man with grey hair gone white at his temples. Anne stepped into his path and pumped his hand hello. She began praising Chase. He agreed. She suggested Mr. Kauffman might like a tour of the Bronx. He politely demurred, saying he'd been up there three years earlier. "But, oh," said Anne, "we've done so much since then." Lois said hopefully, "This is our special tour." The Exxon president was edging away, singing Chase's praises and encouraging the coalition in its pursuit of companies that *lend* money. Before he slipped away, Jim Buckley asked if they couldn't arrange a meeting. Kauffman said to keep meeting with the executives they had been in touch with. They all smiled, for it meant the dialogue was still open.

Then they gathered up their rumpled coats and papers and trooped out, leaving the plush, moneyed corridors of Chase to descend into the grimy bowels of the rush hour subway. Everyone felt pleased with the day's results and they were laughing and joking as the train rumbled north toward their beloved Bronx. "That's what makes America great still," said Anne, "the little guy can still take on the big guy."[14]

They had reason to feel good. All the Alinsky "brushfires," started almost a decade earlier, were burning brightly in the coalition neighborhoods, devotedly tended by the organizers and local leaders. Indeed, some people had learned to help themselves. Rich Gallagher works in the post office, but he also chairs the Reinvestment Committee and helps run a local housing corporation. "We're bringing back to life an apartment house that was really the pits. Now that's a sense of accomplishment. That's something nobody can take away from you."[15]

When arson reared its ugly head in 1982, organizer Lois Harr had led the campaign to get the New York fire department's antiarson squad, the Red Caps, assigned to the Bronx for the first time. The coalition went further and collaborated with the Bronx district attorney, the fire department, and the U.S. Fire Administration to rate fire-prone buildings by a computer analysis of tax arrears, vacancy rates, and previous fires. Those considered at risk became coalition targets for organizing, for loans, or for administrators. One such building celebrated being fixed up by throwing a birthday party for an elderly white woman. Most of the families were black and Hispanic. "They learned there was something to be gained by working together," said Lois. "It was a thrill to go to her birthday party. It was the first winter in four years they had had heat and hot water."[16]

Paul Brant, who had started it all, says proudly; "I suspect it's the largest sustained Alinsky-style organizing effort in the United States. The organizers just fell in love with the place."[17] Monsignor McCarthy, Brant's first "recruit" and a longtime coalition leader, says of his troops; "They've never done anything but good. They've taken the system and shown that if you use it properly, it works for everyone."[18]

34

White Picket Fences
1984

O N an overcast August day in 1984 Edward J. Logue, head of New York City's South Bronx Development Organization (SBDO), surveys the ten cream-and-coffee-colored ranch houses improbably plunked down on Charlotte Street, a startling vision of suburbia in an old Bronx neighborhood. A stocky man of medium height with a square-jawed face and silver-grey hair, Logue runs his hand along the top of a neat, white picket fence enclosing a large, grassy backyard. "This whole job, these houses, got famous because of these white picket fences," he says. "People said they'd be covered with graffiti and we should make them black or green. Who ever heard of a black picket fence?"[1]

He rounds the corner to face the first five houses that went up, all immaculately maintained and alive with the cozy signs of family life: knickknacks in a lace-curtained window, a plastic wading pool in a driveway, a swing set in the back. "When we had the dedication for Charlotte Gardens," says Logue, "I remember a guy at the back of the crowd yelling, 'These houses will be torn down in a week,' and Koch screaming back, 'The people who have bought them will defend them with their lives.'"[2] He laughs delightedly at the recollection as children swirl by on roller skates.

Down and across Boston Road, Logue wades into waist-high weeds to show more sites prepared for the eighty houses that will complete Charlotte Gardens. All the abandoned tenements have been razed clear through to Jennings Street. Only the occasional rumbling of the elevated train and the muted, back-and-forth roar of a bulldozer demolishing vacant buildings intrude on the stillness of lower Charlotte Street and its enormous meadows. (The police station, blocks south, formerly referred to as Fort Apache, has been rechristened "The Little House on the Prairie.") "I need one piece of paper from Chemical Bank," says Logue, shaking his head in frustration, "and then the rest of these houses could be up by Christmas."[3] He trudges back up the street into Crotona Park, lush from plentiful summer rains, and over to Indian Lake. After years of neglect, it has been dredged and the muck conveniently dumped as fill for Charlotte Gardens. Yellow paddle boats ripple gaily across the lake's cool, dark surface.

A year earlier, Logue, an urban planner and builder *extraordinaire* who in his long career in New Haven, Boston, and New York State has reshaped cities and produced more than 40,000 units of housing, had declared, "Nothing I've done was as difficult as building those two goddamn houses [the original models] on Charlotte Street."[4] Of all the efforts confirming the renaissance of the South Bronx, none has been more heralded than Charlotte Gardens, where the mere completion of two American Dream houses on an infamous street spurred a front-page story in the *New York Times* and coverage around the world. (Congressman Bobby Garcia, disgusted by the self-serving political grandstanding on Charlotte Street, had warned the presidential hopefuls for 1984 early on that they were persona non grata in the Bronx. Only Senator Alan Cranston, perhaps unaware of the verbal "Politicians Not Welcome," had made the pilgrimage and seen firsthand the much-touted progress.)

Logue had worked closely with Gennie Brooks's and Father Smith's MBD Development Corporation, which culled the most promising homeowners from a deluge of applicants delighted to resettle this urban frontier in a fifty-two-thousand-dollar three-bedroom manufactured house set on a seven-thousand-square-foot lot. One-shot state and federal subsidies and below-market New York State mortgages kept the purchase prices low. MBD and Logue were also aided mightily by Anita Miller of the Ford Foundation–backed Local Initiatives Support Corporation (LISC).

She had first become interested in the grassroots groups of the South Bronx in the 1970s while an officer at the Ford Foundation. "At that time," she says, "the general feeling was that the problem was so large that, without concerted government effort, no one could do anything. Carter's visit helped change the whole environment. When I came back from Washington, D.C. [where she served in the Carter administration as a bank regulator] Frank Thomas, the new president at Ford, said, 'Let's take another look.' " Toward the end of 1980, LISC was born under the leadership of Mitchell Sviridoff. It sold big corporations on the idea that they should use LISC as their vehicle for social-responsibility spending in cities all over the country. Over the next four years, LISC leveraged $60 million into the South Bronx, mainly to support neighborhood groups, which needed low-interest loans, loan guarantees, outright grants, and technical assistance. "We came to the rescue of the local groups when they ran into legitimate problems. We helped them to dream and then carry out their dreams," says Miller.[5] She watched and encouraged the evolution of the best of them into entrepreneurs and business folk. MBD Development Corporation, for instance, is marketing what is really a suburban subdivision. On Vyse Avenue, they have redeveloped an entire block with hundreds of apartments that they manage. Says LISC President Sviridoff, "As the perception changes of the Bronx, the investment starts to flow in."[6]

Logue has nothing but admiration for LISC's clever approach to the private sector. "There is a do-good component in most corporations today. LISC said, 'Give us your money. We have the confidence to spend it usefully.' It's an idea that borders on genius, and LISC has created miracles with it."[7] Three hundred thousand dollars from LISC was critical to making Charlotte Gardens a reality. Earlier, as Logue had maneuvered his battered blue official City car through the streets farther south, describing the recovery of this block or street or business, he frequently mentioned the contributions of both LISC (go-between, handholder, and bankroller) and the Port Authority of New York and New Jersey, ever-powerful and wealthy.

In Logue's pantheon of local heroes, the Catholic clergy of the South Bronx occupy a high place. He sings their praises constantly, with special hosannahs for Brother Patrick Lochrane of Belmont, and Sister Thomas and Father Gigante of Hunt's Point, locally referred to these days as Giganteland. This outpost of urban resurrection is an oasis of twenty-one hundred new and renovated apartments, two dozen single-family homes, and clean steets shaded by gingko trees. At Tiffany Plaza, in front of Saint Athanasius Church, the honey locust trees sway full and green in the breeze, a lively counterpoint to the solemn lions' heads set against a pale pink wall.

In this restful setting, two well-behaved lines form at a truck that serves a free lunch, underscoring the poverty that still permeates the South Bronx. It would be hard to say which of its social ills is the worst — welfare dependency and joblessness, the epidemic of teenage pregnancy (a special Bronx high school was established for these women, some as young as thirteen and fourteen), school dropouts, poor health, alcoholism, or drug abuse. SBDO has inaugurated and coordinated efforts aimed at all these woes, but, no one can quantify their success. Bronx Frontier has been active here, with its gardens, nutrition classes, and pregnancy prevention programs in the elementary and junior high schools. A spirit of hope prevails.

In the Bronx, as elsewhere, success engenders its own momentum, as witness Father Gigante's fulfillment of his vow to recreate his neighborhood. Logue, the professional builder, is profoundly impressed. "This is the most successful critical mass of neighborhood rebuilding in the whole City. I have a stock line about Gigante. I always say I wish I could clone him. Actually, I wish he'd run for borough president. He'd be great."[8]

Logue turns into Tiffany Street and gestures excitedly at a row of simple, red-brick houses, which were developed several

ABOVE: These houses on Tiffany Street were built in the early 1980s under the now-defunct "235" program and sold to families. Homeowners have been adding jaunty awnings, wrought-iron fences, statuary, and flower gardens.

OPPOSITE, ABOVE: Ed Logue at Charlotte Street, where suburban-style ranch houses have risen from the rubble. The houses, with big backyards and white picket fences, sold rapidly. The first families moved in in 1984.

OPPOSITE, BELOW: A woman keeps an eye on her block amidst her sunflowers

years ago by SBDO for Father Gigante, under a now-defunct low-interest program, and then sold to families. The pride of ownership is manifest in the elaborate wrought-iron fencing and gates supporting statuary, in the charming flower gardens of hollyhocks, roses, and zinnias, and in the old-fashioned bright awnings shielding the windows. "When I first started going around the South Bronx," says Logue, "in the midst of the worst abandonment, you'd see these houses and the owners still in them, hanging on. So we started doing more like these in the '235' program. Well, look at them. It's wonderful."[9] Across the street, more large weedy meadows await houses. Beyond that grassy landscape, the familiar vista of bombed-out buildings shimmers in the August haze.

Just down the way, on banana-shaped Kelly Street, rehabilitation is noisily under way on the last big apartment building being rehabbed with Section 8 subsidies. (The incredible expense of the federal Section 8 program, where tenants pay a third of their income in rent while the feds make up the difference, spelled its doom. By the time it ended, the government subsidy cost in New York City had soared to ten thousand dollars a year per unit.)

Back in his car and driving north toward Charlotte Street, Logue explains how Father Gigante's organization, SEBCO, is collaborating with Gennie Brooks and Father Smith to fill the many acres between their respective developments with 250 owner-occupied ranch houses like those that proved so popular in Charlotte Gardens. As the transformation takes place, this landscape of disemboweled buildings, shuttered shops, and vacant lots thick with weeds and rubbish will give way again to civilization.

The transformation will occur slowly, however, for the bureaucracies that govern these endeavors are cumbersome and painfully lethargic. "Perhaps it is the shellshock of Mr. [Robert] Moses, but it is almost impossible to get things done in this city," laments Logue. "I remember sitting in the City Planning Commission where the seven holy commissioners who rule New York pass on issues. On a pile of agenda papers sat a closely spaced page and a half on opening a curb cut on Queens Boulevard. A curb cut! My God! Every world city has decentralization, but we have a planning commission ruling on every curb cut. The reformers brought us to this, especially Mayor Wagner, for he put all the power in City Hall, and now the borough president cannot be held accountable for the cleanliness of the streets, for potholes, or for the maintenance of the schools. The delivery system in this city is crazy."[10]

In his agency's 1983 report, Logue pleaded for a reconstituted Redevelopment Corporation with enough clout to cut through the red tape and get things done. To make sure no one dismissed this as hoped-for self-aggrandizement, Logue swore he would not head the newly empowered entity. In a city where power is jealously hoarded, his proposal evoked chuckles.

In fact, Logue does not preside over SBDO any longer. The Reagan administration has divvied up the agency's meager $1.3 million federal budget among four other South Bronx groups. City Hall is making up part of the difference and the state continues to ante up $1.5 million a year. (So Logue left, partly in frustration and partly because his wife has a new job in Massachusetts.) The unexpected windfall (in a Reagan era of cutbacks and more cutbacks) yielding $284,500 to Gennie Brooks's MBD for its next 250 houses, $149,000 to Bronx 2000 on East Tremont Avenue for a new business venture and further redevelopment, $376,000 to the Northwest Bronx Community and Clergy Coalition for rehabbing forty apartment buildings and creating a minimall, and the largest sum, $541,000, to the South Bronx Consortium, made up of Bronx Venture Corporation, the South Bronx Overall Economic Development Corporation, and the borough president's Economic Development Corporation.

This last generous award was dismissed in the Bronx as pure pork barrel, for the consortium's officers include Stanley Friedman, Bronx County Democratic leader, and Ramon Velez, who as a longtime Democrat wooed the Puerto Rican

vote on Ronald Reagan's behalf. Logue denounced the award
as "straight whoredom," the blatant and clumsy buying-off of
Velez, whom he deems "incompetent or worse."[11]

The blue official car swerves onto Bathgate Avenue, once
the home of a bustling Jewish market but now the site of the
twenty-one-acre Bathgate Industrial Park. Immediately south
of the Cross-Bronx Expressway, the eight blighted blocks were
laboriously cleared and readied to lure businesses into the
Bronx. The Port Authority actively promoted the development of seven spacious industrial buildings, now occupied by
such firms as Aircraft Supplies, Majestic Shapes, Amco Printers, Collectors Guild, Clay Park Labs, and South Bronx
Greenhouses, Inc. "When I first came to this job in 1978,"
says Logue, "the attitude of businesses was 'Get the hell out
before you get burned.' There were three million square feet
of empty industrial space. Today that's down to five hundred
thousand square feet. I think we have convinced industry that
the South Bronx is a safe place to remain in, grow in, and
come into." Logue instructs, "The Eleventh Commandment
is, 'Thou Shalt Not Speak Ill of the South Bronx.' "[12]

Peter Goldmark, executive director of the Port Authority,
readily admits that "we avoided the Bronx at first. We assessed Bathgate Industrial Park as a gigantic unknown, a big
risk. But it happened. The City should open another five or
ten such parks."[13]

Bathgate might be seen as something of a reproach to the
Reagan White House, a missed opportunity to put theory into
practice. Early on, the Republicans espoused Urban Enterprise Zones as *the* solution to inner-city ills. The unlikely duo
of Representative Jack Kemp, Republican of Buffalo, and
Representative Bobby Garcia, Democrat of the South Bronx,
sponsored legislation that would have offered tax breaks and
cheap loans to encourage businesses in impoverished neighborhoods. But this bill, the administration's most ballyhooed
urban legislation, seems to have died from Republican neglect. Instead, the Democrats of New York City and State
acted on the idea and brought it to fitting fruition in the South
Bronx, where candidate Reagan once electioneered.

The success of Bathgate Industrial Park (where, for example, the herb garden is now going big time with hydroponic technology and a Dutch partner) has helped spawn a second Mid-Bronx Industrial Park, just east of Charlotte Street on ten and a half acres between the Cross-Bronx Expressway and 174th Street. Twenty-five abandoned buildings are being cleared to make way for low-level industrial buildings with rents of four and five dollars a square foot. "It's so simple," says Logue. "Give business as much as they can get in the suburbs."[14] Down in Port Morris, a decaying industrial area on the Bronx's Long Island Sound waterfront, big warehouses and factory buildings are being reoccupied and refurbished, as skyrocketing rents in Manhattan ineluctably push industry north into the Bronx.

Passing beneath the Cross-Bronx Expressway, whose noise spews over its concrete banks, Logue spies an abandoned apartment building. Its blank windows are neatly disguised with decals showing shutters, pots of flowers, and the half-pulled blind. "Now that offends," he says vehemently. "It's pure Potemkin village, just for the benefit of the people passing on the highway."[15] The hundred-thousand-dollar decal effort in the South Bronx stirred a storm of derision and indignation in the national press. South Bronxites wondered, why stop here? How about designer-clothes decals for their wardrobes and sirloin strip decals for their refrigerators?

Logue accepts decals only as a temporary band-aid until an apartment is renovated. "But that building is going nowhere. I say pull it down."[16] That leads to another can of worms: "turfing" and warehousing. Neighborhood powers are loath to let any apartment house — no matter how stripped and vandalized — be demolished, for it might one day be salvaged and repopulated. Because the Reagan administration slashed all rental housing subsidy programs, however, the prospects for further rehabbing are nearly nil. (In the South Bronx, the number of units slated for rehab is a tenth of what it was.) The lead time for housing renovation is so long — four or five years — that even if all money were restored tomorrow, buildings would sit vacant for years. Logue sees no point in

Herbs destined for Manhattan restaurants were being grown in formerly abandoned lots on Bathgate Avenue by GLIE Farms, a local group

clinging to these depressing hulks, two thousand of which blight the South Bronx, potential havens for villainy, illegal dumping, and rats. He advocates methodical clearing and site preparation (which involves pulverizing the rubble) for future building or parks. Enroute now to the Grand Concourse, we see abandoned buildings on block after block that testify to the blight that swept through and killed them. These neighborhoods lack local champions, and they languish accordingly. In the new Bronx, grassroots neighborhood advocacy is all.

Sweeping onto the Grand Concourse, the greatest of all the borough's boulevards, one notices the love and money lavished on its rebirth. "The first thing I said when I got up here," says Logue, "is the Concourse is not going to die,"[17] Fordham Road bustles with shoppers, and the many stores lining the upper Concourse appear properous. (In October 1984 ground would finally be broken for the long-delayed Fordham Plaza, a major office building.)

Along the boulevard, virtually all the enormous apartment houses and edifices that made the Concourse so grandiose have been, or are now being, restored to their former splendor, thanks to City and federal rent-subsidy programs and low-interest improvement loans. The Lewis Morris Building, the mecca of medical practitioners that stood almost empty for several years, is being rehabilitated. Roosevelt Gardens, that most public of disastrous abandonments, reopened in 1981. It has been completely renovated, down to the formal shrubbery out front.

Down and across the busy boulevard, a block of abandoned walk-ups, primly decaled into pseudo-life and waiting resuscitation by private developers, offers haunting evidence of how perilously close the Grand Concourse came to succumbing to blight. Only concerted reinvestment has revived the neighborhood. Black and Hispanic professionals, including Congressman Bobby Garcia, have discovered the glories of the boulevard's extraordinary apartments, with their spacious foyers, sunken living rooms, formal dining rooms, and eat-in kitchens.

Further south, the Andrew Freedman Home stands as impeccably elegant as ever, but for an ugly chain-link fence topped with barbed wire. The board of directors closed its doors in 1983, concluding that it could no longer afford its mission as the "home for poor millionaires." It is slated to become housing for the elderly. Across the street, the Jewish Y, long a temple to athleticism, retains that role as a Girls' Club.

The Bronx Museum of the Arts, jaunty banners waving, has installed itself on the Concourse in the former Temple Emmanuel. At 161st Street, the Concourse Plaza reopened its sedate doors in 1982 as housing for the elderly. Several women live there who happily remember celebrating their weddings in the hotel ballroom (now an open-air courtyard). And so the Concourse is slowly reclaiming its identity as the Grand Concourse, center of the borough and home to the upwardly mobile, though now they are black and Hispanic, not Jewish.

Logue begins cruising back toward Manhattan, pointing out this and that work-in-progress. "The principal thing we have done," he says, "has been changing the perception within the community and outside about the prospects here." He turns east onto 149th Street, the Hub shopping area that is thriving as it had not in years, and then heads south again toward the bridge to Manhattan. "When I came up here everyone thought I'd be eaten alive," he laughs. "I've had frustrations and that's why I'm getting out, but I've had fun with it. It's been a fascinating experience and I love the folks. There is nowhere like the South Bronx. I only wish it well."[18]

Notes

1. "IT IS A VERITABLE PARADISE"

1. Cook, *Borough of the Bronx,* p. 11.
2. *Ibid.,* p. 10.
3. Barbara Tuchman, *The Proud Tower* (New York: Macmillan, 1966), p. 119.
4. Jenkins, *Story of the Bronx,* p. 3.
5. Roosevelt, *Gouverneur Morris,* p. 143.
6. Wells, ed., *Bronx and Its People,* v. I, p. 142.
7. Roosevelt, *Gouverneur Morris,* p. 96.
8. *Ibid.,* p. 95.
9. Cook, *Borough of the Bronx,* p. 367.
10. Lockwood, *Manhattan Moves Uptown,* p. 111.
11. North Side Board of Trade, *Great North Side,* p. 16.
12. *Ibid.,* p. 29.
13. *Ibid.,* p. 39.
14. *Ibid.,* p. 41.
15. *Ibid.,* p. 21.
16. *Ibid.,* p. 93.
17. Lockwood, *Manhattan Moves Uptown,* p. 114.
18. *Ibid.,* p. 116.
19. Riis, *How the Other Half Lives,* pp. 2–3.
20. North Side Board of Trade, *Great North Side,* p. 109.
21. *Ibid.,* p. 192.
22. Johnston, "New York Botanical Garden," p. 3.

2. THE FIRST BOOM

1. Coates, "King of the Bronx."
2. *Ibid.*
3. Flynn, *You're the Boss,* p. 5.
4. Risse, *True History,* p. 3.
5. *Ibid.,* p. 7.
6. *Ibid.,* p. 9.
7. North Side Board of Trade, *Great North Side,* p. 53.
8. "Puerto Rican Immigration," *New York Times,* 11/23/77.
9. James Ford, *Slums and Housing* (Westport, Conn.: Negro University Press, 1971), p. 174.
10. *Ibid.*
11. Burton J. Hendrick, "Great Jewish Invasion," *McClure's,* 1/28/08.
12. Bennett, "Human Citizens — Your United States."
13. Trotsky, *My Life,* p. 271.
14. M. Brenman-Gibson, *Clifford Odets: American Playwright* (New York: Atheneum, 1981), p. 34.
15. "The Concourse Plaza," *Bronx in Tabloid,* 1923.

16. *Ibid.*
17. Durso, *Yankee Stadium,* p. 8.

3.   BOSS FLYNN

1. Flynn, *You're the Boss,* pp. 10–11.
2. Rovere, "Nothing Much to It," p. 33.
3. Flynn, *You're the Boss,* p. 28.
4. *Ibid.,* p. 31.
5. Rovere, "Nothing Much to It," p. 30.
6. Flynn, *You're the Boss,* p. 14.
7. *Ibid.,* p. 33.
8. Interview with Judge David Ross, 10/13/82.
9. Howe and Libo, *How We Lived,* p. 220.
10. Flynn, *You're the Boss,* p. 60.
11. Rovere, "Nothing Much to It," p. 30.

4.   "THE BRONX IS A GREAT CITY"

1. "Yankee Stadium Opens," *New York Times,* 4/24/23.
2. *Ibid.*
3. "Concourse Plaza Opens," *North Side News,* 10/23/23.
4. *Ibid.*
5. Pamphlet on the Concourse Plaza from private collection of Harry T. Johnson.
6. Hotel advertisements from private collection of Harry T. Johnson.
7. Ladies' Luncheon reported in *Bronx Home News,* 11/2/24.
8. Moscow, *What Have You Done,* p. 86.
9. Simon, *Bronx Primitive,* pp. 58–59.
10. Howe and Libo, *How We Lived,* p. 232.
11. Ladies' Luncheon reported in *Bronx Home News,* 11/4/28.
12. Flynn, *You're the Boss,* p. 132.
13. *Ibid.,* p. 72.
14. *Ibid.*

5.   "HARD HIT BY THE DEPRESSION"

1. *New York Times,* 10/30/29.
2. *Bronxboro,* 1/1931.
3. Berg shows at the Museum of Broadcasting, 1 East Fifty-third Street, New York City.
4. Columbia University Oral History of Edward J. Flynn.
5. Flynn, *You're the Boss,* p. 82.
6. *Ibid.,* p. 215.
7. *Ibid.,* p. 140.
8. Rovere, "Nothing Much to It," p. 35.
9. Moley, *Twenty-seven Political Masters,* p. 113.
10. Edward J. Flynn file, FDR Library, Hyde Park, New York.
11. Rovere, "Nothing Much to It," p. 28.
12. Moley, *First New Deal,* p. 379.

13. Lorena Hickock file, FDR Library, Hyde Park, New York.
14. Interview with Judge David Ross, 10/13/82.

6. THE NEW DEAL YEARS

1. Bergman, "The World's Capital."
2. "Courthouse Dedicated," *Bronx Home News*, 6/16/34.
3. "Post Office Started," *Bronx Home News*, 6/14/36.

7. WAR FEVER

1. Radio broadcast reprinted in *Bronxboro*, 6/1939, pp. 1–2.
2. Rovere, "Nothing Much to It," p. 33.
3. Walter Propper, "Footnote to Bronx History," *Bronxboro*, 6/1960.
4. Ultan, *Beautiful Bronx*, p. 45.
5. "Remembering Pearl Harbor," *Bronx Home News*, 12/7/42.
6. Flynn, *You're the Boss*, p. 206.

8. THE DIASPORA AFTER THE WAR

1. *Bronxboro*, 1–2/1944.
2. Bennett Schiff, "City-Owned Houses Boarded Up," *New York Post*, 7/25/46.
3. Glazer and Moynihan, *Beyond the Melting Pot*, p. 28.
4. Brown, *Manchild in the Promised Land*, p. 291.
5. *Ibid.*, p. 292.
6. "Puerto Rico to Harlem," *New York World-Telegram*, 5/1/47.
7. Rodriguez, "Growing Up in the Forties and Fifties," pp. 45, 49.
8. "First Houses" (New York City Housing Authority, 1935).

9. "THERE WAS NO STANDING STILL"

1. "Kridel Buys Hotel," *Bronx Home News*, 12/31/44.
2. Interview with Paula Levison, 1/26/82.
3. Chambers, "Bronx Home News."
4. Samuel Lubell, *Future of American Politics* (New York: Doubleday Anchor, 1955), p. 88.
5. *Ibid.*, p. 89.
6. *Ibid.*, p. 91.
7. Interview with Bob Munoz, 3/14/82.
8. "Puerto Rico to Harlem," *New York World-Telegram*, 5/1/47.
9. "Tide of Migrants Pushing Relief Load through the Roof," *New York World-Telegram*, 10/22/47.
10. Marcantonio, *I Vote My Conscience*, p. 437.
11. Thomas, *Down These Mean Streets*, p. 126.
12. Mohr, *El Bronx Remembered*, p. 92.
13. Interview with Father Joseph Banome, 11/5/81.
14. Obituary for Edward J. Flynn, *New York Times*, 8/19/53.
15. Telephone interview with Cherney Berg.

10. "MOSES THINKS HE'S GOD"

1. Rodriguez, "Growing Up in the Forties and Fifties," p. 50.
2. Interview with Warren Moscow, 11/8/82.
3. *Bronxboro*, 2–3/1945.
4. Caro, *Power Broker*, p. 839.
5. Berman, *All That Is Solid Melts into Air*, p. 292.
6. *Ibid.*
7. "Moses Threatens to Halt Bronx Job," *New York Times*, 3/12/53.

11. THE NEW BOSS

1. Harrison Salisbury, "Kennedy Tours City Area," *New York Times*, 11/6/60.
2. "Buckley Ready to Battle," *New York Times*, 1/25/64.
3. Interview with Judge David Levy, 5/3/82.
4. *Time*, 6/12/64, p. 23.
5. "Troubled Bronx Boss," *New York Times*, 9/30/64.
6. Interview with Jonathan Bingham, 10/28/82.

12. "HORSE WAS THE NEW THING"

1. Lockwood, *Manhattan Moves Uptown*, p. 116.
2. Asbury, *Gangs of New York*, p. 48.
3. Riis, *How the Other Half Lives*, p. 164.
4. Brown, *Manchild in the Promised Land*, p. 103.
5. *Ibid.*, p. 187.
6. *Knapp Commission Report*, p. 97.
7. Thomas, *Down These Mean Streets*, p. 195.

13. THE NEW "OTHER HALF"

1. Harrington, *Other America*, p. 10.
2. Lyndon B. Johnson, *A Time for Action* (New York: Atheneum, 1964), p. 164.
3. Harrington, *Other America*, p. i.
4. Clayton Knowles, "Wagner Opens $18M Attack on City Poverty," *New York Times*, 3/24/64.
5. "Poverty in New York," *New York Post*, 2/22/64.
6. Kitty Hanson, "Death, Divorce, Desertion and Fatherless Kids," *New York Daily News*, 6/24/64.
7. *Ibid.*
8. *New York Times*, 8/21/64.
9. Klein, *Lindsay's Promise*, p. 171.
10. Breslin, "Velez for Congress."

14. THE PONDIAC'S LAST HURRAH

1. Interview with Winnie Corbin, 5/23/82.
2. Interview with Rep. Robert Garcia, 11/14/81.
3. Joseph Wershba, "Relocation Chief," *New York Post*, 12/3/62.
4. Arthur Greenspan, "Badillo Stands for Change," *New York Post*, 4/28/67.

5. Interview with Judge David Ross, 10/13/82.
6. Trial records, Bronx County Court, N.Y.S. v. Eugene Rodriguez (66-CV-2565).
7. Interview with Ross, 10/13/82.
8. Interview with Iris Rivera, 5/13/82.
9. Interview with Judge David Levy, 5/3/82.
10. Obituary for Charles Buckley, *New York Times,* 1/23/67.

15. THE PUERTO RICAN AND THE PRIEST

1. Interview with Michael Nunez, 3/9/82.
2. *Ibid.*
3. Beagle, "Good-bye to the Bronx," p. 96.
4. Interview with Father Louis Gigante, 9/8/83.
5. Interview with Rev. Kenneth Folkes, 5/16/82.
6. Interview with Ramon Velez, 12/8/81.

16. MAU-MAUING THE CITY

1. Demonstration Cities and Metropolitan Development Act of 1966 in Vizbaras, *Bronx Plan,* p. 4.
2. Interview with Carmen Arroya, 4/12/82.

17. WHO WILL BE CAUDILLO?

1. Memos from files of Ralph Alvarado.
2. Vizbaras, *Bronx Plan,* p. 5.
3. Letters from files of Ralph Alvarado.
4. Interview with Ramon Velez, 12/8/81.
5. Letter from files of Ralph Alvarado.
6. Hamill, "Death of Edwin Rivera."
7. Gus Dallas, "Fight for Fund Power Perils Antipoverty Programs," *New York Daily News,* 11/30/69.
8. Interview with Father Louis Gigante, 9/8/83.
9. *Ibid.*
10. Martin King, "War on Dope," *New York Daily News,* 3/8/70.
11. Interview with Victor Marrero, 8/21/81.
12. *Ibid.,* 1/29/82.
13. Interview with George Batista, 5/17/82.
14. Interview with Marrero, 1/29/82.

18. "THE WHOLE PLACE WAS CAVING IN"

1. Interview with Robert Esnard, 7/30/81.
2. "Blue Moerdler," *Newsweek,* 3/28/66.
3. Telephone interview with Charles Moerdler, 3/19/84.
4. Internal memos of 3/13/70 from Board of Education, Office of School Planning.
5. *Ibid.,* 10/6/70.

19. INTERLUDE: SWEET DAYS ON CHARLOTTE STREET

Much of the material for this chapter came from questionnaires filled out by former residents of the Charlotte Street neighborhood.

1. Steven J. Zeitlin, *A Celebration of American Family Folklore* (New York: Pantheon, 1982), p. 118.
2. Rosen, "Glory That Was Charlotte Street."
3. Herman Ridder Yearbook, 1957.
4. Gornick, "You Can Go Home Again."

20. CHARLOTTE STREET: IT WAS NOT A "GOOD" NEIGHBORHOOD

1. A survey by honor students of Hunter College for the Mayor's Committee on Unity (1946).
2. Interview with Carmen Rodriguez (pseud.), 5/6/83.
3. Interview with Father William Smith, 3/17/82.

21. CHARLOTTE STREET: "WHAT A MADHOUSE IT WAS"

1. Interview with Father William Smith, 3/17/82.
2. Interview with Charles Lefkowitz, 4/25/82.
3. Interview with Officer Samuel Strassfield, 4/21/82.
4. *Ibid.*

22. CHARLOTTE STREET: THE FIRES

1. Interview with personnel at Engine Company 82, 6/28/82.
2. *Ibid.*
3. Wallace and Wallace, "Bronx Fire Disaster," p. 3.
4. *Ibid.*
5. Smith, *Report from Engine Company 82*, p. 38.
6. *Ibid.*, p. 132.

23. CHARLOTTE STREET: THE GANGS

1. Newton, "New York's Street Gangs," 6/28/72.
2. *Ibid.*
3. Interview with Louis Lugo, 3/24/83.
4. *Ibid.*
5. *Ibid.*
6. Interview with Father William Smith, 3/17/82.
7. Interview with Elizabeth Martinez, 3/3/82.
8. *Ibid.*
9. *Ibid.*
10. Interview with Lugo, 3/24/83.

24. CHARLOTTE STREET: THE COLLAPSE

1. Interview with John Pratt, 12/7/81.
2. Interview with Charles Lefkowitz, 4/25/82.
3. Interview with Pratt, 12/7/81.

4. *Ibid.*
5. Interview with Genevieve Brooks, 11/16/81.
6. Posters obtained from Captain John Ruffin.
7. Files of Togetherness Management, Inc., letter dated 4/30/74.
8. *Ibid.*, letter dated 8/21/75.
9. Interview with Jack Flanagan, 10/30/81.
10. Interview with Father Louis Gigante, 9/8/83.
11. From files of Rev. Neil A. Connolly.
12. Interview with Rev. Neil A. Connolly, 3/18/83.
13. From files of Mario Merola.
14. Speech delivered 5/10/75 at Cathedral of St. John the Divine; copy provided by bishop's office.
15. News release, Archdiocese of New York, 5/20/75.
16. From files of Mario Merola.
17. Vincent Lee and Frank Lombardi, "Seek Strike Force to Fight South Bronx Arson," *New York Daily News*, 6/8/75.
18. Joseph B. Treaster, "Bronx Boy Says He Set 40 to 50 Fires for $3 Up," *New York Times*, 7/16/75.
19. Interview with Ramon Velez, 5/2/83.
20. *Ibid.*
21. Interview with Michael Nunez, 3/9/82.
22. Interview with Herman Badillo, 6/2/82.
23. Interview with Mario Merola, 3/24/82.

25. THE GRAND CONCOURSE

1. Interview with Gerry Doyle, 3/3/82.
2. "Hotel Rebuilt with Heart," *New York World-Telegram*, 9/28/57.
3. Interview with Winnie Corbin, 5/23/82.
4. Interview with Joseph Caspi, 6/9/82.
5. "Once-Grand Concourse," *New York Times*, 2/2/65.
6. Interview with Donald Darcy, 1/11/82.
7. *Ibid.*
8. Interview with Alan V. Davies, 6/11/82.
9. Interview with Irma Fleck, 11/21/81.
10. John Garabedian, "Elevator Slaying Stirs Divided Neighborhood," *New York Post*, 2/15/67.
11. "City Fights White Exodus," *New York Post*, 3/9/67.
12. Steven V. Roberts, "Integration of Races Sought," *New York Times*, 4/30/67.
13. "The Grand Concourse: Promise and Change" (Commission on Community Interrelations, 1967), p. 5.
14. *Ibid.*
15. *Ibid.*
16. Interview with Simeon Goldstein, 7/20/81.
17. Samuel Goodman, "The Golden Ghetto," master's thesis, University of Bridgeport, 1981, p. 87.
18. Isa Kapp, "American Scene: By the Waters of the Grand Concourse," *Commentary*, 9/1949, p. 269.
19. "Grand Concourse: Hub of Bronx Undergoing Changes," *New York Times*, 2/2/65.

26. THE HOTEL AND THE CONCOURSE

1. Interview with Joseph Caspi, 6/9/82.
2. *Ibid.*
3. *Ibid.*
4. *Ibid.*
5. *Ibid.*

27. ROOSEVELT GARDENS

1. Interview with Robert Abrams, 5/23/83.
2. Stevenson, "Abandonment of Roosevelt Gardens," p. 73.
3. *Ibid.*, p. 74.
4. *Ibid.*
5. *Ibid.*, p. 75.
6. *Ibid.*, p. 79.
7. *Ibid.*
8. *Ibid.*, p. 80.
9. Cataldo, *Yankee Stadium.*
10. "Planned Shrinkage," *Real Estate Weekly*, 2/4/76.

28. THE GRASS ROOTS

1. Interview with Irma Fleck, 11/21/81.
2. Winston, "Bronx Community Groups."
3. *Ibid.*
4. Cole, "Ramon Rueda."
5. CBS News, "The Fire Next Door," broadcast 3/22/77.
6. *Ibid.*
7. *Ibid.*
8. *Ibid.*
9. *Ibid.*
10. Roger M. Williams in *Saturday Review,* 7/1977.
11. Housing Preservation and Development Department files on the Concourse Plaza Hotel.

29. THE PRESIDENT'S MAGIC VISIT

1. CBS News, "The Fire Next Door," broadcast 3/22/77.
2. "Carter Takes Sobering Trip," *New York Times*, 10/6/77.
3. *Ibid.*
4. *Ibid.*
5. Editorial, *New York Times,* 10/6/77.
6. Interview with Lloyd Kaplan, 11/27/81.
7. *Ibid.*
8. *Ibid.*
9. Thomas Glynn, "Charlotte St.," *Neighborhood,* 8/1982, p. 27.
10. Katz, "Faded Dream of Washington Avenue."
11. Interview with Jack Flanagan, 10/30/81.

12. Calvin Tomkins, "The Art World — Alternatives," *New Yorker,* 12/26/83, p. 55.

30. DISENCHANTMENT

1. "White House Tackles the Bronx," *Riverdale Press,* 10/26/78.
2. Anna Quinlan, "The Politics of Charlotte Street," *New York Times Magazine,* 10/7/79.
3. Interview with Herman Badillo, 11/24/82.

31. CHARLOTTE STREET AND NATIONAL POLITICS

1. "Reagan in South Bronx," *New York Times,* 8/7/80.
2. *Ibid.*
3. "In the Bronx, Thousands Cheer," *New York Times,* 10/3/79.
4. *Ibid.*

32. "THE NEXT PART OF THE SOUTH BRONX"

1. Interview with Rev. Paul Brant, 8/29/83.
2. *Ibid.*
3. *Ibid.*
4. *Ibid.*
5. Interview with Msgr. John McCarthy, 3/23/83.
6. Interview with Brant, 8/29/83.
7. Northwest Bronx Community and Clergy Coalition files, position paper of 5/1974.
8. *Ibid.*
9. Interview with Jim Mitchell, 3/22/83.
10. From Northwest Bronx Community and Clergy Coalition files.
11. *Ibid.*
12. Interview with Roger Hayes, 9/6/83.
13. From Northwest Bronx Community and Clergy Coalition files.
14. Interview with Hayes, 9/6/83.
15. Interview with Brant, 8/29/83.
16. Interview with Hayes, 9/6/83.
17. Interview with Mitchell, 3/22/83.
18. Interview with Hayes, 9/6/83.
19. From Northwest Bronx Community and Clergy Coalition files.
20. Interview with Anne Devenney, 4/4/83.
21. Interview with Richard Gallagher, 9/26/83.
22. Interview with Bill Frey, 9/7/83.
23. *Ibid.*
24. Interview with Devenney, 4/4/83.
25. Interview with Hayes, 9/6/83.
26. *Ibid.*
27. Interview with Gallagher, 9/27/83.
28. *Ibid.*
29. Interview with Frey, 9/7/83.
30. *Ibid.*

33. "WE'RE STILL HERE"

1. Interview with Anne Devenney, 4/4/83.
2. Interview with Jim Buckley, 9/6/83.
3. Chang, "Real Grass Roots."
4. Interview with Father John Jennick, 4/18/83.
5. Interview with Buckley, 9/6/83.
6. Interview with Mary McLoughlin, 4/16/83.
7. *Ibid.*
8. Interview with Msgr. John McCarthy, 3/23/83.
9. Northwest Bronx Community and Clergy Coalition videotape.
10. Interview with Jim Mitchell, 3/22/83.
11. Interview with Bill Frey, 9/7/83.
12. Author's notes from stockholders' meeting.
13. Interview with Devenney, 4/4/83.
14. *Ibid.*
15. Interview with Richard Gallagher, 9/26/83.
16. Interview with Lois Harr, 9/6/83.
17. Interview with Rev. Paul Brant, 8/29/83.
18. Interview with Msgr. McCarthy, 3/23/83.

34. WHITE PICKET FENCES

1. Interview with Edward J. Logue, 8/9/84.
2. *Ibid.*
3. *Ibid.*
4. *Ibid.*, 5/18/83.
5. Interview with Anita Miller, 3/5/82.
6. Interview with Mitchell Sviridoff, 9/6/84.
7. Interview with Logue, 8/9/84.
8. *Ibid.*
9. *Ibid.*
10. *Ibid.*
11. *Ibid.*
12. *Ibid.*
13. Interview with Peter Goldmark, 11/17/84.
14. Interview with Logue, 8/9/84.
15. *Ibid.*
16. *Ibid.*
17. *Ibid.*
18. *Ibid.*

Bibliography

As the ensuing bibliography shows, the sources for this book range from early histories to newspaper articles to a multitude of interviews. While the most important print sources are detailed here, the amount of source material used precludes listing everything. For instance, to reconstruct the War on Poverty in New York City and the Bronx in particular, I assembled a chronological "book" of hundreds of newspaper and magazine clips. Similar "books" were compiled for my use on the Concourse Plaza Hotel, whose history I found so intriguing, and on Bronx fires and arson.

In a county that so many people have abandoned and where so much has been destroyed, locating material (not to mention people) can be frustrating and difficult. For instance, I had hoped to track down the morgue of the *Bronx Home News,* which was supposedly left to Fordham University. No one knows what has become of it.

Such disappointments were offset by unexpected windfalls. I had been laboriously looking for former residents of Charlotte Street, when I heard of a reunion to be held in April of 1983. Suddenly I had an entire ballroom full of people whose recollections considerably enriched the book.

For future researchers into New York City history or the Bronx, the files assembled in researching this book (including all the files of the Northwest Bronx Community and Clergy Coalition) will be given to the Bronx Archives of the Herbert H. Lehman College of City University in the Bronx as part of the Harry T. Johnson Collection. The archive is actively seeking to build its collections of Bronxiana. Anyone with memorabilia or photographs to donate should contact the archive c/o The Library, Lehman College, Bedford Park Boulevard West, The Bronx, NY 10468.

BOOKS

Addams, Jane. *Twenty Years at Hull House.* New York: New American Library, 1981.

Adler, Norman, and Blanche Blank-Davis. *Political Clubs in New York City*. New York: Praeger, 1975.

Andersen, Martin. *The Federal Bulldozer*. Cambridge, Mass.: MIT Press, 1964.

Asbury, Herbert. *The Gangs of New York*. New York: Knopf, 1927.

Auletta, Ken. *The Streets Were Paved with Gold*. New York: Random House, 1979.

Banfield, Edward. *The Unheavenly City*. Boston: Little, Brown, 1968.

———. *The Unheavenly City Revisited*. Boston: Little, Brown, 1974.

Barth, Gunther. *City People: The Rise of Modern City Culture in Nineteenth-Century America*. New York: Oxford, 1980.

Berman, Marshall. *All That Is Solid Melts into Air*. New York: Simon and Schuster, 1982.

Bird, Caroline. *The Invisible Scar*. New York: McKay, 1966.

Birmingham, Stephen. *"Our Crowd."* New York: Harper and Row, 1967.

Brown, Claude. *Manchild in the Promised Land*. New York: Signet, 1965.

Caro, Robert. *The Power Broker*. New York: Vintage, 1975.

Colon, Jesus. *A Puerto Rican in New York*. New York: Mainstream, 1961.

Comfort, Randall. *The Borough of the Bronx*. New York: North Side News Press, 1906.

Cook, Harry T. *The Borough of the Bronx, 1639–1913*. New York: privately printed, 1913.

Corman, Avery. *The Old Neighborhood*. New York: Simon and Schuster, 1980.

Curvin, Robert, and Bruce Porter. *Blackout Looting!* New York: Gardner Press, 1978.

Drake, Leonard A. *Trends in the New York Printing Industry*. New York: Columbia University Press, 1940.

Durso, Joseph. *Yankee Stadium: Fifty Years of Drama*. Boston: Houghton Mifflin, 1972.

Fitzpatrick, Joseph P. *Puerto Rican Americans*. Englewood Cliffs, N.J.: Prentice-Hall, 1971.

Flynn, Edward J. *You're the Boss*. New York: Viking, 1947.

Gale, William. *The Compound*. New York: Rawson Associates, 1977.

Glazer, Nathan, and Daniel Patrick Moynihan. *Beyond the Melting Pot*. Cambridge, Mass.: MIT Press, 1963.

Gordon, Milton. *Cultural Assimilation in American Life*. New York: Oxford, 1981.

Goro, Herb. *The Block*. New York: Vintage Books, 1970.

Gould, Heywood. *Fort Apache, The Bronx*. New York: Warner Books, 1981.

Handlin, Oscar. *The Newcomers: Negroes and Puerto Ricans in a Changing Metropolis.* Cambridge, Mass.: Harvard University Press, 1959.

Harrington, Michael. *The Other America.* Baltimore: Penguin, 1963.

Heckscher, August, and Phyllis Robinson. *When La Guardia Was Mayor.* New York: Norton, 1978.

Hentoff, Nat. *A Political Life: The Education of John V. Lindsay.* New York: Knopf, 1969.

Hoenig, Gary. *Reaper: The Story of a Gang Leader.* Indianapolis: Bobbs-Merrill, 1975.

Howe, Irving, and Kenneth Libo. *How We Lived.* New York: Richard Marek, 1979.

Jackson, Anthony. *A Place Called Home: A History of Low-Cost Housing in Manhattan.* Cambridge, Mass.: MIT Press, 1976.

Jackson, Larry R., and William A. Johnson. *Protest by the Poor: The Welfare Rights Movement in New York City.* New York: Rand Institute, 1973.

Jacobs, Jane. *The Death and Life of Great American Cities.* New York: Random House, 1961.

———. *The Economies of Cities.* New York: Random House, 1969.

Jacobs, Julius. *Bronx Cheer.* Monroe, N.Y.: Library Research Associates, 1976.

Jenkins, Stephen. *The Story of the Bronx.* New York: Putnam, 1912.

Klein, Woody. *Let in the Sun.* New York: Macmillan, 1964.

———. *Lindsay's Promise.* New York: Macmillan, 1970.

Knapp Commission Report. New York: Braziller, 1973.

Kunnes, Richard, M.D. *The American Heroin Empire.* New York: Dodd, Mead, 1972.

Latimer, Dean, and Jeff Goldberg. *Flowers in the Blood: The Story of Opium.* San Francisco: Franklin Watts, 1981.

Lewis, Gordon R. *Puerto Rico: Freedom and Power in the Caribbean.* New York: MR Press, 1963.

Lewis, Oscar. *La Vida: A Puerto Rican Family in the Culture of Poverty — San Juan and New York.* New York: Random House, 1965.

Lindsay, John V. *The City.* New York: Norton, 1969.

Lockwood, Charles. *Manhattan Moves Uptown.* Boston: Houghton Mifflin, 1976.

McNamara, John. *History in Asphalt: The Origin of Bronx Street and Place Names.* Harrison, N.Y.: Harbor Hill, 1978.

Marcantonio, Vito. *I Vote My Conscience.* Clifton, N.J.: A. M. Kelley, 1973.

Mohr, Nicholasa. *El Bronx Remembered*. New York: Harper and Row, 1975.

Moley, Raymond. *The First New Deal*. New York: Harcourt, 1966.

———. *Twenty-seven Political Masters*. New York: Funk and Wagnalls, 1949.

Morris, Charles R. *The Cost of Good Intentions: New York City's Liberal Experiment, 1960–1975*. New York: Norton, 1980.

Moscow, Warren. *What Have You Done for Me Lately?* Englewood Cliffs, N.J.: Prentice-Hall, 1967.

Moynihan, Daniel Patrick. *Maximum Feasible Misunderstanding*. New York: Free Press, 1969.

Mumford, Lewis. *The City in History*. New York: Harcourt Brace Jovanovich, 1961.

North Side Board of Trade. *The Great North Side, or the Borough of the Bronx*. New York: North Side Board of Trade in the City of New York, 1897.

Padilla, Elena. *Up from Puerto Rico*. New York: Columbia University Press, 1958.

Peel, Roy V. *Political Clubs of New York*. New York: I. J. Friedman, 1968.

Price, Richard. *The Wanderers*. Boston: Houghton Mifflin, 1974.

Puzo, Mario. *The Godfather*. New York: Putnam, 1969.

Rainwater, Lee, and William L. Yancey. *The Moynihan Report and the Politics of Controversy*. Cambridge, Mass.: MIT Press, 1967.

Ravitch, Diane. *The Great School Wars: New York City, 1805–1973*. New York: Basic Books, 1974.

Riis, Jacob A. *How the Other Half Lives*. New York: Hill and Wang, 1957.

Risse, Louis. *The True History of the Conception and Planning of the Grand Boulevard and Concourse*. New York: Bell Press, 1902.

Roosevelt, Eleanor. *This I Remember*. New York: Harper, 1949.

Roosevelt, Theodore. *Gouverneur Morris*. Boston: Houghton Mifflin, 1888.

Salins, Peter D. *The Ecology of Housing Destruction*. New York: NYU Press, 1980.

Silberman, Charles. *Criminal Violence, Criminal Justice*. New York: Random House, 1978.

Simon, Kate. *Bronx Primitive*. New York: Viking, 1982.

Smith, Dennis. *Report from Engine Company 82*. New York: Pocket Books, 1973.

Sowell, Thomas. *Ethnic America*. New York: Basic Books, 1981.

Sternlieb, George. *The Ecology of Welfare*. New York: Dutton, 1973.

Stimmel, Barry, M.D. *Heroin Dependency*. New York: Stratton, 1975.

Thomas, Piri. *Down These Mean Streets*. New York: Signet, 1968.

Trebach, Arnold. *The Heroin Solution*. New Haven: Yale University Press, 1982.

Trotsky, Leon. *My Life*. New York: Scribner, 1930.

Tugwell, Rexford. *The Stricken Land: The Story of Puerto Rico*. New York: Doubleday, 1947.

Ultan, Lloyd. *The Beautiful Bronx*. Westport, Conn.: Arlington House, 1979.

Wakefield, Dan. *Island in the City*. New York: Corinth, 1957.

Walker, Tom. *Fort Apache*. New York: Crowell, 1976.

Washnis, George J. *Community Development Strategies: Case Studies of Major Model Cities*. New York: Praeger, 1974.

Wells, James Lee, ed. *The Bronx and Its People, 1609–1927*. New York: Lewis Historical Publishing Company, 1927. 4 vols.

WPA Writers Guild. *New York City Guide*. New York: Random House, 1939.

PERIODICALS, REPORTS, AND UNPUBLISHED MATERIAL

Advisory Services for Better Housing. *Progress Report: Inventory and Analysis of the Grand Concourse and Publicly Assisted Housing in the South Bronx*. 7/1979.

Alsop, Stewart. "The City Disease." *Newsweek*, 2/28/72.

———. "The Road to Hell." *Newsweek*, 6/6/72.

Beagle, Peter. "Good-bye to the Bronx." *Holiday*, 12/1964.

Bennett, Arnold. "Human Citizens — Your United States." *Harper's Monthly*, 11/1912.

Bergman, Lewis. "The World's Capital — the Bronx." *New York Times Magazine*, 3/17/46.

Breslin, Jimmy. "Velez for Congress from the Bronx? No Thonx!" *New York Daily News*, 2/2/76.

Bronx Frontier. Annual reports, 1878–1982.

"Bronx Golden Jubilee." Special section of *New York Post*, 5/25/64.

Bronx 2000. Annual report, 1982.

Capa, Cornell. "Melting Pot Politics." *Life*, 10/27/52.

Cataldo, Angelo. "Yankee Stadium." Master's project, Columbia Journalism School, 1977.

CBS News. "The Fire Next Door." Broadcast 3/22/77.

Chambers, Gilbert. "The Bronx Home News." *American Mercury*, 7/1955.

Chang, Julia MacDonnell. "The Real Grass Roots: Anne Devenney." *City Limits*, 3/1983.

Children's Aid Society. *The Negro Children of New York*. Report issued in New York City, 1932.

Clapp, John McMahon. "The Determinants of Housing Abandonment in New York City." Doctoral thesis, Columbia University, 1974.

Clines, Francis X. "About New York: More Heavenly Pursuits Beckon a Pragmatist." *New York Times*, 8/30/77.

Coates, Robert M. "The King of the Bronx." *New Yorker*, 12/7/29. (Profile of J. Clarence Davies.)

Cole, Rick. "Ramon Rueda." Master's project, Columbia Journalism School, 1979.

"Concourse Plaza, The." *Bronx in Tabloid*, 1923.

Devine, Richard James. "Institutional Mortgage Investment in an Area of Racial Transition: A Case Study of Bronx County, 1960–1970." Doctoral thesis, New York University, 1974.

Finder, Alan. "Farming the Ghetto." *Bergen Record*, 3/19/78.

Fried, Joseph P. "South Bronx Story: Logue Returns." *New York*, 10/16/78.

Golden, Martha. *The Grand Concourse: Tides of Change*. New York City Landmarks Preservation Committee, spring 1976.

Goodman, George W. "Rehabilitation Holding Bronx Blight at Bay." *New York Times*, 6/12/83.

Goodman, Senator Roy. *Report on Model Cities*. State Charter Revision Commission, 11/1973.

Goodwin, Michael. "Controversial Father Gigante Wins Applause." *New York Times*, 7/15/81.

———. "Mr. Urban Renewal Acts to Rebuild His Image." *New York Times*, 5/5/80.

Gornick, Vivian. "You Can Go Home Again — But Don't." *Village Voice*, 11/6/69.

Hamill, Pete. "The Death of Edwin Rivera." *Village Voice*, 9/13/76.

Hendrick, Burton J. "Great Jewish Invasion." *McClure's*, 1/28/08.

Janoff, Joe. "Priest's Good Works Atone for Brother Who Went Wrong." *New York World-Telegram*, 6/19/61.

Johnston, Mea. "The New York Botanical Garden." *Historical Society of New York*, 7–8/1981.

Katz, Steve. "The Faded Dreams of Washington Avenue." *City Limits*, 4/1983.

King, Nicholas. "South Bronx: A Crusade Goes Sour." *National Review*, 2/20/81.

Klein, Joe. "The Last of the Bigtime Spenders." *New York*, 6/18/84. (Profile of Logue.)

Ledwith, Tim. "Organizing the North West Bronx." *City Limits*, 3/1983.

Levitt, Leonard. "The Rebirth of the Gangs." *New York Daily News Sunday Magazine*, 8/20/72.

Lockwood, Charles. "Taming the South Bronx Frontier." *Quest*, 12/1977–1/1978.

Lopez, Alfredo. "In Search of Ramon Velez." *Village Voice*, 6/11/70.

McMillan, Penelope. "The Boss and the Priest: A Tale of Two Politicians." *New York Daily News Sunday Magazine*, 12/9/73.

Magnuson, Robert. "The People's Development Corporation." Master's project, Columbia Journalism School, 1977.

Meyer, Herbert E. "How Government Helped Ruin the South Bronx." *Fortune*, 11/1975.

Montgomery, Paul L., and Francis X. Clines. "Thousands Riot in Harlem Area." *New York Times*, 7/16/64.

Municipal Art Society. *The Livable Society*, 7/1979. (Issue on the South Bronx.)

"New Day for the Bronx, A." *New York Daily News Sunday Magazine*, 3/20/83.

Newton, Edmund. "New York's Street Gangs." *New York Post* series starting 6/26/72.

New York City Commission on Intergroup Relations in East Tremont. Report, 1961.

New York City Housing Authority. "A Legislative and Fiscal History." 30-page mimeographed report, undated (probably 1974).

New York City Planning Commission. *Plan for New York City*, II: "The Bronx: A Proposal," 1969.

New York City Police Department. "Homicide Analysis." Office of Management Analysis, Crime Analysis Unit, 1980.

New York Urban Coalition. *Neighborhood*, 8/1982. (Issue on the South Bronx.)

Oser, Alan S. "Housing Supply in City Eroding Amid Construction Standstill." *New York Times*, 2/8/70.

Pilot, Oliver. "Buckley of the Bronx." *New York Post* series, 1/3–1/8/61.

Pringle, Henry F. "Roosevelt's Flynn." *Collier's*, 10/12/40.

"Puerto Ricans in New York, The." Series in *New York Post*, 6–7/1953.

"Puerto Rico to Harlem." Series in *New York World-Telegram* beginning 5/1/47.

Rodriguez, Clara. "Growing Up in the Forties and Fifties." *Devastation/Resurrection* (Bronx Museum of the Arts catalogue, 1979).

Rosen, Ira. "The Glory That Was Charlotte Street." *New York Times Magazine*, 10/7/79.

Rosenblum, Constance. "A Street of Dreams." *New York Daily News Sunday Magazine,* 4/6/80.

Rovere, Richard. "Nothing Much to It." *New Yorker,* 9/8/45.

Scheer, Robert. "Bronx — Landscape of Urban Cancer." Series in *Los Angeles Times* starting 8/6/78.

Schoenberg, Samuel. "An Historical Analysis of the Changing Business Life of New York City, 1820–1937." Doctoral thesis, New York University, 1940.

Shenon, Philip. "Pioneer Settlers Bring Glow to South Bronx." *New York Times,* 1/14/84.

South Bronx Development Organization. *Areas of Strength / Areas of Opportunity: South Bronx Revitalization Program and Development Guide Plans.* 12/1980.

———. *Meanwhile, in the South Bronx.* Summer 1983.

Stevenson, Gelvin. "The Abandonment of Roosevelt Gardens." *Devastation/Resurrection* (Bronx Museum of the Arts catalogue, 1979).

Tabor, George. "Badillo: Orphan at 5, to BP." *Bronx Press-Review,* 5/4/67.

———. "Boss Charles A. Buckley." Series in *Bronx Press-Review,* 1/26, 2/2, 2/9/67.

Tolchin, Martin. "South Bronx: A Jungle Stalked by Fear, Seized by Rage." *New York Times* 4-part series starting 1/15/73.

U.S. Bureau of Labor Statistics. "A Socio-Economic Profile of Puerto Rican New Yorkers." Pamphlet, 1970.

U.S. House of Representatives. "Prohibiting the Importation of Opium for the Manufacture of Heroin." Hearings before Ways and Means Committee, 4/3/24.

Vizbaras, Jonas, Office of. *Bronx Plan: A Report on Physical Development Planning.* Bronx Model Cities Neighborhood, 8/15/69.

———. *Bronx Plan, 1968–1972.* A report to the Bronx Model Cities Neighborhood, 1972.

Wallace, Rodrick, and Deborah Wallace. "The Bronx Fire Disaster: A Study of Urban Ecological Collapse." Public Interest Scientific Consulting Service (New York), 1983.

Weingarten, Gene. "East Bronx Story." *New York,* 3/27/72.

Williams, Robert, and Peter J. McElroy. "The Flynn Machine." Series in *New York Post* beginning 5/18/53.

Winston, Diane. "Bronx Community Groups." Master's project, Columbia Journalism School, 1982.

Women's Club of New York. *With Love and Affection: A Study of Building Abandonment.* Report, 1977.

OTHER SOURCES

Bronx Home News.

Bronxboro, magazine of the Bronx Chamber of Commerce.

Edward J. Flynn, Columbia University Oral History Project, 3/1950.

Files from the FDR Presidential Library at Hyde Park, New York, on Edward J. Flynn, the Democratic National Committee, and Lorena Hickock. The Flynn family donated all of Edward J. Flynn's papers to the FDR Library in 1983.

New York City Board of Elections, election figures, courtesy of Ray Staib.

Files of the Northwest Bronx Community and Clergy Coalition.

INTERVIEWS

Robert Abrams, 5/23/83; Carmen Allende, 6/21/82; Ralph Alvarado, 1/7/82, 3/5/82; Evalina Antonetty, 3/17/82; Carmen Arroya, 4/12/82, 5/15/82; Judge Sidney Asche, 4/22/82; Herman Badillo, 6/2/82, 11/24/82; Father Joseph Banome, 11/5/81; George Batista, 11/16/81, 5/17/82; Louis Benza, 12/8/81; Cherney Berg (telephone); Rep. Mario Biaggi, 11/30/81; Mrs. Logan Billingsley, 10/28/81; Rep. Jonathan Bingham, 10/28/82; Dennis Boyle, 4/16/83; Rev. Paul Brant, 8/29/83; Genevieve Brooks, 11/16/81; Jim Buckley, 3/24/82, 9/6/83; Basil Campbell, 3/22/82; Judge John Carro, 6/1/82; Joseph Caspi, 6/9/82; Megan Charlop, 4/16/83; Roy Cohn, 4/20/83; Rev. Neil A. Connolly, 3/18/83; Winnie Corbin, 5/23/82; Aureo Cordona, 3/22/82; Patrick Cunningham, 1/6/82; Donald Darcy, 1/11/82; Frazier Davidson, 11/18/81; Alan V. Davies, 6/11/82; George DeLuca, 3/20/82; Anne Devenney, 4/4/83; Walter Diamond, 3/12/82, 5/12/82; Isadore Dollinger, 5/5/82; Gerry Doyle, 3/3/82; Carlton Dukess, 11/20/81; Julius Edelstein, 11/15/82; firemen of Engine Company 82, 6/28/82; Robert Esnard, 7/30/81; Leonard Fastenberg, 11/29/81; Rev. Joseph Fitzpatrick, 9/15/82; Jack Flanagan, 10/29/81, 10/30/81, 12/1/81; Eugenia Flatow, 3/26/82; Irma Fleck, 11/21/81; Monserrate Flores, 3/8/82; Richard Flynn, 3/3/82; Rev. Kenneth Folkes, 5/16/82; Councilman Wendell Foster, 10/10/81; Tom Fox, 4/1/82; Bill Frey, 9/7/83; Rep. Richard Gallagher, 9/26/83; Robert Garcia, 10/21/81, 11/14/81; Jim Gelbman, 4/19/83, 12/26/83; Gilberto Gerena-Valentin, 12/14/81; Father Louis Gigante, 9/8/83; Mr. and Mrs. Ben Gilhooley, 6/28/82; Philip Gilsten, 6/23/82; Peter Goldmark, 11/17/84; Simeon Goldstein, 7/20/81, 10/8/81; Albert Goodman, 1/19/82; Arthur Goodman, 7/21/81, 8/9/81; Samuel Goodman, 8/9/81; Morris Greenstein, 3/30/82; Eleanor Greenthal, 3/8/82; Veralyn Hamilton, 3/16/82; Lois Harr, 9/6/83; Roger Hayes, 9/6/83; Robert Hazen, 6/9/82; Maria Hernandez (pseud.), 5/6/83;

William Hubbard, 8/5/81; Bob Jacobsen, 10/29/81; Mike Jacobsen, 12/3/81; Rev. John Jennick, 4/18/83; Harry Johnson, 3/9/84; Helen Johnson, 3/9/84; Lloyd Kaplan, 11/27/81; Elias Karmon, 3/10/82, 3/30/82; George Kinderman, 11/19/81; Judge Martin Klein, 11/9/82; Ruben Kline, 8/6/81; David Krakow, 11/27/81; Sam Kramer, 11/4/81; Steven Lambert, 6/8/82; Mr. and Mrs. Charles Lefkowitz, 4/25/82; Andrew Levison, 1/17/82; Paula Levison, 1/26/82; Stuart Levison, 1/8/82; Judge David Levy, 5/3/82, 5/11/82; Edward J. Logue, 5/18/83, 8/9/84; Father John Luce, 11/23/81; Louis Lugo, 3/24/83; Frank Lugovinia, 3/16/82, 3/20/82, 4/21/82; Eugene Lynn, 1/6/82; Msgr. John McCarthy, 3/23/83; Christopher McGrath, 6/23/83; Kevin McGrath, 4/2/82; Mary McLoughlin, 4/16/83; Michael McManus, 3/30/83; Victor Marrero, 8/21/81, 11/23/81, 1/25/82, 1/29/82, 2/5/82, 3/5/82; Elizabeth Martinez, 3/3/82; Adolph Menendez, 4/18/82, 4/28/82; Mario Merola, 3/24/82; Linda Meyers, 5/20/82; Anita Miller, 3/5/82; Eae James Mitchell, 3/9/82; Jim Mitchell, 3/22/83; Charles Moerdler, 3/19/84 (telephone); Assemblyman Armando Montana, 3/9/82; Preston Moore, 1/13/82; Warren Moscow, 11/8/82; David Muchnik, 3/18/83; Bob Munoz, 3/14/82; Joseph Muriana, 3/22/83; Paul Muscillo, 3/17/82; Assemblyman Louis Nine, 3/13/82; Michael Nunez, 3/9/82; Ted Panos, 3/22/83; John Patterson, Jr., 12/3/81; Ralph Porter, 6/7/82; Seymour Posner, 7/27/81, 11/11/81; John Pratt, 12/7/81; Frank Puig, 10/8/81; Iris Rivera, 5/13/82; Carmen Rodriguez (pseud.), 5/6/83; George Rodriguez, 3/8/82; Capt. Paul Roshkind, 1/7/83; Judge David Ross, 4/15/82, 10/13/82; Capt. John Ruffin, 5/20/82; William Salinger, 4/30/82, 2/20/83; June Salters, 3/15/82; John Santiago, 4/29/83; Mary Sayres, 4/23/83; Rep. James Scheuer, 3/3/82; Sheila Shapiro, 3/31/83; Herbert Siegal, 10/13/81; Father William Smith, 3/17/82, 4/15/82, 3/24/83; Roger Staff, 10/15/81; Officer Samuel Strassfield, 4/21/82; Mitchell Sviridoff, 9/6/84; George Tabor, 5/13/82; Carlos Tejade, 10/29/81; Dennis Terry, 1/27/82; Ted Tiah, 3/11/83; Judge Felipe Torres, 5/13/82; Sherman Tufel, 4/23/83; Ramon Velez, 12/8/81, 5/2/83; Gary Waldron, 3/16/83; Henry Waltemade, 8/11/81, 10/28/81; Richard Weekes, 2/22/82; Alan Weiner, 7/2/81; Carolyn Weiss, 4/19/83; Officer Marty Zloch, 4/30/82.

INDEX

Page numbers in italics indicate photographs.

abandonment of buildings, 7, 199–200, 229–230, 265, 296–299
and insurance, 365
Abrams, Robert, 180, 285, 288, 354
and battle against arson, 259, 260–261, 264
Abrams, Marty, Fur Company, 208
Action (newspaper), 359
Addams, Jane, 139
Adopt-an-Executive program, 374
Aetna Life and Casualty Company, 365–366, 368, 369
African People's Revolutionary Party, 341
Ahearn, Eddie, 46
Ahearn, John, 46
Ahearn, Bishop Patrick V., 349, 350, 351, 352, 355, 358
Aid to Dependent Children, 146, 177
Albert, Jerry, 231
Albert Einstein College of Medicine, 148
Aldrich, Richard S., 145
Ali, Lateef, 185
Alinsky, Saul, 350
Allee, Dennis, 197–198
All That Is Solid Melts into Air (Berman), 121–122
Almanac of American Politics, xvi, xxiv
Almeida, Salvador, 174, 184, 186–188
Alvarado, Ralph, 184, 185, 186
Amco Printers, 384
American Jewish Congress report on Grand Concourse, 275–277
American Labor party, 48, 88, 108
American Real Estate Company, 206
Anderson, Martin
The Federal Bulldozer, 182
Andrew Freedman Home, 278, 312, 387–388
antipoverty programs, 147, 148–149, 152, 164, 166–168, 170–171, 173–174, 188–189
anti-Semitism, 85–86
apartment buildings, 7, 29, 35–37, 49, 83–84
Aquahung River (Broncks' River), 12

Arroya, Carmen, 178–179
arson, 7, 231–235, 252–253, 363–364
incentives for, 259–261, 265–267
task force report on, 258–259
war on, 261, 264–266, 267, 375
Arson Suppression Team, 310
Asbury, Herbert
Gangs of New York, 137
Asencio, Ánibal, 184, 185, 190
Astor, Vincent, 103
Astor, Vincent, Foundation, 322
Astor, William Waldorf, 40

Bacall, Lauren, 4
Badillo, Herman, 155–159, *157,* 164, 174, 176, 274, 333
and City Hall, 180
in Congress, 196, 251, 267
as deputy mayor, 318–319, 324–325
mayoral campaign of, 193, 277
Bailey, William O., 366
Banana Kelly, 322–323
Bancroft, Anne, 4
Bank of the United States, 214
banks, 356–359, 360–361
and arson, 266
see also savings banks
Banome, Father, 114
Barinoff (slumlord), 291
Baruch, Bernard, 90, 101, 103
Bathgate, Alexander, 206
Bathgate Avenue, *76,* 327, 384, *386*
Bathgate Industrial Park, 384, 385
Batista, George, 197
Beagle, Peter, 168
Beame, Abraham, 149–150, 158, 299, 309–310, *314,* 317
and Carter's visit, 311–312
and coalition, 352, 355, 362
Beautiful Bronx, The (Ultan), 88
Beckhardt, Rabbi, 65
Bedford Stuyvesant Restoration Corporation, 197
Belmont, 4, 379
Bennett, Arnold, 36
Berg, Cherney, 116
Berg, Gertrude, 67, 115–116

Berman, Marshall
  All That Is Solid Melts into Air, 121–
    122
Berra, Yogi, 106
Beth Israel Hospital, 225
Beth Israel Temple, 65
Better Concourse, Inc.. A (ABC), 277
Beyond the Melting Pot (Glazer and
    Moynihan), xvii
Biglaiser, Harry, 215
Billingsley, Logan, 289
Bingham, Jonathan, 134–135
Bird, Isabella Lucy, 24, 137
blackout of 1977, 308–310
blacks, 5, 6, 96–98, 102, 177
  and antipoverty programs, 164, 168,
    170
  on Charlotte Street, 219–224
  discrimination against, 111–112, 152
  on Grand Concourse, 273, 282, 284
  struggle of, for political control, 171,
    174, 175–177, 189–190
Black Spades (gang), 245
block grants, 257
block patrols, 350, 357
Bob's Bar, 110
Boggs Act, 142
Borough Hall, 78, 207
Boston Road, *21*, 202, 206, 313, 376
Bouza, Anthony, 260
Brant, Paul, 345–348, 351, 352, 375
Breslin, Jimmy, 151
breweries, 19
Brightside, 20
Bronck, Antonia Slagboom, 11
Bronck, Jonas, xv, 11–12
Bronx, 4
  founding of, 11–15, 19–20, 22–26
  growth of, 27–29, 32–33, 35–37, 39–
    40, 49–50
  heyday of, 51, 53, 56, 60–62, 205–206,
    208–218
  topography of, 11, 60
  see also Bronx areas
Bronx areas
  East Bronx, 5, 148, 261, 344
  North Side (Annexed District), 22
  northwest Bronx, 344, 345–348, 365–
    368
  West Bronx, 218, 229, 298, 306, 344
  see also South Bronx
Bronx Arson Task Force, 258–259, 260,
    265
Bronx Board of Realtors, 285
Bronx Board of Trade, 23, 49, 51, 85–
    86
  and Moses, 119, 120, 122
Bronxboro, 87, 119, 120
Bronx Boys' Club, 245, 249

"Bronx Browning Literary Society," 107
Bronx Central Post Office, 80, 81
Bronx Cheer (Jacob), 61
Bronx County Bar Association, 32
Bronx County Building, 80, 81
Bronx County Courthouse, 278
Bronx County Democratic dinner, 130–
    131
Bronx County Veterans Co-ordinating
    Council, 121
Bronx Frontier Development Corpora-
    tion, 301, 320–322, 379
Bronx Home News, 44–45, 88–89, 107–
    108, 115, 359
Bronx Museum of the Arts, 289, 388
Bronx Park, 11, 25
Bronx Primitive (Simon), 60
Bronx River, 11, 205
Bronx Rotary Club, 52, 57, 282
Bronx Savings Bank. *See* Eastern Sav-
    ings Bank
Bronx 2000, 322, 383
Bronx Venture Corporation, 383
Bronx-Whitestone Bridge, 119
Bronx Zoo, 26, 50, 80, 301
Brook Avenue, 100
Brook Club, 128
Brooks, Genevieve, 249, 250–252, 260,
    267, 317, 377, 382
Brothers Construction, Inc., 346
Brown, Claude
  Manchild in the Promised Land, 98,
    141, 142
Brown, Jim, 42, 43
Brown v. *Board of Education of To-*
    peka, 220
Bruckner, Henry, 78
Bruckner Boulevard, 123, 125
Buckley, Charles A., xviii, 114, 127–
    128, *129,* 130–136, 153, 163
Buckley, James, 366, 367, 370, 372, 374
BUILD, 370
building inspectors, 201, 350, 355
building services breakdown, 229–230,
    270, 273, 289, 350–354, 368
bureaucracy, 178–181, 359, 368, 382–383
burglaries, 225, 227, 337
burning buildings. *See* arson
Burnside Avenue, 69
Business Confidence Week, 66
business growth, 15, 20, 23
Butcher, William C., 372

Campaign for Human Development,
    352
Cantor, Eddie, 62
Cardinal Hayes High School, 344
Carnegie, Andrew, 26
Carney, George M., 160–162

Caro, Robert
  The Power Broker, 120–122
Carruthers, Francis, 260
Carter, James E., *314*
  and aid efforts, 319–321, 324–327
  Bronx visit of, 8, 311–313, 316–317
  failure of, 333, 341, 343–344
Caspi, Joseph, 270, 281, 284–285
Catholic Charities, 178
Catholic church. *See* Roman Catholic
  church
Cavanaugh, James, 352–353
CBS television, 67, 115
  broadcasts "The Fire Next Door,"
    306–307, 312
Central Savings Bank, 105
Chambers, Gilbert, 107
Charlotte Gardens, 376–378
Charlotte Street, xxi, *21,* 202–204, 205–
    206, 208, 214–218, *314, 315, 335*
  arson on, 231–235
  Carter and, 8, 313, 316, 324–325
  drug addiction on, 225–230
  gangs on, 237
  Jewish exodus from, 219–224
  and 1980 presidential campaign, 333–
    343
  rebuilding on, 376–378
Chase Manhattan Bank, 371–372
Chatfield-Taylor, Adele, xxi
Chayefsky, Paddy, 4
Chemical Bank, 249, 250, 377
children, 210–214, 221, 228
Christian Science Monitor, 344
Chuck Wagon program, 321
Churchill, Winston, 90
Church of the Immaculate Conception,
  19
Citizens' Union, 43
City College, 216, 217
City Limits (magazine), 320
Civilian Works Administration, 80
Claremont Park, 25
Claremont Parkway, 313
Claremont Village housing project, 324
Clay Avenue, 290–292
Clay Park Labs, 384
Cloward, Richard A.
  "A Strategy to End Poverty," 177–
    178
clubhouses, political, 45–47, 128, 134,
  136
cocaine, 139, 140
Cohn, Albert, 45
Collazo, Oscar, 100
Collectors Guild, 384
College Avenue, 318
Commentary, 278
Community Affairs Associates, 188

community block grants, 257
Community Board 5, 351
"community corporations," 151, 173,
  174
Community Development Committee,
  359
Community Development funds, 355,
  356, 359, 369–370
Community Planning Board 3, 327
community progress centers, 149, 150,
  151
Community Reinvestment Act, 369
compost production, 301, 321
Concourse Plaza Hotel, 37, 39, 53, *54–
    55, 56–59,* 63, 70, 105–107, 130, 278
  downfall of, 268–270, 281–286, 312
  reopened for housing for elderly, 388
Concourse Village, 275
Congress, U.S.
  Eighteenth District, 9
  Twenty-first District, 192, 193–194
Connolly, Neil A., 258, 259–261, 344
Consolidated Laundries, 66
Construction for Progress, 331
consultants, 188
Consumer-Farmer Foundation, 304, 305
Cooke, Cardinal Terence, 264, 342, 349
Cooney, Joan Ganz, 371
Co-op City, 6–7, 273–276, 289, 290,
  294, 346
Corbin, Winnie, 270
corruption, 142
Cost of Good Intentions (Morris), 180
Coulter's Brewery, 18
Counter Convention of the Coalition for
  the People's Alternative. *See* Peo-
  ple's Convention
Courier and Enquirer, 15, 18
Courtlandt Avenue, 48
Cranston, Alan, 377
crime, 6–8, 24, 137–139
  in Bronx, 271–272, 276, 283, 350
  and drug addiction, 141–143, 225–229
Criminal Justice Coordinating Council,
  304
Crosetti, Frank, 106
Cross-Bronx Citizens' Protective Associ-
  ation, 121
Cross-Bronx Expressway, 5, 119–123,
  124, 384, 385
Crotona Park, xxiv–xxv, 11, 24, 80, 206,
  207, 211–212, 222–223, 313, 329,
  377
Croton Aqueduct, 14–15
Cunningham, Patrick, 302, 353
Curran, Paul, 259
Curtis, Tony, 4
CWA (Civilian Works Administration),
  80

Daily News, 146, 150, 252
Darcy, Donald, 271, 272, 360–361
Davidson, Joan, 300
Davidson Avenue, 306
Davies, Alan V., 272
Davies, J. Clarence, 27–29, 272
Davis, Albert, 24–25
Davis, Gordon, 362
Davis, John W., 58–59
Deadman's Hill, 211
Death and Life of Great American Cities, The (Jacobs), 182
decals program, 385
Decatur Avenue, 367
Deegan, Major, Expressway, 123
Democratic National Committee, 62–63, 86
Democratic National Convention, 1980, 333, 341
Democratic party
  growth of, 41–45, 59, 71, 73, 74
  Irish control of, 18
  machine of, 5, 45–49, 128, 194
  1948 defeat of, 108–109
  Puerto Ricans in, 154–156, 158–160, 164, 173–174
  weakness of, 353–354
Democratic State Committee, 64
Demonstration Cities and Metropolitan Development Act (Model Cities), 175
Depression, the, xv, 65–67, 69, 74–75, 97, 214–215
Devenney, Anne, 355–356, 358, 363, 365, 366, 371–372, *373,* 374
Diamond, Walter, 158
discrimination, 18, 110–114, 152
Disraeli, Benjamin
  Sybil, xxv–xxvi
Dobinsky, Mrs., 107
Doc Fisher's Saloon, *21*
Dollar–Dry Dock, 370
Dollar Savings Bank, 349, 356, 361, 369, 370
Donleavy, J. P., 4
Dougherty, Sister Eleanor, 371–372
Down These Mean Streets (Thomas), 113, 142–143
Doyle, Gerry, 268–269
drug addiction, xviii–xix, 6, 137, 139–143, 225–230, 337–339, 379
  and arson, 7, 232
  and gangs, 237, 245, 246
drug pushers, 141, 143, 225, 236, 339–340
drugs. *See entries for specific drugs*
Drummond, Malcolm, 51
Dry Dock, 370
Dryfoos, Orville, 272

dumping buildings, 357, 358
Durso, Joseph
  Yankee Stadium, 40
Durso, Mike, 369
Dutch West India Company, 11

Eastern Savings Bank (Bronx Savings Bank), 356, 357
  vs. coalition, 360–361
  picketed, 358–359
East Harlem, 5, 99
East Harlem for Kennedy for President Committee, 156
Eastman, Monk, 138
East 163rd Street Improvement Association, 185
East River, 11
East Tremont, 4, 122, 344
East Tremont Avenue, 322, 383
Economic Development Corporation, 383
Economic Opportunity Act of 1964, 145, 148
Economic Opportunity Corporation, 149
Edelstein, Julius, 145
education, 34, 95–96, 217
  importance of, 210–211
Eighteenth Congressional District, 9
Eighth Avenue IND subway, 80–81, 83
Eins, Stefan, 323
Einstein, Albert, College of Medicine, 148
Elmwood, 20
Emergency Financial Control Board, 305
Emergency Repair Program (ERP), 353, 354, 356
Emergency Work Bureau, 65
Emmaus, 12
Esnard, Robert, 199–200
Everart, George, 56
Exxon Corporation, 352, 371–372, *373,* 374

Faile Street, *254–255, 343*
Fair Access to Insurance Plan, 364
Farley, James, 69, 70, 72, 81–82, 86, 114
Farm, the, 307–308
Farrell, Thomas F., 120
Fashion Moda, 323
FBI, 264–265
Federal Bulldozer, The (Anderson), 182
Federal Deposit Insurance Corporation, 360, 361
Feiffer, Jules, 4
Fekner, John, 333
Ferry Point Park, 298

"finishers," 7
  and Roosevelt Gardens, 297–298
Finletter, Thomas K., 133
Fire, Safety, and Educational Program, 250
Fire Administration, U.S., 375
Fire Department, New York City, 194, 232, 250–251, 258
  Engine Company Eighty-two, 7, 231, 233–235
  Red Caps, 375
fire marshals, 231, 250, 265
"Fire Next Door, The," 306–308, 312
fires, 7–8, 231–235, 261–267, *262–263*, 306, 310, 317
  decline in, 363–364
  campaign for prevention of, 251–252, 310
First Houses, 103, 183
First New Deal, The (Moley), 73
fiscal crisis, 286–287, 298–299, 304–305, 352
Fitzpatrick, Joseph P., xxiv
Five Points, 18
Flanagan, Jack, 249, 256, 301, 320, 321
Flatow, Eugenia, 176, 184, 188
Fleck, Irma, 272–273, 300–301
Flores, Monserrate, 166, 167
Flynn, Edward J., xvi, xvii, 5, 59, *68*, 69, 114–115, 127, 136
  elected Democratic leader, 37, 41–45, 48–49
  promotes Lyons, 78, 82
  supports Roosevelt, 62–64, 70–75, 77, 86–90
  You're the Boss, 42
Flynn, Fred, 115
Flynn, Richard, 131
Folkes, Kenneth, 171
Foote, Aston, 283
Ford Foundation, 377, 378
  study of blackout, 309
Fordham-Bedford Neighborhood Association, 365
Fordham Plaza, 387
Fordham Road, 8, 362, 370, 387
Fordham University, xvii, 50, 244, 345, 349
Forest Houses, 117
Fort Apache, 226–227, 294, 377
Fox, Tom, 321
Fox, William, 205, 206
Fox Funeral Home, 163
Fox Street, 110, 166, 240, 241, 325
Franco, Thomas, 296
Freedman, Andrew, Home, 278, 312, 387–388
Freedomland, 274
Frey, Bill, 356, 358, 361, 370

Friedman, Stanley, 265, 353, 356, 383
Fuchs, Charles, 269, 270, 285
Fulton Avenue, 308
Future of American Politics, The (Lubell), 5, 108–109

Gaines, Edythe J., 203
Gallagher, Richard, 357, 360, 361, 369, 375
Gallent, Martin, 300
gangs, 9, 137–138, 236–240, *238–239*, 242, 244, 245–248
  and gang wars, 109–110, 114, 222–223
Gangs of New York (Asbury), 137
Garcia, Bobby, 99, 154, 160, 162, 164, 318
  as congressman, 377, 384, 387
garment industry, 34, 93
Gelbman, Jim, 240–245
Gerena-Valentin, Gilbert, 341
Germans, 18–20, 74
  Jewish, 33–34
Gerosa, Lawrence, 131
GI Bill, 95–96, 217
Gigante, Father Louis, 168–170, 189–191, *195*, 257–258, 317, 344, 348, 349, 379
  runs for Congress, 193–194, 196
  and SEBCO, 302–303, 382
  rivalry of, with Velez, 184, 187
Gilbert, Jack, 171
Gilhooley, Ed, 154
Giovinazzi, F. Giles, 260
Glazer, Nathan, xvii, xx
"Glory That Was Charlotte Street, The" (Rosen), 215
Glynn, Thomas, 319
Godfather, The, 141
Goldbergs, the, 67, 115–116
"Gold Coast," 84
Goldmark, Peter, 384
Goldstein, Simeon H. F., 277
Goldwater, Monroe, 59
Goldwater and Flynn, 59
Gompers, Clara, 153–154
Goodman, Al, 184–185
Goodman, Samuel M., 277
"good repair clause," 357, 364, 368
Gornick, Vivian, 216
Gottlieb, Bluma, 293
Gouverneur Morris housing project, 14
Grand Boulevard and Concourse, 4, 11, *30–31*, 32, 37, 83–84
  abandonment on, 298, 343
  exodus from, 268, 271–280
  rebirth of, 387–388
Grand Jurors Association, 78
grassroots groups, 9, 300–306, 320–323, 343, 351, 356, 387

Gray Panthers, 341
Great Society programs, 6, 149, 164
Green Guerrillas, 321
Greenspan, Arthur, 159

Halper, Morris, 296
Halprin, Esther, 336
Hamill, Pete, 150
Hamilton, Charles V., xxiii–xxiv
Hamilton, Veralyne, 327–332
Hammer, Armand, 4
Hans, Hyman, 273
Hanson, Kitty, 146–147
Harlem
  overcrowding in, 5, 97–100, 147–148
  Spanish, 100, 111
Harlem Renegades (gang), 303
Harlem River, 11, 14, 346
Harlem River Houses, 103
Harper's Monthly, 36
Harr, Lois, 374, 375
Harriman, Averell, xviii
Harrington, Michael
  The Other America, 144, 145
Harris, Patricia, 311, 313, *314*
Harrison Narcotic Act, 139, 140, 142
"Haryou-Act," 148
Hayes, Cardinal, High School, 344
Hayes, Roger, 346, 350, 351, 353–354,
  355
  and Morris Heights, 359–360
Health, Education and Welfare, U.S.
  Department of, 196–197
Hebrew Y, 278–279
Heiman, John G., 198
Heine, Heinrich, 278
Heintz, Louis, 23, 29
Henkel, Paul Revere, 39
Herman Ridder Junior High School,
  216, 220, 240, 241–245, *315*
Hernandez, Maria (pseud.), 336–341
heroin, 6, 140–143, 225, 227, 236, 338
Hickock, Lorena, 75
Highbridge (neighborhood), 4, 8, 19,
  344
High Bridge, 14, 19
High Bridge aqueduct, 74
highway construction, 119–123, 125, 126
Hispanics, 153, 159, 326
  see also Puerto Ricans
Hoe, Richard March, 20
Holden, Missy, 296
Holiday, Billie, 141
Holy Spirit parish, 345
Home Mortgage Disclosure Act of
  1975, 356
homesteading, 303–306, 307, 308
homicides, 138, 226, 227, 228

Hone, Philip, 24
Hoover, Herbert, 63, 65, 69
Hoovervilles, 69
House of Representatives Public Works
  Committee, 128, 130
housing, xxii–xxiii
  deterioration of, 199, 200–204
  importance of, 194, 197, 198, 351
  inspectors of, 201, 350, 355
  postwar shortage of, 95–96
  preservation of, 351–352
  projects, public, 5, 102–104, 117–119
  rehabilitation of, 302–303, 364–365,
    366, 370, 379, 382
Housing and Urban Development, U.S.
  Department of, 257
housing corporations established by co-
  alition, 370
housing court, 351, 364
Howard, Elston, 106
Howe, Irving, 4
Howe, Louis, 63
How the Other Half Lives (Riis), 24
How We Lived (Schimmel), 46
Hub, the, 48, 193, 388
Hudson River, 11
Hudson River Railroad, 19
Human Resources Administration, 151
Hunter College, 80, 95, 293
Hunt's Point, 4, 100, *195*, 240, 344
  destruction of, 8, 261
  and SEBCO, 301–302
  urban resurrection in, 379
Hunt's Point Community Corporation,
  167, 186, 190, 191
Hunt's Point Community Progress Cen-
  ter, 167, 173–174
Hunt's Point Multi-Service Center, 167,
  170–171, 173, 183, 196–197, 303
Hunt's Point Produce Market, 301, 321
Huston, Colonel Tillinghast l'Homme-
  dieu, 39, 40

illegitimacy, 177, 227, 339, 340
immigration
  to Bronx, 4, 5, 6, 19–20, 33, 35–37,
    219, 220
  to New York City, 15, 23–24, 34–35
Impelliteri, Vincent, 114
Indian Lake, *207*, 211, 212, 377
Indian Rock, 212
Indian tribes of the Bronx, 11
industry
  in Bronx, 14, 19, 20, 23
  in New York City, 15, 91, 94
  regrowth of, 327, 384–385
inspectors, building, 201, 350, 355
Institute for Local Self-Reliance, 321

insurance companies
  and arson, 232, 259–260, 265–267
  crackdown on, 364
  redlining by, 365–366
  reinvestment by, 368–369, 370–371
Interim Operations, Inc., 269
Interior, U.S. Department of, 321
Irish, 14, 15, 18, 19–20, 34, 74
  political power of, 18, 41, 128, 152,
    154, 159
  vs. Puerto Ricans, 110, 114, 222–223
Irving, Albert (pseud.), 208–209, 214
Irving, Sarah (pseud.), 209, 210
Isacson, Leo, 108, 109
Italians, 4, 33, 35, 74, 138, 152, 222–223

Jacobs, Jane
  The Life and Death of Great American Cities, 182
Jacobs, Julius
  Bronx Cheer, 61
Jake the Pickle Man, 208, 211, 226
James Monroe High School, 220
Janes and Kirtland Iron Works, 23
Javits, Jacob, 197–198, 250
Jazz Singer, The, 37
Jennick, John, 366–367
Jennings Street, 205, 226, 228, 376
Jennings Street Market, 202, 208, 220
Jerome Avenue, 29
Jerome Cafeteria, 287
Jerome Park Reservoir (racetrack), 80
Jewish Daily Forward, 138
Jewish War Veterans, 95
Jews, 4, 97, 206, 208–213
  and anti-Semitism, 85–86, 217
  leave Charlotte Street, 219–224
  and crime, 138
  Eastern European, 33–35, 74
  German, 33–34
  and Grand Concourse, 271, 273, 277–280
  in politics, 128, 132–134
John Paul II, 341
Johnson, Harry, 291, 292, 294
Johnson, Helen, 289–295
Johnson, James Weldon, 97
Johnson, Lyndon B., 135
  and war on poverty, 144–146, 148
Johnston, Mary, 282
Jolson, Al, 37
Jones Act of 1917, 99
Jordan, Vernon, 311
Joyce Kilmer Park, 271, 278
Justice Department, U.S., 259

Kahn, Joseph, 270, 281–282
Kane, Patrick J., 43–44, 45

Kaplan, Lloyd, 316, 317, 318–319
Katz, Steve, 320
Kauffman, Howard C., 372, 374
Kelley, Clarence, 264
Kelly Street, 382
Kemp, Jack, 384
Kennedy, John F., *129*, 144
  endorses Buckley, 133, 163
  presidential campaign of, 128, 130–131
Kennedy, Joseph, 128
Kennedy, Robert, 163, 197
Kennedy, Ted, 333
Kilmer, Joyce, Park, 271, 278
King, Martin Luther, Jr., 147–148
Kingsbridge, 22
Kingsbridge Heights, 349, 367
Kirby, Charles F., 233–234
Kitchenwonks, 11
Klein, Woody
  Lindsay's Promise, 151
Knapp Commission, 142
Koch, Edward I., 310, 318, 319,-325,
  326, 327, 362, 364, 376
Kridel, Frank, 105, 268–269, 270
Kristof, Frank S., 199
Kubrick, Stanley, 4

labor unions
  and minorities, 98, 194, 196
  strength of, 91, 93, 147
Labrecque, Thomas G., 372
Ladies' Luncheons (Concourse Plaza),
  58–59, 63, 70, 87, 130–131
LaGuardia, Fiorello, *68*, 81, 83, 102
LaMotta, Jake, 4
Landis, Kenesaw Mountain, 53
landlords, 213, 220–221, 350–351
  abandon buildings, 199–202, 265,
    296–299
  arson and, 7, 232–233
  loans to, 364–365, 370
  "milk" buildings, 7, 229–230
  and welfare families, 253, 256, 282–284, 295–297
Lang, Martin, 356
Lefkowitz, Charles, 226, 249–250
Leggett, Charlotte, 205
Lehman, Herbert H., 114–115, 133, 134
Leventhal, Nathan, 362
Levison, Paula, 105–106
Levy, David, 133–134, 163
Lewis, Philip, 273
Lewis Morris Apartments, 279, 387
Liberty League, 82
Life and Death of Great American Cities, The (Jacobs), 182
Lincoln Hospital, 80

Lindsay, John V., 149–151
  administration of, 180–181, 189, 190,
    201, 228, 277
  and purchase of hotel and Yankee
    Stadium, 285, 286
Lindsay's Promise (Klein), 151
Lions Club, 57, 66
LISC (Local Initiatives Support Corpo-
    ration), 377–379
Livable City, xxi
Lloyd's of London, 364, 365
loans
  for rehabilitation, 364–365, 366, 368,
    370
  for weatherization, 371–372, 374
Local Initiatives Support Corporation
    (LISC), 377–379
Lochrane, Patrick, 379
Lockwood, Charles
  Manhattan Moves Uptown, 15, 18
Loeb, Henry, 198
Loeb, Phil, 115–116
Loew's Paradise Theater, 279
Logue, Edward J., 319, *381*
  and SBDO, 325–327, 376–379, 382–
    385, 387–388
Lorelei Fountain, 278
Lorillard family, 20, 26
Louisiana-Pacific Lumber Company, 320
Lubell, Samuel
  The Future of American Politics, 5–6,
    108–109
Lugo, Louis, 245–246, 248
Lydig Estate, 28
Lynn, Eugene, 269
Lyons, James J., xvii, 78, 91, *92*, 119,
    122, 123, 125, 132

McCarthy, Monsignor John, 345–349,
    353, 358, 369, 375
McCloskey, Mark, xviii
McClure's magazine, 35
McCombs Dam Park, 80, 287
McGrath, Christopher, 71
McGraw, John J., 39–40
McLean, Malcolm, 93
McLoughlin, Mary, 367–368, 370
McSherry's Bar, 110
Magnani, Peter, 298
Mahopac, Lake, 72, 89
Majestic Shapes, 384
Major Deegan Expressway, 123
Maldonada, Antonio, 161
Manchild in the Promised Land
    (Brown), 98, 141, 142
Manhattan Indian tribes, 11
Manhattan Moves Uptown (Lockwood),
    15, 18
Manhattantown, 125

Manhattan Valley, 100
Manheimer, Bernard, 132
Marcantonio, Vito, 111
Marin, Luis Munoz, 99
Marrero, Victor, 192–193, 194–198, 256,
    311, 326
Martinez, Elizabeth, 247–248
Marty Abrams Fur Company, 208
Maryknoll Brothers, 318
"mau-mauing," 176, 180
"maximum feasible participation," 149
Maynicke and Franke, 39
MBD Development Corporation, 377,
    378, 383
Meany, George, 4
media
  and coverage of fires, 261, 264, 265
  and coverage of gangs, 237, 240, 245–
    247
Mejias Brothers, 220
Melrose, 4, 8, 19, 117
Menendez, Adolph, 286
Merola, Mario, 259, 260–261, 264, 267
Methodist Church, Mott Avenue, 65
Mid-Bronx Desperados Development
    Corporation, 317
Mid-Bronx Industrial Park, 385
migration to New York City, 5–6, 96–
    100, 102, 110–112, 165
Milbrook Houses, 117
"milking" buildings, 7, 229–230
Miller, Anita, 377–378
Miller, Simeon, 283
Mineo, Sal, 4
Minford Place, 205, 225, 237, 245
Minford Place synagogue, 217, 229
minorities, 5
  discrimination against, 110–114, 152
  unions oppose, 98, 194, 196
  receive voting rights, 153, 158
  see also blacks; Puerto Ricans
Misericordia Hospital, 292
Missionaries of Charity, 318
Mitchell, Eae James, 249, 252, 253, 256
Mitchell, Helen, 167
Mitchell, Jim, 346, 349, 352, 370
Mobilization for Youth, 148, 177
Model Cities program, 6, 175–176, 180–
    181, 182–183
  Hamilton on, 330–331
  replaced, 257–258
  South Bronx program of, 184–189,
    190–198, 203
Moerdler, Charles G., 201
Mohegans, 11, 12
Mohr, Nicholasa
  "Uncle Claudio," 113–114
Moley, Raymond, 72
  The First New Deal, 73

Monroe, James, High School, 220
Moore, Bishop Paul, Jr., 264
Morgan, J. Pierpont, 26
morphine addiction, 139–140
Morris, Charles R.
  The Cost of Good Intentions, 180
Morris, Gouverneur, 13–14, 206
Morris, Gouverneur, II, 14, 106
Morris, Gouverneur, housing project,
  14
Morris, Colonel Lewis, 12
Morris, Lewis, xv, 12–13
Morris, Lewis, Apartments, 279, 387
Morrisania
  arson in, 8, 261, 344
  Hamilton on, 327–328
  history of, 4, 12–14, 22
Morris Avenue, 14
Morris Heights, 8, 14, 345, 359–360
Morris Heights Neighborhood Improve-
  ment Association, 346, 353
Morris High School, 14, 220
Moscow, Warren
  What Have You Done for Me Lately?,
  59, 118
Moses, Robert, xxv, 64, 298
  highway and bridge projects of, 83,
  119–123, 125
  slum clearance projects of, 125–126
Mott, Jordan L., 14
Mott Avenue Methodist Church, 65
Mott Haven, 4, 8, 14, 100, 344
  vest pocketing in, 182
Mott Haven Housing Development
  Fund, 325
Mott Haven Plan Committee, 182, 183,
  184
Moyers, Bill
  "The Fire Next Door," 306–308, 312
Moynihan, Daniel Patrick, 177, 179
Muchnik, David, 322
Municipal Housing Authorities Law,
  102
Munoz, Bob, 110, 190
murders. *See* homicides
Murphy, Arthur, 42, 43, 44, 127
Murphy, Charles F., xvi, 41, 42, 44

Narcotics Bureau, U.S., 139, 140
Nash, Ogden (quoted), 79
Nassau Management Company, 268,
  269
Nation, 177
National Association of Lesbian and
  Gay Filmmakers, 341
National Association of Neighborhoods,
  341
National Association of Puerto Rican
  Affairs (NAPRA), 166

National Council on Drug Abuse, 142
National Housing Act, 102
National People's Action, 356, 365–366
National Recovery Act, 75
National Task Force on Prostitution,
  341
National Urban League, 333
National Welfare Rights Organization,
  178
NBC radio, 67
Neighborhood Counseling Center, 190
Neighborhood Project No. 1, 287
"Neighborhood Strategy Area," 370
neighborhoods vs. City Hall, 131, 185,
  188–190, 197, 352–356, 383
Nesbitt, A. Hamilton, 65
New Deal, xvi, 75, 77, 78–84, 128
New Frontiersmen, 145
New Jersey Tenants' Organization, 341
newspapers, 19, 88–89
  see also entries for individual newspa-
  pers
New York and Harlem Railroad, 14, 19
New York Botanical Garden, 26, 50,
  80, 321
New York City, 5–6, 15, 22
  breakdown in services in, 273, 299,
  351, 352–354
  fiscal crisis in, 286–287, 298–299, 304–
  305, 352
  immigration to, 23–24, 34–37, 219,
  220
  migration to, 96–100, 102, 110–112,
  165
  postwar changes in, 91, 92–96
  see also New York City agencies;
  New York City government
New York City agencies
  Board of Education, 203, 204
  Board of Estimate, 78, 81, 325,
  351
  Buildings Department, 296
  City Council, 191, 302, 351
  City Council Against Poverty, 149,
  150, 174, 189
  Housing and Development Authority,
  103, 118–119, 176, 182, 194, 200,
  259–260, 303, 353–355
  Housing Preservation and Develop-
  ment, 304, 364, 372
  Parks Department, 23, 206
  Planning Commission, 286, 298, 300,
  351, 382
  Real Estate Department, 156, 285–
  286
  Redevelopment Corporation, 383
  Relocation Department, 156, 282
  Sanitation Department, 194
  Social Services Department, 229

New York City agencies (*continued*)
Welfare Department, 69, 178–180,
253, 256, 260, 266
see also Fire Department, New York
City; Police Department, New
York City
New York City government vs. neigh-
borhoods, 6, 131, 188–190, 197,
352–356, 383
Seabury investigates, 67
Third Assembly District of, 45, 47, 75
New York Daily News, 146, 150, 252
New Yorker, 28–29, 73, 144, 323
New York Giants (baseball team), 39
New York Giants (football team), 106,
286
New York Port Authority, 93, 94, 327,
379, 384
New York Post, 108, 146, 159, 273–274
New York Post–Bronx Home News, 108
New York Property Insurance Under-
writing Association, 364
New York *Staats-Zeitung*, 216
New York State agencies
Banking Department, 360
Division of Housing, 322
New York State legislature
imposes flat-grant system, 179
Fourth District of, 155
Twenty-ninth District of, 160
New York Times, 8, 65, 114
on the Bronx, 79, 100, 270–271, 272–
273
on Buckley, 163
on fires, 310, 316
on Velez, 192
New York Times Magazine, 215, 265
New York University, 50, 346
University Heights campus of, 360
New York Urban Coalition, 303, 319
New York World-Telegram, 100, 110–
111, 169, 269
New York Yankees, 52, 53, 57, 106,
281, 286, 287
Welcome Home dinners for, 106, 269
New York Zoological Society, 26
Nine, Louis, 316
Nixon, Richard M., 179, 256, 299
North Side News, 32
North Side Savings Bank, 271, 356–357,
360
Northwest Bronx Clergy Conference,
347
Northwest Bronx Community and
Clergy Coalition, 317–318, 349–354,
359–362, 366–372, *373*, 374–375,
383
City Services Committee of, 354–356
Energy Committee of, 374

Housing Committee of, 354–355
Insurance Committee of, 365–366
Reinvestment Committee of, 357–358,
360–362, 375
Youth Development Program of, 359
Nunez, Michael, 164, 266–267

Odets, Clifford, 4, 37
Office of Economic Opportunity, 151,
175
Office of Management and Budget,
U.S., 359
O'Hagan, John T., 233
Open Space Task Force, 321
Operation Bootstrap, 110
opium, 139–141
Orchard Beach, 80
Orchard Hill, 89
Ostroff, Harold, 275
Other America, The (Harrington), 144
Ottinger, Albert, 63
Our Lady of Angels Church, 349
Our Lady of Refuge parish, 366

Panitz, William, 198
Parker, Charlie, 141
parks, 25–26, 321, 355–356
patronage, 45, 48–49, 86, 128, 173
Patterson housing project, 117
"paving block" scandal, xvii, 89
Pelham Bay Park, 25
People's Convention, 333, 341
People's Development Corporation,
303–306, 307–308, 312, 320, 321
breakup of, 326
Periconi, Joseph, 132, 156, 158
piano factories, 19
picketing, 358–359, 360–361
Pius XII, 90
Piven, Frances Fox
"A Strategy to End Poverty," 177–
178
"planned shrinkage," 298–299
Plenty Commune, 307–308
Poe, Edgar Allan, 15
Police Department, New York City,
140, 194, 245, 258, 266
Forty-first Precinct of (Fort Apache),
226–227, 249, 294, 377
Forty-fourth Precinct of, 294
Narcotics Division of, 142
politics, national, and Charlotte Street,
333, 336, 341–343
Pondiac Club, 45–47, 153–155, 162–163,
302
Popham Avenue, 346
population growth in Bronx, 35, 49, 74,
221
Porter, Ralph, 249

Porter, Stephen, 140
Port Morris, 385
Posner, Seymour, 295, 297
Post, Langdon, 103
Powell, Adam Clayton, 173
Power Broker, The (Caro), 120–121, 122
Pratt, John, 249–250, 251
Pratt Institute Center, 305
press. *See* media; newspapers
printing industry, 23, 91, 94
Prospect Avenue, 329
Public Housing Law of 1939, 103
Public School 61, 203, 211, 220, 233, 250
public works, 80–83, 131–132
Puerto Ricans, xix, xx, 5, 6, 98–100, 101, 102, 110–114, 165
    and antipoverty programs, xxiv, 164, 166–168
    move to Charlotte Street, 219–224
    discriminated against, 152
    family life and structure of, 113–114, 223, 336–341
    take over Pondiac Club, 153–155, 159–163
    struggle for control of South Bronx, 171, 173–174, 183–190

Ramos, Jack, 186
Ranachqua, 12
Raskob, John J., 62
Reagan, Ronald, 333, 334, 336, 344
    cutbacks of, 371, 383, 385
    and urban legislation, 384
real estate development
    and land boom, 4, 27–29, 84–85
    and market collapse, 75, 276
Real Estate Weekly, 298
Red Caps, 375
redlining, 356, 360, 365–366
reform movement, 131–136
rehabilitation
    of buildings, 302–303, 379, 382
    loans for, 364–366, 368, 370
    and tax shelter aspect of arson, 259–260
reinvestment
    drive for, 356–361, 368–371
    by government, 356
    on Grand Concourse, 387
rent
    control of, 7, 103–104, 199
    nonpayment of, 201, 229, 253, 256
    stabilization in, 200
    strikes in, 350
Report from Engine Company 82 (Smith), 234–235
Republican-Fusionists, 111, 156

Ridder, Herman, Junior High School, 216, 220, 240, 241–245, 315
Rider and Driver Club of Manhattan, 29
Riis, Jacob
    How the Other Half Lives, 24, 137–138, 246–247
riots
    1964 in Harlem, 147–148
    1977, 308–310
Risse, Louis A., 29, 32, 278
Rivera, Edwin, 187–188
Rivera, Geraldo, 246
Rivera, Iris, 162–163
Riverdale, 115, 156
Riverdale Press, 324
Roberts, Burton, 160–161
Robinson, Rabbi Theodore, 273
Rodriguez, Carmelotta, 162
Rodriguez, Carmen (pseud.), 221–222, 227
Rodriguez, Clara, 117–118
Rodriguez, Eugene, 155, 159–162, 302
Rodriguez, George, 186, 187, 198
Rodriguez, Mrs. Lucy, 261, 264
Roman Catholic church
    work of clergy in, 9, 266, 347, 348, 379
    and the Irish, 18
    power of, 112
    work of, in South Bronx, 317–318
Roosevelt, Eleanor, 68, 72, 87, 133, 134
Roosevelt, Franklin Delano, xvi, xvii, 5, 32, 67, 68
    elected president, 67, 69–70, 72
    and Flynn, 62–64, 70–75, 77, 86–90
    second presidential campaign of, 82–83, 214–215
Roosevelt, James, 63
Roosevelt, Theodore, Apartment Hotel, 58
    see also Roosevelt Gardens
Roosevelt Gardens, 279, 288–289, 294–298, 312
    renovation of, 387
Rose, Daniel, xxii–xxiii
Rosen, Ira
    "The Glory That Was Charlotte Street," 215
Rosenman, Samuel, 90
Ross, David, 46, 75, 154, 159–160, 162, 174
Rovere, Richard, 73
Royal Charmers (gang), 249, 250
Royal Javelins (gang), 237, 245
Rueda, Ramon, 303–305, 312–313, 316, 320–321, 326
Ruffins, John, 250
Ruppert, Jacob, 37, 39–40

Ruth, Babe (George Herman), 39, 53, 57
Ruth, Helen, 57

Sachs, Richard, 198
Saint Ann's Church, 13
Saint Athanasius Church, 168–169, 302, 342, 379
Saint Brendan's parish Altar and Rosary Society, 355
Saint Jerome's, 115
Saint John Chrysostom's parish, 223
Saint Joseph's Church, 114
Saint Mary's Park, 25, 117
Saint Rita's parish, 318
Saint Thomas Aquinas parish, 223, 366
Salinger, William, 188
Salk, Jonas, 4
Sasse syndicate, 364
Saturday Review, 307
Savage Nomads (gang), 245
savings banks, 356–359
    picketed, 358–361
    reinvestment by, 368, 369, 370
SBDO. *See* South Bronx Development Organization
Schimmel, Henry
    How We Lived, 46
Schmertzler, Jack, 270, 281–285
school districts, 203, 244
school dropouts, 102, 146–147, 236, 379
schools. *See entries for individual schools*
Screvane, Paul, 158
Seabury, Amelia, 205
Seabury, Samuel, 67, 69
Seabury Day-care Center, 249, 250
Seabury Place, 202, 203, 205
SEBCO, 301–303, 382
Section 8 program, 382
security programs, 352, 354, 359
    block patrols, 350, 357
Sedgwick Avenue, 367–368, 370
Segal, George, 4
Senate Foreign Relations Committee, 89
Seventh Avenue Express, 209
Seventh Regiment Band, 53
Shapiro, Sheila, 214, 215, 219–220
Shertzer, Jacob, 226
shipping, 93–94
Shriver, Sargent, 145
Simon, Kate
    Bronx Primitive, 60
Simpson family, 20
Simpson Street, 100
Simpson Street Development Association, 170
Sint Sincs, 11

Siwanoy, 11
slavery, 96
slums, 18, 23–25, 102, 112, 168
    and clearance projects, 125–126
    and slumlords, 291, 350–351, 357
Smith, Alfred E., xvi, 43, 53, 56–57, 59, 62–63
Smith, Dennis
    Report from Engine Company 82, 234–235
Smith, Father William, 223, 225, 247–249, 258, 317, 348, 377, 382
socialism, 74
Socialist party, 47–48, 77
Social Security Act of 1935, 177
social workers, 146, 166
Sousa, John Philip, 53
South, the, 96–98
South Bronx, 3–4, 7–9, 168
    Carter's visit to, 311–313, 316–317
    expansion of, 306–307, 344
    and federal aid, 325–327, 333, 336, 341–342
    and planned shrinkage, 298–299
    rebuilding of, 377–379, 382–385
South Bronx Church Coalition, 259–261
South Bronx Community Housing Corporation, 189, 198, 256, 257
South Bronx Consortium, 383
South Bronx Development Organization, 325, 327, 344, 370, 379, 382
    dismantled, 383
South Bronx Greenhouses, Inc., 384
South Bronx Model Cities Policy Committee, 184, 185, 190
South Bronx Neighborhood Orientation Center, 166, 168
South Bronx Overall Economic Development Corporation, 383
South East Bronx Community Organization (SEBCO), 301–303, 382
Southern Boulevard, 38, 202, 206
South Fordham, 350–351
Spanish Harlem, 100, 111
speculators, 357–358
Spofford, Paul N., 20
Starlight Studios, 210
Starr, Roger, 298–299, 354–355
Steinbrenner, George, 286
    and Neighborhood Project No. 1, 287
Stephens, Roderick, 85
step streets, 60
Stevenson, Gelvin, 289, 295, 296, 297
Strassfield, Sam, 226–229
"Strategy to End Poverty, A" (Cloward and Piven), 177–178
strippers, building, 232, 266
    see also "finishers"
subway lines, 4, 28, 80, 81, 83–84, 206

Suerth, Curtis, 301
Sullivan, Donald, 4
Sullivan, John, 132
Sullivan, Mrs. (Highbridge resident), 306–307
Summer in the City program, 170
Sviridoff, Mitchell, 150–151, 378
Sybil (Disraeli), xxv–xxvi

Tackamuck, 12
Taekmucks, 11
Tammany Hall, 41–42, 138
Tankitekes, 11
tax delinquency, 7, 202, 253, 269, 296–297, 363
tax shelters, buildings as, 259–260, 295
Taylor, Louis Fess, 160–161
teenage pregnancies, 177, 379
Teichner, David, 297
Temple Emmanuel, 388
tenant associations, 350–351, 354, 359, 368
tenements, 14–18, 24, 25, 74
Teresa, Mother, 318
Theodore Roosevelt Apartment Hotel, 58
  see also Roosevelt Gardens
Third Alarmers, 281, 313
Third Assembly District, 45, 47, 75
Third Avenue subway, 28
Thomas, Frank, 378
Thomas, Norman, 77
Thomas, Piri
  Down These Mean Streets, 113, 142–143
Thomas, Sister, 379
Tiffany Plaza, 379
Tiffany Street, 379, *380,* 382
Time magazine, 86, 108
Tishman, John, 198
Title I slum-clearance projects, 125–126
Togetherness Management, Inc., 249
topography of Bronx, 11, 60
Torres, Felipe, 154, 155
Torres, Frank, 154, 155
trade, 15, 27, 93, 94
traffic, automobile, 83
traineeships, 194
Travelers Insurance Company, 366
Treasury Department, U.S.
  Narcotic Bureau of, 139, 140
Tremont, 8
Tremont Avenue, 312
Triborough Bridge, 80, 82–83
Triborough Bridge Authority, 83
Trotsky, Leon (on Bronx), 36–37
Truman, Harry S., 90, *92,* 100, 109
Tunnel (disco), 284
Turbans (gang), 237, 245, 337, 338

"turfing," 385
Twenty-first Congressional District, 192, 193–194

Ultan, Lloyd, xv
  The Beautiful Bronx, 88
"Uncle Claudio" (Mohr), 113–114
unemployment, 146, 147, 312, 379
Unemployment Sunday, 65
Union Avenue, 329
unions. *See* labor unions
United Housing Foundation, 274, 275
United States Housing Act, 103
Unity Park, 304
Urban Development Corporation, 199, 319
Urban Enterprise Zones, 384
Urban Guerrillas, 301

Vallone, Peter, 194, 196
Van Cortlandt Park, 25
Vanderbilt, Cornelius, II, 26
Velez, Ramon, 164–168, 170–171, *172,* 173–174, 183, 303, 318, 383–384
  on arson, 266
  vs. Logue, 326
  and Model Cities program, 184–193, 196–198, 256–257
Venice Hall, 303–306, 312, 326
"vest pocketing," 182, 193
Vincent Astor Foundation, 322
"voting clubs," 156
Voting Rights Act of 1965, 153, 158, 223
Vyse Avenue, 237, 378

Wagner, Robert, 114, 154, 383
  and Badillo, 155, 156
  opposes political machine, 131–134
  and war on poverty, 145–149
Wakefield, 11
Waldorf-Astoria Hotel, 282
Walker, James J., 46, 59, 64, 67, 69
Wallace, Henry A., 90, 108, 109
Waltemade, Henry, 349, 361, 369
Walton Avenue, 279
War Assets Administration, 90
warehousing, 385
Warner, Ivan, 158
war on poverty, 6, 144–146, 148–152
Washington Avenue, 119, 303, 307
Watson, Jack, 319, 324
weatherization loans, 371–372, 374
Weckquaesgeeks, 11
Weekes, Richard, 185
Weiner, Alan, 311
Weinreb, Wolf, 289, 290, 295–297
welfare
  and arson, 232–233

welfare (*continued*)
  dependency on, 6, 146, 178, 180, 229
  families on, xx–xxi, 229–230, 253,
    256, 282–284, 295–297
  mothers on, 113, 177–179
  and "welfare dumping," 180, 379
"welfare rights movement," 176–180,
  229
West Farms, 4, 8, 22, 206, 344
  elevated line, *16–17*
West Indies, 97, 98
West Side Story, 109
West Tremont Neighborhood Preserva-
  tion Office, 359
What Have You Done for Me Lately?
  (Moscow), 59
White Construction Company, 40
white flight, 6, 220–222, 223, 271–275
WHOM radio station, 166
Wilkins Avenue, 202, 205, 226
Williams, Joseph, 194
Williams, Roger M., 307
Williamsburg Houses, 103
Willkie, Wendell, 86

windmills, 322
Women's City Club Bronx report, 362
World-Telegram, 100, 110–111, 169, 269
World War II, 85, 87, 88–89, 216–217
Worm World, Inc., 320
Wouk, Herman, 4
WPA (Works Progress Administration),
  80, 83, 103
Wright, Hamilton, 139

Yankee Stadium, 39–40, 51, *52,* 53, 278,
  317
  City buys, 286–287, 298
Yankee Stadium (Durso), 40
Yeshiva University
  Albert Einstein College of Medicine,
    148
You're the Boss (Flynn), 42

Zipes, Philip P., 269
Zombie Bar, 213
ZooDoo, 321
Zuccotti, John, 198, 251, 311, 351, 355